Flash 4!

Creative Web Animation

Derek Franklin
Brooks Patton

D1712256

macromedia®
PRESS

Flash 4! Creative Web Animation
Derek Franklin and Brooks Patton

Published by Macromedia Press, in association with Peachpit Press,
a division of Addison Wesley Longman

Macromedia Press
1249 Eighth Street
Berkeley, CA 94710
(510) 524-2178
(800) 283-9444
(510) 524-2221 (fax)

http://www.peachpit.com
http://www.macromedia.com

Editor	Clifford Colby
Copyeditor	Jill Simonsen
Production Coordinator	Amy Changar
Compositor	Magnolia Studio
Interior Design Modifications	Owen Wolfson
Cover Design	TMA Ted Mader Associates
Indexer	James Minkin
Tech Reader	Dave Baldeschwieler

ISBN 0-201-35470-5

9 8 7 6 5 4 3

Printed and bound in the United States of America.

Dedications

I would like to dedicate this book to the Flash community, which not only inspired me in my own work but made me realize the enjoyment and excitement that comes with helping someone else achieve success. Thanks to all of you!

—Derek

I'd like to dedicate this book to four critical people in my life. To my wonderful wife, Leslie, whose love and optimism has shaped the person that I am today and who believed in me long before I did. To my son, Brooks Jr., who has shown me the true wonder of life by being the most important part of mine. To my mother, Jane, who brought me into this world and taught me that faith can be stronger than fact. And to my sister, Melissa, who through her own life has taught me that success isn't achieved just through effort but through perseverance as well. I love ya, sis!

—Brooks

Acknowledgments

Thanks to Marjorie Baer, Cliff Colby, Nancy Ruenzel, and the entire wonderful staff at Peachpit Press for their endless patience. I may now be an author, but I still can't come up with enough glowing words to describe my appreciation to you all.

Finally, thanks to Derek Franklin, my coauthor, business partner, and great friend. Because of you this experience was as fun as it was rewarding. I could have asked for no greater partner to weather the storm with.

—Brooks

Before actually coauthoring this book (which is my first) the idea of writing one was something that appeared to be a simple process of writing some words about what I love and taking some screen shots. No big deal, right? Wow! Was I wrong (See Kathy, I admitted it!). A project of this magnitude requires sacrifices from nearly everyone around you. And to say that my friends and family understood would be a shameful understatement.

My most-excellent wife, Kathy, has been so incredibly supportive. She's endured my bad moods and long nights and has basically sacrificed a summer of fun to allow me to pursue one of my life-long dreams—getting my name in the amazon.com author database. She did whatever she could to make sure I had as few distractions as possible so I could concentrate on the task at hand. Thanks, Lovie! As for my daughter, Ashlie Russell, thanks for always being a good sport and laughing even when I was being a jerk, which of course happens so seldom. I know you're glad this book is finished: It opens up more time for me to concentrate on your homework for the coming year. One of these days you're going to have to actually do it yourself. To my dad, Roy: Well, Pop, I didn't make it as a rock star as I had once hoped, but those woopin's you gave me sure helped me form the proper mindset that I needed to pull this author-thing off. Although I don't say this as often as I should, I love you and wish I was a kid again so we could spend more valuable time together like we always used to. To my sister, Marliese, I just want to say I'm proud to have you as my sis. Thanks for my two wonderful nieces, Jasmine and Cecilia. And lastly from my family, I'd like to thank Sue Stailey, my favorite mother-in-law. Although becoming your favorite son-in-law wasn't a hard task to accomplish, it's the thought that counts. Thanks for all your excitement and enthusiasm.

The Peachpit Press gang have been awesome! Marjorie Baer: It took a while, but here are the fruits of our labor. Thanks for giving us the ultimate opportunity. When we make it to Berkeley, dinner is on me (literally, have you ever seen me eat!). To Cliff Colby, our editor, I know my English ain't no good, but thanks for making it read more better. Awesome job on the editing. I appreciate your hard work. To Jill "Eagle Eye" Simonsen, good eye on the copy editing. To Amy Changar, our production coordinator, you did a fabulous job keeping us all on our toes and making this come together so well. Thank you. The whole staff at Peachpit Press deserves a hand. Thanks to all of you!

And to my great friend Brooks: Well, I'm glad I listened to you. Your efforts are what made this possible. You really made my part in this very easy at the cost of your own sanity, and I want to say I really appreciate it. One last request though, just let Gary win at Quake for once, will ya?

—Derek

Contents

Introduction

We're often asked why, as professional developers in a competitive market, we'd write a book that gives away the very secrets that ensured our success. The answer is simple: For us, the Flash learning process was extremely painful. Documentation was scarce and resources almost nonexistent (at least back in the good ol' Flash 2 days). After months of sleepless nights, accelerated hair loss, and diminishing pizza budgets, we decided that once we had mastered the program, we would give something back to the development community. It seemed senseless, if not downright inhumane, to knowingly allow our peers to suffer the same agony we experienced—especially when the same basic questions appeared to be perplexing everyone. A visit to the Flash newsgroup provided clear evidence of this: There we found users starved for samples, examples, explanations—anything to make the going a little easier.

Flash isn't a difficult program, but it is a powerful one—and there's a certain order to the process of creating Flash content. Not knowing that order can lead to headaches and frustration. As we learned through training our own staff, the real key to mastering Flash is a solid comprehension of its various aspects, gained in a sequential manner.

Our first pass at teaching Flash came in creating interactive Flash tutorials—made with Flash—for our Web site, http://www. crazyraven.com. The response was immediate and enthusiastic; users reported that concepts, which had eluded them for months, were finally crystal clear. We felt tremendously rewarded—and for a brief time we thought we had done our duty. It didn't take long, however, for requests for further interactive tutorials to begin flooding in. While we wanted to help, we did, after all, have a business to run.

Feeling an obligation to what had become a very loyal following, we took our message to Peachpit Press/Macromedia Press with the idea of expanding our scope.

What you'll learn...

How to use the book

What's in the chapters and sections

Fast-forward to the present, and you have in front of you the third edition of Flash Creative Web Animation (Darrell Plant wrote the first two editions). This volume represents a total rewrite, complete with a new approach and fresh methods of learning. Just as important, it includes a CD-ROM disc containing our interactive lessons, QuickTime tutorials, and source files. Now you can see how tasks are accomplished rather than just read about them.

To us, the interactive tutorials form the heart of this book. While the text provides a foundation and basic knowledge of the application and its tools, the tutorials teach you how to transform this understanding into powerful multimedia capabilities. This is where the magic and cool effects come to life.

Naming of the Parts

Before you dive in, we should explain some terminology. First, the terms *movie, presentation, content,* and *project* all refer to basically the same thing: the Flash file you create to show to the world. *Animation* in this context means any kind of onscreen movement you intentionally create (no, monitor crashes *do not* qualify). *Interactivity* here refers to anything you create in Flash that reacts to viewer input—via keyboard or mouse. And, finally, *multimedia* is where all of these things, plus sound, come together.

Now take a look at the following list of chapters to see what's in store:

1. **Why Flash?** As if you had to ask. Here you'll find out why Flash 4 is the tool of choice for creating high-impact Web sites and multimedia presentations.

2. **Getting Started.** If you want to find out what's new in Flash 4 as well as familiarize yourself with the authoring environment and all its enhancements, this is the place to go.

3. **Drawing.** Although some find Flash's drawing tools limited, we believe just the opposite to be true. Here we'll show you why as well as provide an in-depth discussion of Flash's powerful tool set.

4. **Text.** Although not the most exciting part of a movie, text is sometimes necessary to get the message across—and it doesn't have to be boring. In this chapter, we'll show you how to use it to receive user input and liven up your presentation.

5. **Sound.** Visual effects are great, but if you can learn to use sound in conjunction with them, your Flash movies will have a tremendous impact. Here we show you how to harness the power of audio.

6. Bitmaps. Although Flash's drawing tools are great, they're not always enough. However, when you add bitmaps (or photos) to your Flash presentations, there's no limit to the visual effects you can achieve. Here, we'll show you how and then detail some of their really great uses.

7. Symbols. These make up the heart of Flash's Web multimedia capabilities. If you can master them, you're halfway to handling most of what you'll encounter in Flash.

8. Library. When it comes to Flash organization, the library can be your best friend. In this chapter, we'll acquaint you with it as well as show you ways to manipulate it to your liking. If only all friends were this easy!

9. Layers. An integral part of animation, layers are sometimes required to make full use of Flash's capabilities. Here, we'll help you get a handle on them as well as show you some of the great things they can enable you to do.

10. Animation. Animation involves not only movement but timing as well. Combine the two, and you won't believe the results.

11. Interactivity. This is where you provide your creation with some direction and manners. Although Flash's capabilities for interactivity may at first seem overwhelming, once you understand their underlying logic, you're likely to be unstoppable.

12. Testing Your Work. You need to consider many things when creating a Flash movie and—not surprisingly—any number of small things can easily slip through the cracks. Here, we'll show you how to use the Flash testing tools to create smooth-running, error-free compact Flash movies in no time.

13. Publishing Your Work. All your hard work is for naught if you're unable to share the final product. Here we'll familiarize you with the many ways Flash allows you to present your work as well as the possibilities and appropriate uses of each.

14. Planning Your Project. You want to think about several things before even opening the program. In this chapter we'll make you aware of some factors that will make the development process flow easier and more efficiently.

How to Use this Book

Although we recommend going through this book from front to back, sections are organized so that they can be easily referenced in the future. Plus, the book has plenty of tips, tricks, warnings, and other learning aids to keep you on track. The CD-ROM disc contains associated QuickTime video tutorials for most chapters. The CD also contains associated source files for you to open in Flash itself so that you can then tear them apart to see what makes them tick. This icon precedes a section in the book that refers to material on the CD.

We've tried to make this book as easy, enjoyable, and informative as possible. Now it's up to you to take the information and run with it. We'd love to hear of your successes as well as view what you've accomplished by using this learning aid. Don't let us think all of our hard work was for nothing: Contact us at flash4@crazyraven.com. Although we may not be able to respond to all emails, we'll certainly do our best. Tell us what you think of the book, what you thought was cool, or what you'd like to see in future editions. We'll be listening.

Why Flash?

Multimedia is just as its name implies: an experience that uses multiple forms of media to convey a message, idea, or thought in a manner that requires the use of many senses. Movement, sound, interaction, and the passage of time are the basic elements; life itself is the ultimate multimedia experience.

It's human nature to want use every one of our senses to experience life. Although we love to look at a beautiful picture, that experience pales in comparison to watching the sun set over the ocean while feeling a gentle breeze against our cheek and hearing the waves beat against the shore. We enjoy listening to our favorite musician's latest CD, but it doesn't compare to seeing the artist perform live, where he or she might dance on stage and interact with the audience against the backdrop of a perfectly timed light show. Nothing moves us more than an experience that engages as many of our senses as possible—which is what multimedia attempts to do in digital form.

Although digital multimedia has been around for several years, it didn't blossom until CD-ROM drives became integrated into personal computers. Prior to that, practical limitations made it difficult to experience good multimedia presentations. This is because the elements that make up multimedia—pictures, sound, and animation—require a large amount of disk space. So in many ways the CD-ROM disc itself—which can hold as much as 640 megabytes of information—sparked the multimedia revolution. In the intervening years, multimedia has become a way of life for many computer users, making programs and games more exciting and enjoyable. Today, in fact, multimedia is de rigueur for such programs—anything less is simply unacceptable.

In 1994 another revolution was about to begin: that of the World Wide Web. Although scientists and educators had been using the Web for several years, the public was just beginning to understand its attraction. And although computer users the world over were enticed by the thought of accessing a massive worldwide computer network, the delivery of this information was somewhat disappointing: The Internet was largely a text-only medium—a far cry from the multimedia world they had grown accustomed to.

It didn't take long, though, for graphics to move from novelty to necessity on the Web: Users simply weren't interested in looking at text-only pages. Yet the transition was hindered by the fact that most Web surfers had slow connections—no small obstacle since graphics, by nature, are bandwidth intensive. To solve this problem, image viewers using the GIF and JPEG standards were introduced into browsers, allowing graphics and even some animation to be added to Web pages without making them ridiculously large and slow to download.

For the multimedia neophytes, however, satisfaction remained elusive. Graphics had to be small and few, and adding sound—let alone *synchronized* sound—was impractical if not impossible. User interaction was also almost nonexistent. Web pages were simply a collection of useful but static documents. With bandwidth at a premium, creating full-blown multimedia Web pages seemed a distant, if not unobtainable, dream. How could you incorporate compelling graphics, synchronized sound, and interactivity into a medium with so many limitations?

If the Internet craze has taught us anything, it's that the world of cyberspace is all about speed and accelerated evolution: If a task needs to be accomplished on the Web, the solution is generally just around the corner. Building a technology for multimedia delivery over the Internet would have to rely on a process that would minimize the bandwidth problem by incorporating various compression methods for graphics, sound, and overall development.

Enter Macromedia Flash!

Speed

With Flash, Macromedia combined a number of powerful ideas and technologies into a single program that allows users to deliver full multimedia presentations over the Web.

One thing that makes Flash an incredible development tool for the Web is its use of vector graphics as the default graphics mode. Vector graphics are objects defined by mathematical equations, or vectors, that include information about the object's size, shape, color, outline, and position. This is an efficient way of handling graphics and often results in relatively small file sizes—even when dealing with complex drawings. Furthermore, vector graphics are resolution independent, which means that a vector graphic the size of a pinhead will retain the same file size even when enlarged to fit your entire screen with no quality degradation.

Traditionally (and on the Web in particular), graphics have been delivered primarily in the form of *bitmaps*. Although effective and often quite artistic, bitmaps are bandwidth intensive and share none of the benefits of vector graphics. Bitmap graphic files, for example, are almost always larger than their vector counterparts (even though they appear similar)—a fact that becomes more apparent as the physical dimensions of the graphic increase. The construction of bitmaps accounts for this difference. (**Figure 1.1**).

Figure 1.1
Comparison of enlarged vector circle (left) to an enlarged bitmap circle (right).

Unlike vector images, which use mathematical equations, bitmaps are made up of a collection of dots, or *pixels,* placed in a grid formation, or pattern, one right next to another. These pixels are usually so small that from a distance, the pixels in the pattern that make up a bitmap blend seamlessly to form a picture. However, if you were to zoom in on this picture, the tiny square pixels would become apparent. Each pixel in a bitmap has associated information that relates to its color. Most images comprise thousands, hundreds of thousands, or even millions of pixels. Obviously, the larger the graphic, the more pixels it contains. Hence, even a small bitmap 100 pixels tall by 100 pixels wide would have to store information for 10,000 pixels. You can begin to see the benefits of using vector graphics wherever possible. Although vector graphics offer file size advantages, you can achieve some graphic effects only with bitmaps. Fortunately, Flash supports bitmap graphics. And because it uses the latest compression technologies, Flash helps you keep file size to a minimum even when using bitmaps.

Flash's development approach also facilitates the creation of complex multimedia presentations while still maintaining small file sizes. Because such elements as vectors, bitmaps, and sounds are usually employed more than once in a given movie, Flash allows you to make a single version of an object, which you can then reuse elsewhere rather than re-create the object each time you wish to use it—a capability that goes a long way toward conserving file size. For example, if you wanted to use a 10-KB bitmap logo in ten locations in your Flash presentation, it would *appear* to require 100 KB (10 KB used 10 times) of file space. However, Flash requires just one actual copy of the 10-KB logo; the other nine instances are simply references to the main file. Although these "references" appear just as the actual file would, less than 100 bytes per instance are required to reference the actual file. So, you would save nearly 90 KB in file size—a considerable amount on the Web. You can use this powerful capability with vectors, bitmaps, sounds, and more.

A final—and perhaps the defining—factor in Flash's ability to create fast-loading multimedia over the Web is *streaming content*. Despite its other benefits, without this capability, Flash would probably not be practical for the Web.

Streaming content is another example of a technology born out of necessity on the Web. Before streaming, bandwidth issues prevented users from viewing or listening to files until all of their contents had been downloaded. Engineers, however, realized that users don't see or hear every byte in a file simultaneously: Users can experience the full impact of the content by receiving it incrementally. For example, when reading a book, you view only a page at a time. So, if your book were delivered over the Web, you would probably appreciate being able to read the first few pages while the rest of the book downloaded in the background. If you had to wait for the whole book to download before you could begin reading, you might give up and click elsewhere.

Flash's streaming capabilities mean that even large files with sound, animation, and bitmaps can begin playing almost instantaneously. If you plan your project precisely, your audience can view a 10- to 15-minute presentation over the Web without noticing that content is being downloaded in the background.

Web Standard

As most Web developers will attest to, browser and software manufacturers frequently tout Web standards even as they continue to define their own *versions* of those standards. Not surprisingly, we all have our own ways of doing things, and nowhere is this more apparent than in the browser itself. Take the following scenario: After spending hours creating the perfect Web page, with graphics placed just so and perhaps some JavaScript added for a bit of simple interactivity, you view your work in your favorite browser, where it looks and functions just as it should. You feel pretty good until you decide to view the page through your *least favorite* browser: Now you're mortified. Besides not looking anything like it should, your Web page is producing JavaScript error after JavaScript error. Your beautiful interactive page has fallen victim to a compatibility problem between browsers—one that may well send you back to the drawing board and cause you to lose a few hairs.

Since the Web continues to evolve at a phenomenal rate, the lack of universal standards continues to be a roadblock to a number of powerful technologies. Many developers are sticking to the basics rather than run the risk of creating compatibility problems by including fancier features.

As if that weren't enough, there's also the problem of dealing with different versions of the same product. For example, Both Netscape and Microsoft 4.x and 5.x browsers include numerous features and improvements that the 3.x version of the same software lacks. Although you can develop a page to take specific advantage of the new versions' powerful features, users viewing your work through 3.x browsers will see a considerably less interesting page. So, developers who want their pages to appeal to a wide audience must create multiple versions of the same content—a time-consuming task to say the least.

Standards, if implemented properly, eliminate this problem, making it possible to create "one size fits all" pages. Flash addresses this issue by using its own plug-in, which provides the browser with special capabilities. Although not everyone in the world has acquired the Flash plug-in, it's been around long enough that millions of Internet users certainly have (and if they haven't, it's easy to download and install). What's more, such major companies as Audi, Casio Electronics, Disney, and Paramount Pictures (to name just a few) use the technology on their own sites. And most important, current (and future) versions of the major browsers include the Flash plug-in, and current versions of Windows and Macintosh operating systems ship with it pre-installed: If that doesn't make Flash a standard, we don't know what would.

So what does this mean to Flash developers? It means they can create content once—with all the design and interactive wizardry they wish—and know that it will look and act the same, regardless of browser or version (3.x and above).

And we don't need to tell you that *that's* good news for developers.

Interactive and Engaging

Humans find few things as captivating as movement and interaction. As kids, a butterfly or a favorite animated show could hold our attention for hours. And although it's certainly not exciting to look at a rock, we could watch time and again a cartoon in which a rock was being obliterated by all kinds of explosions. Add to that the way we're engrossed by buttons. Just look at our toys: As we grow older, the buttons seem to multiply (think remote control or stereo system). We all like to provoke a response with our actions—even if it's not the precise reaction we were looking for. Perhaps that's because it makes us feel powerful, or in control. However, it's one thing to have this power and another to endow someone else with it: That is what Flash provides, giving you the ability to create a user-controlled experience that is directly tied to your creativity in presenting an interactive offering.

You can create buttons that display information, play sounds, take you to different points in your movie, and react to mouse events. Your movie can be a presentation that moves along at a predefined pace or one that follows a path defined by viewer input. Flash 4 supports if-then-else interactivity through a basic but powerful scripting engine, which means your movie can move along in the following fashion: "*If* Button A is pushed *then* do Action 1, *else* (or otherwise, such as if Button B, C, or D is pushed) do Action 2."

The more you engage your audience, the more they will enjoy themselves and the greater their message retention will be. In addition to the elements already discussed, one more factor will play a large part in determining the effectiveness of your Flash presentation: Sound.

Sound has a profound effect on how we react to things. Without it, even the most phenomenal visual display seems lacking. Flash allows you to use sound to enhance the user experience, adding sound effects or synchronizing the onscreen action with any soundtrack you wish to use—all of which translates into a truly memorable experience.

Ease of Use

As cool as all of the above sounds, the icing on the cake is that all of these elements are easy to create: You can produce a full-blown multimedia extravaganza, complete with interactive controls and buttons, without opening another graphics program or scripting anything in HTML. And your creation will work in any browser that has the Flash plug-in installed.

For creating graphic content, Flash provides a wide range of tools that enable you to produce professional-looking designs without having to learn new skills or techniques. Although these tools share a number of concepts with other vector drawing programs, Flash handles some drawing tasks in a unique fashion, which may require some adjustment on your part. If you've used an illustration program before, though, not to worry: You should be up and running with Flash's drawing tools in no time. And even if you haven't used a drawing program, the concepts are simple and easy to pick up.

When Flash's own drawing tools are insufficient (such as when you need a bitmap graphic), you can take advantage of the program's strong import capabilities. This way, you can create artwork in your favorite illustration or photo editing program and then import it into Flash for use in your movie.

In addition, Flash's use of timelines make animations easy to conceptualize: You should be able to readily determine when, where, and how long a certain element appears.

Few Design Limitations

When the Web was in its infancy, layout and design were minor concerns. Most pages had colored backgrounds, a few centered graphics, and some text—not very engaging visually but effective (to some degree) nonetheless. Then came the introduction of frames and tables into browsers, and Web page creation became an art. Suddenly complex pages were the standard—and one that wasn't necessarily easy to live up to since methodology was tricky and browsers remained limited in their graphics presentation.

Designers learned that by chopping, slicing, and precisely positioning graphics, they could emulate the beauty of the printed page—a popular though limited approach to Web page design. Certain key elements—such as exact positioning and the use of layers to stack page elements on top of one another—were still missing.

Both major browsers tackled these issues in their 4.0 editions by introducing *Dynamic HTML,* or DHTML, which allows for exact positioning of elements, the incorporation of layers, and a number of other long-requested capabilities. Although these capabilities opened many doors, there are still associated challenges. For one, a thorough understanding of DHTML and scripting is a necessity. Some design tools make the process easier, yet even they are occasionally cryptic in themselves. And compatibility, too, remains an issue: Pre-4.0 browsers will not recognize DHTML (not to mention that the browsers themselves handle DHTML differently); so, your hard work will be left unappreciated unless you take the time to create another version to accommodate these older browsers. And, as mentioned earlier, many designers simply choose to design for the least common denominator—that is, 3.x browsers.

In contrast, Flash-designed content has few design limitations. Graphic elements can be placed precisely, anywhere on the page. And you can stack elements. You can also create online forms in Flash that can receive information from your users. In addition, Flash has transparency capabilities, which give your layouts depth and make them more visually appealing. You can even use a background that doesn't tile across the screen.

You can use Flash to easily achieve all the wonderful layout possibilities of printed material. Moreover, you can animate your material as well as make it interactive. You can even choose to forego Flash's multimedia capabilities: That's OK too.

The best thing about all of these capabilities is that they are not complex to achieve. You simply place a graphic on the page, add some interactivity (if you wish), and then rest assured that it will look exactly as you created it—regardless of which browser or version your audience is viewing it with.

Versatility

Flash can handle jobs of all sizes and proportions. For example, you can use it to create a full multimedia Web site with tons of cool graphics, form elements, and interaction, or you may employ it simply to create a navigation bar or banner. The choice is yours. Your presentation or movie can serve nearly any function you desire—an informational vehicle, an advertisement, a button, or even just a way of putting background music on your Web site. You can also use it for a corporate site or to present a slide show of your last vacation that includes music and interesting transitions. There's no end to the possibilities.

Flash integrates easily with HTML, so incorporating it into your Web pages is almost seamless. This means that nothing special is required for Flash to follow a hyperlink, open up a new browser window, or accomplish anything through the use of HTML. For more advanced interactivity, Flash can interact with JavaScript and VBScript. It should be stressed, however, that you don't have to use these additional scripting capabilities to create a multimedia site. Scripting with Flash allows your creation to react to actions taken with the browser or any of the HTML elements on the page.

Widespread Viewability

The Internet is the future of communications. Even now, it allows us to see video from anywhere in the world, send messages with pictures, and make Internet phone calls and hold international meetings. However, not everyone has an Internet connection, and even if they do, it may not always be available to them.

Although Flash was designed to create compact, fast-loading multimedia—which makes it an ideal technology for the Web—you are not restricted to delivering your Flash content over the Internet. Any Flash-created content can be exported as a multimedia movie for use on the Web, as video that can be viewed on both Windows and Macintosh computers, or even as a stand-alone program that you can distribute on floppy disks or CDs. (**Figure 1.2**)

Figure 1.2
On the top is Flash content delivered over the Web; on the
bottom is Flash content delivered via its stand-alone player.

With Flash, you no longer have an excuse for delivering boring, static, or uninterest-
ing content. It's easy to use, powerful, interactive, and just plain fun. If you're the least
bit creative, you'll be amazed at what you can come up with—and seeing someone else
enjoying your work is a satisfying feeling you won't soon forget.

Getting Started

In this chapter we'll help to establish momentum by providing a basic understanding of the way Flash works—a few simple concepts, without which you won't get very far. We'll then take a look at some of the enhancements included in this new version that will make your projects even more powerful and interactive. Finally, we'll show you how to create your first interactive Flash movie by means of an interactive tutorial—a chance to get your feet wet, if you will.

By the time you finish this chapter, you'll have the basic knowledge necessary to work through the rest of this book. Fortunately, Flash isn't rocket science, so don't get discouraged. Remember, you build momentum by starting slowly and gradually gaining speed. Don't expect to be a Flash master overnight. If you stick with us, you'll get there soon enough.

How Flash Works

The first thing to be aware of when creating Flash content is that you need *two files* to make the process work: an authoring file (where you create content, animation, and interactivity) and a compressed and optimized version of this file, better known as a Flash movie.

The authoring file (which has an *.fla* extension) is where you store your work so that you can tinker with it later—it's the file you actually work on when Flash is open. It contains all the sounds, bitmaps, drawings, text, and interactivity you want your final movie to contain. The authoring file is your movie in its *preoptimized* state—which means it can balloon to well more than several megabytes.

When you've gotten your authoring file to look and work the way you want, it's time to turn it into a Flash movie. This is known as *exporting*. When you export your authoring file to a movie (which has an *.swf* file extension), Flash compresses and optimizes it so that the Flash movie file is dramatically smaller than the original authoring file. You place this smaller file on your Web page or distribute it on disk or CD. For the most part, the exported movie cannot be edited. If you wish to edit your movie's content, you must reopen the original authoring file, make your changes, and then export the authoring file to a Flash movie.

Many factors will affect the size of your Flash movie—most of which you can control. Getting the smallest file size for your final movie usually involves balance and an occasional compromise. You must decide when and where to sacrifice quality—such as sound clarity or picture sharpness—in your quest for a smaller exported movie. We'll show you how to use Flash's tools to get the best-quality final movie while still retaining a reasonable file size.

You can not only create Flash movies from your authoring files but also export these same files to produce QuickTime movies, animated GIFs, and even static or nonanimated graphics—and you can have Flash create all of these simultaneously! This means you can create once (the authoring file) and distribute many ways (Flash movie, QuickTime movie, animated GIF, JPEG, and so on).

Content Creation

When considering Flash content, you must remember three key elements: movement, time, and interactivity—the same principles that define life itself.

Take driving your car: That task requires both *movement* (on the part of your car) and *time* (to get from one intersection to the next). When you reach an intersection with a traffic light, *interactivity* kicks in. If the signal is red, you stop your car, yet time continues to tick away. When the light turns green, you know to move your car and proceed to work. Life revolves around movement and interactivity across the passage of time. Movement is what you see, interactivity is what you do, and time is when you do it. If you understand these three principles, you should have no trouble catching on to Flash.

The program's basic components are a timeline and stage. You draw or import objects and place them on the stage, where you then make them move or react based on the passage of time (on the timeline) or audience interaction. You determine the speed—frames per second—at which the timeline moves. (You'll learn more about these principles in the Chapter 11, "Interactivity.")

Projects can take the form of presentations, tutorials, or even games. Some Flash projects use interactivity but little or no animation—in which case all you need to do is create an interface with buttons users click to perform specific actions. Buttons can also be used to accept information from the user, such as on a form. Flash can send the information on a form off for processing or use it to trigger something in a movie. To help you create content, Flash allows you to split the authoring file up into *scenes.* You can think of scenes as pages within your authoring file, each of which looks completely different than the others. A single authoring file can have as many scenes as you wish; however, all of the scenes are part of a single exported movie. Scenes merely simplify content creation in the authoring environment.

Content Distribution

After you've created your content and exported it as a Flash movie, you must decide what you want to do with the final optimized .swf file. One option is to embed your movie in a Web page, where it will appear just as a regular graphic—only animated and interactive. You can, in fact, create an entire Web site based solely on a single Flash movie. If this is how you wish your audience to view your movie, however, be aware that they must have the Flash plug-in installed to view it. Your Flash movie will be streamed over the Web, which means that viewers can begin playing it almost immediately while the rest of the movie is being downloaded in the background—no more waiting for the entire file to download before it can play. Once the movie is playing, you can tell Flash to open and close browser windows, accept information from your user (which can be processed by a CGI script), play sounds, interact with the user, and more.

Another popular way of delivering your Flash movie is to turn it into a *projector,* or stand-alone player, which transforms it into a self-running application. This means you can put your movie on a disk or CD, and anyone can view it immediately just by opening it. Unfortunately, projectors don't work on Web pages, so don't even try that.

Because Flash movies can be exported in multiple formats and delivered over the Web or through a projector, you can create your Web site entirely in Flash and then put it on the Web *and* give it to your customers on disk or CD. This way, they can view it without connecting to the Internet if they so desire.

What's New in Flash 4

Newcomers to Flash probably will have a hard time appreciating how Macromedia transformed this version. Flash veterans, however, will quickly see that nearly every aspect of the program—from the its tools and the way it looks to the features it provides—has been improved or enhanced. In addition, the program contains a slew of new features. With this version, Flash has moved beyond a simple tool for creating awesome but basic multimedia content to a full-blown development platform for producing high-powered, highly interactive multimedia content. The following touches on these enhancements and additions, and the rest of the book looks at the tools in detail.

The tool set. One look at Flash's new tool set will reveal that it gives the program a more professional feel and is organized to increase your productivity. For example, the Line, Oval, Rectangle, Pencil, and Hand tools that were once modifiers have been promoted to individual tools. A new modifier for the Rectangle tool allows you to create rectangles with rounded corners.

Color. Color values can now be entered using hexadecimal code, enabling users to easily match Web page colors with those in their Flash projects. Users can also now create, import, or export special color palettes, simplifying color management.

Curve effects. You can use the Lines to Fills effect to turn lines into filled shapes, the Expand shape effect to create larger or smaller shapes from an original shape, and the Soften Edges effect to quickly give a shape to a vector drop shadow.

Editable text fields. You can specify that audience keyboard input affect your movie internally or information entered into a text field be sent to a CGI script for processing (as in a regular HTML form). Text fields also allow you to display dynamically generated text.

Editing. You can now use the new Edit in Place command to edit Symbols in the context of where they are located on the stage.

Timeline. As with the rest of the Flash interface, the timeline has been transformed to increase your productivity, allowing you to quickly see and assess your project's structure. Frames now have drag-and-drop functionality and are color-coded, which allows you, at a glance, to determine empty, static, motion-tweened, or shape-tweened frames. In addition, the timeline can now be docked to any side of the Flash interface or float in its own window.

Layers. Flash 4 gives you much greater control over layers. For example, with one click, you can create, delete, hide, show, lock, and unlock layers. Multiple layers can now be linked to a singular mask or motion guide layer. The update also comes with an enhanced Layers Properties dialog box.

Library. The library has been redesigned from the ground up to offer many organizational improvements. For example, the library is now based on a hierarchical structure (similar to your computer's operating system), which means you can organize items within folders and even folders within folders. It also offers at-a-glance information on how many items are in the Library and how many times each one is used in your project.

Inspectors. Flash 4 comes with four new inspectors, the Frame, Transform, Scene and Generator inspectors, as well as the enhanced Object inspector.

Sound. The ability to export sound in the MP3 format facilitates more sophisticated soundtracks, and the redesigned interface for adjusting sound and compression settings is easier to follow.

Actions. This is probably where the most dramatic changes have taken place. New Flash actions along with new ActionScripting gives users the ability to assign variables and write expressions, to evaluate actions taken by their audience, and to react to the timeline's movement. New tricks can be performed with movie clips, including the ability to drag them or duplicate them, all possible while the movie is playing.

Publishing. You can now publish your project to multiple formats—including HTML, GIF, JPEG, and QuickTime—easily and simultaneously from within Flash.

If you've used previous versions of the program, you'll see many other small improvements when working with Flash. Overall, you should find the development of Flash content has become easier and more streamlined.

Interface

It's time to get acquainted with Flash's interface and learn how to customize it. We'll take a general look at the interface before we go on to examine each area in more detail. Some areas, such as the timeline and the layer interface, are covered in more depth in the chapters on animation and layers.

The interface is made up of the following areas (**Figure 2.1**):

Toolbars

Flash's toolbars provide quick access to many of the functions that are otherwise available from the menus. Although the Macintosh version of Flash provides a drawing toolbar and controller, the standard toolbar and status bar are only available in the Windows version.

The standard toolbar includes buttons for quickly starting a new project and for opening, saving, printing, cutting, copying, pasting, and several other commonly used commands. The drawing toolbar includes a complete set of Flash's creation tools. The controller is a VCR-like control pad for playing, stopping, rewinding, and fast-forwarding your movie within the authoring environment. The status bar provides information about the status of the Caps lock and Num lock keys.

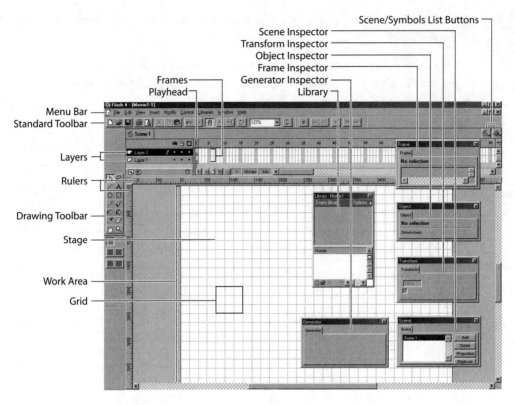

Figure 2.1
The parts of the Flash interface.

In Windows, the standard, drawing, and controller toolbars can be docked to a screen edge or float above it.

To dock a toolbar on another edge of the screen:

1. Click and hold on an area on the toolbar with no buttons.

2. Drag the toolbar to an edge of the screen and release.

The toolbar runs horizontally when docked to the top or bottom of the screen and vertically when docked to the left or right part of the screen.

The Windows toolbars also have several configurable options.

> **TIP** *To make a toolbar float separately on the screen, place the pointer over an area on the toolbar with no buttons. Then, while holding down the Control key click. The docked toolbar becomes a floating toolbar (Figures 2.2 and 2.3).*

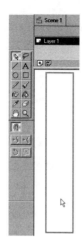

Figure 2.2
The drawing toolbar
docked and...

Figure 2.3
...the drawing toolbar
floating.

To configure which toolbars are visible and how they appear:

- From the Window menu choose Toolbar.

The Toolbar dialog box appears and offers the following options:

Show

Standard. Check to display the standard toolbar.

Drawing. Check to display the drawing toolbar.

Status. Check to display the status toolbar.

Controller. Check to display the controller.

Options

Large Buttons. Check to display larger toolbar buttons.

Show Tooltips. Check to display "tooltips" when the pointer hovers over a button.

Menu Bar

The menus provide access to many of Flash's commands. An arrow to the right of a selection in the menu bar indicates a submenu (**Figure 2.4**). Keyboard shortcuts for menu commands are shown to the right of the commands. For clarity, the terms *Flash project* and *project* denote Flash-authoring documents—that is, the place where you create the content that you eventually export as a Flash movie.

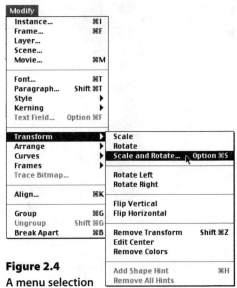

Figure 2.4
A menu selection from the Menu bar that has submenus associated with it.

File menu

Use the File menu to create, open, and save files (**Figure 2.5**).

New. Creates a new Flash document.

Open. Opens an existing Flash project.

Open as Library. Makes another Flash project library available for the current project.

Close. Closes the current Flash project.

Save. Saves the current project.

Save As. Lets you name a new project or rename an existing one.

Revert. Returns to the last saved version of a project.

Import. Imports sounds, bitmaps, QuickTime video, and other files.

Export Movie. Exports the current Flash project to a Flash movie, QuickTime movie, animated GIF, or other animated sequence.

Export Image. Creates a nonanimated image from content on the stage.

Publish Settings. Adjusts settings for publishing your Flash project to HTML, QuickTime, and more.

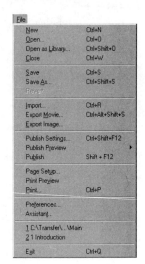

Figure 2.5
The parts of the File menu.

Publish Preview. Opens a submenu that allows you to create a temporary preview file or files based on settings you've selected with the Publish Settings option.

Publish. Creates a file based on settings you've selected with the Publish Settings option.

Page Setup. Sets printing options.

Print Margins (Macintosh). Sets margins when printing your Flash project.

Print Preview. Shows a preview of your project with the Page Setup settings.

Print. Prints project frames.

Send (Windows). Attaches the current document to an email message.

Preferences. Lets you personalize Flash.

Assistant. Allows you to set drawing-tool parameters.

Recent File List. Displays the four most recently opened files.

Exit. Closes the program.

Edit menu

The selections on the Edit menu help you work on your files (**Figure 2.6**).

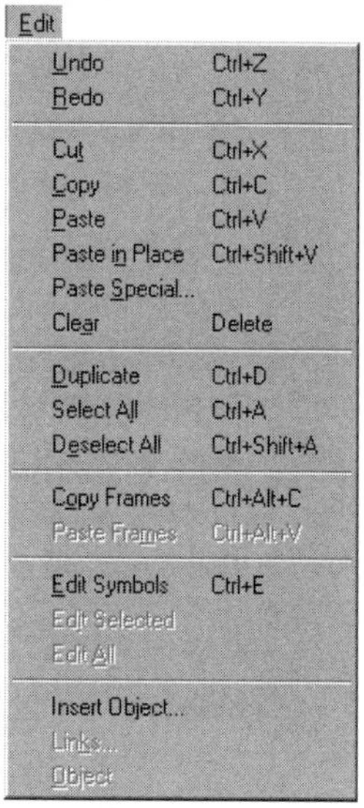

Undo. Reverses your last action.

Redo. Reinstates the action you just reversed.

Cut. Cuts the selected content and places it on the clipboard.

Copy. Copies the selected content and places it on the clipboard.

Paste. Pastes the current clipboard content.

Paste in Place. Pastes content on the clipboard into the same relative position that it was cut or copied from.

Paste Special. Pastes content from other programs.

Clear. Deletes selected items on the stage.

Duplicate. Creates a copy of selected items on the stage.

Select All. Selects everything on the stage.

Deselect All. Deselects anything selected on the stage.

Figure 2.6
The parts of the Edit menu.

Copy Frames. Copies frames selected on the timeline and places them on the clipboard.

Paste Frames. Pastes frames on the clipboard onto the timeline.

Edit Symbols. Places the last edited symbol back into symbol-editing mode so that you may edit its stage and timeline. (Item changes to Edit Movie when editing a symbol.)

Edit Selected. Places a selected symbol into symbol-editing mode.

Edit All. Makes all content available for editing.

Insert Object, Links, Objects (Windows). Windows commands not related to Flash.

View menu

The parts of the View menu can control how your files look (**Figure 2.7**).

Goto. Brings up a submenu to navigate to frames or scenes in your movie.

100%. Sets the view to the movie's actual size.

Show Frame. Makes the entire stage visible.

Show All. Makes all objects on the stage and in the Work Area visible.

Outlines. Turns all stage objects into outlines (no fills) for fast object redraw.

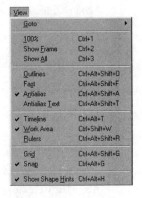

Figure 2.7
**The parts of the
View menu.**

Fast. Turns off antialiasing for fast object redraw.

Antialias. Smoothes the edges of all stage objects except text.

Antialias Text. Antialiases all stage objects including text.

Timeline. Displays or hides timeline.

Work Area. Displays or hides the work area.

Rulers. Displays or hides horizontal and vertical rulers.

Grid. Displays or hides the grid.

Snap. Turns on or off snapping.

Show Shape Hints. Shows where shape hints are placed on objects.

Insert menu

The Insert menu gives you control over frames and layers (**Figure 2.8**).

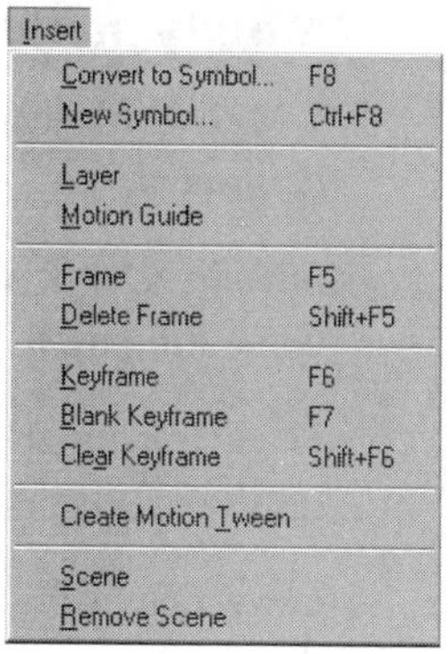

Convert to Symbol. Converts all selected objects on the stage into a new symbol.

New Symbol. Creates a new, empty symbol.

Layer. Creates a new, empty layer above the current layer on the timeline.

Motion Guide. Creates a new Motion Guide layer above the current layer.

Frame. Creates a new, empty frame to the right of the selected one.

Delete Frame. Deletes the selected frame.

Keyframe. Converts the selected frame on the timeline to a keyframe, which contains the same content as the last keyframe on the layer.

Blank Keyframe. Converts the selected frame on the timeline into a blank keyframe.

Clear Keyframe. Converts the selected keyframe to a regular frame.

Create Motion Tween. Coverts all objects on the selected layer and frame to a symbol so that it may be motion-tweened.

Scene. Inserts a new scene into your Flash project.

Remove Scene. Removes the current scene from your Flash project. (Not available if your project contains only one scene.)

Figure 2.8
The parts of the Insert menu.

Modify menu

Use the Modify menu to set various Flash properties (**Figure 2.9**).

Figure 2.9
The parts of the Modify menu.

Instance. Opens the Instance Properties dialog box, where you configure the properties of the selected instance.

Frame. Opens the Frame Properties dialog box, where you set the properties for the selected frame.

Layer. Opens the Layer Properties dialog box, where you set the properties for the current layer.

Scene. Opens the Scene Properties dialog box, where you change the name of the current scene.

Movie. Opens the Movie Properties dialog box, where you set the properties of your movie.

Font. Opens the Font dialog box, where you set the properties of the selected text.

Paragraph. Opens the Paragraph properties dialog box, where you set the properties of the selected text block.

Style. Opens a submenu with options for setting the style and alignment properties of the selected text.

Kerning. Opens a submenu, where you set the kerning of the selected text.

Text Field. Opens the Text Field Properties dialog box, where you set the properties of the selected text fields.

Transform. Opens a submenu with options for transforming, editing, and reshaping the selected object or shape.

Arrange. Opens a submenu with options for changing the "stacking order" of objects or to lock and unlock them.

Curves. Opens a submenu with options for performing editing tasks on lines and shapes.

Frames. Opens a submenu with options for modifying the selected frames on the timeline.

Trace Bitmap. Opens the Trace Bitmap dialog box, where you adjust the settings for turning the selected bitmap into a vector.

Align. Opens the Align dialog box, where you align selected objects.

Group. Groups selected objects.

Ungroup. Ungroups selected group.

Break Apart. Converts selected text to shapes, breaks a selected symbol into its individual shapes, or turns a bitmap into an editable object.

Control menu

The Control menu lets work with your movie (**Figure 2.10**).

Play. Plays the timeline from its current position.

Rewind. Rewinds the timeline to the first frame of the current scene.

Step Forward. Moves the timeline forward one frame from its current position.

Step Backward. Moves the timeline backward one frame from its current position.

Figure 2.10
The parts of the Control menu.

Test Movie. Allows you to test your exported .SWF file in the authoring environment.

Test Scene. Allows you to test your exported .SWF file in the authoring environment.

Loop Playback. Plays the timeline again when it has reached its last frame.

Play All Scenes. Plays all scenes in the project. When turned off, playback will end on the last frame of the current scene.

Enable Frame Actions. Lets the timeline react to any frame actions that have been set up.

Enable Buttons. Enables buttons in the authoring environment to reflect their Up, Over, Down, and Hit states in reaction to the pointer and perform some button actions.

Mute Sounds. Mute all sounds.

Libraries menu

The reusable library items that come with Flash are available via the Library menu. You can add library items by placing a Flash file with the library items into the Libraries folder in the Flash 4 folder (**Figure 2.11**).

Figure 2.11
The parts of the Libraries menu.

Window menu

The Window menu give you access to the various toolbars and dialog boxes in Flash (**Figure 2.12**).

New Window. Opens the current scene in a new window.

Arrange All. Arranges all open windows vertically.

Cascade. Cascades all open windows so they appear stacked on top of each other.

Toolbar. Opens the Toolbars dialog box, where you configure what toolbars are visible and how they look. On the Mac, determines whether the drawing toolbar is visible.

Figure 2.12
The parts of the Window menu.

Inspectors. Opens a submenu with options for choosing which inspectors are available onscreen.

Controller. Displays or hides the controller.

Colors. Opens the Colors dialog box for selecting, creating, and editing colors and gradients.

Output. Opens the Output window, which allows you to preview Generator variables used in the authoring environment and other information such as Flash 4 variables.

Generator Objects. Works with Generator-related content.

Library. Opens the Library window for working with reusable objects in your movie.

Open File List. Displays all the currently open Flash files.

Help menu

Use the Help menu for guidance (**Figure 2.13**).

Flash Help Topics. Opens the Flash online help within a browser window.

Register Flash. Opens the Macromedia Registration Web site.

Flash Developers Center. Opens the Flash Developers Center Web site in your browser.

Figure 2.13
The parts of the Help menu.

Lessons. Provides access to step-by-step lessons.

Samples. Provides access to Flash projects.

About Flash. Opens the About Flash dialog box.

Context-Sensitive Menus

Several additional menus are not available from the main menu bar. Known as context or contextual menus, they provide commands based on the pointer's position. So, if you access a context menu while your pointer is over a toolbar, you will be able to access commands pertaining to that toolbar.

To access a context menu:

- Right-click (Windows) or Control-click (Macintosh) a toolbar, a frame on the timeline, a layer, the stage or an object on the stage, any area in Flash that can accept or display text, the library preview window, or an item in the library.

Timeline

The timeline is where you work with the frames and layers that make up your project's content and animation. When you select a layer and then draw on the stage or import content onto the stage, that content becomes part of that layer, since it is currently selected. Frames on the timeline allow you to change content over time. What appears on the stage at each frame represents a "snapshot" of all the content contained in the layers at that point in time. You move, add, change, and delete content from layers on various frames to create movement and animation. Using multiple layers stacked from top to bottom on the timeline allows you to place different content on different layers to create depth in your animation—for example, objects that appear above a background. For more information about the timeline, see Chapter 10, "Animation."

You can resize the timeline to display as few or as many timeline layers as you wish by adding or removing screen space allocated to the stage and work area. You can also move the timeline from its default position at the top of the authoring environment to any edge of the screen.

To resize the timeline:

1. Place your pointer over the line that separates the timeline from the stage; the pointer turns into a double-sided arrow (**Figure 2.14**).

2. Click and drag the separating bar to a new location and then release.

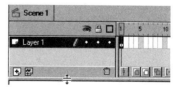

Figure 2.14
By placing your pointer over the line that separates the timeline from the stage, the pointer turns into a double-sided arrow.

To move the timeline to another edge of the screen:

1. Place the pointer over the area above the time ruler, and then click and drag. An outline of the timeline appears as you drag (**Figure 2.15**).

2. Once you've reached the edge of the screen, release the mouse. The timeline docks there.

   TIP *You may turn the timeline docking feature off if it interferes with how you work. From the File menu choose Preferences and check the Disable Timeline Docking option.*

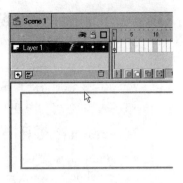

Figure 2.15
Dragging the timeline to another area creates a floating timeline.

Stage

The stage is the rectangle-shaped area where you draw and place the content of your movie. What you see on the stage at any given time represents the contents of the current frame.

The stage—with its default color of white—serves as the background for your movie. The background will be visible in any areas of your final movie that an object does not cover. You can import a bitmap into Flash and place it on the bottom-most layer of a scene so that it covers the stage and becomes a background.

To change the background color of the stage:

1. From the Modify menu choose Movie to open the Movie Properties dialog box.

2. To make the Flash color palette appear, click the Background button (**Figure 2.16**).

3. Click the color you wish to use, and click OK.

   The stage color changes to the color you selected.

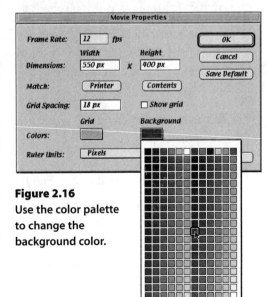

Figure 2.16
Use the color palette to change the background color.

Work Area

The work area is the gray area surrounding the rectangle that represents the stage. The work area is commonly used as a starting or ending point of an animation where an object slides in or out of a movie.

> **TIP** *If you don't wish to be distracted by elements in the work area, from the View menu choose Work Area to pick whether you want to view it.*

Library

The library helps you organize reusable elements of your Flash project. For more detailed information about the library, see Chapter 8.

Inspectors

Flash's five Inspectors—Object, Frame, Transform, Scene, and Generator—are accessible from tabs in the inspectors window and help you in the following ways:

Object Inspector

The Object Inspector shows the size (vertical and horizontal) and position (from the top and left sides of the stage) of the currently selected object. You can also enter new values into the text boxes and click Apply to resize or reposition any selected objects. By clicking Reset, you remove any transformations made to a selected instance of a symbol, including resizing, rotating, or skewing (**Figure 2.17**).

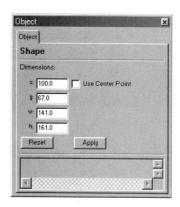

Figure 2.17
The Object Inspector.

If you select an instance of a symbol, the lower half of the Object Inspector will display its properties and any actions it has been set up to perform. If you select a regular text object, it will display that object's font as well as the size, alignment, and style used. In addition, if you select an editable text object, the Object Inspector will also display its variable name and any other configurable options you have set up for it.

Frame Inspector

The Frame Inspector provides detailed information about the currently selected frame on the timeline, including type, sound properties (if applicable), associated label or comments, and any actions it's set up to perform (**Figure 2.18**).

Transform Inspector

The Transform Inspector reacts to objects in two ways: If you select a regular shape, you can enter precise scale, rotation, and skewing amounts and then click Apply to make your settings take effect. If you click Copy, your settings will be applied to a copy of the selected shape, which is automatically created and placed on the stage (**Figure 2.19**).

If you select an instance of a symbol, the values that initially appear reflect how much (in terms of size and rotation) the instance of the symbol has deviated from the original. You can change these values and click Apply to make your settings take affect. As with regular shapes, clicking Copy will apply your settings to a copy of the selected instance, which is automatically created and placed on the stage.

Scene Inspector

The Scene Inspector helps you work with and organize scenes in your project, allowing you to create, delete, reorganize, and switch between scenes (**Figure 2.20**). For a more detailed description of the Scene Inspector, see Chapter 10, "Animation."

Generator Inspector

You use the Generator Inspector to work with Generator-related content. This inspector is not functional unless you have Generator installed.

Figure 2.18
The Frame Inspector.

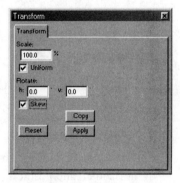

Figure 2.19
The Transform Inspector.

Figure 2.20
The Scene Inspector.

Working with Inspectors

You can display any or all of the inspectors at once, and they can appear separately or as a group.

To display an inspector:

1. From the Window menu choose Inspectors.

2. From the submenu that appears choose the inspector you wish to display.

To ungroup one inspector from another:

• Click the tab of the inspector you wish to ungroup, and drag it away from the group.

    The tab you dragged is now separated from the group.

To group inspectors:

• Click the inspector's tab, and drag it on top of another inspector.

    The tab you dragged and the one you dragged it over become a group of tabs. You can drag as many tabs to a group as you wish.

Grid

Using a grid in Flash places a set of intersecting horizontal and vertical lines over the stage and work area. The grid is useful for aligning, scaling, and placing objects precisely. The grid is never exported in your final movie; it's only visible in the Flash authoring environment.

To set up and view the grid:

1. From the Modify menu choose Movie.

    The Movie Properties dialog box appears and offers you several grid configurations:

    Grid Spacing. Sets the amount of space between lines in the grid (the same amount is used both vertically and horizontally).

    Show Grid. Lets you choose whether you want the grid to appear.

    Grid Color. Lets you choose the color of the grid by clicking the color box, which brings up a color palette.

2. When you have completed adjusting you settings, click OK. Your grid adjustments are now reflected onscreen.

> **TIP** *The grid is only useful as an alignment tool if you've turned "snapping" on. To turn it on, from the View menu choose Snap. For more information, see the "Snapping" section of Chapter 3, "Drawing."*

> **TIP** *If the grid is the same color as the work area, it may not be visible over the work area. You can change the color of the grid, as described above, to alleviate this problem.*

> **TIP** *You can quickly turn the grid on and off by checking or unchecking the Grid command in the View menu.*

Rulers

Rulers provide a visual cue to objects' placement on the stage. When you move, scale, or rotate an object on the stage, lines indicating the width and height of the object appear on the top and left rulers, respectively. The rulers can be changed incrementally in any unit you choose.

To set ruler units:

1. From the Modify menu choose Movie to make the Movie Properties box appear.

2. From the Ruler Units pop-up box, select the unit you wish to use, and click OK.

If the rulers are visible, they will reflect your setting adjustments.

> **TIP** *Whatever unit you choose will be the default unit used throughout Flash in the dialog boxes that reflect size values.*

To view rulers:

- From the View menu choose Rulers.

  The rulers appear along the left and top part of the stage/work area.

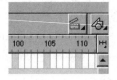

Figure 2.21
Scene (left) and symbol (right) list buttons.

Scene and Symbols List Buttons

The Scene and Symbol buttons (**Figure 2.21**) provide pop-up menus that allow you to quickly navigate to and edit scenes or symbols in your project.

Viewing Options

In Flash, you can zoom into areas for more detailed work or zoom out for an overall look. You can control both with the View pop-up menu (**Figure 2.22**). In Windows the View pop-up menu is part of the standard toolbar; on the Macintosh it's part of the drawing toolbar. It functions the same in both systems: Choose a percentage from the pop-up menu to enlarge or shrink the stage. The Show Frame option sets the view to make the entire stage visible. The Show All option sets the view to make all objects on the stage and the work area visible.

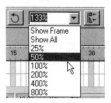

Figure 2.22
The View pop-up menu.

You can also adjust the view via the Hand or Magnifier tools (available on the toolbar).

Preferences

By choosing Preferences from the File menu, you bring up the Preferences settings dialog box, which lets you control clipboard image placement, the number of available undo/redo levels, and several other settings that affect how you work (**Figure 2.23**).

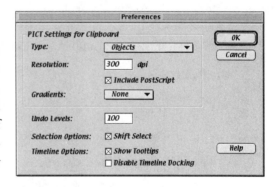

Figure 2.23
The Preferences dialog box.

Clipboard

When you copy a drawing and place it on the clipboard, Flash actually puts two versions there: one based on metafile information (useful for pasting into another vector program) and a bitmap version for pasting into a bitmap program.

Windows settings for bitmaps on the clipboard:

Color Depth. Sets the color depth.

Resolution. Sets the resolution of the bitmap.

Size Limit. Allows you to set the maximum RAM you wish to allocate for placing the bitmap on the clipboard. (Higher resolutions require more RAM.)

Smooth. Antialiases, or smoothes, the bitmap.

Mac settings for bitmaps on the clipboard:

Type. Lets you choose whether to create a bitmap out of objects selected or to just leave them as vectors when copying to the clipboard.

Resolution. Sets the resolution of the bitmap.

Including PostScript. If you are exporting a PICT file as object-, or vector-based, including PostScript information will optimize the graphic for PostScript printing.

Gradients. Sets the quality of the gradients in PICT files created by copying objects to the clipboard. You should choose "none" for this setting if you will be copying and pasting within Flash. This will speed the time it takes to copy complex, gradiated drawings.

Gradients on the Clipboard (Windows)

Sets the quality of the gradients in files created by copying objects to the clipboard. Choose "none" for this setting if you will be copying and pasting within Flash itself. This speeds up copying complex, gradiated drawings.

Undo Levels

Allows you to set the levels of undo/redo available in Flash. The higher the setting, the more memory is required and so the more performance degradation your computer may suffer. The maximum setting is 300.

Printing Options (Windows)

Enables or disables PostScript output when printing to a PostScript printer.

Selection Options

Sets how you select objects on the stage and work area. If this option is checked (the default setting), you need to hold down the Shift key to select multiple objects. If it's not checked, you need only click additional objects to add them to the current selection.

Timeline Options

When you disable Timeline Docking, the timeline will detach from the main Flash window and remain free-floating—a useful feature if you move the timeline much and don't want it to snap into place at the top of the screen as it usually would.

When you choose Show Tooltips (Macintosh), information balloons appear when you hold your pointer over items such as the drawing tools and timeline elements.

Setting Up Your Movie

To begin your Flash project, you must set its play speed and its vertical and horizontal size. You should have a clear idea of what you want these to be right from the start because changing them halfway into your project can adversely affect whatever you've already created. For example, if you've placed objects on the stage and animated them to look just right at a 12 frames per second (fps), changing the fps setting will alter animation speed throughout the movie, making your movie appear different than your original conception. Sure, you could reedit to compensate, but that could take a considerable amount of time—especially if your movie is long. Plan so that the settings you choose are the ones you can stick with.

You set up a movie through the Movie Properties dialog box.

To set your movie's dimensions and speed:

1. From the Modify menu choose Movie to bring up the Movie Properties box.

2. In the Frame Rate box type the number of frames per second you would like your movie to play.

The default setting of 12 is sufficient for most projects, though you can choose a higher or lower number if you wish. Remember, the higher the frame rate, the more difficult it will be for slower machines to play back your movie.

3. In the Dimension boxes, enter values for the width and height of your movie.

The minimum width or height is 18 pixels; the maximum is 2880 pixels.

4. Adjust any of the other settings, and click OK.

The screen now reflects any changes you made.

These are not the only settings that affect the way your movie looks and works. Several other settings are available when you finally export your project to a movie. We'll look at these in more detail in Chapter 13, "Publishing Your Work."

Your First Interactive Flash Movie

Alright, it's initiation time: We promised an interactive tutorial at the end of this chapter to take you through the process of creating your first interactive animation—and here it is.

 The interactive tutorials on the accompanying CD-ROM disc are the best way to apply what you've learned in the chapters—and the next best thing to us showing you in person how to perform the tasks. Watch the tutorial while you have the program open, and pause it to perform the same task on your own computer. Replay sections as many times as you need to feel you've grasped the concept and are ready to move on.

Now, go!

You will find the following interactive tutorial on the CD along with the source files:

Your First Interactive Flash Movie. This tutorial guides you through the steps of creating your first interactive Flash movie. You'll see how drawing works, create movement, assign variable names for interactivity, and test your project.

Drawing

Who as a kid didn't love getting a brand-new box of crayons? The smell, the colors, the way they melted in the sunlight—all of these things combined to make them a treasured object of our childhoods. Crayons weren't expensive or fancy, but they helped us bring the world of our imaginations to life—and we never tired of producing artwork for the refrigerator door.

Now that we're older, the tools haven't changed much—except now they're digital and they're part of Flash. They still open up a world of possibility yet are simple to use. In fact, employing Flash's tool set to draw has got to be the easiest part of creating a presentation. With Flash's drawing tools, you can draw perfect squares and rectangles, paint with colors, erase mistakes, and much more. If you can point and click the mouse, you should be able to create graphics in Flash. But don't be fooled: With Flash's easy-to-use tool set, you can produce artwork that rivals in complexity that created by some of the leading vector art tools.

If you've used other drawing programs, you'll soon discover that Flash handles some aspects of graphics creation in a unique fashion. While it may seem awkward at first, once you've used the tool set enough, you may just decide that the Flash way is the *only* way.

Flash drawing tools create *vector graphics,* which are simply mathematical equations that your computer translates and displays as drawn objects. This equation contains all the information your computer needs to display the object accurately, including its size, shape, and position; whether it has a fill (and if so, what color); and whether it has an outline (and if so, what type). And the best part is, you never even see the mathematical equation; all you see is the *computer representation* of the equation. If only all math were so easy.

Let's take a look at the way the tool set works.

Tools and Modifiers

The Flash drawing toolbar actually consists of two areas: the toolbar buttons and the modifier controls (**Figure 3.1**). When you click a tool, it becomes active, displaying a set of modifiers you can use to adjust its settings. Select the Eraser tool, for example, and modifiers applicable to it appear in the modifier section of the toolbar. This type of context-sensitive interface makes numerous options readily accessible without having to go up to the menu bar—a clutter-free and time-saving feature that surprisingly few other programs incorporate.

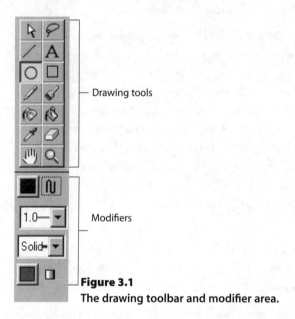

Drawing tools

Modifiers

Figure 3.1
The drawing toolbar and modifier area.

First, let's look at the tools and their modifiers (in the order they appear on the toolbar); later, we'll explore drawing tasks in depth. Because the Text tool has so many unique settings and uses, we discuss it at length in the next chapter. Also, you'll notice that we mention *stage-level objects* and *overlay-level objects* several times in our discussion of the tools. Briefly, a stage-level object can be thought of as something drawn directly on the stage, whereas an overlay-level object "floats" above it. You don't need to understand much about these concepts at this point; however, if you want more information, you can look ahead to the information on stage- and overlay-level objects later in this chapter.

The letter in parentheses following each tool name represents a keyboard shortcut: Simply press that letter on the keyboard to quickly switch between tools.

Arrow Tool (A)

There's a reason this is the first tool in the toolbar: It's the one you'll use the most. Acting as your "hands" inside of Flash, the Arrow tool is what you use to grab, select, move, and reshape your graphics (**Figure 3.2**). However, you must select an object before you can do anything with it—and you usually do so by clicking it.

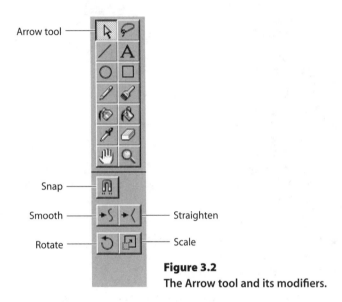

Arrow tool

Snap

Smooth ——————— Straighten

Rotate ——————— Scale

Figure 3.2
The Arrow tool and its modifiers.

The Arrow tool includes five modifiers:

Snap. If you choose this option, objects that you draw, move, rotate, or resize will "snap" into place.

Smooth. Allows you to smooth lines and simple shapes.

Straighten. Allows you to straighten lines and simple shapes.

Smooth and Straighten will only work on lines on the stage level; they will not affect overlay-level objects such as groups, text, symbols, and bitmaps that have not been broken apart.

Rotate. Allows you to rotate objects.

Scale. Allows you to resize objects.

> **TIP** *All the Arrow tool modifiers expect Snap will be grayed out until you first select an object.*

Lasso Tool (L)

The Lasso tool (**Figure 3.3**) resides next to the Arrow tool because you also use it to select objects on the stage. It's a bit more specialized, however. With the Lasso tool, you define odd-shaped areas of stage-level objects to select them for editing. You also use it to select areas in bitmaps based on color if they've been broken apart.

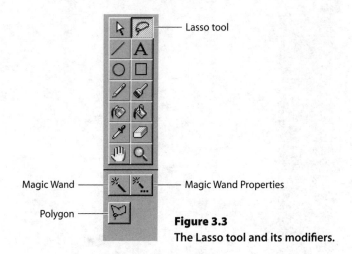

Lasso tool

Magic Wand

Magic Wand Properties

Polygon

Figure 3.3
The Lasso tool and its modifiers.

The Lasso tool includes three modifiers:

Magic Wand. It allows you to select odd-shaped areas of objects based on color.

Magic Wand Properties. Allows you to adjust Magic Wand tool settings.

Polygon. Allows you to select polygon-shaped areas.

Line Tool (N)

The Line tool (**Figure 3.4**) is as straightforward as its name suggests: You use it to draw straight lines, which are initially stage-level objects.

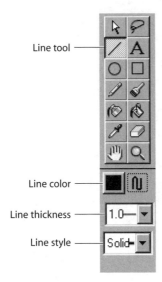

Line tool

Line color

Line thickness

Line style

Figure 3.4
The Line tool and its modifiers.

The Line tool includes three modifiers:

Line Color. Allows you to select the color to use when creating lines. You may choose any color on the palette except gradients (which can't be used as line colors so don't appear).

Line Thickness. Allows you to select line thickness.

Line Style. Allows you to select line style, such as solid, dotted, or dashed. You can even create custom styles.

> **TIP** *To color a line with a gradient or even a bitmap fill, you must first convert it into a fillable area by selecting the line with the Arrow tool and then choosing Modify > Curves > Lines to Fills.*

Text Tool (T)

We cover the Text tool in detail in Chapter 4, "Text."

Oval Tool (O)

Use the Oval tool (**Figure 3.5**) to create ovals and perfect circles—which are initially stage-level objects—and perfect circles.

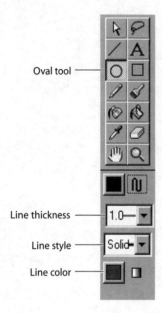

Oval tool

Line thickness ——— 1.0

Line style ——— Solid

Line color

Figure 3.5
The Oval tool and its modifiers.

The Oval tool includes four modifiers:

Line Color. Allows you to select the line color to use when creating ovals. You can choose any color available on the palette except gradients (which can't be used as line colors so don't appear) or "no color."

Line Thickness. Allows you to select the line thickness of your oval's outline.

Line Style. Allows you to select line style, including solid, dotted, dashed, and custom styles.

Fill Color. Allows you to select the oval fill color. You can choose any color available on the palette, including gradients and "no color."

> **TIP** *To color a line with a gradient or even a bitmap fill, you must first convert it into a fillable area by selecting the line with the Arrow tool and then choosing Modify > Curves > Lines to Fills.*

Rectangle Tool (R)

Use the Rectangle tool (**Figure 3.6**) to create rectangles—which are initially stage-level objects—and perfect squares.

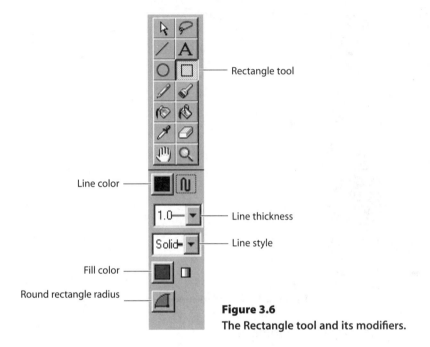

Figure 3.6
The Rectangle tool and its modifiers.

The Rectangle tool includes five modifiers:

Line Color. Allows you to select rectangle line color. You can choose any color available on the palette except gradients (which don't appear since they can't be used as line colors) or "no color."

Line Thickness. Allows you to select the line thickness of your rectangle's outline.

Line Style. Lets you select line style, including solid, dotted, and custom styles.

Fill Color. Allows you to select a rectangle's fill color. You can choose any color available on the palette, including gradients or "no color."

Round Rectangle Radius. Allows you to create rectangles with rounded corners. You can set the amount of radius for the corners via the Radius Settings dialog box.

> **TIP** *To color a line with a gradient or a bitmap fill, you must first convert it into a fillable area by selecting the line with the Arrow tool and then choosing Modify > Curves > Lines to Fills.*

Pencil Tool (P)

Use the Pencil tool (**Figure 3.7**) to draw freehand straight or curved lines, which are initially stage-level objects.

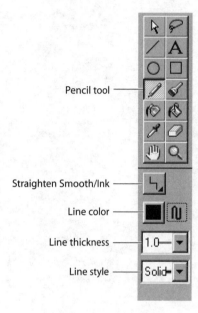

Figure 3.7
The Pencil tool and its modifiers.

The Pencil tool includes four modifiers:

Pencil Mode. Lets you choose from three modes to set how Flash modifies drawn lines:

Straighten performs shape recognition: If you draw a rough square, circle, straight line, or curve, Flash will perfect the shape based on what it thinks you're drawing.

Smooth does just what its name implies: It smoothes jagged lines.

Ink does nothing to your line, which means you can draw a line and be assured Flash won't modify it.

Line Color. Allows you to select the line color. You can choose any color on the palette except gradients (which don't appear since they can't be used as colors).

Line Thickness. Lets you set the line thickness.

Line Style. Allows you to select line style, including solid, dotted, dashed, and custom styles.

> **TIP** To color a line with a gradient or a bitmap fill, you must first convert it into a fillable area by selecting the line with the Arrow tool and then choosing Modify > Curves > Lines to Fills.

Brush Tool (B)

Use the Brush tool (**Figure 3.8**) to fill, or *brush,* areas with a solid color, bitmap, or gradient. Brush strokes are initially stage-level objects.

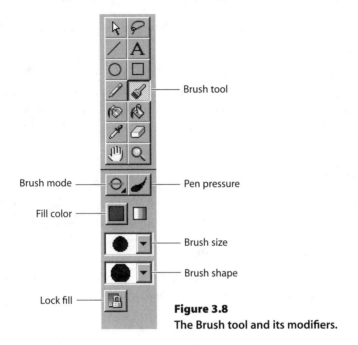

Figure 3.8
The Brush tool and its modifiers.

The Brush tool includes six modifiers:

Brush Mode. The five brush modes allow you to determine how brush strokes are applied when drawing:

Paint Normal paints over any area on the stage.

Paint Fills paints filled areas but not lines.

Paint Behind paints around stage-level objects but not over them, giving the appearance of painting behind a shape.

Paint Selection paints only inside filled areas that are selected.

Paint Inside allows you to begin a brush stroke inside a filled area and thereafter paint only inside that filled area without affecting any lines. If the point where you begin does not have a fill, your brush stroke will not affect previously filled areas.

Use Pressure. Available only for pressure-sensitive graphics tablets, this modifier allows you to create pressure-sensitive brush strokes. (A mouse can't make use of this feature.)

Fill Color. Allows you to select the fill color for brush strokes. You can choose any color on the palette, including gradients.

Brush Size. Lets you set the size of the brush stroke. Employed with the Use Pressure modifier, it defines the maximum size of the pressure-sensitive stroke.

Brush Shape. Lets you set the shape of your brush so you can create all sorts of interesting effects.

Lock Fill. Allows you to control how Flash paints areas with gradients. When turned on, all brush strokes that use the same gradient will appear to be part of one large gradient stretching across the stage. When turned off, each stroke will be distinct and display the entire gradient.

Ink Bottle Tool (I)

The Ink Bottle tool (**Figure 3.9**) lets you create and modify the color, size, and style of the lines surrounding a shape. The tool affects only stage-level objects.

The Ink Bottle tool includes three modifiers:

Line Color. Allows you to select line color. You can choose any color on the palette except gradients (which don't appear since they cannot be used as line colors).

Line Thickness. Lets you select line thickness.

Line Style. Allows you to select line style, including solid, dotted, dashed, and custom styles.

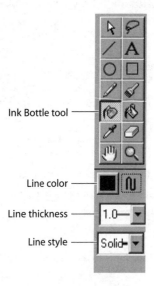

Figure 3.9
The Ink Bottle tool and its modifiers.

Paint Bucket Tool (U)

Use the Paint Bucket tool (**Figure 3.10**) to fill shapes made up only of an outline or to change a shape's existing fills. It affects only stage-level objects.

The Paint Bucket tool includes four modifiers:

Fill Color. Allows you to select the fill color. You can choose any available color on the palette, including gradients.

Gap Size. Lets you adjust the way the Paint Bucket tool handles outlines that are not completely closed.

Lock Fill. Allows you to adjust the way Flash fills areas with gradients.

Transform Fill. Allows you to resize, rotate, and skew gradients or bitmap fills within shapes.

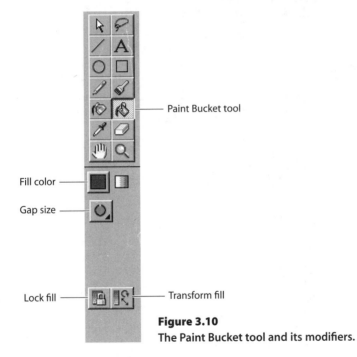

Paint Bucket tool

Fill color

Gap size

Lock fill — Transform fill

Figure 3.10
The Paint Bucket tool and its modifiers.

Dropper Tool (D)

The Dropper tool (**Figure 3.11**) Lets you *sample,* or pick up, the fill or line style of a stage-level object that's already on the stage and then apply that sampled fill or line style to another stage level-object. This time-saving tool has no modifiers.

Dropper tool

Figure 3.11
The Dropper tool.

Eraser Tool (E)

The Eraser tool (**Figure 3.12**) does just that: It erases. You can use it to completely or partly erase lines and fills and shapes. The eraser tool only affects stage-level objects.

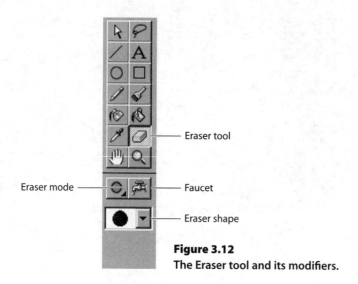

Eraser tool

Eraser mode

Faucet

Eraser shape

Figure 3.12
The Eraser tool and its modifiers.

The Eraser tool includes three modifiers:

Eraser Mode. This modifier includes five options, which control how Flash erases areas of your drawing:

Normal erases lines and fills.

Erase Fills erases only fills, leaving lines untouched.

Erase Lines erases only lines, leaving fills untouched.

Erase Selected erases only currently selected fills, leaving lines unchanged.

Erase Inside lets you begin erasing inside a filled area and thereafter erase only within that filled area without affecting any lines.

Faucet. Allows you to erase a line or fill just by clicking somewhere on the line or in the fill. (It acts the same as if you had selected a line or fill and then pressed the Delete key.)

Eraser Shape. Configures the shape of your eraser and lets you erase with precision.

Hand Tool (H)

The Hand tool (**Figure 3.13**) serves only one purpose: to help you easily move around your work area in any direction by grabbing the stage (click and hold anywhere) and then dragging. The Hand tool has no modifiers.

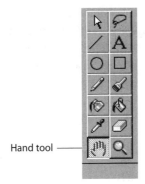

Hand tool

Figure 3.13
The Hand tool.

TIP *For this tool to work, you must make the work area viewable by selecting View > Work Area.*

TIP *Any time you are drawing with another tool, you can hold down the spacebar to activate the Hand tool. Releasing the spacebar returns you to the tool you were previously using.*

Magnifier Tool (M)

The Magnifier tool (**Figure 3.14**) allows you to zoom in or out of your drawing to work on fine details or to get a good overall look.

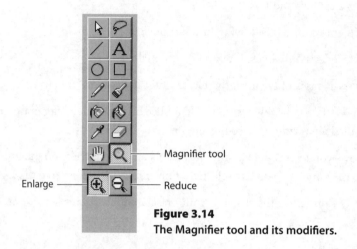

Enlarge —

Reduce

Magnifier tool

Figure 3.14
The Magnifier tool and its modifiers.

The Magnifier tool has two modifiers:

Enlarge. Zoom in on your drawing.

Reduce. Zoom out on your drawing.

> **TIP** *To enlarge an area of the stage, select the Magnifier tool and then click and drag on the stage. The area you're defining will be identified by a thin black outline. Release the mouse to complete your selection. Flash will automatically zoom in on the area you defined. (The maximum zoom amount is 2000 percent.)*

Drawing Tasks

Now that we've introduced you to all of the drawing tools, let's dig a little deeper: It's time to learn the ins and outs of graphic creation and page layout. By the time you've completed this section, you should be able to bring your ideas into being. So sit back, put on your beret, and get ready to create your first masterpiece.

Stage and Overlay Levels

When you're drawing or working with shapes and objects on the stage, you need to be aware that they can appear on two levels: the stage level and the overlay level.

> **TIP** *Although easy to confuse, levels and layers are not the same thing. Each layer on the timeline has two levels. For more information, see Chapter 9, "Layers."*

Imagine a sheet of glass on the floor. The glass represents a layer. Now, if you took a crayon and drew on the glass, you would be drawing on the *stage level* of the layer, and your crayon marking would be a *stage-level object*. If, however, you drew the same marking on a sheet of transparency paper and then placed it on the glass, your crayon marking would be an *overlay object* placed on the *overlay level*.

All stage-level objects can interact with one another. If, for example, you used a blue crayon to draw over a red crayon mark on the stage level, the wax from the two crayons would interact with each other. If instead you made your blue crayon mark on a sheet of transparency paper—an overlay-level object—the two markings wouldn't touch and thus could not interact.

> **TIP** *Although you can do some editing on overlay-level objects, you can apply most effects (for example, reshaping and adding gradients) only to stage-level objects.*

So why two levels, and what differentiates stage-level objects from overlay-level objects? The answer to these questions is simple: When you use the drawing tools to create graphics, you may sometimes want your shapes to interact to simplify editing. Once you're satisfied with your graphic's appearance, you can turn it into an overlay-level object. By so doing, you make your graphic a self-contained entity, no longer able to interact (from a drawing perspective) with other objects.

Types of objects

Comprising simple shapes such as lines, circles, and squares, stage-level objects are normally drawn with a tool from the Flash tool set. The most important thing to remember about stage-level objects is that they can affect each other and can be manipulated and reworked more than overlay-level objects can. You can turn stage-level objects into overlay-level objects by grouping them or by turning them into symbols. For our discussion, *simple shapes* and *stage-level objects* describe the same thing.

Overlay-level objects can contain any of the following:

Groups. Groups allow you to *group* together several simple shapes or other overlay-level objects so that they act as a single object. You can convert groups into stage-level objects simply by ungrouping them, or breaking them apart.

Text. Unless broken apart (see "Breaking Up Is Not Hard to Do"), text blocks are similar to groups but are just sections of editable text. Breaking text apart turns letters into stage-level objects so that you can edit them in ways not available to overlay-level objects (for example, reshaping them or adding gradient fills).

Symbols. You can turn any simple shape into a symbol. Similar to groups, you can use symbols in your movie. For more information, see Chapter 7, "Symbols."

Imported graphics. Flash imports all graphics, including bitmaps, as overlay-level objects. Only after you break apart an imported graphic does it becomes a stage-level object.

Stage-level objects will always appear below overlay objects if they are all on the same layer.

Breaking Up Is Not Hard to Do

*Although it may sound harsh, breaking apart graphics is actually a gentle process (**Figure 3.15**). It's what you do to turn overlay-level objects—including bitmaps, text, and symbols—into stage-level objects, thus reducing them to their most basic elements so that you can edit and control them, as you will learn in this chapter.*

To break apart a graphic, select it and then from the Modify menu choose Break Apart.

Figure 3.15
Select Break Apart from the Modify menu to break up a selected graphic.

TIP *To change the stacking order of over-lay objects on the same layer, select one of the objects, and then from the Modify menu choose Arrange and from the submenu choose one of the following (Figure 3.16):*

- *Bring to Front moves the selected over-lay object to the top of the stacking order of the layer it resides on.*

- *Move Ahead moves the selected overlay object up one position.*

- *Move Behind moves the selected over-lay object down one position.*

- *Send to Back moves the selected overlay object to the bottom of the stacking order of the particular layer it resides on.*

Figure 3.16
The Arrange submenu from the Modify menu.

Creating Objects

This is where the fun begins. Now that you know a bit about your tool set, it's time to experiment. In this section we'll show you how to create all kinds of objects that you can use in your movie.

Creating stage-level objects

All lines, circles, squares, and brush strokes you create with the Flash drawing tools are initially stage-level objects. It's only after you group them or turn them into symbols (which you'll learn about later) that they become overlay-level objects.

To create straight lines:

1. From the toolbar select the Line tool, or press the N key.

2. From the modifiers that appear in the lower part of the toolbar, choose a line color, thickness, and style.

   Move the pointer to the stage area, and you'll notice it changes to a crosshair (**Figure 3.17**).

Figure 3.17
The pointer changed to a crosshair on the stage when you select the Line tool.

3. Click and drag, and you'll see a basic representation of your line. Release when your line is at the angle and length you want (**Figure 3.18**).

> **TIP** *If you've turned on Snapping, the beginning and ending point of the line, along with the angle, will "snap" to the gird of the stage. (See the Snapping section later in this chapter.)*

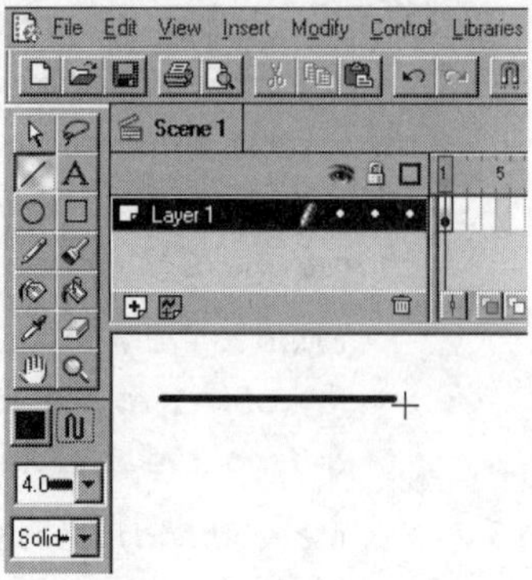

To create regular lines:

1. From the toolbar select the Pencil tool, or press the P key.

2. From the modifiers that appear, choose a pencil mode and line color, size, and style.

   Move the pointer to the stage area, and you'll notice it changes to a pencil (**Figure 3.19**).

3. Click and drag to create a line, and then release to finish drawing. Depending on the pencil mode, Flash straightens or smooths the line (**Figure 3.20**).

Figure 3.18
A line drawn on the stage.

Figure 3.19
The pointer changed to a pencil.

Figure 3.20
The line being smoothed.

To create ovals:

1. From the toolbar select the Oval tool, or press the O key.

2. From the modifiers that appear, select a line color, size, and style as well as a fill color.

   If you want your oval to have a fill but not an outline, or vice versa, select the No Color chip in the top left corner of the Line Color or Fill Color palette, respectively.

   Move the pointer to the stage area, and you'll notice it changes to a crosshair (**Figure 3.21**).

3. Click and drag, and you'll see a basic representation of your oval. Release when your oval is the size and shape you desire (**Figure 3.22**).

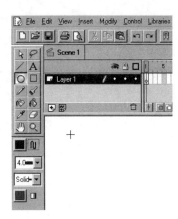

Figure 3.21
The pointer changed to a crosshair with the Oval tool selected.

TIP *To draw circles, turn on Snapping or hold down the Shift key when dragging.*

To create rectangles:

1. From the toolbar select the Rectangle tool, or press the R key.

2. From the modifiers that appear select a line color, size, and style, as well as a fill color.

   If you want your rectangle to have a fill but not an outline, or vice versa, select the No Color chip in the top left corner of the Line Color or Fill Color palette, respectively.

   Move the pointer over to the stage area, and you'll notice it changes to a crosshair (**Figure 3.23**).

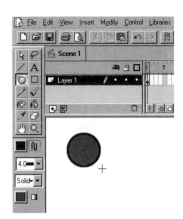

Figure 3.22
The oval drawn on the stage.

3. If you want your rectangle to have rounded corners, click the Round Rectangle Radius modifier, and set a radius amount.

4. Click and drag, and you'll see a basic representation of your rectangle. Release when your rectangle is the size and shape you desire (**Figure 3.24**).

Figure 3.23
The pointer changed to a crosshair with the Rectangle tool selected.

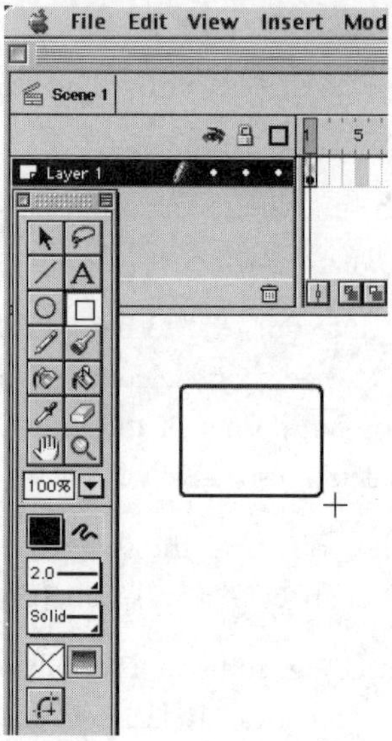

Figure 3.24
The oval rectangle on stage.

TIP *To create perfect squares, turn on Snapping or hold down the Shift key when dragging.*

TIP *An easier way to create a rectangle with rounded corners is, while dragging, to press the down-arrow key for corners with a larger radius and the up-arrow key for sharper corners.*

To create shapes with the Brush tool:

1. From the toolbar select the Brush tool, or press the B key.

2. From the modifiers that appear select a fill color, brush size, and brush shape. You can set how the tool applies brush strokes and handles gradients. (See the Tools and Modifiers section earlier in this chapter for more information.)

3. If you use a pressure-sensitive tablet, you can select the Use Pressure option to create brush strokes of varying widths based on the pressure you apply on your tablet. This option is not available if you use a mouse.

Figure 3.25
The Pressure modifier poised for use.

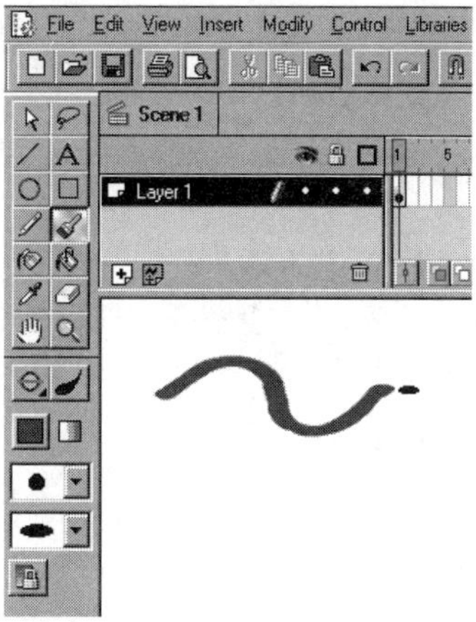

Figure 3.26
The brush stroke on the stage.

Move the pointer to the stage area, and you'll see it change to a representation of what your brush looks like based on the size and shape you selected. If you selected the Use Pressure modifier, the pointer will look like a circle with a crosshair inside.

4. Click and drag, and you'll see a basic representation of your brush stroke (**Figure 3.25**). Release when your brush stroke looks the way you desire (**Figure 3.26**).

TIP *If you break apart a bitmap, you can use it as a fill if you select it with the Dropper tool and then switch to the Oval, Rectangle, or Brush tool. The bitmap becomes the selected fill for any new ovals, rectangles, or brush strokes you create—that is, at least until you select a different one.*

Selecting Objects

When it comes to selecting things, many of us can be quite indecisive: Heads or tails, stripes or solids, Yahoo or Infoseek. It can all be too much. Not to fear, though: Selecting anything in Flash is pretty much a no-brainer—and it only takes a few seconds.

Before you move, resize, or rotate an object, you must first select it. A selected object is easily identifiable: Stage-level lines and fills take on a textured look, and overlay objects (such as groups or symbols) are surrounded by a textured outline of a box (**Figure 3.27**). You can select as many objects at once as you wish, which is useful for changing several objects together.

You'll use the Arrow tool for most of your selecting; however, you'll also use the Lasso tool for a few selections. For now, though, we're going to concentrate on the Arrow tool.

Before trying any of the following tasks, click the Arrow tool on the toolbar or press A on the keyboard to activate the tool.

Normal selecting

To select a line, fill, or overlay object such as a group or symbol, click it once.

To select a line and fill of an object simultaneously, double-click the fill.

To select same-colored lines that touch each other, double-click one of the lines.

To include more than one object in your selection, click once on any other object to select it and then shift-click on as many additional objects as you wish.

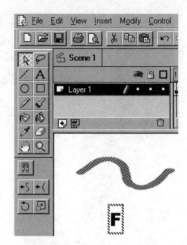

Figure 3.27
Comparison of selected lines and selected group.

> **TIP** *Flash has a Preferences setting that allows you to choose whether you wish to add multiple selections by clicking each additional object or by Shift-clicking. To reach this setting, choose File > Preferences, then check or uncheck the Selection Options: Shift Select checkbox (**Figure 3.28**). When you uncheck, or turn off, this option, you'll add objects to your selection by just clicking additional objects.*

> **TIP** *To select every object on the stage, choose Edit > Select All.*

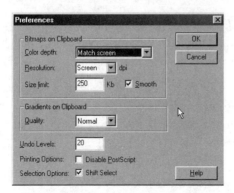

Figure 3.28
The Preferences dialog box.

Marquee selecting

Marquee selecting, or drag selecting, allows you to select whole areas or parts of lines and shapes on the stage level.

To marquee select an area:

1. From the toolbar select the Arrow key, or press the A key.

2. Click and drag in any direction. You see the outline of the selection box (**Figure 3.29**).

3. Once you've made your selection, release the mouse button (**Figure 3.30**).

   You must completely enclose overlay-level objects with the selection box to select them. If you do not do so, they will remain unselected. Stage-level objects, however, are a bit different: You select the portion of a stage-level object that's inside the selection box, not what's outside. This allows you to select parts of a stage-level object.

   TIP *Once you've made a selection using this method, you can add to the selection by holding down the Shift key and marquee selecting another area.*

Figure 3.29
Marquee selecting
multiple objects.

Selecting with the Lasso tool

Using the Lasso tool, you can select nonuniform areas of stage-level objects such as polygon-shaped areas and colors in bitmaps. Think of it as a specialized Arrow tool since its sole purpose is to select areas that would be otherwise impossible to define with the Arrow tool. (You can only select stage-level objects with the Lasso tool.)

Figure 3.30
Multiple objects
selected.

To select an area with the Lasso tool's Magic Wand modifier:

1. From the toolbar select the Lasso tool, or press the L key.

2. From the modifiers that appear, select the Magic Wand tool.

   Move the pointer to the stage area, and you'll notice it changes to a Lasso icon.

3. Click a color in a broken-apart bitmap.

The area you clicked becomes selected (**Figure 3.31**).

To select a polygon-shaped area with the Polygon modifier:

1. From the toolbar select the Lasso tool, or press the L key.

2. From the modifiers that appear, select the Polygon modifier.

3. Click, release, and drag, and you'll see a basic representation of one side of your selection area.

4. To add another side to your selection, click, release, and drag again. You can add as many sides as you wish by continuing to click, release, and drag.

5. Make sure you end close to the point where you started in Step 3. Double-click, and the area you have outlined becomes selected (**Figure 3.32**).

To select colors in a bitmap using the Lasso tool:

Make sure that the bitmap from which you wish to select colors has been broken apart.

1. From the toolbar select the Lasso tool, or press the L key.

2. From the modifiers that appear, choose Magic Wand properties.

3. In the dialog box, you can set two Magic Wand properties (if you so desire): Threshold and Smoothing.

Threshold allows you to define a range that determines how closely an adjoining pixel color must match the color you selected to also be selected. Using "0" selects pixels of the *exact* color of the one you picked. Using "100" selects *all* pixels (**Figure 3.33**).

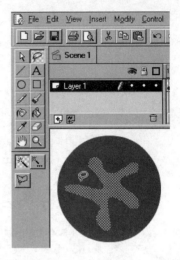

Figure 3.31
Area selected with the Lasso tool.

Figure 3.32
Area selected with the Lasso tool and the Polygon modifier selected.

Smoothing allows you to set how Flash deals with the edge of selected color areas. The setting can range from Pixel, which means the selected pixels perfectly define the edge of the selected area, to Smooth, which creates a very smooth selection edge.

4. Click OK.

5. Click a color in the bitmap to select it. Any pixels that fall within the Threshold range also is selected.

You can move or delete any selected areas (**Figure 3.34**).

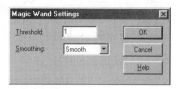

Figure 3.33
The Magic Wand Settings dialog box.

Figure 3.34
A selected area ready to be moved or deleted.

Deselecting

To deselect a selection, click on an empty space on the stage or choose Edit > Deselect All (**Figure 3.35**). To deselect an individual object, such as a part of a multiple selection, Shift-click the object.

Shape Recognition

Not many of us were born with surgeon's hands. And even if we were, we *still* wouldn't likely be able to draw perfect circles, squares, triangles, and straight lines. But don't despair: We know you have the *brains* of a surgeon since you were smart enough to get Flash 4—which takes care of drawing for you.

With shape recognition, you draw a rough idea of what you want and Flash cleans it up. You can create perfect objects with shape recognition as well as remove any roughness your object contains. Shape recognition does have its limits, however. You must give it a legitimate rough shape to work with—that is, you can't just close your eyes, draw a shape, and expect Flash to turn it into a square. You need to draw something *approaching* a square for shape recognition to work properly—and it works only on stage-level objects. You can use shape recognition while you're drawing a shape or after you've already created one.

Figure 3.35
Choosing Deselect from the Edit menu.

To use shape recognition while drawing:

1. From the toolbar select the Pencil tool, or press the P key.

2. From the modifiers that appear, select the Pencil Mode modifier pop-up menu and choose Straighten.

3. Select a line color, size, and style.

4. Draw a rough shape (for example, a square, triangle, or circle), and when you release the mouse, Flash attempts to recognize what you've drawn and create a more perfect version of it (**Figure 3.36**).

Figure 3.36
A shape without (left) and with (right) shape recognition enabled.

To use shape recognition on already drawn shapes:

1. From the toolbar select the Arrow tool, or press the A key.

2. Select the shape or line you want to modify, remembering that shape recognition works only on stage-level objects (**Figure 3.37**).

3. With your shape selected, press the Straighten modifier button. If your shape was rough in the first place, you'll now see a more perfect version (**Figure 3.38**).

> **TIP** If one click of the Straighten button doesn't perfect your shape, you can keep pressing it because it has an accumulative effect. You will, however, reach a point when the square or circle is perfect or the line is straight.

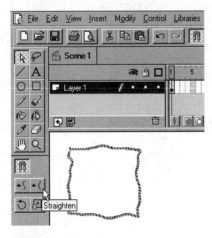

Figure 3.37
A shape before straighten.

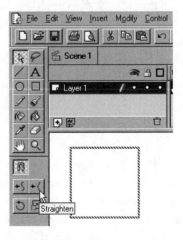

Figure 3.38
A shape after straighten.

TIP *You can also straighten an object by selecting the shape or line and then choosing Modify > Curves > Straighten. However, we don't really recommend this method since using the Straighten modifier on the toolbar is so much quicker and more efficient.*

Working with Line Attributes

While you may not think you can accomplish much with lines, the styles, shapes, and sizes Flash can apply to them open up a wealth of creative possibilities. Before you know it, you will have transformed your "simple lines" into artistic elements within a dynamic design. To find out how, read on.

In Flash you work with lines and outlines. A line is just a line, but an outline is a line with no beginning or end (like that which surrounds an oval or rectangle). While *lines* and *outlines* refer to essentially the same thing, you should understand the above distinction if you plan to work with them in Flash.

You work with lines and outlines to create new lines and edit existing ones. You use the Line, Oval, Rectangle, and Pencil tools to create new lines, and you edit existing lines with the Ink Bottle or Arrow tools. Either way, your choices for how you want your line to appear are basically the same: You control the line's attributes. Let's take a look at some of the attributes you can set for lines.

Line Color. Allows you to select any color from the current palette. If you don't like any of the colors on the palette, you can always create your own (see the Color section later in this chapter). You can also choose the No Color chip when creating ovals and rectangles to create an object without an outline.

Line Thickness. Allows you to select a line size and includes several preset choices. If you don't like any of the choices, you can scroll to the bottom of the pop-up list and select Custom. A dialog box appears allowing you to enter a custom size.

Line Style. Offers a handful of line styles. If you don't see one you want, you can create a custom style by scrolling to the bottom of the pop-up list and selecting Custom. A Line Style dialog box appears allowing you to create your own custom styles. For a detailed view of the effect of your custom settings on the line, check the Zoom 4x box.

TIP *Any settings you choose for one tool's line attributes will be reflected in the other tools that have line attributes.*

TIP *You can set line attributes when you create the object. To add to or change a line or outline setting, you'll need to use the Ink Bottle tool.*

To add or change a line or outline using the Ink Bottle tool:

1. From the toolbar select the Ink Bottle tool, or press the I key.

Move the pointer over to the stage area, and you'll notice it changes to an ink bottle (**Figure 3.39**).

2. From the modifiers that appear, choose your settings.

3. Use the tip of the bottle (where it looks like ink is pouring out) to click a line to change its attributes, or use it to click the edge of a filled shape to add an outline using the Ink Bottle tool's current settings (**Figure 3.40**).

The Ink Bottle tool also allows you to modify lines; however, it works differently than the other tools. You can use it to copy a line's color, thickness, and style and then easily apply those characteristics to another line.

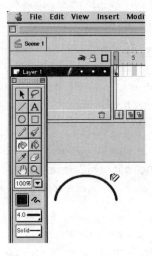

Figure 3.39
The pointer has changed to an ink bottle.

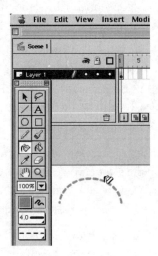

Figure 3.40
The line attributes changed after using the Ink Bottle.

To copy one line's attributes and apply them to another:

1. From the toolbar select the Dropper tool, or press the D key.

Move the pointer over the stage, and you'll see that it changes to a dropper.

2. When you position the dropper over the line with the attributes you wish to copy, a Pencil icon appears next to the dropper. Click once, and the Ink Bottle tool becomes active (**Figure 3.41**).

3. Click an existing line once to change it, or click the edge of a fill to create a line with the same attributes as those you picked up with the Dropper tool.

TIP *For information on reshaping lines and outlines, see the Reshaping section in this chapter.*

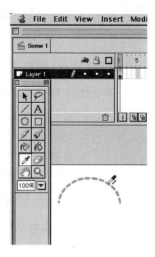

Figure 3.41
A pencil icon appearing next to the dropper.

Working with Fill Attributes

Although lines and outlines go a long way toward sprucing up designs, you really need to mix them with something of substance. Think how scary it would be if we were all skeletons with no meat on our bones. Adding fills is a graphical way of adding meat. Combine several filled objects with the right colors and gradients, and you have the potential for some very lifelike graphics.

Fills come in four flavors:

Solid. Color fills such as red, green, and blue.

Linear gradient. Special fills where one color fades into another from top to bottom or side to side.

Radial gradient. Similar to linear gradients except that they fade from inside out.

Bitmap. Fills created from a bitmap that has been broken apart. You can make a bitmap fill look however you want; you can even tile it inside a shape. For more about creating and editing bitmap fills, see Chapter 6, "Bitmaps."

We get more into the creation of colors and gradients later in the chapter. For now, you just need to be aware that solid-color fills are simple to create (as are gradient and bitmap fills) and that you can customize them.

You use the Oval, Rectangle, and Brush tools to create new filled objects, and you use the Paint Bucket tool to edit filled objects.

You can use four settings to create or edit fills.

For the Oval, Rectangle, Brush, and Paint Bucket tools:

Fill Color. Allows you to select any color from the current palette as your line color. If none of the colors are what you want, you can create your own (see the Color section of this chapter). When you create an oval or rectangle, a No Color color chip also becomes available; if you select it, you can create an outline shape with no fill.

For the Brush and Paint Bucket tools:

Lock Fill. Allows you to adjust how Flash fills areas with gradients. When turned on, all fills that use the same gradient will appear to be part of one large gradient stretching across the stage. When turned off, each fill will be distinct and display the entire gradient.

For the Paint Bucket tool:

Gap Size. Allows you to adjust how the Paint Bucket tool handles unclosed outlines. You can choose from four modes (**Figure 3.42**):

Don't Close Gaps.

Close Small Gaps.

Close Medium Gaps.

Close Large Gaps.

TIP *Although it can close many gaps, the Close Large Gaps mode only works within reason. If you find that it isn't doing its job, you may need to manually close gaps— or at least make them smaller for this mode to work.*

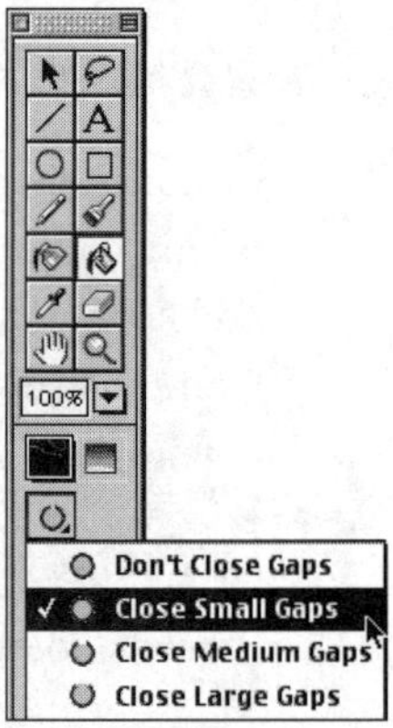

Transform Fill. Allows you to resize, rotate, and skew linear or radial gradients or bitmap fills.

Figure 3.42
The four Gap
Size modes.

TIP *Any settings you choose for one tool's fill attributes will be reflected in the other tools that have fill attributes.*

TIP *Although you can select a fill color or gradient when you create an object, you can also add a fill to an outline or change an existing fill with the Paint Bucket tool.*

To add or change a fill using the Paint Bucket tool:

1. From the toolbar select the Paint Bucket tool, or press the U key.

    Move the pointer over the stage, and you'll see that it changes to a paint bucket.

2. From the modifiers that appear, select your settings.

3. With the edge of the bucket (where paint is pouring out), click in a fill to change its attributes or click inside an outline to add a fill using the Paint Bucket tool settings. If you are using a linear gradient as a fill, you can click and drag to set the angle. If you are using a radial gradient, you can click and drag to set its center point (**Figure 3.43**).

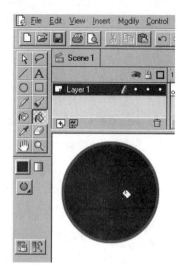

Figure 3.43
The Paint Bucket tool in use.

To edit a linear gradient fill:

1. From the toolbar select the Paint Bucket tool, or press the U key.

2. From the modifiers that appear, press the Transform Fill button. For this demonstration, make sure the Lock Fill button next to it is not selected.

    Move the pointer over the stage, and you'll see that it changes to an arrow with a small gradient symbol next to it.

3. Click anywhere on a linear gradient to make it editable.

    Editing handles appear (**Figure 3.44**), which allow you to move, rotate, and resize a gradient's center point. If you move your pointer over one of the handles, the pointer changes to reflect what the handle does.

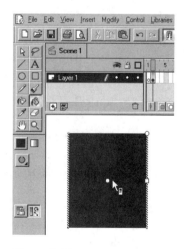

Figure 3.44
The gradient editing handles.

4. Edit the gradient:

To move the gradient's center point, click and drag the center handle with the four-headed arrow.

To rotate the gradient, click and drag the handle with the circling arrow.

To resize the gradient, click and drag the handle with the two-headed arrow.

To edit a radial gradient fill:

1. From the toolbar select the Paint Bucket tool, or press the U key.

2. From the modifiers that appear, press the Transform Fill button. For this demonstration, make sure the Lock Fill button next to it is not selected.

3. Click on a radial gradient. The gradient becomes editable, displaying editing handles that allow you to move, rotate, resize, and reshape a gradient. If you move your pointer over one of the handles, it changes to reflect what the handle does.

4. Edit the gradient:

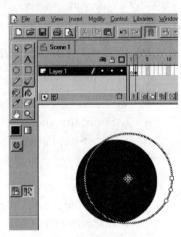

To move the gradient's center point, click and drag the center handle with the four-headed arrow (**Figure 3.45**).

To rotate the gradient, click and drag the small circle handle with the circling arrow.

To resize the gradient, click and drag the small circle handle with an arrow inside.

To reshape the gradient, click and drag the small square handle with the two-headed arrow.

Figure 3.45
Moving the gradient center point.

TIP *Remember, you can edit fills only in stage-level objects—not in groups and symbols or text unless the text is first broken apart.*

The Dropper tool also allows you to modify fills, though not in the same way the other tools do. With the Dropper, you can copy one fill's color or gradient and apply it to another fill.

To copy the attributes of one fill and apply it to another:

1. From the toolbar, select the Dropper tool, or press the D key.

Move the pointer over the stage, and you'll see it change to a dropper (**Figure 3.46**).

2. When you position the Dropper over the fill that has the attributes you wish to copy, a Brush icon appears next to the Dropper. Click once, and the Paint Bucket tool becomes active.

3. Click on a fill to change it, or click inside an outline to create a fill with the attributes you picked up with the Dropper tool.

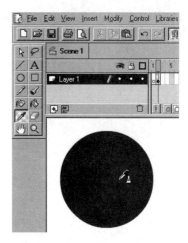

Figure 3.46
The pointer changed to a dropper.

> **TIP** *If you break apart a bitmap, you can use the Dropper tool to fill a shape by using the method just described. For more information see the Chapter 6, "Bitmaps."*

> **TIP** *For information on reshaping fills, see the Reshaping section of this chapter.*

Line and Fill Effects

Flash provides a few simple but useful goodies to help you in the design process. For example, although you can't usually fill lines with a gradient, Flash lets you turn a line into a shape that can have a fill of any kind, including a gradient or bitmap. This allows you to spice up those boring one-color lines.

You can also quickly create a larger or smaller version of a shape—a process known as *contouring* in some illustration programs. Referred to in Flash as *expanding* a shape, this process is a bit different than resizing (see the Resizing section in this chapter). Whereas resizing makes a shape proportionally larger or smaller, expanding a shape makes it appear swollen—it looks bigger and fatter but loses some of its detail and crispness.

A third Flash effect allows you to give a shape a soft edge. Flash does this by automatically creating a series of incrementally larger versions of the shape, each a little more transparent than the last. This makes the edge of the shape blend more easily with shapes or graphics behind it and gives vector shapes a more realistic look.

To turn a line or outline into a fill:

1. Select one or more lines on the stage that aren't part of a group or symbol.

2. Choose Modify > Curves > Lines to Fills to convert the line into a fillable shape (**Figure 3.47**).

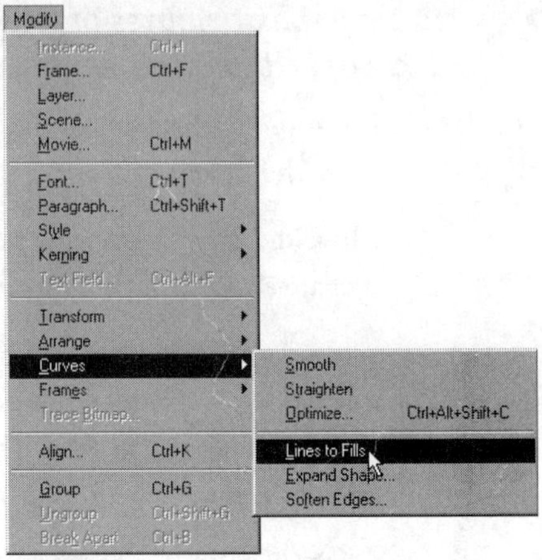

To expand a shape:

1. Select one or more shapes on the stage that aren't part of a group or symbol.

2. Choose Modify > Curves > Expand Shape.

3. In the dialog box that appears, choose your settings (**Figure 3.48**).

Distance. Allows you to set how far, in pixels, the expanded shape will be from the outside edge of the original shape.

Direction. Allows you to choose whether you want the shape to expand outward or inward. (Expand will make the shapes appear fatter, and Inward will make it look skinnier.)

4. Click OK.

Figure 3.47
Choosing Lines to Fills from the Curves sub-menu of the Modify menu.

Figure 3.48
The Expand Path dialog box.

To soften the edges of a shape:

1. Select one or more shapes on the stage that aren't part of a group or symbol.

2. Choose Modify > Curves > Soften Edges.

3. In the dialog box that appears, choose your settings (**Figure 3.49**):

Distance. Allows you set how far, in pixels, the soft edge will be from the outside edge of the original shape.

Figure 3.49
The Soften Edges dialog box.

Steps. Lets you set the number of steps from the original edge of the shape to the end of the softened edge. You get a smoother edge with a greater number of steps; however, this also results in a larger file size. Using too many steps can adversely affect the playback of you movie because Flash has to calculate an individual shape for each step. If you're setting 20 to 30 steps, you're using a lot of processing power.

Direction. Allows you to choose whether you want the soft edge to go outward or inward. (Expand will soften from the outside edge of the shape outward, and Inward will soften from the outside edge inward.)

4. Click OK.

TIP *Use the Soften Edges effect to give your shapes a drop-shadow effect. An interactive tutorial on how to do this can be found on the CD.*

Groups

Creating groups allows you to work on multiple objects as a single unit—for example, applying the same formatting, such as moving or resizing, to several objects at once.

Each object in the group retains its individual properties as well as its relation to the other objects when you edit the group. For example, if you move a group, all of the elements of the group retain their positions relative to each other. Likewise, if you resize the group, all of its elements are resized the same relative amount.

To create groups, the only drawing tool you use is the Arrow tool, which you use for selecting. This is because groups consist of objects already on the stage, including stage- and overlay-level objects. And groups can be part of other groups—a function called *nesting*.

You can also ungroup a group (for example, if you wished to edit individual objects).

To create a group:

1. Select the objects you wish to be part of this group. You can select anything on the stage, including simple shapes, other groups, bitmaps, and even symbols.

2. From the Modify menu choose Group (**Figure 3.50**).

TIP *Anytime you wish to revert a group back to its individual objects, select the group and from the Modify menu choose Ungroup.*

Figure 3.50
Creating a group from multiple objects.

Editing Objects

You'll rarely build anything that doesn't need some cleanup or fine-tuning—and Flash projects are no exception. Once your ideas begin to come to life, you may find that something that looked great on paper looks terrible on stage. Luckily, you can edit your objects. And in Flash such tasks as changing your object's color or reshaping, rotating, resizing, or moving it are all just a couple of mouse clicks away.

Moving objects

Consider yourself lucky when you create an object that is perfectly positioned and never needs to be moved: It won't happen often. Fortunately, Flash allows you to easily move objects with a great deal of precision.

You can move both stage- and overlay-level objects. To move a fill or an overlay object, simply click the object and drag it to a new location. To move a line, first select it and then click and drag it to a new location.

You can also select an object and press the arrow keys to move it up, down, left, and right a pixel at a time. If you hold down the Shift key while pressing an arrow key, your object moves 8 pixels at a time.

When you need to place an object with more precision than any of the above methods allow, you can use the Object Inspector.

To place an object precisely using the Object Inspector:

1. Select an object on the stage.

2. Choose Window > Inspectors > Object.

   The Object Inspector appears and offers four adjustable object properties: *x, y, w,* and *h.* The *x* field sets how many pixels separate the object from the left side of the stage; *y* sets the pixel distance between the object and the top of the stage. The *w* and *h* properties refer to width and height, respectively (**Figure 3.51**).

3. In the *x* and *y* fields enter your values, and press enter.

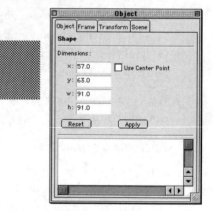

Figure 3.51
The Object Inspector.

TIP *Because the Object Inspector is context sensitive, you can select an object on the stage and the Object Inspector will reflect that object's properties. This makes it easy to adjust individual object settings by selecting them and then adjusting the settings.*

TIP *You can also select multiple objects (see the Selecting section of this chapter) and move them with the Object Inspector.*

Resizing objects

When you resize or rescale objects, you make them proportionately or disproportionately bigger or smaller by adjusting their width or height. Scaling changes an object's dimensions without changing its basic shape. You can resize both stage- and overlay-level objects.

Just as with moving, you can resize or scale a shape freehand (where you basically eyeball it), or you can precisely resize a shape using the Object Inspector or Transform Inspector.

To freely resize or scale a shape:

1. Select the shape on the stage.

2. Choose Modify > Transform > Scale, or from the toolbar's Arrow tool modifiers, choose the Scale modifier.

   Eight small boxes surround the shape.

3. Place your pointer over one of these boxes (it will change into a two-headed arrow), and click and drag.

   If you drag one of the corner boxes, you will scale the object's width and height proportionately. If you drag one of the side handles, you will adjust only the object's width or height, depending on which side handle you choose (**Figure 3.52**).

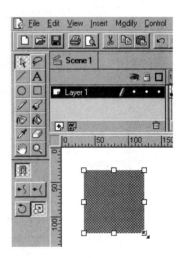

Figure 3.52
Resizing or scaling a shape.

To precisely scale or resize an object using the Object Inspector:

1. Select an object on the stage.

2. Choose Windows > Inspectors > Object.

The Object Inspector appears on the stage with four adjustable properties: *x, y, w,* and *h.* We discussed the *x* and *y* properties in the section on moving objects. The *w* field sets the width of the object in pixels; the *h* field sets its height in pixels.

3. Enter your new values in the *w* and *h* fields, and press enter.

To precisely scale or resize an object using the Transform Inspector:

1. Select an object on the stage.

2. Choose Windows > Inspectors > Transform.

The Transform Inspector appears on the stage and offers several settings: a percentage amount and the Uniform setting. If you enter a percent greater than 100 in this field, your object will become bigger; if you enter a percent less than 100, it will become smaller. Check the Uniform option if you want the amount you enter in the percentage field to be the same for width and height. If you leave this option unchecked, Flash shows you two percentage fields, one for scaling the width and another for scaling the height (**Figure 3.53**).

3. Enter your new values, and click the Apply button or press enter.

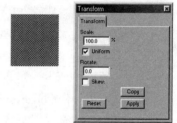

Figure 3.53
The Scale Inspector.

TIP *Flash offers you another way to transform an object using a percentage. Select the object, and then choose Modify > Transform > Scale and Rotate. A dialog box will appear. Enter a number in the Scale field, and click OK (**Figure 3.54**).*

TIP *By selecting multiple objects (see the Selecting section of this chapter) you can resize and scale them with the Object Inspector.*

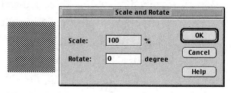

Figure 3.54
The Scale and Rotate dialog box.

Segmenting and connecting

Here's where Flash really differentiates itself from other drawing programs—and where you'll begin to understand why the application offers two levels (stage and overlay).

When you segment something, you cut off part of it or divide it. In Flash, segmenting and connecting allow you to create complex shapes with ease, putting a great deal of power at your fingertips.

Imagine rolling out a sheet of cookie dough and then using a cookie cutter to cut out shapes in the dough. You can do the same thing in Flash: When you fill in a rectangle (or any shape for that matter), you can place a circle partly over it or completely inside it and then remove the circle to reveal a hole or cutout section.

Likewise, you can cut a cake in half to make two separate sections. In Flash, you can draw a line completely through a circle to slice it into halves, which you then can treat as separate shapes. Once you've segmented a shape with a line, you can give the parts of the shape different fill colors or outlines. This is the interaction we referred to earlier when we discussed what you can do with shapes on the stage level.

You can only segment and connect stage-level objects.

To segment shapes:

1. With the Oval tool, draw an oval on the stage with a red fill and no outline.

2. With the Rectangle tool, draw a blue rectangle in the center of the oval you just created.

3. Select the blue rectangle in the center, and move it elsewhere on the stage.

    The oval now has a hole that shows the stage background color. This is the cookie-cutter effect produced by shape segmenting (**Figure 3.55**).

    TIP *Shapes can segment lines as well. By placing a shape on top of a line and then deselecting the shape, you can make the portion of the line that was underneath the shape disappear.*

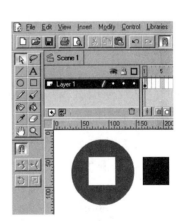

Figure 3.55
The cookie-cutter effect produced by shape segmenting.

To segment lines:

1. With the Oval tool, draw an oval with a red fill and a solid black outline.

2. Select the Pencil tool, and from the Pencil Mode modifier choose Ink. Draw a horizontal line completely across the oval you just created.

3. Select the top half of the fill: It is now a separate object, as is the bottom half.

   This is the slicing effect produced by line segmenting (**Figure 3.56**).

Figure 3.56
The slicing effect produced by line segmenting.

If you select any of the lines, you will notice that they have been segmented as well. Line segmentation like this occurs wherever lines intersect.

You can only segment two shapes if they are on same layer, are both stage-level objects, and are different colors. They must also have been deselected.

TIP *You can also segment a bitmap if you first break it apart.*

Connecting shapes has the opposite effect of segmenting: It can be likened to welding two shapes together so that they become one, allowing you to create shapes that you couldn't otherwise make with the Flash drawing tools.

To connect two shapes:

1. Select one shape and drag it on top of another.

2. Deselect the shape that you dragged.

   The two shapes automatically connect and become a single shape (**Figure 3.57**).

You can only connect two shapes if they are on the same layer, are both stage-level objects, and are the same color (gradients will not work). In addition, they cannot have outlines, and they must have been deselected.

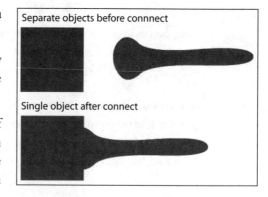

Figure 3.57
Separate shapes joined as one.

You can segment and connect any shape, including ovals, rectangles, lines, and brush strokes as long as they are not part of a group or symbol.

Aligning objects

Most designs require perfectly aligned and spaced graphics—a tedious task if it weren't for the automation Flash provides. With it, you can line up any number of objects—both overlay level and stage level—in a perfectly straight row or column. You can also align objects to the left, right, top, bottom, and center of each other as well as create even spacing between your objects.

What's more, Flash allows you to make selected objects match the size—horizontally, vertically, or both—of the largest selected object. You can even perform multiple alignment tasks simultaneously.

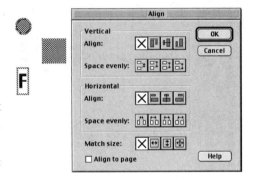

Flash's Button icons will help you to determine your alignment options. The boxes on the buttons represent objects, and the lines in the buttons represent the point at which the objects will be aligned or spaced. The Align dialog box offers eight buttons each for vertical and horizontal alignment and spacing; however, you can choose only one button at a time. Each button set, in turn, provides four alignment options for any objects you've selected (**Figure 3.58**):

Figure 3.58
The Align dialog box.

no alignment (the X buttons), edge alignment (top and bottom for vertical; left and right for horizontal), center alignment, and spacing.

(To understand how each option affects the objects you've selected, see **Figure 3.59**.)

First, be aware of two aspects of alignment: *edge reference* and *center reference*. In other words, what determines the edge or center that objects are aligned to?

Edge reference. When you select several objects on the stage, one of these objects is going to be the left-, right-, top-, or bottom-most object of the selection. Depending on which edge you choose to align to, this object's edge will be the edge all other objects align to. For example, if you choose to align the objects to the left edge, the left edge of the left-most selected object is the point all of the objects will be aligned to. That is, unless you've selected the Align to Page option, which aligns all selected objects to the edge of the page (stage).

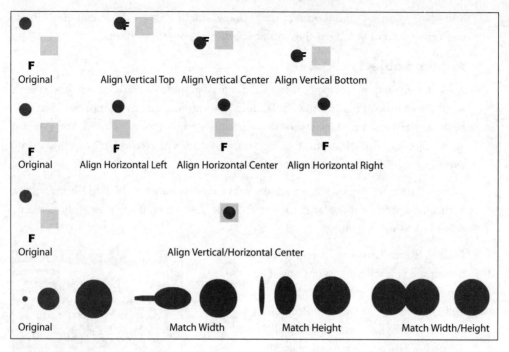

Figure 3.59
The effects of alignment options.

Center reference. When you select several objects on the stage, Flash creates an invisible center point, which represents the middle of the overall width and height of all of the selected objects. When you choose to align objects to the center, this is the center that the objects align to—that is, unless you've selected the Align to Page option, which aligns all selected objects to the center of the page (stage).

The "Match size" buttons all indicate which dimensions the objects will share. The largest object is the reference size that all others will match. Click the X button if you want all selected objects to remain their current size.

> **TIP** *To make aligning objects easy, you can turn on Snapping (see the Snapping section in this chapter) and the Grid (see the Using Rulers and the Grid section in Chapter 2, "Getting Started"). These options automate the alignment process.*

To align or space objects:

1. Select the objects you want to align.

2. From the Modify menu choose Align, or press the Align button on the toolbar.

   The Align dialog box appears.

3. Select the appropriate options, and click OK.

Rotating and skewing objects

Rotating, as you may have guessed, allows you to spin an object completely around based on a center point. Skewing allows you to distort, or bend, a shape at a vertical or horizontal angle. Just as with moving and scaling, rotating and skewing can be accomplished in free-form fashion or precisely.

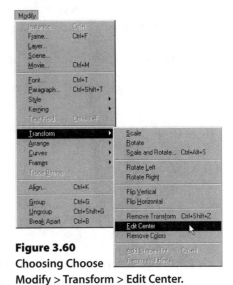

Figure 3.60
Choosing Choose Modify > Transform > Edit Center.

By default, the point that defines each object's center of rotation is the actual center of the object. With overlay-level objects such as groups and symbols, you can move this center point anyplace on the stage. You can rotate and skew both stage level-objects and overlay-level objects.

To change an overlay object's center point:

1. On the stage, select an overlay object.

2. Choose Modify > Transform > Edit Center (**Figure 3.60**).

   A small plus (+) sign appears in the middle of the object. This represents the object's center point (**Figure 3.61**).

3. Click and drag the center point anyplace on the stage, and then release.

   Whenever this object is rotated, the center of rotation will be wherever you placed it.

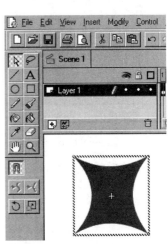

Figure 3.61
An object's center point.

To freely rotate or skew an object:

1. Select the shape on the stage.

2. From the Arrow tool modifiers, choose the Rotate modifier, or choose Modify > Transform > Rotate.

   Eight small circles surround the shape (**Figure 3.62**).

3. Rotate or skew your object in one of the following ways:

   Place your pointer over one of the corner circles (it changes into a circling arrow), and then click and drag. By clicking and dragging one of the corner circles, or *handles,* you can rotate the object clockwise or counterclockwise around its center point.

   Place your pointer over one of the side handles (it changes to a double-sided arrow), and then click and drag. You can skew the object vertically or horizontally, depending on which side handles you move: top and bottom or left and right.

To precisely rotate and skew an object with the Scale Inspector:

1. Select an object on the stage.

2. Choose Window > Inspectors > Scale.

   The Scale Inspector appears, offering two initial settings for rotating and skewing: the rotation angle setting and the Skewing option. By entering a nonnegative rotation angle (0 to 360), you

Figure 3.62
The eight circular rotation handles around a selected object.

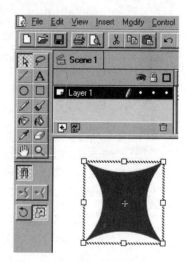

Figure 3.63
The skewing handles.

78

rotate the object clockwise that amount. By entering a negative rotation angle (-1 to -360), you rotate the object counterclockwise that amount. When you check the Skew option, you get two fields in which you can enter a horizontal skewing angle and a vertical skewing angle (**Figure 3.63**).

3. Enter your new values, and click the Apply button or press enter.

To quickly rotate an object at a 90-degree angle:

1. Select an object on the stage.

2. Choose Modify > Transform > Rotate Left or Rotate Right.

Rotate Left rotates the selected object 90 degrees clockwise; Rotate Right rotates it 90 degrees counterclockwise. You can choose this option multiple times to quickly rotate the object 180 or 270 degrees (**Figure 3.64**).

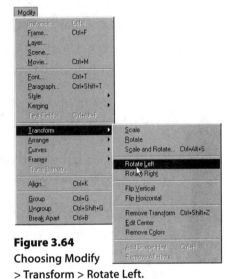

Figure 3.64
Choosing Modify > Transform > Rotate Left.

TIP *You can also rotate an object in Flash by entering a rotation angle. Select the object, and choose Modify > Transform > Scale and Rotate. In the dialog box that appears, enter a rotation angle in the Rotate field and click OK.*

TIP *By selecting multiple objects (see the Selecting section of this chapter), you can rotate and skew them using the steps above. The center point of multiple selected objects is the overall center of all the objects selected, and it cannot be moved.*

TIP *The Transform Inspector has a button labeled Copy. After you've selected an object on the stage, click this button to create a copy of the selected object. You can then apply the settings to the copy instead of the original.*

Flipping objects

Flipping an object creates a reflection effect, similar to holding the object up to a mirror. Flash allows you to easily flip both stage- and overlay-level objects horizontally and vertically.

To flip an object:

1. Select the object on the stage.

2. Choose Modify > Transform > Flip Vertical or Flip Horizontal (**Figure 3.65**).

   TIP *The way in which you flip an object is largely based on its center point. By moving the center point, you can change the point you flip it from.*

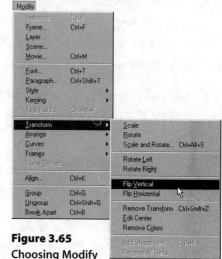

Figure 3.65
Choosing Modify > Transform > Flip Vertical.

Removing transformations

We all know about 20/20 hindsight. If we could just rewrite history, life would be so much better. Well, if you've ever resized, skewed, and rotated an object to death, only to find out it's *still* not what you want, it's time to rejoice because Flash lets you return a group or symbol to its original size and shape so that you can begin the editing process all over again. Keep in mind, however, that you can only remove transformations from overlay-level objects.

To remove transformations from an object:

1. Select the groups or symbols on the stage.

2. Choose Modify > Transform > Remove Transform.

   The object reverts to its original state (**Figure 3.66**).

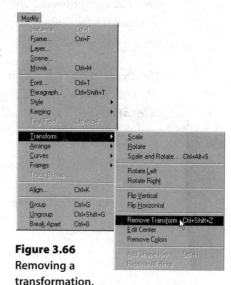

Figure 3.66
Removing a transformation.

TIP *You can accomplish the same thing from the Transform or Object Inspectors by first selecting the object and then clicking the Reset button on the Inspector.*

Reshaping objects

Just as a sculptor transforms a lump of clay into something incredible, as a digital artist working in Flash, you get to transform basic shapes such as squares, circles, and brush strokes into all sorts of things—and you don't even have to get your hands dirty.

Of course, squares, rectangles, and brush strokes aren't the only things you can use as starting points. You can also use broken-apart text to create some cool typography effects. Just remember: You can only reshape stage-level objects.

To reshape a stage-level object:

1. From the toolbar, select the Arrow tool, or press the A key.

Move your pointer over a line or along the edge of a filled shape, and it will change to indicate the type of reshaping you can do at that point.

2. Choose what area you want to reshape:

Sides of filled shapes and lengths of lines (**Figure 3.67**).

Corners of filled shapes (**Figure 3.68**)

Ends of lines (**Figure 3.69**).

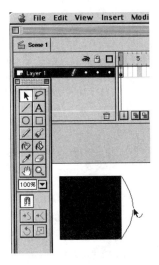

Figure 3.67
Reshaping the side of an object.

Figure 3.68
Reshaping the corner of an object.

3. Once you're at a point you would like to reshape, click and drag the pointer until the point is where you want it, then release.

TIPS *If you hold down the Control key (Windows) or Command key (Macintosh) when dragging a side, you can add a new corner point to the shape.*

If you find that a shape you want to work with has an unreasonable number of corner points, select it and press the Arrow tool's Smooth modifier to eliminate some of them.

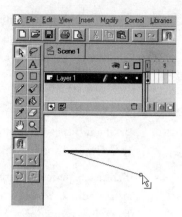

Figure 3.69
Reshaping the end of a line.

Snapping

Snapping allows you to easily create perfect shapes and align objects with each other or with points on the grid by "snapping" your pointer's movement to specific points on the grid or on objects. You can apply snapping to both stage- and overlay-level objects.

You can enable snapping in several ways: On the toolbar click the button with the magnet on it, choose the Arrow tool's Snap modifier, or from the View menu choose Snap.

You can apply snapping when you create a new shape or when you start to drag a side or corner of a stage-level object; a side, corner, or center point of an overlay-level object; or a line end.

You can make an item snap to:

Lines and intersecting points on the grid (the grid must be visible).

Edges of filled shapes.

The length and ends of lines.

An invisible line that follows the horizontal and vertical center of an overlay-level object.

The center point of an overlay-level object.

Points that are part of a symmetrical shape, such as a perfect square or circle.

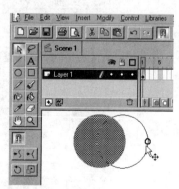

Figure 3.70
Reaching a point where reshaping can occur.

When you turn on snapping, you will notice a small ring underneath the pointer when you drag to create or edit an object. When you reach a point where snapping can occur, the ring grows larger (**Figure 3.70**).

Duplicating objects

If you weren't aware of Flash's built-in copy machine, you will be now. With Flash, there's no reason to create a graphic more than once. Take, for example, columns on a building or stars in the sky: Since they all look pretty much the same, you can draw just one and then make duplicates with the same size, shape, and proportions. You can create as many duplicates of an object as you wish, and you can even make copies of copies. You can duplicate both stage-level objects and overlay-level objects.

To duplicate objects:

1. Select the objecton the stage that you wish to duplicate.

2. Choose Edit > Duplicate, or press Control-D (Windows) or Command-D (Macintosh).

   A duplicate of your object appears on stage, offset slightly from the original.

   TIP *A quicker way to duplicate an object is to hold down the Control key (Windows) or Option key (Macintosh), place you pointer over the object, and click and drag a duplicate to any point on the stage (Figure 3.71).*

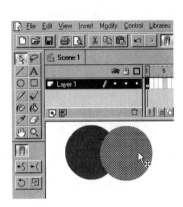

Figure 3.71
Duplicating an object.

Erasing

Erasing allows you to precisely remove portions of shapes or lines. You can change the size and shape of the eraser as well as the portions of any object you want to erase by adjusting the modifiers. You can only erase stage-level objects.

To erase with the Eraser tool:

1. From the toolbar select the Eraser tool, or press the E key.

2. From the modifiers that appear, select an Eraser mode.

3. Choose an eraser size and shape.

   (If you have the Faucet modifier on, size and shape settings won't work.)

Move the pointer to the stage area, and it will change into a representation of your eraser settings.

4. Click and drag.

5. Release when you've erased the portions you want remove (**Figure 3.72**).

> **TIP** *By selecting the Faucet modifier, you can delete complete lines and fills just by clicking them. This is similar to selecting a particular line or fill and then pressing Delete on the keyboard.*

> **TIP** *To delete everything on the stage at once, simply double-click the Eraser tool.*

Figure 3.72
Erasing a portion of an object.

Cutting, copying, deleting, and pasting

If you've ever cut, copied, and pasted information in another program, you'll find that Flash works the same way. You can cut, copy, delete, and paste both stage- and overlay-level objects.

You can employ these functions to perform any of the following:

Move objects to a different frame, layer, scene, or even movie.

Place a copy of an object in a different frame, layer, scene, or movie.

Delete an object.

Import text or graphics from other programs.

Cutting, copying, and deleting is pretty straightforward. Pasting, on the other hand, can produce different results, depending on what you're pasting and where you're pasting it. Here's what to expect:

Anything you cut or copy from Flash will be the same object when you paste it back into Flash—whether in the same movie or in another one.

Text you copy from an application such as a word processing program will be pasted in Flash as editable text if you paste it inside an existing text block. Otherwise, it will be pasted as a group, and you will need to ungroup it before you can edit it. For more information about working with text, see Chapter 4, "Text."

Vector objects you copy from other vector-based drawing programs such as Macromedia FreeHand, Adobe Illustrator, and CorelDRAW will be pasted as groups. If you ungroup them, you can edit them just as you would any other shape in Flash. You may need to ungroup imported vectors several times to turn them into stage-level objects.

Bitmaps are pasted into Flash as groups and may appear jaggy at first.

> **TIP** *Although you can copy from another program and paste into Flash, we recommend importing vector objects and bitmaps instead because the results are more predictable.*

To cut or copy an object:

1. Select it.

2. From the Edit menu choose Cut or Copy, depending on what you wish to do.

To delete an object:

1. Select it.

2. From the Edit menu choose Clear, or press the Delete key.

To paste an object:

From the Edit menu choose Paste, to paste the object in the center of the stage of the current scene.

By default, any object you paste is placed in the middle of the stage. The problem is, you may not want it in the middle of the stage. You may instead want to copy an object from one scene to the exact same position in another scene. This is where Paste in Place can help. By using Paste in Place instead of just Paste, you can paste your object in the same relative position form the top-left corner as you cut or copied it from.

Locking objects

Sometimes you'll want to work on a drawing without having to worry about selecting the wrong object. You can solve this problem by simply locking objects: This way, you can't select, move, or edit them until you unlock them again. You can, however, still see them. You can only lock overlay-level objects.

To lock a group or symbol:

1. Select the groups or symbols you wish to lock.

2. Choose Modify > Arrange > Lock (**Figure 3.73**).

To unlock all locked objects:

Choose Modify > Arrange > Unlock All.

You can't unlock individual objects because you can't select them when they are locked.

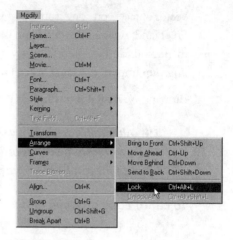

Figure 3.73
Locking a group.

Editing Groups

Have you ever wanted to edit the various elements of a group without actually ungrouping them? With Flash, you can do just that, editing just the elements of a group and nothing else on the stage. But what, you ask, is gained by doing this rather than just ungrouping, editing, and regrouping? By isolating a group, you avoid making unwanted changes to other elements on the stage.

To edit a group:

1. Select the group:

Double-click the group.

or

Click the group, and from the Edit menu choose Edit Selected.

2. Make your changes with the Flash drawing tools.

Anything on the stage that is not part of the group is dimmed to indicate that you cannot edit it.

3. When finished, double-click an empty place on the stage, or from the Edit menu choose Edit All.

Edit in Place

This is similar to editing groups. The difference is, you use Edit in Place only for symbols. Using Edit in Place, you can alter your symbol in the context of the rest of the stage. In other words, you can edit a symbol while other content on the stage remains visible.

To use Edit in Place:

1. Right-click (Windows) or Control-click (Macintosh) a symbol, and from the contextual pop-up menu select Edit in Place.

   Anything on the stage that is not part of the symbol is dimmed to indicate that you cannot edit it (**Figure 3.74**).

2. Make your changes using Flash's tools.

3. When finished, return to the entire scene by clicking the Scene button and choosing the Scene you would like to return to.

Figure 3.74
Choose Edit in Place from a symbol's pop-up menu.

Importing Vectors

Even with all of Flash's powerful capabilities, some tasks you still can't easily accomplish via its toolset.

For example, you may wrestle with creating polygons, spirals, or 3D objects. Or maybe you've created a bunch of artwork in FreeHand for a client, and now that client wants you to develop a Flash presentation that will take his breath away. There's no need to re-create the logo, Web graphics, and experimental concept in Flash—you can simply reuse your FreeHand artwork in Flash.

Or perhaps you just spent some of your hard-earned cash on one of the many wonderful clip-art collections that exist. It's a good bet that little, if any, of the clip art on those 14 CD-ROMs was created in Flash—yet that doesn't mean you'll need to convert any of those graphics to use in your Flash presentation.

Importing can help in each of these scenarios.

Importing allows you to take graphics created outside of Flash and bring them into Flash, where you can work with them and animate them just as if Flash had made them.

Most vector graphics programs on the market today—including Adobe Illustrator, CorelDRAW, Deneba Canvas, Macromedia FreeHand, and even Flash—can import and export vector graphics, so you can easily create a graphic in one program and use it in another. And when you import and export files, the vector format most accurately reproduces artwork, including layers.

Although the Adobe Illustrator format may be the most popular means of working with graphics between programs, it's not the only way. **Table 3.1** lists the vector graphic formats that Flash can import.

Table 3.1

Vector Formats Supported by Flash

Type	Windows	Macintosh
Enhanced Metafile (.emf)	X	
Windows Metafile (.wmf)	X	
Adobe Illustrator (.ai, .eps)	X	X
Flash Player (.swf, .spl)	X	X
AutoCAD DXF (.dxf)	X	X

To import vector graphics into Flash:

1. From the File menu choose Import.

The Import dialog box appears.

2. Locate the file you wish to use, and click Open.

If the imported file's name ends with a number—for example, Ball1.ai—Flash will look for a related sequence of files, such as Ball2.ai and Ball3.ai. If it finds a sequence, it will ask whether you want to import the single file you first specified or the whole sequence of files.

For 3D, if you use Adobe Dimensions to create animated 3D objects, you can export each animation frame as a separate .ai file of a sequence. You can then import the sequence into Flash and open up the world of 3D for your projects.

TIP *If you choose to import a .swf file, which is actually a Flash movie, you can't import individual layers, actions, or tweening. The .swf format is best if you export from FreeHand (using the Flash Xtra) and then import into Flash.*

Optimizing Graphics

When you create or import an object, you may sometimes need to optimize it, basically eliminating some of the unnecessary vector curves. You can think of it as removing "vector splinters"—things you can't see from a distance but are noticeable up close. This is important because fewer curves means smaller files, and small files usually indicate well-done Flash projects. In addition, graphics with lots of vector curves require a lot of processing power and can thus slow down your presentation's animation.

Imported graphics, such as those from a clip-art gallery, are good candidates for optimization. (We've seen a file reduced by as much as 70 percent after being optimized.) However, imported files aren't the only graphics that can benefit from optimizing. Believe it or not, even objects you create with Flash's own drawing tools can be optimized. For example, hand-drawn lines that appear smooth from a distance may look crooked when you zoom in on them; to make them smoother, you can optimize them.

Because optimization actually edits the vectors that make up a shape, it can sometimes change a graphic's appearance, especially with pieces of clip art. Usually, though, such changes aren't too noticeable. And fortunately, Flash lets you control how much optimizing actually occurs, so you can keep distortion to a minimum.

You can optimize graphics only on the stage level.

To optimize a graphic:

1. On the stage, select the line or fill you wish to modify.

If you want to optimize an imported graphic, which is normally imported as a group, make sure you completely ungroup it first.

2. Choose Modify > Curves > Optimize.

3. In the Optimize Curves dialog box, select your settings (**Figure 3.75**):

Smoothing. Use this to set the amount that Flash will smooth, or optimize, the item.

Use Multiple Passes. Select this to have Flash optimize, scan, and then reoptimize an item until it can't be optimized any more. (This just automates the process.)

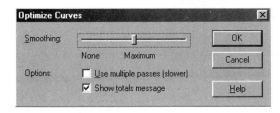

Figure 3.75
Optimizing curves.

Show Totals Message. Employ this if you want to see a breakdown of just how much optimizing Flash was able to do. It gives you that same satisfied feeling you get from cleaning a filthy house.

4. Click OK.

Flash optimizes the shape based on your settings. If you don't like the results, simply select Undo and pick new settings.

The Assistant

With all that drawing power at your fingertips, you may find that you need help figuring things out now and again. Fortunately, Flash comes with a helpful assistant. OK, it can't get coffee or even send memos, but it can assist you with most of your drawing tasks. In fact, it can even help you set personal preferences for the drawing tools. To get to your own assistant, from the File menu choose Assistant.

Let's take a look at the options (**Figure 3.76**):

Snap to grid controls how near to the grid a line's end points can be before snapping to it.

Connect lines determines how close two end points must be before Flash will connect them.

Smooth curves sets the degree of smoothing Flash will apply to lines drawn with the Pencil tool when you select the Straighten or Smooth modifiers.

Recognize lines controls how straight a line drawn with the Pencil tool must be for Flash to recognize and straighten it.

Recognize shapes sets how close you have to come to a Pencil-drawn shape—such as an oval or a square—for Flash to recognize and perfect it.

Click accuracy determines how close you can click to an object to select it.

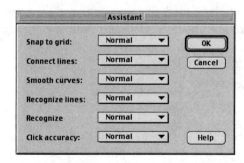

Figure 3.76
The Assistant.

Color

Who can forget the moment in *The Wizard of Oz* when the dull, lifeless, black-and-white world of reality is replaced by the beautiful, full-color world of Oz? Sixty years ago, those filmmmakers understood something we still know to be true: Color affects us. It provokes an emotional response.

Thus, by using color effectively, you can grab your audience's attention and guide their reactions to your presentation. Why is it then that much of the content on the Web looks like designers aren't giving color much thought at all?

Although we don't intend to get into the finer points of color theory here, an understanding of some basic principles can go a long way toward making your designs pleasing and effective. First off, let's take a look at what precisely it is that makes up a color.

What Makes a Color?

All colors comprise three elements:

Hue is the most obvious characteristic and gives colors their names: red, yellow, and blue, for example. Every color falls into a hue category in the spectrum, or range, of colors.

Saturation describes the intensity of hue. Saturated colors are intense and deep; less saturated colors are washed out or dull.

Luminance describes a color's brightness of illumination and locates its position in relation to a scale of grays between black and white.

Some graphic programs allow you to enter HSL (hue, saturation, and luminosity) values to achieve the color you desire. Flash is not one of them. Instead, it lets you define a color in one of three ways: The first is through the Color dialog box, which lets you define a color by moving your pointer through a rainbow of colors and adjusting sliders. We'll come back to this at the end of the chapter.

The second and third methods are by entering RGB values and hex values. *Relax*—it's not as bad as it sounds. These methods just describe different ways to create a color's hue, saturation, and luminance; they are not additional color characteristics.

RGB stands for red, green, blue. Your computer monitor displays every color you see by using a mixture of these three colors. The amount of each color used is based on a value between 0 and 255. Mixing colors on a monitor is different than mixing them on paper with watercolors. Using watercolors, the darker or blacker we want something, the more color we add; the whiter we want something, the less color we use. It works just the opposite way with your monitor and RGB values. If R, G, and B each has a value of 0 (represented as 0-0-0), your screen will be black. If each has a value of 255 (or 255-255-255), your screen will be white. The value 255-0-0 is pure red because the first number value in the sequence represents red. Likewise, 0-255-0 equals pure green, and 0-0-255 is pure blue.

You may find it takes some practice to mix red, green, and blue to create colors if you used the primary colors red, yellow, and blue to paint with in art class. While in art class you may have created orange by mixing the primary colors of red and yellow, with RGB, you create orange using the value 255-177-0—the maximum value of red, half the value of green, and no blue. If this seems confusing, experiment a bit, and you'll begin to get the hang of it.

The third method Flash uses to create, or define, color is via hex values. *Hex,* short for *hexadecimal,* is a six-digit value that describes a color. Most HTML documents and Web pages use hexadecimal values to describe colors. Being able to enter the same color value on a Web page as you do in your Flash movie makes it easy to maintain color consistency.

With hex, instead of assigning a value of from 0 to 255 to R, G, and B, you assign a value of 00 to ff. Let us explain.

We're used to the base ten system, where the numerals run 0 to 9 and then repeat with a *1* attached to them—10 to 19—and repeat again with a *2* attached —20 to 29—and so on. Hex values are a little different. Instead of going from 0 to 9 and then repeating, hex values run 0 to 9 but continue on with *a* to *f*—...8, 9, a, b, c, d, e, and f— before repeating. The hex system is base 16, so *15* in base 10 is equivalent to f in base 16. When you've run through the first 16 0 to f hex values, they repeat with a *1* attached: 10, 11, 12, 13, 14, 15, 16, 17, 18, 19, 1a, 1b, 1c, 1d, 1e, 1f. The value 1f is equal to 31 in our more familiar numbering system, and ff is equal to 255. **Table 3.2** shows the complete hex values for 0 to 255.

An RGB value of 100-255-0 converted to hex is 64ff00. You'll use this later in the color creation process. Now let's move on to another aspect of color that plays a major role on the Web.

Table 3.2
Hex-to-Decimal Conversion Table

	0	1	2	3	4	5	6	7	8	9	a	b	c	d	e	f
0	0	1	2	3	4	5	6	7	8	9	10	11	12	13	14	15
1	16	17	18	19	20	21	22	23	24	25	26	27	28	29	30	31
2	32	33	34	35	36	37	38	39	40	41	42	43	44	45	46	47
3	48	49	50	51	52	53	54	55	56	57	58	59	60	61	62	63
4	64	65	66	67	68	69	70	71	72	73	74	75	76	77	78	79
5	80	81	82	83	84	85	86	87	88	89	90	91	92	93	94	95
6	96	97	98	99	100	101	102	103	104	105	106	107	108	109	110	111
7	112	113	114	115	116	117	118	119	120	121	122	123	124	125	126	127
8	128	129	130	131	132	133	134	135	136	137	138	139	140	141	142	143
9	144	145	146	147	148	149	150	151	152	153	154	155	156	157	158	159
a	160	161	162	163	164	165	166	167	168	169	170	171	172	173	174	175
b	176	177	178	179	180	181	182	183	184	185	186	187	188	189	190	191
c	192	193	194	195	196	197	198	199	200	201	202	203	204	205	206	207
d	208	209	210	211	212	213	214	215	216	217	218	219	220	221	222	223
e	224	225	226	227	228	229	230	231	232	233	234	235	236	237	238	239
f	240	241	242	243	244	245	246	247	248	249	250	251	252	253	254	255

The Web-Safe Palette

By combining the 256 values each of red, green, and blue value, you can create 16,777,216 (256 x 256 x 256) colors. It would be great if you could use all of these possible colors without thinking about it. Unfortunately, you do have to think about it because although you have more than 16 million colors to choose from, some of your audience will be using computers that can only display 256 without dithering.

Dithering is a way your computer tries to simulate colors that it can't normally display. It does this by mixing colors it *can* display to approximate other colors, creating a similar illusion to viewing a newspaper from a distance. From a distant vantage point, the newspaper appears to be full of colors; up close, however, you see that all of those colors are made up of little dots of only a few colors that blend together seamlessly when observed from far away.

Most designers don't look on dithering favorably because dithered solid colors can sometimes appear snowy or speckled, which can detract from a wonderful design. However, dithering is less noticeable in graphics (such as photographs) where numerous colors are dithered rather than just one (**Figure 3.77**).

The only way to avoid dithering is to use the same 256 colors your viewer's computer uses. However, if you're designing for the Web, this number drops to 216 because the major browsers and operating systems have only 216 Web-safe colors in common. With all other colors, you're taking your chances with color inconsistencies and dithering.

The Web-safe palette, although small, does offer a variety of color choices. You'll find black, white, greens, reds, pinks, blues, yellows and many colors in between. **Table 3.3** lists the six values you can use for R, G, and B to give you all 216 (6 x 6 x 6) Web-safe colors.

To make it easier to find the right Web-safe color, Flash does two things: By default it loads Web-safe colors, so you can select any of them and know they won't dither. And its snap-to feature "snaps" the colors you select to the nearest Web-safe color.

Although the Web-safe palette is important, you shouldn't feel completely restricted by it. After all, computers are becoming more capable and can display more colors every day. Besides, there are times when only a color that is not Web safe will do. Use it, and don't worry. At least you're informed enough to make the choice.

Web-safe   Dithered

Figure 3.77
Web-safe versus dithered colors.

Table 3.3
Web-Safe Values

RGB	Hex
0	00
51	33
102	66
153	99
204	cc
255	ff

Working with Solid Colors and Gradients

The Color dialog box is where you actually get your hands dirty, adding, changing, and deleting colors and gradients on the color palette. One of the first things you'll notice about the Color dialog box is that it has two tabs, Solid and Gradient.

The Solid tab contains the following (**Figure 3.78**):

Current color palette. This scrollable palette displays the available solid colors for creating fills and outlines. Select a color by clicking it.

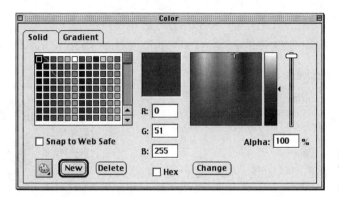

Figure 3.78
The Solid Color
dialog box.

Snap to Web Safe. When you choose a color, this option will snap it to its closest Web-safe equivalent. What's the point of having this if the palette is already made up of all 216 Web-safe colors anyway? Convenience, really. Sometimes you may wish to just enter an RGB value rather than calculate which Web-safe color is the closest. Check this option, and Flash takes care of it for you.

Color preview box. This box displays a large representation of the color you've selected as well as the effects of your editing. If the color is transparent, a grid will show through it.

RGB value fields. Enter individual RGB values here to create colors. If you leave the Hex option unchecked, use values from 0 to 255. If you check the Hex box, you'll need to enter values in hex format.

Hue and saturation definition area. Click and drag inside this multicolored square on the right side of the dialog box to select a color. A small crosshair indicates where the color is in the area.

Luminosity definition slider. Click and drag inside this rectangle or on the arrow to the right of it to set the luminosity value of your color.

Alpha slider. Drag this slider to define your color's transparency value. If the slider is at its top-most position your color will be completely opaque. At its bottom-most position your color will be completely transparent.

Alpha value field. You can also enter a percentage in this box to set your color's transparency.

Color set button. This pop-up menu lets you work with color palettes—which we'll cover shortly.

New button. Adds a currently defined color to the palette.

Delete button. Deletes a selected color from the palette.

Change button. Updates a selected color with editing changes you've made to it.

To edit or create a new color:

1. Bring up the Color dialog box:

From the Window menu choose Colors.

or

With a tool that uses color, select the Color modifier pop-up menu, and click the Color Palette icon at the top of the menu.

2. In the Color dialog box, click the Solid tab, and select a color on the color palette (**Figure 3.79**).

3. If you've edited a color, click the Create button to add your new color to the end of the color palette or click the Change button to replace the original color you selected with your edited version.

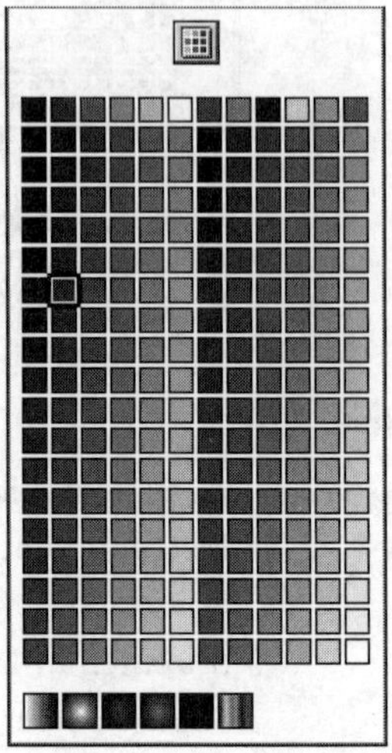

Figure 3.79
Selecting a color
on the Solid palette.

To delete a color:

1. In the Color dialog box, select the color you wish to delete from the palette.

The color is surrounded by a black border.

2. Click the Delete button.

Flash deletes the color from the palette.

Let's look at the Gradient tab now (**Figure 3.80**). As you can see, it's slightly different from the Solid colors tab. The Gradient tab of the Color dialog box contains the following:

Current gradient palette. This scrollable list displays the available gradients for creating fills and outlines. Select a gradient by clicking it.

Pointer well and color pointers. Use this area to define where a color in the gradient changes.

Gradient definition bar. This bar displays the effects of your editing on the selected gradient.

Gradient type pop-up menu. You can choose between two gradients: *Linear gradients* create a parallel blend of colors, and *radial gradients* create a circular blend of colors.

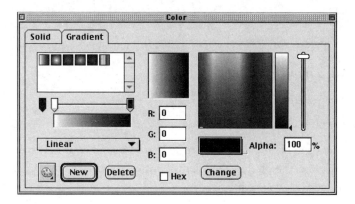

Figure 3.80
The Gradient Color dialog box.

Gradient preview box. This box displays a large representation of the gradient you've selected and shows the effects of your editing. If the gradient is transparent, a grid will show through it.

RGB value fields. Enter individual RGB values here to create colors of the gradient. If you leave the Hex option unchecked, use values from 0 to 255. If you check the Hex box, you'll need to enter values in hex format.

Hue and saturation definition area. Click and drag inside this multicolored square on the right side of the dialog box to select a color for your gradient. A small crosshair indicates where the color is in the area.

Luminosity definition slider. Click and drag inside this rectangle or on the arrow to the right of it to set the luminosity value of your gradient color.

Alpha slider. Drag this slider to define your color's transparency value. If the slider is at its top-most position, your color will be completely opaque. At its bottom-most position your color will be completely transparent.

Alpha value field. You can also enter a percentage in this box to set your color's transparency.

Solid color pop-up menu. This pop-up menu displays the solid colors on the current palette. Use this to define the colors of your gradient.

Color set button. This pop-up menu lets you work with color palettes. We'll cover this shortly.

New button. Adds a currently defined gradient to the palette.

Delete button. Deletes a selected gradient from the palette.

Change button. Updates a selected gradient with editing changes you've made to it.

To edit or create a new gradient:

1. In the Color dialog box, click the Gradient tab.

2. Click a gradient in the palette to edit it.

3. If you've edited a gradient, click the Create button to add your new color to the end of the color palette or click the Change button to replace the original gradient you selected with your edited version.

To delete a gradient:

1. In the Color dialog box, select the gradient you wish to delete from the palette.

The gradient is surrounded by a black border.

2. Click the Delete button.

Flash deletes the gradient from the palette.

TIP *The Color dialog box remains available until you close it, which means you can continue to modify colors and perform on-the-spot color and gradient editing.*

Importing and Exporting Palettes

Flash allows you to easily import color palettes created for other Flash projects or in different programs such as Macromedia Fireworks. This means you don't need to tediously re-create a custom palette from another project. You can export your current color palette from Flash to use it elsewhere as well.

Flash can export a palette in two formats, .CLR (.FCLR for Macintosh) and Adobe color tables, or .ACT files. CLR files save both solid-color and gradient information, but only Flash can use this type of palette. ACT files cannot store gradient information but can be used in such programs as Flash, Macromedia Fireworks, and Adobe Photoshop. Consider your needs to determine which format is best.

When importing, you can bring in .CLR or .ACT palettes, or import the color palette of a .GIF graphic file. This means all of the colors in a .GIF file will import as a palette.

The Color set pop-up menu is where you import and export palettes. The options available include:

Add Colors. Allows you to import a palette from a .CLR, ACT, or .GIF file and add it to the current palette. Selecting this option opens the Import Color Swatch dialog box, where you can locate the palette you want.

Replace Colors. Lets you replace the current palette with an imported one. Selecting this option opens the Import Color Swatch dialog box, where you can locate the palette you want.

Load Default Colors. Loads the default color palette that comes with Flash or one you defined with the Save as Default option (see below). Selecting this option automatically updates the current palette with the default one.

Save Colors. Allows you to save the current palette as a .CLR or .ACT file for use in either other Flash projects or in other programs. Selecting this option opens up the Export Color Swatch dialog box, where you can name your palette and choose a format (.CLR or .ACT).

Save as Default. Lets you save the current palette as the one Flash uses automatically when you start a new Flash project. Selecting this option opens an alert box asking you to confirm your decision. Choose Yes or No.

Clear Colors. Clears all colors from the current palette except black and white and one gradient.

Web 216. Loads the Web-safe palette of 216 colors that Flash ships with.

Sort by Colors. Sorts the colors on the current palette by their luminosity values.

Drawing Tutorials

 To help you put all of these things together, we've assembled the following interactive tutorials (which you'll find on the CD along with the resulting source files):

Basic Drawing in Flash. This tutorial guides you through the basic concepts behind Flash's drawing tools.

Chrome Text. This tutorial shows you how to create text in Flash with the look of chrome. You'll see the reasons behind breaking text apart and view segmenting in action.

Glowing Text. This tutorial shows you how to create text that appears to be glowing. You'll learn how to add outlines to text and work with groups.

Drop Shadows. This tutorial shows you how to create drop shadows on objects in Flash to give them more depth.

Text

Since the days of the Ten Commandments, text has played a major role in our lives. Sure, graphics are great, but they can't always get our ideas across quickly and clearly. After all, if they did, wouldn't we have had the Ten Pictographs?

Text is necessary to eliminate ambiguity. For example, while a picture of the sun could indicate any number of things—including heat, nuclear energy, or the solar system—put the word *summer* next to it and your message is suddenly clear.

Together, text and graphics convey ideas clearly and concisely. Take, for example this book: The text you're reading right now doesn't do much besides just sit on the page. Put it in Flash, though, and it can slide in, fade in or out, grow or shrink, and even explode if that's what you want. Though not a full-featured word processor by any stretch of the imagination, Flash lets you control your text in a number of ways. The most important thing to remember about Flash text is that it can be both active and interactive.

In addition, Flash 4 introduces a new element of interactivity—editable text fields. Opening up all sorts of possibilities for developing dynamic Web sites, editable text fields allow you to accept keyboard input from your audience—previously most commonly achieved with the use of HTML form elements, which were interactive but dull. Toward the end of this chapter we'll discuss some of the many things made possible by this great new enhancement.

What Is Text?

Because Flash more closely resembles a graphics program than a word-processing one, it handles text in a unique way. Any group of characters you type in Flash (such as a paragraph) starts out as a self-contained entity on the stage. As discussed in the preceding chapter, blocks of text and labels can be considered overlay-level objects that act similar to groups or symbols. Such blocks are resized and moved as a single object. As long as they remain in their original state, you can reedit these text objects using any of the available text tools. However, if you break apart a text object, you can no longer edit it as text. Instead, the individual characters are converted into shapes, which you can reshape and dress up in ways you can't with normal text. Later in the chapter, we'll discuss the implications of breaking up text objects as well as some of the ways you can improve the look of your text by doing so. For now, though, let's take a look at the Text tools and settings available in Flash.

Text Tool and Its Modifiers

Just as with the other tools on the Flash drawing toolbar, clicking the Text tool activates it for use in creating text objects and makes available all of that tool's modifiers. Most of the common tasks you'll perform with text, such as selecting a font or font color, are just a click away. Other tasks require that you click a modifier button to be presented with more choices. Once we've looked at the options, we'll show you how to use them to get the precise effects you desire (Figure 4.1).

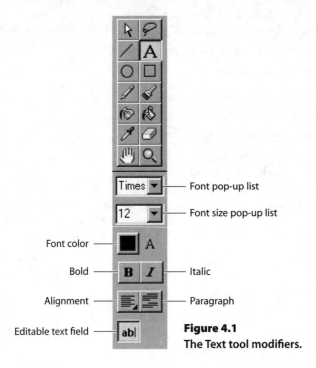

Figure 4.1
The Text tool modifiers.

Font pop-up list. Displays the current default font and lets you change the default font for new text objects and the font of selected text. The list includes all currently installed fonts that Flash can use.

Font size pop-up list. Displays the current default font size and lets you change the default size for new text objects and the size of selected text. If none of the available sizes meets you needs, you can type a size into the box and then press the Enter key.

Font color. Opens the Color pop-up menu, which displays your current font color palette. If none of the available colors meets your needs, click the Colors window button to open the Colors window where you can create your own. You'll notice gradients are not available for text objects. We discuss a way around this later in the chapter.

Bold. Changes the currently selected style to bold. All new text objects as well as any selected text or text blocks will now be boldface.

Italic. Changes the currently selected style to italic. All new text objects as well as any selected text or text blocks will now be italic.

Alignment. Changes the current default alignment setting used to create new text objects. It also lets you change selected text to that alignment setting.

Paragraph. Changes the current default paragraph properties used to create new text objects. You can also use it to change selected text to the properties you set.

Editable text field. Sets whether you want new or selected text objects to be editable—that is, whether text can be updated as a result of user input or scripts built in to your Flash movie. (For a better understanding of this, read on.)

> **TIP** *Most of these settings and more can be found on the Modify menu.*

Creating Text Blocks

Flash contains three types of text objects: text labels, text blocks, and editable text fields. We'll discuss editable text fields later in this chapter; the following describes the other two types of text objects and how they work.

A text label, or variable-width text block, is simply text that continues on a single line until you manually insert a line break by pressing the Enter or Return key. This type of text object does not wrap text automatically as do most word-processing applications. Instead, text labels allow you to determine what word appears at the end of each line (**Figure 4.2**).

To create a text label:

1. On the toolbar, choose the Text tool, or press the T key.

2. From the modifiers that appear, set the text attributes—including, font, font size, and color—that you want for this label, or variable-width text block.

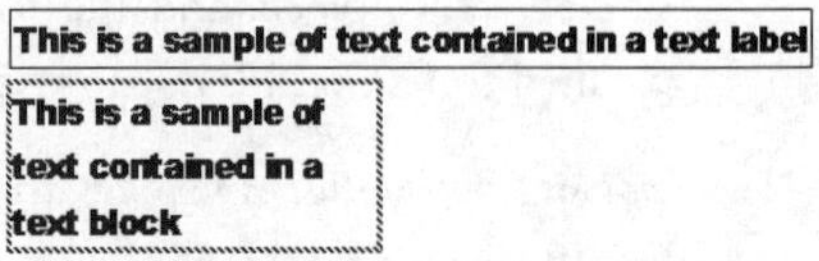

Figure 4.2
Comparison of text label versus text block.

Move the pointer to the stage area, where it turns into a crosshair with a small *a* in its bottom right corner. The center of the crosshair indicates the bottom left corner of any new text labels created (**Figure 4.3**).

3. Click on the stage where you want to place your text label.

   A small box with a circle in its top right corner and a blinking insertion point appears. This is an empty text label (**Figure 4.4**).

4. Enter whatever text you desire, and the text label automatically expands to accommodate it.

   TIP *If you click elsewhere before entering text, your empty text label will disappear.*

   TIP *Be careful in choosing your font for creating text objects. Due primarily to antialiasing (see Chapter 2, "Getting Started"), some fonts are hard to read at small sizes—especially when viewed in the final presentation. If you can't enlarge your text, you can select one of three special fonts from the font pop-up list: _sans, _serif, or _typewriter. These fonts will always be displayed with antialiasing turned off.*

Figure 4.3
The Text tool crosshair.

Figure 4.4
An empty text label box.

To create a text block:

1. On the toolbar select the Text tool, or press the T key.

2. From the modifiers that appear, set the text style for your fixed-width text block.

   Move the pointer to the stage area, where it turns into a crosshair with a small A in its bottom right corner.

3. Click and drag from left to right to define the width of your text block; then release to complete the action.

   A rectangle with a small square in its corner and a blinking insertion point appears. This is an empty text block (**Figure 4.5**).

   Figure 4.5
   A text block being dragged to a width.

4. Enter the text you want, and the text block automatically wraps text to the width you defined.

   TIP *Once you've adjusted any of the modifier settings (as in Step 2), these settings will be used for all new text objects (until you change them again).*

   TIP *There's an easy way to distinguish between text objects: A small circle on an object's top right corner indicates a text label, or variable-width text block, and a small square in the same position indicates a fixed-width text block.*

   TIP *Any text you type may initially appear rough. To obtain smoother-looking text, from the View menu choose Antialias Text. (For more information about antialiasing see Chapter 2.)*

   TIP *When transferring a Flash authoring file from one computer to another, the second computer must be able to make use of all of the fonts used to create the file on the first computer. If a font isn't available, you will see blank places where text should appear. You can avoid this problem by breaking the text apart on the first computer before opening the file on the second computer. (See "Breaking Text Apart" later in this chapter.)*

Editing Text Objects

You can edit text labels and text blocks in two ways: as single units (for example, moving, rotating, resizing, or aligning the blocks as you would a group or a symbol) or as text within the block (for example, correcting spelling or changing words). Fortunately, when editing the text itself, Flash closely mimics the way you work in your favorite word processor.

To edit a text object as a whole:

1. On the toolbar, choose the Arrow tool, or press the A key.

2. Move your pointer onto the stage, and click on any text (**Figure 4.6**).

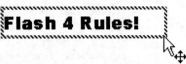

Figure 4.6
Selecting the entire text object.

A thick, checked outline defines the text object, showing that it is selected.

3. Resize, move, rotate, or align the text object just as you would a group or symbol.

> **TIP** *By selecting a text object and then immediately choosing the Text tool from the toolbar, you can change any of the text-modifier settings such as font, size, and color, and they will affect all currently selected text objects.*

To edit the text inside a text object:

1. On the toolbar, select the Arrow tool.

2. Move the pointer to the stage and double-click any text to place it in text-edit mode; you can then edit individual letters, words, or paragraphs in the text block.

   or

   On the toolbar, select the Text tool.

   When you move the pointer to the stage, it changes into an I-beam when it is over a text object.

3. Click between characters to place the insertion point for entering more text.

4. In text-edit mode, do any of the following (**Figure 4.7**):

   Select a letter, word, or paragraph for editing by click-dragging from the first letter you wish to edit to the last; then release.

Figure 4.7
Selecting specific text for editing.

This highlights and selects the text, which you can then edit in all sorts of ways (changing font, font size, color, and so on).

Delete text by click-dragging to select it, and then pressing the Delete or Backspace key.

Copy text by click-dragging the text you wish to copy and choosing Copy from the Edit menu.

Paste text by clicking once to place the insertion point where you would like the pasted text to begin; then, from the Edit menu choose Paste.

Convert a text label to a text block and vice versa. To convert a text label to a text block, place the pointer over the small circle on the top right corner of the label. When the pointer changes to a double-sided arrow, click and drag. This automatically converts the text label into a text block, the width of which is determined by where you release the mouse. To convert a text block to a text label, place the pointer over the small square on the top right corner of the text block and then double-click when the pointer changes into a double-sided arrow.

TIP *While working with a text object in text-edit mode, clicking anywhere on the stage outside the object's outlined area will cause it to drop out of text-edit mode.*

Formatting Text

Although Flash cannot offer the same type of text control that a dedicated word processor can, it can handle some of the more common text-formatting tasks, such as setting margins, line spacing, and kerning.

Basic Formatting

Basic formatting includes things such as changing the font size, color, and style.

To perform basic formatting on text:

1. Select the text object or individual text you wish to change.

2. Select the Text tool (if not already selected).

The different modifiers reflect the current settings for the selected text.

3. Adjust the modifiers to fit your needs; any changes are immediately reflected on the selected text.

Paragraph Properties

By setting paragraph properties, you can adjust the appearance of text paragraphs in new objects as well as in selected text (**Figure 4.8**):

Margins. Sets the distance between the text object's outer border and the text itself. There are individual settings for both the left and right margins.

Indentation. Sets the indent amount, in relation to the left margin, for the first line of every new paragraph.

Line space. Sets the amount of space between the individual lines in the paragraph.

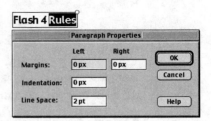

Figure 4.8
The paragraph properties dialog box.

To adjust paragraph properties:

1. Select a text object or any individual paragraph text you wish to change.

2. Select the Text tool (if not already selected).

3. Click the Paragraph modifier button.

4. In the dialog that box appears, adjust the paragraph settings to your liking; then click OK.

The selected text reflects your changes.

> **TIP** *These settings are also available on the menu bar. From the Modify menu choose Paragraph.*

> **TIP** *With the exception of line spacing, which always defaults to points, the measurement units for paragraph settings default to the measurement-unit settings the rulers use. You can, however, mix and match units by employing the appropriate abbreviation: " for inches, pt for points, cm for centimeters, mm for millimeters, and px for pixels.*

> **TIP** *You can apply different settings to individual paragraphs within the same text block.*

Text Alignment

Aligning text—or defining the way individual lines of text align—is similar to aligning objects (see Chapter 3, "Drawing"). You can choose from four options (**Figure 4.9**):

Left justification. By far the most common alignment option, it aligns the beginning of each line of text with the left margin.

Center justification. Aligns the horizontal center of every line of text.

Right justification. Aligns the end of each line of text with the right margin.

Full justification. Adjusts word spacing so that the left and right sides of text are flush with the left and right margins.

Figure 4.9
The text alignment dialog box.

> **TIP** *These settings are also available on the menu bar. From the Modify menu choose Style. A checkbox appears next to the current setting.*

Kerning

Kerning lets you control the spacing between characters so that you can make them appear closer together or farther apart.

To change character spacing by one-half pixel:

1. Select a text object or any individual text you wish to change, or place the pointer between the characters whose spacing you wish to change.

2. From the Modify menu choose Kerning and pick Narrower or Wider from the submenu, depending on your needs (**Figure 4.10**). The text reflects the change.

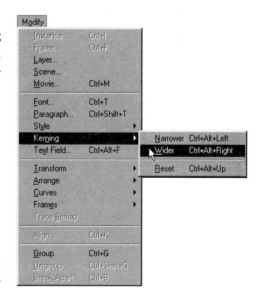

Figure 4.10
By using the commands on the Kerning submenu, you can tighten up or loosen text.

TIP *An even quicker way to alter kerning is to follow Step 1 above (to select text) and then press Control-Alt-left arrow or -right arrow (Windows) or Command-Option-left arrow or -right arrow (Macintosh). If you hold down the respective arrow key, kerning will continue.*

To change character spacing by 2 pixels:

1. Select a text object or any individual text you wish to change, or place the pointer between the characters whose spacing you wish to change.

2. Press Shift-Control-Alt-left arrow or -right arrow (Windows) or Shift-Command-Option-left arrow or -right arrow (Macintosh).

To reset character spacing to normal:

1. Select a text object or any individual text you wish to change, or place the pointer between the characters whose spacing you wish to change.

2. From the Modify menu choose Kerning-Reset or press Control-Alt-up arrow (Windows) or Command-Option-up arrow (Macintosh).

Editable Text Fields

Flash's editable text fields transform text into much more than a simple information-al tool for clarifying your message: Editable text fields, or simply *text fields,* open up a whole new realm of interactive possibilities. Because they work in a fashion similar to browser form fields, you can constantly update the information they display or even allow your audience to input information that triggers a reaction in your movie.

Although you use the Text tool to create editable text fields just as you would to pro-duce text labels and blocks, you work with and format these fields a bit differently. However, before we discuss those variations, let's take a look at a few of the many ways you can employ this new addition to Flash.

Uses

Here are some specific uses for editable text fields:

User input. By using editable text fields, you can employ audience input to trigger your movie to react in a specific way or to submit information for processing (in much the same manner that Web page forms do). Imagine the great-looking forms you'll be able to create. Used in conjunction with Flash's other programming features (which you'll learn about later), your forms can be validated completely in Flash. What's more, they can offer interactivity unparalleled by normal HTML forms (which goes a long way toward alleviating the need for HTML content in the first place).

Updated information. In projects such as Flash games, editable text fields provide a means for tracking and displaying scores in real time. In fact, Flash is likely to be a good bet for any project that requires constantly updated information.

Password fields. While password fields are similar to basic form fields in their implementation, Flash offers a setting that allows you turn regular text fields into password fields. Doing so causes any text entered into the text field to be hidden through the use of asterisks (similar to the way password fields work in most other programs as well as on the Web).

Creating Editable Text Fields

Creating an editable text field is similar to creating a text label or text block: The main difference is that text fields have configurable properties that let you determine their functionality and appearance.

To create an editable text field:

1. On the toolbar select the Text tool, or press the T key.

2. Choose the Text Field modifier, and then set the font style, size, color, and so on for your text field.

Note that the options you choose here and the way the text field actually appears in your final movie depend on the property settings you assign.

Move the pointer to the stage area, where it turns into a crosshair with a small *a* in its bottom right corner.

The center of the crosshair indicates the bottom right corner of the new text labels created.

3. Click and drag from left to right to define the width and height of your text block, and then release to complete the action.

A rectangle with a small square on its bottom right corner and a blinking insertion point appears. This is an empty text field.

4. Enter your text.

TIP *You can leave the text field empty and, if you wish, use some advanced interactivity to dynamically fill it with text once your audience has viewed it. You can also use an empty text field for user input; we'll discuss that in detail in Chapter 11, "Interactivity."*

TIP *You can resize the text field by placing the pointer over the small square at its bottom right corner and—once it has turned into a double—sided arrow—clicking and dragging it to a new size.*

TIP *You can easily change a text field into a text block by selecting the text field on the stage and then clicking the Text Field modifier on the toolbar.*

Text Field Properties

As one of the more dynamic elements in Flash, text fields include a set of properties that can be used to determine not only how they look but also the way they work. Each text field on the stage can be configured independently. To reach the Text Field Properties dialog box, right-click (Windows) or Control-click (Macintosh) the text field object, and select Properties from the pop-up menu. The following options and settings are available (**Figure 4.11**):

Variable. This is where you assign a variable name to your text field. It must begin with a letter—not a number or space (You may use a number after the first character). By naming your text field, you enable Flash to identify it—important when you want to get it to do something. We'll discuss this in greater detail in Chapter 11.

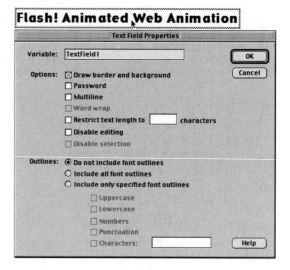

Options

This part of the Text Field Properties dialog box is where you define your text field.

Figure 4.11
The Text Field Properties dialog box.

Draw border and background. Allows you to have your text field identified in Flash itself, and in your final movie, by a solid thin outline and a background. If you leave this option unchecked, your text field will still be identified within Flash itself by a dotted outline; however, once you export, it will have no border. If you choose the "no border" option, make sure your text field is clearly identified if you plan to use it for user input—you don't want to confuse your audience.

Password. Allows you to determine the appearance of sensitive text inside the text field. If checked, asterisks (★) will replace actual characters entered into the text field.

Multiline. Lets you determine whether line breaks will be allowed in the text field.

Word wrap. Automatically creates line breaks in the text once the line has reached the right margin of the text field. It is only available if you've checked the Multiline option.

Restrict text length to. Allows you to set the maximum number of visible characters in the text field.

Disable editing. Prevents your audience from editing text that appears in the text field. You might select this option if you were using a text field to display dynamically generated text that the user would not need to edit.

Disable selection. Normally, if the "Disable editing" option is checked, the text within the text field can still be copied. This option, when checked, allows you to prevent your audience from doing even that. It is only available if the "Disable editing" option has been checked first.

Outlines

This critical last set of options determines how text appears within the text field and how it affects your movie's overall size.

Choosing outlines is primarily a matter of preference. Without them, your text will appear rough and jaggy in your final presentation—still acceptable in most cases, but jaggy nonetheless. In contrast, outlines make your text appear smooth and readable. The trade-off is that outlines increase your presentation's size—and on the Web, size is everything. Luckily, you can pick some settings to minimize outline overhead. Just be aware of how different options affect the look of your text field and your movie's overall size.

Do not include font outlines. If checked, Flash will not include font outlines in the final movie—the result being text-field text that appears rough and jaggy. Trade-off? Overall size is minimized.

Include all font outlines. Includes all font outlines in your final movie. Doing so will make your text-field text appear smooth and antialiased but could also increase you file size 35Kb to 60Kb on average, depending on what fonts are used.

Include only specified font outlines. Allows you to specify which of a font's characters you want to include. This in turn leads to great-looking text with minimal overhead (since there are fewer outlines).

> **TIP** *Once you've added the complete or partial set of outlines for a particular font within a text field, you can use those same font outlines in any other text field without increasing the size of your final movie.*

> **TIP** *Some additional things to remember about text fields:*
> - *Kerning is not supported.*
> - *Full justification is not supported—just left, right, and center.*
> - *Rotation and alpha-color transformations cannot be accomplished unless you include font outlines.*
> - *You cannot select multiple fonts or styles for the same text field.*

How Text Fields Work in the Player

When using text fields in your movie, it's important to understand the interactivity they provide when viewed through a Web browser or the Flash stand-alone player (fortunately, the latter resembles other programs that deal with text).

The Pointer

When you position the pointer over a text field, it turns into an I-beam. If you click a character in a text field, the caret, or blinking horizontal line, will be placed in front of that character. If you click between two characters, the caret will be placed between them.

Moving Around Text Fields

When you place the pointer inside a text field, it becomes the currently selected text field. Your audience can maneuver between text fields by pressing the Tab key (this causes Flash to cycle through fields from the top left-most text field to the bottom right-most text field). Pressing Shift-Tab cycles you through the text fields in the opposite direction.

Selecting

You select text inside a text field by clicking the character you wish to begin the selection and dragging to the last character you want included. Once selected, you can cut, copy, and paste as you would normally.

Scrolling

Flash Player does not provide a visual mechanism for scrolling; however, it's still easy to scroll inside a text field. To scroll a text field vertically, click inside the text field and drag up or down. To scroll a text field horizontally, click inside the text field and drag left or right. With data entry, if the Multiline option was selected from this text field's property box, text would automatically scroll to accommodate the text being entered.

Breaking Text Apart

Some effects cannot be directly performed on text objects in their initial state. This includes giving text a gradient or bitmap fill, providing an outline for text, or even reshaping or tweaking individual characters. To edit text in this way you need to convert or break the text apart first. Doing so transforms the text object from a group of editable and configurable characters to its most basic form—a bunch of vector shapes. The text must be in this form to be considered a simple shape or stage-level object that can be reshaped and graphically edited in any way you choose. Notice we only said *graphically* edited; this is because once text has been broken apart it can no longer be edited as text. So, font changes, paragraph settings, and other normal textural configurations are no longer possible. In other words, there's no going back—make sure your text reads and looks just the way you want before you break it apart.

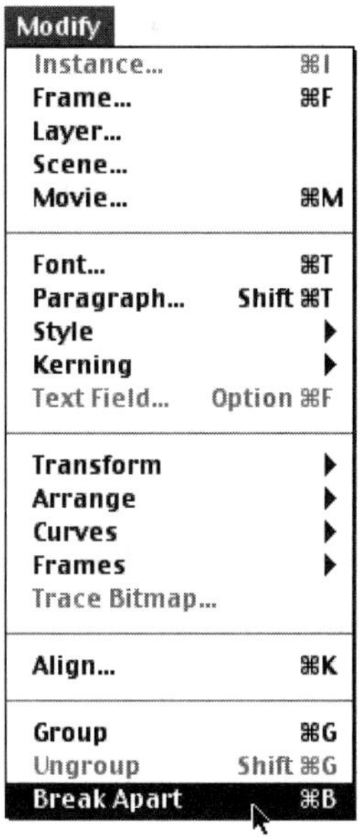

To break text apart:

1. Select any text object on the stage.

   A textured selection box surrounds it.

2. From the Modify menu choose Break Apart (**Figure 4.12**).

   Once broken apart, you can give your text a gradient fill and outline as well as perform many other graphical edits that were previously impossible.

Figure 4.12
Breaking apart
selected text.

Animation Considerations

Now that you've learned to control your text and its appearance, there's only one thing left to do—animate it! By bringing your text to life, you can create visual effects such as stock tickers, scrolling text, and other cool yet informative animations. As exciting as this sounds, though, you still need to achieve a balance between your text requirements and processor limitations. Here's why.

If you consider each single letter in a text object as an individual vector shape, and you have a text object that consists of, let's say, 100 characters, that's 100 individual vector shapes. As a result, animating this text block essentially entails animating 100 shapes simultaneously. Although Flash can handle this type of visual effect, it's extremely processor intensive—which can slow your movie to a halt, turning an exciting, upbeat, fast-moving presentation into a lesson in patience on a slower machine.

Because each project is different, there are no hard and fast rules to go by in determining when to animate blocks of text; however, the following guidelines should help:

Avoid animating large blocks of text. There are few visual reasons for animating a large block of text. Even if processor speed were not an issue, reading a large block of moving text can be a difficult, and you don't want to frustrate your audience.

For visual effects, animate only a few words or letters (or even just a single letter) at a time. This type of text animation can liven up your presentation in ways that no other graphic element can. This also means that if you want to bring a large block of text to life, bring it into the scene a sentence at a time.

The smaller the text object, the less processor intensive animation will be. This means that if you want a full-screen scrolling text effect, you had better provide your audience with plenty of caffeine to keep them awake while they wait and wait and wait for the text to scroll. If you really want to animate blocks of text, make them as small as possible while maintaining their readability.

When animating text, minimize animating other elements simultaneously. If you choose to animate text, avoid animating other elements at the same time. This allows you to devote as much processing power to the text animation as possible.

Sound

You may have noticed in recent years that producers are no longer content to simply sit back and watch moviegoers shell out $5 for a 20-cent bag of popcorn to munch on while viewing a $7 movie on the silver screen. Instead, the money men are turning their attention to a new type of revenue: *soundtracks*. Great effort goes into creating soundtracks that not only work well within their movies but also promise commercial appeal as stand-alone products.

In addition to playing on our emotions, music can trigger memories. It's not uncommon to relive the experience of watching a favorite movie when you hear a song from its soundtrack. The music may excite you, make you mad, or even reduce you to tears, but it's certain to provoke some sort of response. And think about this: How many people can remember all the words to every song by their favorite musical group but have trouble remembering a phone number? Even simple sounds can affect us. Does your heart race when you hear a police siren? Does the sound of an oncoming train put you on alert? And what about the din of children playing? Does that bring a smile to your face?

There's no denying the power of sound: Not surprisingly, then, the more your movies make use of it, the more powerful the messages they'll convey.

Using sound—via HTML—on a regular Web page, however, can be a nightmare for developers and audiences alike. Because sound is even more download-intensive than bitmaps, small sounds (and especially music soundtracks) are rarely used on the Web.

Flash, in contrast, provides a bit more latitude. You can add small sound effects for things like button clicks and create custom music soundtracks that play in the background. You can even synchronize a sound or vocal track with the visual component of your movie to create a flowing presentation.

Before you add any audio masterpieces to your project, however, you should know a few things about the way sound works in the digital world. Even just a basic grasp of these concepts will help you maximize your ability to use sound.

Understanding Sound

Although sound is invisible, tools exist to help us understand its physical representation. They show us that sound is made up of *waves,* which vary in length (to denote time) and size (to denote volume). When these sound waves hit our eardrums, they cause them to vibrate—thus hearing is born. We're able to distinguish among sounds because each unique one causes our eardrums to vibrate in a different fashion.

Analog sounds, or those we hear naturally, are produced by sound waves that our ears are designed to detect and process. Digital sampling—which transforms analog sound waves into mathematical equations—was invented to record, edit, and play back such sounds. Close examination of a digitally sampled sound (**Figure 5.1**) reveals a bunch of differing-length vertical lines stacked closely together. Each of these lines represents a *sample.* The quality of a digital sound is determined by the number of samples that exist within each *second* of sound (the *sampling rate*) and the number of values each sample can contain (*sample size*). For example, a 16-bit, 44.1-kHz sound contains 44,100 (44.1 kHz) lines, or samples, per second, each of which can have a value between 0 and 65,536 (16 bits). The result? A highly accurate digital sound, but also a large file. On the other hand, an 8-bit, 11.025-kHz sound contains only 11,025 samples per second, each of which can have a value between 0 and 255. The result here is a duller, less clear representation of the original sound—but also a much smaller file.

Figure 5.1
A digital representation of a sound.

As you may have figured out by now, you need to strike the right balance between audio quality and file size to employ sound effects and soundtracks effectively—a trick that may require some experimentation. Here Flash can provide help, offering tools to maximize your audio and also using the leading technologies for compression.

The first thing you need to do, however, is get sounds *into* Flash—which is what we'll discuss next.

Importing Sounds

You cannot record sounds in Flash; in fact the only way you can use sounds in Flash is by importing them. This means you must record your sound files outside of Flash, download them from the Internet, or purchase a sound collection. Flash can import.wav (Windows) and .aiff (Macintosh) sound files.

> **TIP** *You cannot use MIDI files within Flash. The only way to control a MIDI file using Flash is through using JavaScript.*

> **TIP** *With this release, Flash enables you to export to the MP3 format any sound you add to your project. This is the format that's taking the Web by storm due to it's superior compression abilities, which can take a sound file and make it nearly one-tenth it's original size. Because Flash can export files in the MP3 format, you would think it could import MP3 files as well. Think again: Flash does not support MP3 as an import file type.*

To import a sound file into Flash:

1. From the File menu choose Import to bring up the Import dialog box.

2. Select the sound file you wish to import, and click Open.

The sound is imported into the Library but does not initially show up on the timeline (**Figure 5.2**).

Figure 5.2
Initially, importing a sound into Flash places it in the Library. You need to add it to the timeline to actually use it in your project.

Once the sound file is placed in the Library, you can use the whole sound or just sections of it repeatedly in different places in your movie—it will not significantly affect file size. (We'll discuss how to use a single sound for different effects later in this chapter.)

> **TIP** *A sound imported into Flash actually becomes part of the Flash file. This means that large files, such as sound or vocal tracks, may cause your Flash authoring file to become huge.*

Adding Sounds to the Timeline

Once you've imported a sound into Flash, you need to figure out exactly how you want to use it in your presentation. Is it a short sound best suited for an action such as a button-click? Is it a section of music that you want to use in the background? Or is it a soundtrack you need to synchronize with an on-screen animation? Flash deals with sounds differently depending on their use. This, as you're about to learn, helps minimize file size and download time.

Sound Types

When importing, just remember this: A sound is a sound is a sound is a sound. Once in Flash, however, sounds fall into two categories: *event driven* and *streamed*. Event-driven sounds are triggered by an action that has occurred in your movie—for example, a user pressing a button, or the timeline reaching a keyframe in which a sound has been placed. Streamed sounds, in contrast, are downloaded to the user's computer as needed.

Event-driven sounds

You can use event-driven sounds for button-click sounds and looped music clips as well as anywhere you wish a sound to play from beginning to end without interruption. As you work with event-driven sounds, be aware of the following:

- An event-driven sound must be downloaded completely before it can play. Larger sound files may make the download very long.

- Once downloaded into memory, an event-driven sound will not need to be downloaded again, even if it is used repeatedly in your movie.

- Event-driven sounds play from beginning to end, regardless of what's happening around them. It doesn't matter whether the movie slows down, other event-driven sounds are being played, or your navigation structure sends the audience to other sections of your presentation—the sound will just keep playing.

- An event-driven sound needs to be inserted only into a single frame—regardless of the sound's length.

Streamed sounds

You can use streamed sounds for vocal or sound tracks in which sound needs to synchronized with visual elements of your movie as well as for sounds that you'll only use once in your movie. As you work with streaming sounds, be aware of the following:

- You can synchronize streaming sounds to the visual elements of your movie.

- Only a small portion of the sound file needs to be downloaded before it begins to play—even for a large sound.

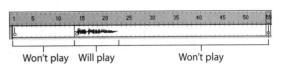

Won't play   Will play   Won't play

- A streaming sound will only play within the frames on the timeline where it is placed (**Figure 5.3**).

Figure 5.3
The frames a streamed sound occupies are the only frames in which it will play.

Since you can use sounds imported into Flash repeatedly and in different ways throughout your presentation, you can use a single file in one place as an event-driven sound and in another as a streaming sound—this is what's known as using an instance of a sound. Because an *instance* is only a copy of the original sound (which resides in the library), any configuration changes you make to it will not affect the original.

When you place an instance of a sound on the timeline, you determine whether it will be event driven or streamed. This is also when you edit it for different effects such as volume fade-in and fade-out. Let's look at how to add a sound and then at the many ways you can modify an instance of it.

You have several ways to place a sound into your timeline.

To place an already imported sound onto the timeline (version 1):

1. Create a new layer on the timeline by pressing the Add Layer button (**Figure 5.4**).

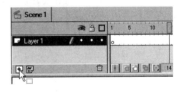

2. Double-click the layer name, and rename it "Sound."

   Although you don't have to make a separate layer for sound, we recommend you do so to make your project more manageable.

Figure 5.4
Clicking the Add Layer button will add a new layer to your scene. It's always a good idea to place sounds on their own layer.

3. Click the frame where you would like the sound to begin playing.

   The frame's color turns black to show that it's been selected.

4. Right-click (Windows) or Control-click (Macintosh) the frame, and from the contextual menu that appears choose Insert Keyframe.

5. From the Modify menu choose Frame to make the Frame Properties box appear.

As you'll learn in Chapter 10, "Animation," this is where you configure the different properties for this particular frame.

6. Click the Sound tab to make the sound property for this frame appear.

7. From the Sound pop-up menu, select an item from the list of imported sounds.

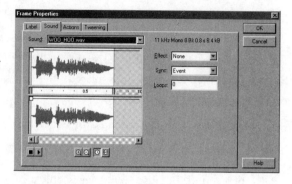

A digital representation of the selected sound appears in the sound editing windows (**Figure 5.5**).

8. Click OK.

The timeline reflects that a sound has been added.

TIP *All sounds are initially event driven.*

Figure 5.5
Selecting a sound from the Sound pop-up menu causes a digital representation of that sound to appear in the sound-editing windows.

To place an already imported sound onto the timeline (version 2):

1. Create a new layer on the timeline by pressing the Add Layer button or by choosing Insert > Layer.

2. Double-click the layer name, and rename it "Sound."

3. Click the frame where you would like the sound to begin playing.

4. Right-click (Windows) or Control-click (Macintosh) on the frame and from the contextual menu that appears choose Insert Keyframe to insert a keyframe onto the timeline.

5. From the Window menu choose Library to open the library window.

6. In the Library locate the sound you wish to use.

7. Click the sound's name, and drag it onto the stage.

An instance of the sound is added to the frame you previously selected. When dragging a sound from the Library to the stage, an outline appears that makes it look as if you're dragging an object onto it—this is not the case. The outline simply indicates that you're dragging something from the Library to be used on the stage or the timeline—in this case a sound.

TIP *You can have as many layers with sound as you wish. Use multiple layers, each with different sounds, to help you keep your project organized. All of the layers will be combined in your final file.*

Configuring or Editing a Sound

More than likely, you'll need to tweak the sound you just added—for example, adjusting how it should fade in or its length or volume. You perform all such sound-editing tasks in the Frame Properties dialog box.

To open the Frame Properties dialog box:

1. Double-click any frame that includes a sound.

Double-clicking a frame always opens its Properties dialog box.

2. Click the Sound tab.

If the frame includes a sound, this is where you configure it; if it doesn't include a sound, this is where you add and configure one.

Now let's take a look at the various ways you can configure your sound using the Sound editing dialog box (**Figure 5.6**):

Sound. You select the sound you wish to use from this pop-up menu of imported sounds.

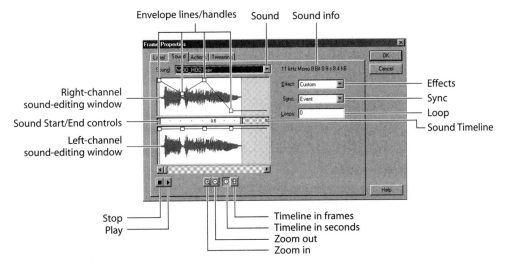

Figure 5.6
The Sound-editing dialog box.

Sound Info. Provides information about the sound you selected from the pop-up menu, including the original sound's sample rate and size, playing time, and file size.

Sound-editing windows. Display a digital representation of the currently selected sound plus the controls for editing it. The top window represents the left channel of stereo; the bottom window the right channel. If you have a mono (nonstereo) sound, each window represents the same mono channel.

> **TIP** *Each channel in a stereo sound file usually contains unique information: This is what enables our ears to distinguish spatiality in the music we listen to. In contrast, the channels in a mono sound file contain identical data. Keep in mind, though, that even if you're not dealing with a stereo sound, you can still create some interesting left-to-right and right-to-left fades as well as a few other effects.*

Sound timeline. Used for sound editing, this timeline initially displays a sound's duration in seconds; however, you can change the unit to frames (see below).

Sound Start/End controls. Also known as Time In/Time Out controls, these allow you to determine how much of an actual sound you wish to use in a particular instance. Click-dragging the Time In control to the right will cause the sound to start playing at the point you dragged it to (rather than its original starting point). Likewise, click-dragging the Time Out control to the left will cause the sound to stop playing at the point you dragged it to (rather than its original end point) (**Figure 5.7**). This is a great way to use different sections of one sound for varying effects—and in so doing dramatically reduce the size of your Flash movie (see "Sound Tutorials" in this chapter).

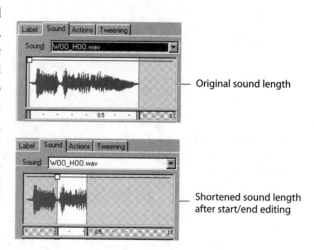

Original sound length

Shortened sound length after start/end editing

Figure 5.7
The sound Start/End controls allow you to set the point at which a sound will start or end.

TIP *Keep in mind that the stopping and ending points, along with any other settings you adjust here, only affect the instance of the sound and not the original that resides in the Library.*

TIP *Some sounds you import may have stretches of silence at the beginning or end of them. Use the Sound Start/End controls to get rid of these silences—another way to dramatically reduce the size of your final movie.*

Envelope lines and handles. Use these to adjust a sound's volume at specific points in its playing time. The higher a handle is in a sound-editing window, the louder the sound will be at that point, and vice versa. The lines represent the transition from one volume to another in relation to the sound's timeline (**Figure 5.8**). You may add as many as eight handles. To add a handle, just click the Envelope line where you would like it to go. To remove a handle, click and drag it out of a sound-editing window.

Stop/Play buttons. Use these to test any adjustments you have made to the sound in the sound-editing window.

Figure 5.8
Envelope handles represent the sound's volume at specific points during the duration of the sound, and the lines represent the transition from one volume to another.

Zoom in/out buttons. Use these to fine-tune your sound. You can zoom in to more precisely place Time In/Out controls and Envelope handles so that you can achieve greater accuracy in your sound editing. When zooming in or out, the sound-editing timeline will also reflect a change.

Timeline in seconds/frames. These let you choose the units used on the sound-editing timeline. Seconds are good for seeing the duration of your sound, whereas frames are useful for synchronizing sound with visual elements on the screen since they show the actual frame numbers in which the sound will play in your movie's timeline.

Effect pop-up menu. Choose from the following sound-envelope presets to quickly adjust the volume of your sound's left and right channels:

None. Use this option if you don't wish to apply a volume, *or envelope,* effect to your sound or to remove a previously configured envelope effect. If you choose this option, the sound will play in its original form.

Left/Right Channel. Use this to configure the sound to play in either the left or right channel (left or right speaker).

Fade Left to Right/Right to Left. Use this to configure the sound to fade from one channel to the other (one speaker to the other).

Fade In/Out. Use this to make the sound fade in or out.

Custom. Use this option—which is automatically displayed if you edit the sound envelope in the sound-editing windows—to create your own effects.

Sync. This is where you set how Flash handles a particular instance of a sound. The options are as follows:

 Event. An event-driven sound will play from beginning to end the moment the timeline reaches the keyframe in which it is placed (for more information, see the "Sound Types" section in this chapter). This option works best for short sounds and short background music tracks you wish to loop. (See the Event Sound.fla source file on the CD-ROM disc as well as "Sound Tutorials" in this chapter.)

Start. If an instance of the sound you select is already playing elsewhere on the timeline, Flash won't play the instance again.

 Stop. When using multiple event-driven sounds on the timeline that are playing simultaneously, you may want to specify one to be silent. To do so, from the Sound pop-up menu choose Stop, and then click OK. By choosing this option, you don't need to edit the sound. (See the Stop Sound.fla source file on the CD-ROM and "Sound Tutorials" in this chapter.)

 Stream. This option ensures that animated elements on other layers remain in sync with the sound track—even if some animated frames must be skipped to do so. Streamed sounds stop any time your movie does, and they only play for the duration of the frames they occupy. (See the Sound Sync.fla source file on the CD and "Sound Tutorials" in this chapter.)

Loop. With this option, you can determine how many times an instance of your sound will play from beginning to end before stopping. You can loop a sound as many times as you wish without affecting file size. This option is often used to create looping sound tracks for background music.

> **TIP** *A looped event-driven sound will continue playing for as many times as you've set it to loop, even if the movie comes to a stop.*

Optimizing Sounds

Although Flash is not a sound-editing program per se, it does provide a means for squeezing as much quality out of your sound as possible while still maintaining a small file size. You optimize sounds through the Sound Properties dialog box. Any editing you perform there will affect every instance of the sound in your movie.

To open the Sound Properties dialog box:

1. From the Window menu choose Library to open the library window.

2. Locate the sound you wish to optimize, and double-click the sound icon to the left of its name to open the Sound Properties dialog box.

> **TIP** *You can also right-click (Windows) or Control-click (Macintosh) the sound's name in the library, then choose Properties from the pop-up menu that appears.*

The Sound Properties dialog box consists of the following areas, settings, and buttons (**Figure 5.9**):

Preview window. Displays a digital representation of your sound. If the file is a stereo sound, a representation of the left and right channels will appear in the preview window. If it's a mono (nonstereo) sound, a single representation will appear.

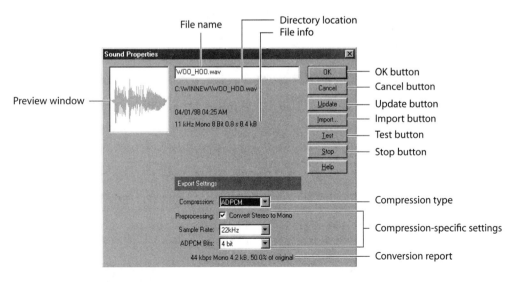

Figure 5.9
The Sound Properties dialog box.

Name. Flash assigns a default name to the sound based on the original file's name, and that is what's used in the library to identify the sound. You can change this name at any time.

Directory path. The directory path the sound was originally imported from.

File info. Provides such file data as sample rate, sample size, duration (in seconds), original size, and date last modified.

Compression type. This pop-up menu allows you to determine what kind of compression you wish to use on the sound when you export your project to create a Flash movie. Each sound can have its own unique settings.

OK/Cancel buttons. Use these buttons to complete or cancel any actions taken within the Sound Properties box.

Update button. If, within a sound-editing program, you changed or edited the original file (the one found at the directory path location) that you had imported into Flash, this button allows you to update the sound used by Flash to reflect your changes.

Import button. Use this button to change the sound file referenced by the directory path information. Importing a sound in this manner changes all references to the current sound to the one you are importing using this button.

Test button. Click to see how different compression settings will affect the sound.

Stop button. Use this button in conjunction with the Test button: Clicking the Test button gives you a full-length preview, and clicking the Stop button halts the preview at any point.

Compressing and Exporting

Let's take a look at the two compression types available for sound—ADPCM and MP3—as well as two additional export settings. All four of these options are available from the Compression pop-up menu. The trick is to find the settings that will keep the file as small as possible while maintaining decent audio quality. Each setting is good for a specific purpose.

Default. Choosing this compression option will compress the sound using the default setting.

TIP *At export time, Flash provides a general compression setting that you can use to compress all of the sounds in your movie the same amount. This can save time by eliminating the need to compress each sound individually to specific settings. However, we don't recommend this course of action for a couple of reasons: For one, to get the most out of your hard work, you'll want to control each aspect of it, including the sound compression settings. Second, the default approach is not always the best one from an audio perspective. Where some sounds may sound good using the general setting, others may degrade terribly. This is one time where one size does not fit all. Set the compression amounts for each sound individually.*

ADPCM. This compression is best for short sounds such as those used for button-clicks and sound effects or for sounds that you plan to use primarily as event sounds. You'll find this option works well for looped soundtracks because it's quicker to decompress than MP3, which may cause *lags* (unwanted intervals of silence) between loops.

To compress a sound using the ADPCM compression option:

- From the Compression pop-up menu choose the ADPCM compression type.

  The following options appear (**Figure 5.10**):

Preprocessing. With this, you can turn a stereo sound into a mono sound, automatically cutting in half the sound's influence on your movie's overall file size. Where a stereo sound file may add 100 KB to your overall file size, checking this option will take that amount down to 50 KB. The trade-off is that you lose the spatiality of a stereo sound.

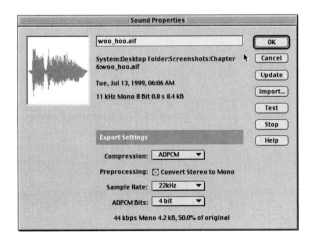

Figure 5.10
ADPCM-specific compression settings.

TIP *You can get immediate feedback on how the options you have selected will affect file size by looking at the conversion report at the bottom of the Sound Properties box.*

Sample Rate. This option allows you to set the sample rate at which a sound is exported in your final movie. Even if the sound file was originally sampled at 22 kHz, you can choose 5 kHz and Flash will resample it at export to reflect the sample rate you choose here (for more information about sample rates, see "Understanding Sound" in this chapter). A smaller sample rate reduces the sound's effect on your movie's overall file size; the trade-off is a loss of sound quality. Be sure to press the Test button to preview any choice you make here. Usually, you can get away with a lower sample rate if the sound is a vocal track, whereas music tracks typically require a higher sample rate to avoid sounding dull.

ADPCM Bits. This allows you to set the sample size at which this sound is exported in your movie. A smaller bit rate will cause the sound to distort but will reduce how it affects overall file size. Again, it's a matter of balance.

MP3. Short for MPEG-1 Layer 3 (MPEG is short for Moving Pictures Expert Group), MP3 is a *lossy* type of audio compression, which means that when sound is compressed in this format, parts of the original file will be lost for the sake of compression. Compressing an uncompressed audio file (WAV) using MP3 can decrease the file size to about one-tenth of the original without any significant loss in quality. This means that a WAV file that was originally 50 MB will end up as a 5 MB MP3 file with hardly any audible loss in quality. Depending on the bit rate you choose, this number can go much lower—though sound quality will degrade at export. MP3 is best used for long nonlooped soundtracks and not short or looped sounds (see the Looping option under "Configuring Your Sound" in this chapter).

To compress a sound using the MP3 compression option:

- Choose MP3 from the Compression pop-up menu.

  The following options appear (**Figure 5.11**):

Preprocessing. Allows you to turn a stereo sound into a mono sound, automatically cutting in half the sound's influence on your movie's overall file size. The trade-off is that you lose the spatiality that comes with stereo sounds. This option will be grayed out if the bit rate chosen is too low to support stereo.

Bit Rate. The bit rate of an MP3 file defines the number of bits the encoder can use to describe 1 second of sound. A high bit rate provides better sound quality; a lower bit rate decreases file size.

Quality. This lets you set the quality of the sound once it's been exported. The setting you choose will depend largely on how you plan to deliver your movie. Use Fast for any movie distributed over the Web and Medium or Best for delivery on a CD.

Raw. Not true compression, this option allows you to resample a sound to a new sample rate at export. For example, if the sound you originally imported was a 22 kHz sound file, this will enable you to convert it to an 11 kHz or 5 kHz file on export. This setting does not compress the sound.

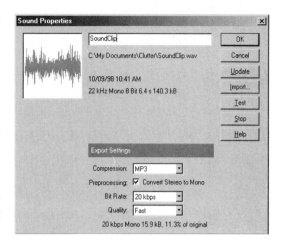

Figure 5.11
MP3-specific compression settings.

Sound Tutorials

To help you put together all of what you've learned here, we've assembled the following interactive tutorials. They, as well as the resulting source files, are on the accompanying CD-ROM disc:

Adding Sound to a Button. This tutorial guides you through the steps entailed in adding sound to a button so that it interacts with your audience's cursor in lively ways.

Editing a Sound. This tutorial shows you how to get the most out of a sound using Flash's own sound-editing capabilities.

Syncing Sound to Animation. This tutorial shows you how to synchronize a simple vocal track to some animated text.

Sound On/Off Button. This tutorial demonstrates how to create a button that will enable your audience to choose whether to listen to a sound track in your movie or not. In the process, you'll also learn how to create and use a variable that tracks whether the music is currently playing or not.

Bitmaps

What you'll learn...

Importing bitmaps

Optimizing bitmaps

Tracing bitmaps

Using animated GIFs

Using PNGs

In designing your presentations, you may find yourself limited in the graphics you can create using Flash's drawing tools. If you require more than simple vector shapes, and ovals, rectangles, and lines just won't cut it, you'll need to turn to bitmaps. With these, you can add more complex images to your project such as photos, scanned images, or other natural-looking graphics.

As mentioned in Chapter 1, "Why Flash," unlike vector graphics, which are based on mathematical equations, bitmaps comprise a bunch of small dots, or *pixels,* that appear as photographic images when viewed from a distance.

Although graphically pleasing, bitmaps can dramatically increase your movie's file size, which in turn lengthens download time. You, however, can minimize this problem. In this chapter, we'll look at several Flash options for optimizing bitmaps so that you can keep file size down—though it's still important to use bitmaps sparingly.

You can use bitmaps for more than just photographs in your movie. You can also employ them as backgrounds and fills, for special effects, or even as buttons. In addition, you can convert a bitmap into a vector graphic, which can sometimes help lessen the bitmap's effect on your movie's file size. But before you do any of this you have to get the bitmap into Flash—which is where importing enters the picture. Since it's the first step in using bitmaps in your Flash movie, let's take a look at it now.

Importing Bitmaps

Getting bitmaps into Flash is straightforward: You simply move the graphic onto your computer's hard drive by scanning it, by creating it in a photo-editing program, or through some other electronic medium; then you import it into Flash.

Table 6.1 lists the Bitmap file types you can import into Flash.

To import a bitmap into Flash:

1. From the File menu choose Import to make the Import dialog box appear (**Figure 6.1**).

2. Navigate to the bitmap file you wish to import.

3. Select the file you wish to import, and click Open.

The image is imported into the current frame and layer, and it appears on the stage (**Figure 6.2**). The image is now considered an overlay-level object, and you can edit it in the same you would any other overlay-level object, as described in Chapter 3, "Drawing."

Table 6.1
Bitmap File Types Supported by Flash

Type	Windows	Macintosh
BMP	X	
PICT		X
JPEG Image	X	X
GIF	X	X
PNG	X	X

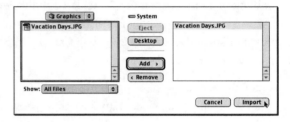

Figure 6.1
The Import dialog box (Macintosh).

Figure 6.2
Bitmaps are imported into the current frame and layer.

Bitmaps, such as GIFs or PNGs, imported into Flash will retain their transparency settings. As you'll learn later, this is a powerful feature.

Any bitmap that you import into Flash is automatically added to the library (**Figure 6.3**). As we explain in greater detail in the following chapter, you can reuse any library object (including bitmaps) as much as you want in different places of your movie—and with varying dimensions—without significantly affecting file size.

Once you've imported a bitmap into your current Flash project, you simply cut and paste it or drag a copy from the library to use it elsewhere in your presentation.

To drag a copy of a bitmap from the library:

1. From the Window menu choose Library to make the Library window appear.

2. Locate the bitmap in the library.

3. Click and drag it from the list or Preview window onto the stage (**Figure 6.4**)

If you choose to copy a bitmap from another program and paste it directly into Flash using the Paste Special command located under the Edit menu, be aware that this pastes the bitmap as an embedded object. Double-clicking an embedded bitmap opens the program that was used to create it so you can edit

Figure 6.3
Imported bitmaps are automatically added to the library.

it. Because embedded bitmaps have a number of limitations, we recommend that you use the Import command on the File menu (as described earlier) to initially get bitmaps into Flash.

Optimizing Bitmaps

Importing bitmaps into Flash is only half the equation of using them in a project. You can do a number of things to minimize file size while maximizing visual impact.

The first thing to be aware of when using bitmaps is their resolution, or the amount of pixels (dots) within each inch of a graphic, both horizontally and vertically. Thus, a 1-inch-by-1-inch graphic with 10 dots per inch (dpi) would comprise 100 pixels (10 pixels vertically by 10 pixels horizontally). If you bump up the dpi of this graphic to 20, the number of pixels it contains increases to 400 (20 pixels by 20 pixels). A higher dpi gives you clearer, sharper graphics—but at a cost. More dots

Figure 6.4
Click and drag bitmaps from the library onto the stage to add them to your project.

per inch also mean a larger file size (See **Figure 6.5**). You shouldn't import bitmaps with resolutions greater than 72 dpi into your Flash project. You will not be able to see the benefits of a higher resolution on your computer monitor; it will only increase file size. You can usually set an image's dpi when scanning or exporting it from another program—you cannot do so in Flash.

Another way to get the best results when importing a bitmap into Flash is to make sure the bitmap is at least as big (in dimension) as the largest iteration of it you'll need in your movie. If you are using more than one copy—in more than one size—of the imported bitmap, make sure that the size of the image you import is based on the larger of the two

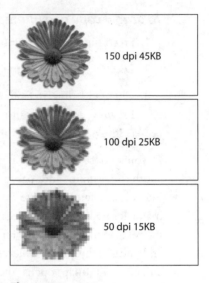

150 dpi 45KB

100 dpi 25KB

50 dpi 15KB

Figure 6.5
Comparisons of resolution versus file size.

bitmaps required by your project. Resizing a larger graphic to a smaller one has less effect on image quality than vice versa (**Figure 6.6**).

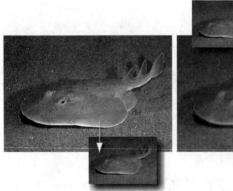

Figure 6.6
Resizing a large image to make it smaller has less influence on image quality than resizing a small image to make it bigger.

Using the fewest number of colors possible in a bitmap is another way to minimize file size. Thus, whenever you're creating paletted graphics such as GIFs, you should export them from your image-editing program with as few colors as you can get away with without sacrificing image integrity.

You can further optimize your graphics (while retaining image quality) by using the Bitmap Properties dialog box.

To open the Bitmap Properties dialog box:

1. From the Window menu choose Library to open the Library window.

2. Locate the bitmap you wish to optimize, and click it to select it.

3. From the Library Options menu choose Properties to open the Bitmap Properties dialog box (**Figure 6.7**).

> **TIP** *You can also right-click (Windows) or Control-click (Macintosh) the bitmap's name in the library, and choose Properties from the menu that appears.*

The Bitmap Properties dialog box includes the following areas, settings, and buttons (**Figure 6.8**):

Preview window. This window provides a preview of your image reflecting any changes you've made to the available settings. Clicking the Test button refreshes the image in the Preview window. You can also click and drag the image in the Preview window to change the image area you wish to preview.

Name. Based on the name of the original file, this is the default name given to the bitmap, which the library uses to identify the image. You can change this name at any time.

Figure 6.7
Selecting a bitmap in the library and choosing Properties from the Library Options menu allows you to adjust individual compression settings.

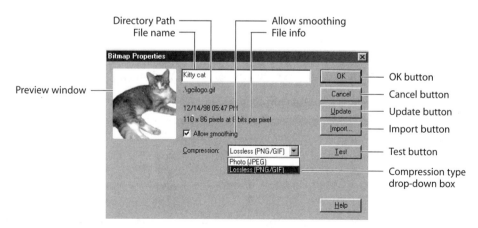

Figure 6.8
The Bitmap Properties dialog box.

Directory path. This is the path from which the image was originally imported.

File info. Provides such file information as its dimensions and color depth and the day it was last modified.

Allow smoothing. Affects the way the image appears inside the Flash authoring environment. Checking it will cause the image to be antialaised, or smoothed (**Figure 6.9**).

Compression type drop-down box. This drop-down box allows you to set the type of compression you wish to use on this image when you export your project to create a Flash movie. Each bitmap can have its own unique settings. (We'll provide a more in-depth discussion of this dialog box later in the chapter since it plays an essential role in image optimization.)

Figure 6.9
A bitmap with smoothing off (left), and the same bitmap using smoothing (right).

OK/Cancel buttons. These buttons perform the obvious actions of completing and canceling any actions taken within the Bitmap Properties box.

Update button. If you've used an image-editing program to change or edit the original file you imported into Flash (the one found at the directory path location), you can employ this button to update the Flash image to reflect those changes.

Import button. This button allows you to completely change the bitmap file being referenced as indicated by the directory path information. Importing an image in this manner will change all references in the movie from the current graphic to the one you import using this button.

Test button. You can use this button in conjunction with the Preview window to see how different compression settings will affect your image.

You need to compress your bitmap image to minimize its affect on the overall size of your project. The Bitmap Properties box is where you choose your compression settings for each individual graphic used in your movie.

You can perform two types of compression on bitmap graphics, *photo* and *lossless*—both of which are available from the Compression drop-down box. The trick is to find the setting that will allow the image to have the least effect on overall file size while maintaining acceptable quality. Photo compression, as its name implies, is best suited for photos or for graphics with numerous colors and subtle blends between them.

To compress an image using the photo compression option:

Choose the photo compression type from the drop-down box.

1. A checkbox appears asking if you want to use imported JPEG data (see tip below). If you leave this box unchecked, a new option becomes available allowing you to set the compression amount, or quality, for your image. The lower the number you enter into this box, the greater the compression—and also the greater the image degradation.

2. Enter a compression amount in this box, and then click Test.

   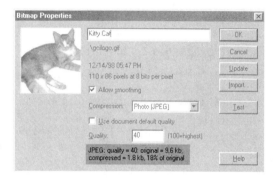

   You can now look at the Preview window to view how the selected settings will affect your image. In addition, a compression results comparison appears at the bottom of the Bitmap Properties box showing the settings' effect on the bitmap's file size (**Figure 6.10**).

   Figure 6.10
   Clicking the Test button after adjusting compression settings allows you to see how the settings change the bitmap's file size.

3. If you're satisfied with your adjustments, click OK.

> **TIP** *At export, Flash provides a general compression setting that you can use to compress all of your movie's graphics simultaneously. However, we don't recommend this course of action. One, to get the most from your hard work, you'll want to control every aspect of it—including bitmap compression settings. Second, some graphics may look good using the general setting, but others may degrade terribly. Set the compression amounts for each graphic individually.*

Lossless compression is best suited for images with limited colors such as logos, line art, and nonphotographic images. If you select this, you are not presented with any additional settings. You may test it on the image, however, by clicking the Test button.

> **TIP** *When adjusting compression settings, remember to click the Test button so that you can use the Preview window to find the best balance between compression and image quality—especially with Photo or JPEG compression.*

Working with Bitmaps

Flash is not an image editor like Adobe Photoshop or Corel Photo-Paint; thus, there are limits to what you can do with bitmaps after importing them into the program. With little effort, though, you can perform some simple tasks, such as using a bitmap as a fill or even erasing part of bitmap.

First, however, you must break the bitmap apart so that it becomes a stage-level object. Once it's in this form, you can use the Flash drawing tools to edit it. (For more on this, see Chapter 3, "Drawing.")

To break apart a bitmap:

1. Select the bitmap on the stage.

2. From the Modify menu choose Break Apart (**Figure 6.11**).

The bitmap takes on a textured look, indicating it has been converted to a stage-level object (**Figure 6.12**).

We're going to look at two basic editing tricks you can perform with a broken apart bitmap: using it as a fill and removing specific colors from it. Since a broken apart bitmap is basically just another stage-level object, you edit it in the same way you would any other stage-level object (see Chapter 3).

Figure 6.11
Selecting a bitmap and choosing Modify >
Break Apart turns the bitmap into a stage-
level object, which allows you to perform
basic editing on it or use it as a fill.

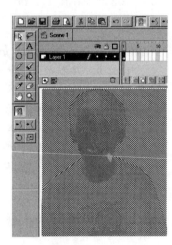

Figure 6.12
A broken apart bitmap will initially appear textured, indicating it is completely selected.

To use a bitmap as a fill:

1. From the toolbar select the Dropper tool.

2. Place the Dropper over the broken apart bitmap on the stage (**Figure 6.13**).

3. Click once, and the pointer changes automatically to the Paint Bucket tool. Click on another stage-level object to fill it with the bitmap image (**Figure 6.14**).

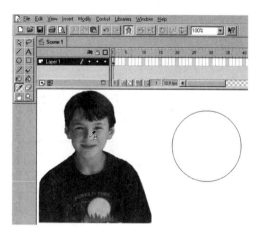

Figure 6.13
With the Dropper tool selected, clicking on a bitmap that has been broken apart makes that bitmap image the current fill.

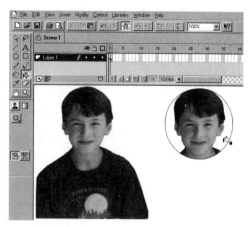

Figure 6.14
You use the bitmap image as a fill on another object on the stage.

While the fill may not look exactly the way you want it to right off the bat, Flash allows you to transform it through handles on the fill (**Figure 6.15**):

Centerpoint. This handle changes the center point of the bitmap fill.

Proportional resize. This handle proportionally resizes the bitmap fill.

Vertical resize. This handle vertically resizes the bitmap fill.

Horizontal resize. This handle horizontally resizes the bitmap fill.

Rotation. This handle rotates the bitmap clockwise and counterclockwise.

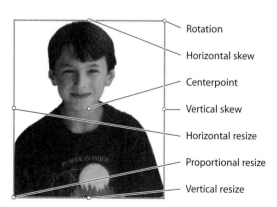

Rotation

Horizontal skew

Centerpoint

Vertical skew

Horizontal resize

Proportional resize

Vertical resize

Figure 6.15
The handles for transforming a bitmap fill.

To transform a fill:

1. From the toolbar select the Paint Bucket tool.

2. From the modifiers that appear, click the Transform Fill modifier.

3. Bring the pointer onto the stage, and click any shape that has a bitmap fill.

The transform handles appear.

4. Click and drag a handle to transform the fill any way you wish.

To select areas in a bitmap based on color:

First make sure the bitmap has been broken apart.

1. From the toolbar choose the Lasso tool.

2. From the modifiers that appear, select Magic Wand Properties modifier.

A dialog box appears, letting you set two properties for the Magic Wand: Threshold and Smoothing. Threshold allows you to set a range for how close an adjoining pixel color needs to be to the original color you click to be selected. A setting of "0" selects only pixels of the exact same color as the one you click; a setting of "100" selects all pixels. Smoothing allows you to set how Flash deals with the edge of the selected color area. The settings for this property range from Pixel, which means that the selected area will have an edge defined perfectly by the selected pixels, to Smooth, which creates a very smooth selection edge (**Figure 6.16**).

3. Adjust the properties according to your preferences, and click OK.

4. From the toolbar select the Magic Wand modifier.

Move the pointer onto the stage area and over your bitmap, where it changes into a magic wand icon.

5. Place the pointer over the colored area in the bitmap that you want to select, and click.

Any pixels that fall within the Threshold range you set earlier is selected. Once selected, you can move or delete them (**Figure 6.17**).

Figure 6.16
The Magic Wand Settings dialog box.

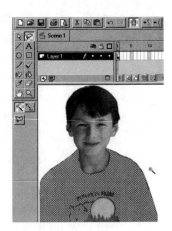

Figure 6.17
Selecting pixels using the Magic Wand tool allows you to edit or delete them.

Tracing Bitmaps

With tracing, Flash offers a powerful way to reduce a bitmap's impact on your project's overall file size. Specifically, tracing allows you to easily convert a bitmap graphic into a vector graphic. It accomplishes this by examining the pixels that make up the bitmap, locating areas with similar-colored pixels, and then attempting to create vector graphics based on the shapes of those colored areas.

TIP *You can only trace a bitmap that you haven't broken apart first.*

You'll get the best results from tracing if you use it on bitmaps with few colors and no gradiated areas—which means steer clear of photographs. Attempting to trace a photo will tax your computer's resources and likely result in a vector graphic that's larger than the original bitmap—hardly a desirable outcome!

To trace a bitmap:

1. On the stage, select the bitmap you wish to convert to a vector graphic.

2. From the Modify menu choose Trace Bitmap to bring up the Trace Bitmap dialog box **(Figure 6.18)**.

   Adjust the settings:

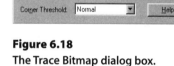

Figure 6.18
The Trace Bitmap dialog box.

   Color Threshold. Lets you set the amount each pixel of the bitmap must vary in color from the other pixels it touches before it is considered a different color. The larger the number, the fewer the vector shapes that will be created.

   Minimum Area. Sets the minimum size of any vector shape created by the trace. You can enter a value between 1 and 1000.

   Curve Fit. Allows you to set how closely the trace-created shapes follow the original bitmap colors.

   Corner Threshold. Lets you set the amount a curve has to bend before it turns into corner.

3. Once you've adjusted the settings, click OK.

   TIP *Tracing a bitmap usually requires some experimentation: Feel free to test your settings and—if you're unhappy with the results—select Undo to start over.*

TIP *Remember that turning a bitmap into a vector graphic doesn't always reduce file size. You can use a before-and-after comparison to test the transformation's change on file size. Before tracing a bitmap, from the Control menu choose Test Scene. From the Bandwidth Profiler, note the scene's overall file size, and then close the window. Now trace your bitmap, and then from the Control menu choose Test Scene again to see whether tracing had a positive or negative affect on file size. To learn more about the Bandwidth Profiler, see Chapter 12, "Testing Your Work."*

Using Animated GIFs

When the animated vectors Flash creates aren't sufficient for your project, animated GIFs could be the solution. These animated bitmaps abound on pages throughout the Web, and tons of cool animated GIF collections are available for download and purchase. GIFs facilitate such visual effects as explosions, fires, and people in motion. They can have transparent backgrounds (just as they would on a regular Web page), which means you can blend them seamlessly into the rest of your layout.

To use an animated GIF in Flash, you must import it. As you are probably aware, an animated GIF comprises several bitmaps, or *frames,* which appear animated when played in succession. The time between frames determines the speed at which the animated GIF plays. When importing an animated GIF into Flash, each of its frames is placed in an individual frame on Flash's timeline. Flash also spaces the animated GIF frames so that the speed at which they play in Flash is as close to the original speed as possible. For example, if you import a 5-frame, 5-second animated GIF into a 15-fps Flash movie, Flash would place the individual GIF frames 15 frames apart on the Flash timeline (**Figure 6.19**).

Figure 6.19
When importing an animated GIF, Flash spaces the individual frames of the GIF so that they appear and play back at the same speed within Flash.

We recommend using animated GIFs as movie clips inside Flash. Because each movie clip is a self-contained animation (see Chapter 7, "Symbols"), you can reuse a movie clip created from an animated GIF repeatedly throughout your presentation without affecting its overall file size. In addition, because it is a movie clip, you can resize, move, or even rotate the entire animated GIF as a single entity within Flash.

To create a movie clip using an animated GIF:

1. From the Insert menu choose New Symbol to bring up the Symbol Properties dialog box.

2. From the behavior options, choose Movie Clip, and give your movie clip a name.

3. Click OK.

You are automatically taken to the movie-clip editing window. The timeline that appears is your movie clip's timeline. This is where the individual frames of the imported animated GIF go.

4. From the File menu choose Import to bring up the Import dialog box.

5. Select an animated GIF, and click Open.

Each individual frame of the animated GIF is imported and placed in a frame on the movie clip's timeline.

6. Click the Scene List button to return to the scene you were in.

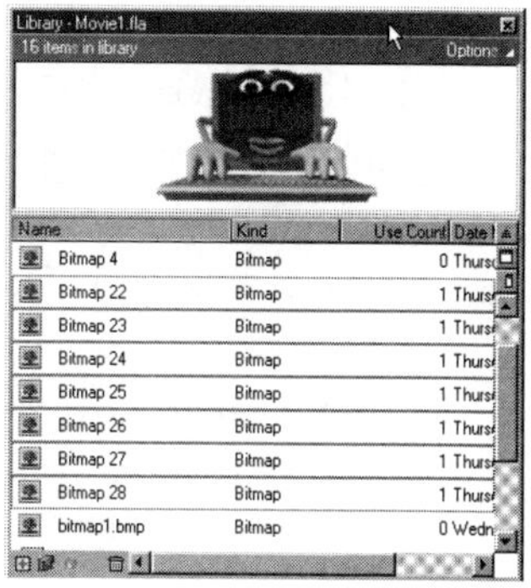

Figure 6.20
When importing an animated GIF, Flash places in the library each of the bitmaps that make up individual frames of the GIF.

> **TIP** *When you are importing an animated GIF to create a movie clip, Flash places the bitmaps that make up its individual frames into the library (**Figure 6.20**). Be sure not to delete any of these bitmaps if you want your movie clip to play properly.*

Now that you've created a movie clip from an animated GIF, it's time to use it in your presentation.

To use an animated GIF/movie clip in your project:

1. From the Window menu choose Library to make the Library window appear.

2. Find the animated GIF/movie clip you created.

3. Click and drag it from the list or Preview window onto the stage (**Figure 6.21**).

> **TIP** *Only the first frame of the imported animated GIF/movie clip will be visible. To see it in action, from the Control menu choose Test Scene. This allows you to preview how your newly created movie clip will appear in your Flash movie. Once you've finished viewing, close the Test window.*

Before moving on to the next topic, we should make one thing clear: Two types of bitmap animations are possible in Flash. One, as just discussed, involves importing an animated GIF, which is a sequence of several images that are "flipped" through in order to make it appear to be animated, and converting it into a movie clip. The other involves actually animating an imported bitmap through movement. This means taking something like a photograph and making it slide from one side of the screen to the other, or even making it appear to grow or shrink. We discuss these affects in greater detail in Chapter 10, "Animation." Just be aware of the distinction now.

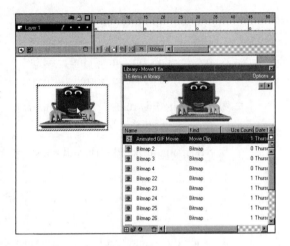

Figure 6.21
Once you've turned an animated GIF into a movie clip, you can drag it from the library onto the stage to use it wherever you want in your project.

Using PNGs

PNG, or Portable Network Graphic, is a relatively new graphics standard that offers numerous advantages over GIFs—especially in compression, color capabilities, and transparency.

Like GIFs, PNGs use a lossless compression algorithm. This means that a PNG file is compressed at the time it is created, in such a way that when it is viewed, there is no loss in quality from its original version. Thus, you can bring in or create a 1-MB bitmap in your favorite image-editing program, export it as a PNG, and end up with a file that is every bit as clear and beautiful as the original—but at a fraction of its size. In fact, PNG compression typically surpasses GIF compression by 5 percent to 25 percent (though on tiny images, that number often rises to 40 percent or 50 percent). Many programs on the market today can export to the PNG format, including Adobe Photoshop, Macromedia Fireworks, and Corel Photo-Paint.

Even more impressive than PNG's compression abilities is the graphic's support for 24- and 32-bit color (in contrast to GIFs, which only support 8-bit color). This means your images aren't limited to a 256-color palette as are GIFs; instead, you can use the full range (in the millions, if that's what you wish).

The icing on the cake, however, is that PNG images support full alpha transparency, which means each pixel can have a transparency value between 0 and 255. (GIFs, in contrast, offer only on/off transparency, which means that a pixel is either transparent or not.)

PNGs' transparency capabilities make it possible to create some impressive effects with bitmaps, including:

Images with gradiated transparencies (**Figure 6.22**).

Figure 6.22

PNGs allow you to use bitmaps with gradiated transparencies. This PNG image was of a single violin with a gradiated mask and was exported from a photo-editing program. Importing it into Flash and stacking copies of the image on top of each other shows the effect that the gradiated mask produces.

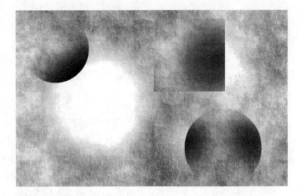

Figure 6.23
PNG images imported into Flash can have transparent backgrounds. This vegetable image has been copied three times and the copies placed on top of each other.

Figure 6.24
You can export PNGs with a gradiated mask from a photo-editing program and import them into Flash to act as gradiated masks in your project.

Objects with transparent backgrounds (**Figure 6.23**).

Gradiated masks (**Figure 6.24**).

Creating a PNG with a graduated transparency in a bitmap editing program usually only involves masking off image areas that you wish to be transparent and then, with the mask still active, exporting your image to PNG.

The moral of the story here is, when you import bitmaps into Flash, use PNG graphics wherever possible—for both photographic images and images with few colors. You can do more with graphics in this format than in any other.

GIFs do, however, offer one advantage over PNGs: You can't import animated PNGs, only animated GIFs. Thus, if you need to use animated bitmaps in your project, don't even bother to look for the animated PNG option—it doesn't exist. However, if your series of PNGs is numbered in a sequence like the previous example, Flash will import the sequence and put them all on separate frames—much like an animated GIF.

Symbols

If you've spent time camping in the great outdoors you've probably come to appreciate the value of a Swiss army knife. Having to already lug around pounds of food and equipment, the compact size yet unending usefulness of the tool is constantly appreciated. For something so small that can fit into your pocket, the fact that a Swiss army knife can perform the same feats that would normally take a whole assortment of tools in a regular, heavy toolbox is absolutely incredible.

The trend lately is to create a single tool that can do-it-all, like the Swiss army knife. This is because these days, time and space are a premium. If you live in a small apartment yet want to create gourmet meals, you probably don't have the room for all kinds of kitchen appliances. One tool that slices, dices, and even makes julienne fries is the way to go. This philosophy is the guiding principle behind one of Flash's core means of delivering compact multimedia over the Web—symbols.

One object, many uses—that best describes symbols' role in Flash projects. Designed to help you easily create dynamic *yet compact* movies, symbols are a key component of any Flash project. As such, an understanding of the way they work is essential if you are to deliver highly interactive, compact Flash movies with the smallest file size possible.

Understanding Symbols and Instances

Simply put, a symbol is a special object you create once in Flash and then reuse throughout your movie—with no significant impact on file size. Symbols can range from a shape you've drawn to an animation of a bird in flight, and any symbol you create automatically becomes part of the library. If, for example, you wish to create a scene with a flock of birds, you

Figure 7.1
One button symbol, each instance of which is a different shade.

could drag *instances* of your in-flight bird symbol from the library. (You'll learn more about this in Chapter 8, "Library."). You can have as many instances of your flying bird as you want—each of which is only a reference to (rather than a re-creation of) your original, which is stored just once in your final Flash file. Referencing a symbol has very little impact on file size—regardless of the number of instances you use. Therefore, if the object you made into a symbol initially added 25 KB (25,000 bytes) to your movie's overall file size, adding 10, 20, or even more instances of that symbol would add less than 100 bytes to the file's overall size—regardless of symbol size. Just remember this: Symbols should be considered master objects, which reside only in the library; you use instances of these master objects, not the master objects themselves, when putting content into your movie.

The real magic of symbols stems from that individual instances don't have to look and act just like the original. Each symbol instance can be a different color and size as well as offer different interactive functions. For example, you could place multiple instances of a button symbol on stage, each with different associated actions and colors (**Figure 7.1**).

Each symbol has a unique timeline and stage, complete with layers. This means that you can view the task of placing a symbol instance in a scene as placing a small movie (the symbol) inside a bigger movie (your Flash project). In addition, you can animate a symbol instance as a whole. For example, if you had a symbol of a bird flapping its wings, you could animate an instance of that symbol (the whole bird) so that it appeared to be moving across the sky in whatever direction you chose. Another thing to be aware of, at least from a graphical standpoint, is that once you've edited a symbol's appearance, each instance of that symbol will reflect those changes. For example, if you decide to change the master artwork of a square symbol that appears several times on the stage into an oval, each instance of that symbol will now appear as an oval as well (**Figure 7.2** and **Figure 7.3**). However, remember that it's only from a graphical standpoint that symbol changes will be reflected in every

Figure 7.2
Multiple instances of a square symbol.

instance; individual symbol instances can still have their own colors, sizes, and functionality.

When creating movies, it's important to understand where and when you can use symbols. First of all, not every graphic in your movie has to be a symbol. Create symbols out of any object you plan to use more than once (with the exception of sounds and bitmaps; see the "Pseudo-Symbols" sidebar for more on this topic). If your movie includes three interface buttons that—apart from their text labels—look alike, separate the labels from the actual button graphic (**Figure 7.4**). This way, only the text label on top of the button changes, not the button itself. You'll learn more about this when we discuss creating symbols later in the chapter.

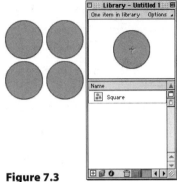

Figure 7.3
The square symbol edited to a sphere affecting the previous instances seen in Figure 7.2.

Symbol Types

You can create three symbol types, or *behaviors,* in Flash.

Graphics. Graphic symbols are often made up of static, or nonanimated, graphics that are used a number of times in your movie. For example, you could create a field of flowers by placing many instances of one flower symbol in your scene—that single, nonanimated flower represents a perfect example of a graphic symbol. This is not to say, however, that graphic symbols cannot be animated. We'll discuss this in more detail in "Working with Symbols" and "Instances" later in this chapter.

Buttons. Button symbols react to pointer movement; your audience can use them to control and interact with your movie. A button can be set to perform all kinds of actions.

Movie clips. As the most interactive, versatile, and powerful element in Flash, movie-clip symbols are basically small independent movies that can contain all of the elements of your main movie, including sound, animation, and buttons. They achieve independence in Flash, however, due to their independent timelines; so, if the main movie's timeline stops, the movie clip's timeline can continue. Think of movie clips as small movies within the

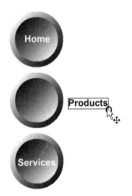

Figure 7.4
The text elements are separate from each button symbol instance.

main movie (**Figure 7.5**). (For more information on movie clips, see Chapter 11, "Interactivity.")

Once you create a symbol with a specific behavior, you can easily assign different behaviors to various instances of it. So, you could make a graphic symbol behave like a button, or vice versa. What's more, each instance of a symbol can have a different color, size, or rotation as well as behave differently than all other instances (see "Changing a Symbol's Behavior" in this chapter).

Whenever you create a new symbol, it is automatically added to the library, which the Flash designers created specifically as a place for users to keep track of their symbols and imported bitmaps and sounds (see the "Pseudo-Symbols" sidebar).

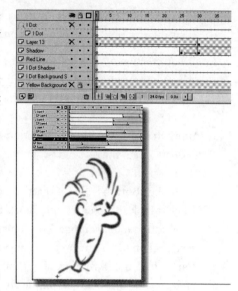

Figure 7.5
A movie clip with its own timeline placed inside the main movie.

One thing that makes symbols quite powerful is that you can place one type of symbol inside another. Thus, you can place instances of buttons and graphic symbols inside movie-clip symbols or instances of movie-clip symbols inside button symbols. You can even place instances of movie clips within movie clips. However, buttons and frame actions don't work inside graphic symbols. (See "Symbol Tutorials" in this chapter.)

Pseudo-Symbols

Although not necessarily defined as symbols, Flash treats bitmaps and sounds similarly. Like symbols, imported bitmaps and sounds are added to the library automatically, becoming reusable elements that don't significantly increase your Flash movie's overall file size if used repeatedly within your project.

Creating Symbols

When you begin to create symbols, keep in mind that you're essentially producing an object with its own timeline that sometimes runs in conjunction with the main timeline (that is, its timeline stops at the same time as the main movie's timeline) and sometimes runs independently (that is, its timeline continues to play even after the main timeline has stopped). You work with this timeline—which has its own set of layers—in much the same way you would with the main timeline. A little later we'll examine each type of symbol's timeline; first, however, we're going to teach you how to create symbols.

General Symbol Creation

Flash offers a couple of ways to create symbols: You can convert stage (or main timeline) content into symbols, or you can create a blank or empty symbol, which you later fill with content. Each approach offers advantages.

To create a symbol using content on the stage:

1. Select the objects on the stage you wish to convert.

   These can include shapes, text, groups, and even other symbols.

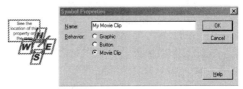

2. From the Insert menu choose Convert to Symbol to bring up the Symbol Properties dialog box (**Figure 7.6**).

Figure 7.6
The Symbols Properties dialog box after a group of objects has been selected for conversion to a symbol.

3. In the dialog box, assign a name and behavior (graphic, button, or movie clip) to your new symbol; then click OK.

4. From the Window menu choose Library to verify that your newly created symbol has been added (**Figure 7.7**).

Figure 7.7
All newly created symbols are automatically placed in the library.

You can now drag instances of this symbol from the library to the stage. For more on this, see Chapter 8.

Although the above-described method provides a quick way to create the three symbol types, it's not the most versatile way of doing so. By creating symbols in this manner, you're placing all of the content you selected from the main stage into the first frame of the newly created symbol's timeline; no animation has taken place yet (**Figure 7.8**). To animate your new symbol, you must edit its time-line and stage (see "Working with Symbols and Instances" later in this chapter). Sometimes it's better to start from scratch by creating a blank or empty symbol, which you can then fill.

Figure 7.8
When using the Convert to Symbol command, all content of the new symbol is initially placed on the first frame of its timeline.

To create an empty or blank symbol:

1. From the Insert menu choose New Symbol to make the Symbol Properties dialog box appear.

2. Assign a name and behavior (graphic, button, or movie clip) to your new symbol; then click OK.

   You are automatically put into symbol-editing mode, which consists of a blank timeline and stage for your newly created symbol.

3. Use the steps you've already learned to draw or import and add content along your symbol's timeline. (See "Symbol-Specific Creation" for more on this.)

4. When you've finished creating your symbol content, from the Edit menu choose Edit Movie.

   This will take you out of symbol-editing mode and return you to the main movie's timeline and stage.

   TIP *When reentering your main movie's timeline and stage, your newly created symbol will not initially appear. To place an instance of it, open the library and drag an instance of it to the stage.*

Duplicating Symbols

If you've ever spent a great deal of time creating a symbol only to find you want to create another symbol that's a little different, duplicating it may be the route to go.

Duplicating a symbol allows you to use an existing symbol as a starting point for a new symbol. Once duplicated, the new symbol is added to the library, and you can change it any way you wish.

To duplicate a symbol:

1. On the stage, double-click an instance of the symbol you wish to duplicate.

The Instance Properties dialog box appears.

2. Click the Duplicate Symbol button (**Figure 7.9**).

The Symbol Properties dialog box appears.

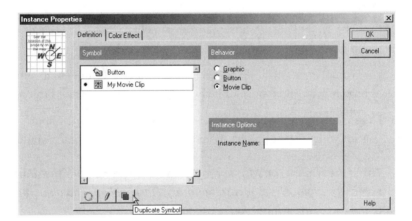

Figure 7.9
The Duplicate Symbol button in the Instance Properties dialog box.

3. Give your new symbol a name, and click OK.

You have now created a new symbol based an existing symbol.

TIP *When duplicating a symbol the original instance you double-click automatically becomes an instance of your duplicated symbol: Graphic- or timeline-related changes will be reflected in this instance as well.*

Symbols from Other Movies

There's no reason to reinvent the wheel: If you want to use a symbol from a previous Flash project in your current movie, Flash makes it easy. And once you bring the symbol into your current project, you work on it in the same way you would any other symbol. There is no link between the symbol in the different files; editing it in one will not affect the other. You can use as many different symbols from as many Flash projects as you wish.

To use a symbol from another movie:

1. From the File menu choose Open as library.

The Open as library dialog box appears.

2. Navigate to the Flash file containing the symbol you wish to use, and click Open.

A library window appears containing all of the symbols used in the Flash file you just opened.

3. Drag the symbol you wish to use from the library onto the stage of your current movie.

The symbol is automatically added (under its original name) to the library of your current project; an instance of it also appears on your current project's stage.

4. Drag as many additional symbols as you wish from the open library onto the stage of your current project. When finished, close the library window.

TIP *If the symbol you wish to drag from a Flash library has the same name as a symbol in your current library, Flash will append a number to the end of the symbol you're dragging.*

Symbol-Specific Creation

As you've just learned, you employ pretty much the same method to create any type of symbol—graphic, button, or movie clip. However, the way you add content as well as the way the symbol's timeline works in relation to the main timeline vary according to symbol type.

Graphic Symbols

When creating graphic symbols, you're presented with a stage and timeline that look just like the main stage and timeline. Not surprisingly, then, you create content on them in much the same way you do in your main movie: The drawing tools work the same, layers work the same, and creating animation across a graphic symbol's timeline is also pretty much the same. The only difference between the way these timelines work is that sounds and interactivity don't function on the graphic symbol's timeline.

This doesn't mean, however, that you can't animate a graphic symbol's timeline; you just need to be aware of a few things. For starters, a graphic symbol's timeline is closely linked to the main timeline. This means that although you can make a graphic symbol's timeline as long (in frames) as you wish, it will only play while the main timeline is playing. If you want your symbol's timeline to move independently of the main timeline, use a movie-clip symbol instead.

Button Symbols

When creating button symbols, you're presented with a unique timeline, whose four frames—Up, Over, Down, and Hit—represent different button symbol states (as explained below) (**Figure 7.10**).

Up. This frame, or *state,* represents the button's appearance when the pointer is *not* over it.

Over. This frame represents the button's appearance when the pointer is over it.

Down. This frame represents the button's appearance when the user clicks it.

Hit. This frame is where you define the area in which the button will respond to a pointer's movement. A solid object—which can be a different size and shape than the button—usually goes here (**Figure 7.11**). Items in the Hit frame will not be visible from your main movie.

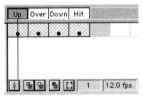

Figure 7.10
The button symbol frames (states).

A button graphic's timeline doesn't actually play; rather, it simply reacts to pointer movement and actions by jumping to the appropriate frame based on the position and actions of the pointer.

Figure 7.11

The Hit state can be any size and placed anywhere on the stage, causing the button to react to a pointer's movement even if the pointer is not directly over the button graphic. In our example shown here, the box represents the hit state. This will not be seen when the movie is exported.

Each state can have a unique appearance, though it's common practice to highlight buttons in their Over state and to make them smaller (or appear pressed) in their Down state—these simply simulate the way most people relate to buttons. To create dynamic-looking buttons, use your drawing tools and layers. If you want your button to make a sound when it's in a particular state, place the desired sound on a layer in that state (**Figure 7.12**). (See "Symbol Tutorials" at the end of this chapter.) You can also place instances of movie-clip symbols into different states of your button symbol to create animated buttons; however, you cannot place buttons inside buttons.

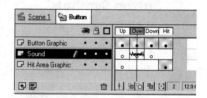

Figure 7.12

The Button Symbol with a sound associated with its Over state.

TIP *For information on adding actions to buttons see "Adding Actions to Buttons" in this chapter.*

Movie-Clip Symbols

As mentioned earlier, a movie-clip symbol is really just a small Flash movie—with all of the interactivity, sound, and functionality of your main movie. You can add to your movie-clip symbol buttons, sounds, graphics, and even other movie clips.

The timeline of a movie clip runs independently of the main timeline. So, if the main timeline comes to a stop, the movie clip's timeline doesn't necessarily have to; it can continue playing.

You create movie-clip content just as you would content for your main movie. You could even convert any or all of the content on your main timeline into a movie clip, say, if you wanted to reuse an animation created on the main timeline in various places within your project.

To convert animation on the main timeline to a movie-clip symbol, you must select the frames and layers that make up the section of animation you wish to use.

To create a movie-clip symbol from animation on the main timeline:

1. On the main timeline, click and drag from the first frame of the top layer to the last frame of the bottom layer to select the timeline frames you wish to convert.

The frames now show that they are selected (**Figure 7.13**).

2. Right-click (Windows) or Control-click (Macintosh) any one of the selected frames, and from the contextual pop-up menu that appears choose Copy Frames.

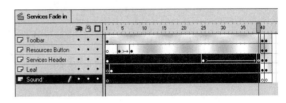

Figure 7.13
The layers and frames of an animation selected in preparation for copying.

3. From the Insert menu choose New Symbol.

The Symbol Properties dialog box appears.

4. Give your new symbol a name and movie-clip behavior.

5. Click OK.

You are taken to symbol-editing mode, where the stage is empty and the timeline has one layer and one frame.

6. On the timeline, right-click (Windows) or Control-click (Macintosh) Frame 1 on Layer 1, and from the contextual menu that appears choose Paste Frames (**Figure 7.14**).

This pastes the frames you copied earlier from the main timeline to the timeline of this movie-clip symbol.
Any animation, buttons, or interac-

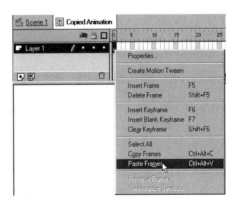

Figure 7.14
Preparing to paste frames into the symbol timeline.

tivity from the frames you copied now becomes an independent animation (a movie-clip symbol) that you can reuse throughout your movie.

Adding Instances of Symbols to the Stage

As mentioned earlier, you never use symbols directly in your movie, only instances of them. This is accomplished mostly by dragging an instance of a symbol from the library to the stage.

To add an instance of a symbol to the stage:

1. From the Window menu choose Library.

This opens the library window.

2. From the list that appears, locate the symbol you wish to use.

3. Click the symbol's name, and drag it onto the stage. An instance of the symbol appears on the stage.

> **TIP** *You can quickly create several instances of the same symbol: On the stage, simply select the instance you wish to duplicate, and press Control-D (Windows) or Command-D (Macintosh).*

Working with Symbols and Instances

Now that you've figured out how to create symbols (and their instances), it's time to learn how to edit and work with them.

Symbol Editing

Symbol editing involves editing a symbol's content and timeline. When you edit a symbol in this manner, all instances of it—regardless of placement—reflect your changes. Symbol instances *will,* however, retain instance-specific edits—for example, their size, overall color, and any interactivity they're set to perform.

To edit a symbol's content and timeline, you must place it in symbol-editing mode.

To edit a symbol by placing it in symbol-editing mode:

1. On the stage, double–click an instance of a symbol.

The Instance Properties dialog box appears.

2. Click the Edit Symbol button (**Figure 7.15**).

This places you in symbol-editing mode, where you can edit the symbol's timeline and stage.

or

1. On the stage select the symbol you'd like to edit.

2. From the Modify menu choose Instance.

or

1. Click the Symbol List button in the upper-right corner of the timeline.

2. From the list of symbols that appears, choose the one you wish to edit.

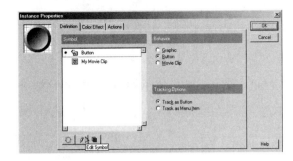

Figure 7.15
The Edit Symbol button in the Instance Properties dialog box.

You have other ways to place a symbol into symbol-editing mode: One is Edit in Place; the other is Edit in New Window. Edit in Place allows you to edit a symbol in the context of the scene in which it is placed. Edit in New Window allows you to enter a symbol's editing mode, just as the name describes, in a new window, so the main timeline and stage will still be visible in the background but a new window for editing the symbol's timeline and stage will also appear.

To Edit in Place:

1. On the stage, right-click (Windows) or Control-click (Macintosh) the symbol you wish to edit.

2. From the contextual menu that appears choose Edit in Place.

   All of the objects on the stage, except for the symbol itself, are lightened to indicate they cannot be edited (**Figure 7.16**). You can, however, edit the objects that make up the symbol and its timeline.

3. Edit the symbol's content or timeline, and then click the Scene button above the Layers interface to return to the main stage and timeline (**Figure 7.17**).

Figure 7.16
The symbol itself is available for direct editing, but other elements are not.

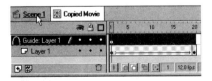

Figure 7.17
The Scene button on the Layers interface.

To Edit in a New Window:

1. On the stage, right-click (Windows) or Control-click (Macintosh) the symbol you'd like to edit.

2. From the contextual menu that appears choose Edit in New Window.

A new window opens with the symbol in symbol-editing mode.

3. From the Window menu choose Arrange All to view the main stage and timeline as well as the symbol's stage and timeline.

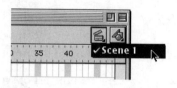

4. Edit the symbol's content or timeline, and then click the Scene list button above the Layers interface on the right corner to return to the main stage and timeline (**Figure 7.18**).

Figure 7.18
The Scene list button.

TIP *In the Flash authoring environment, you can see only the first frame of any symbol instance. This means that only the edits you make to Frame 1 of the symbol's timeline will be visible on the main movie's stage. To view the effect of your edits to other frames, from the Control menu choose Test Movie. This opens up the Test Movie window, which gives you a preview of any changes you've made. For more information on this, see Chapter 12, "Testing Your Work."*

TIP *The way to determine whether you're working with the main time- line and stage or with a symbol's timeline and stage is to look above the Layers interface: Either a scene or symbol name will be highlighted (**Figure 7.19**).*

Figure 7.19
The symbol name is highlighted, indicating that the symbol is being edited rather than the main movie.

Instance Editing

As you learned in Chapter 3, "Drawing," instances of symbols that you place on the stage are simply overlay-level objects. As such, the first thing to remember when working with them is that they are scaled, rotated, moved, copied, pasted and so on in the same way other overlay-level objects are. If you want to edit the symbol's content, you must do so when the symbol is in symbol-editing mode (see "Symbol Editing" in this chapter). Edits to an *instance* of a symbol will not change the original symbol or other instances of it.

> **TIP** *By following two quick steps, you can return to its original state an instance of a symbol that's you've scaled or rotated: Select the instance on the stage; then, from the Modify menu choose Transform > Remove Transformations. This returns the instance to its original size and orientation.*

Color and Transparency

Besides being able to resize, rotate, and edit symbol instances, you can also change their overall color and transparency. Once again, this allows you to use instances of a single symbol in many ways. Although the original symbol may be made up of objects of different colors and transparencies, these settings affect the instance as a whole.

To change the overall color or transparency of an instance:

1. Double-click an instance of a symbol on the stage.

The Instance Properties dialog box appears.

2. Click the Color Effects tab to bring up a pop-up menu, and choose from the options (**Figure 7.20**):

None. Causes the instance to appear as it did originally, without any color or transparency effect.

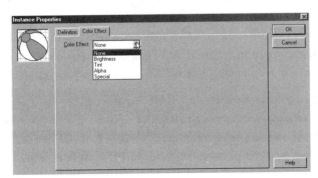

Figure 7.20
The Color Effects pop-up menu in the Instance Properties dialog box.

Brightness. Lets you adjust the overall brightness of the instance. A setting of 100 turns the instance white; a setting of –100 turns the instance black.

Tint. Allows you to tint an instance the color of your choosing. The Tint Amount slider lets you set the tint percentage.

Alpha. Allows you to adjust an instance's transparency. A setting of 0% makes the instance completely transparent; a setting of 100% makes the instance completely opaque.

Special. Lets you simultaneously adjust an instance's tint and transparency. The right slider adjusts the value; the left slider adjusts the percentage of change that value setting will have.

Adjusting any of these parameters will update the Preview Window in the upper left corner of the Instance Properties dialog box.

3. When you've completed your adjustments, click OK.

The instance reflects any changes you made.

TIP *Color effects editing is only possible on symbol instances. You cannot perform such edits on other Flash objects (such as text, groups, or imported bitmaps) unless you turn them into symbols and then drag an instance on stage for editing.*

TIP *You can create various tinted and transparent bitmaps by turning a bitmap into a symbol and adjusting the colors and transparency of various instances of it.*

Defining an Instance

Normally, placing an instance of a symbol on the stage creates an instance defined as the original symbol. Not to worry: It isn't as confusing as it sounds. When you create a symbol and define its behavior—making it, say, a graphic symbol—any instance of that symbol that you place on the stage will initially share the original's behavior. This does not mean, however, that it must retain that behavior. You can turn an instance of a movie-clip symbol into a button, a button into a graphic, a graphic into a movie clip, and so on—this is known as *defining* an instance.

You can define an instance in one of two ways: by fine-tuning the way it works or by changing the way it behaves—for example, making a graphic symbol react like a button or even a movie clip. When you change an instance's behavior, it takes on the functionality of its new behavior type and loses the functionality of its previous behavior.

To define an instance:

- Double-click an instance of a symbol on the stage.

    The Instance Properties dialog box appears.

Selected by default, the Definition tab is where you define an instance's behavior or switch the instance it is derived from. The tab has three sections; the third section varies according to behavior (graphic, button, or movie clip).

In the **Symbol** section of the Definition tab, you'll find a list of your movie's symbols; a dotted rectangle highlights the symbol the selected instance is based on (**Figure 7.21**). If you want to change the symbol this instance points to, click the symbol you would like to switch it to and then click the Switch Symbol button (**Figure 7.22**). The instance you are currently defining will be based on the new symbol you selected.

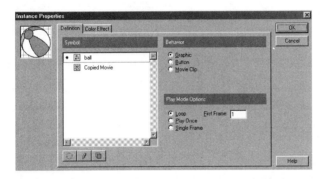

Figure 7.21
The symbol the instance is based on is highlighted by a dotted rectangle.

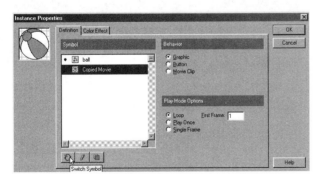

Figure 7.22
The Switch Symbol button.

In the **Behavior** section, you define the behavior for the instance you're editing. (The default behavior is defined by the symbol it was derived from.) Each behavior type then displays additional settings in the section below it that allow you to fine-tune the way the instance works. The additional Play Mode Options settings for the Graphic behavior (**Figure 7.23**):

Loop. Causes the instance to loop repeatedly. Since you're defining this instance as a graphic, and a graphic symbol's timeline plays in sync with the main timeline, the instance will only continue to loop while the main timeline is playing; when it stops, so will the instance.

Play Once. Cause the instance to play once and then stop.

Single Frame. You can choose to show only a single frame of the graphic symbol with this option.

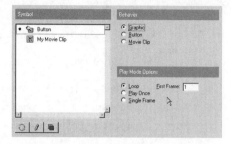

Figure 7.23
When you select Graphic in the behavior section, the section below changes to Play Mode Options and gives you more settings to choose from.

First Frame. Allows you to choose which frame on the instance's timeline will appear first.

The additional Tracking Options setting for the Button behavior (**Figure 7.24**):

Track as Button or *Track as Menu Item.* Lets you set how buttons react to pointer movements and mouse actions. Basically, this involves stacking buttons and assigning to each an action and is used mostly for creating menu bars in Flash (see "Symbol Tutorials" in this chapter).

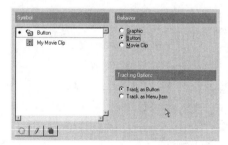

Figure 7.24
When you select Button in the behavior section, the section below changes to Tracking Options and gives you more settings to choose from.

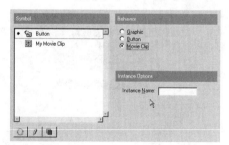

Figure 7.25
When you select Movie Clip in the behavior section, the section below changes to Instance Options which allows you to give the movie clip instance a name when identifying it for ActionScripting purposes.

The additional Instance Options settings for the Movie Clip behavior (**Figure 7.25**):

Instance Name. You can make any movie-clip instance into what's known as a *target*. By doing so, you can tell it to do all kinds of things within Flash. To make a movie clip a target, you assign a name to it from inside this box (for example, MyTarget). When you've done that, using actions you can instruct the target to rotate, move, resize, and so on *while* the Flash movie is playing. You can even give your audience this power by using buttons in conjunction with movie-clip instances that you've turned into targets. We'll discuss this topic in greater detail in Chapter 11, "Interactivity." For now, just be aware that movie-clip instances are the only objects that can be targets and that targets play a major role in Flash movie interactivity.

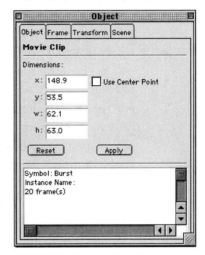

Figure 7.26
The Object Inspector.

> **TIP** *To easily see how a particular instance is defined, from the Window menu choose Inspectors > Object to make the Object Inspector appear. Click symbol instances on the stage and look at the top-left area of the inspector to see how they are defined (graphic, button, or movie clip) (Figure 7.26).*

Adding Actions to Buttons

Each button instance on the stage can be set up to perform a different action—even if more than one instance is derived from the same master symbol. This means you can use one button design for many purposes. Remember, though: You don't place actions (telling your button what to do) in the button timeline; instead, you add them to individual button instances on the stage.

To add an action to a button symbol:

1. Double-click any instance of a button symbol that appears on the stage.

   The Instance Properties dialog box appears.

2. Click the Actions tab.

3. Click the Add an Action button.

4. Choose an action, and configure it as you wish (**Figure 7.27**).

5. Click OK.

You have now assigned an action to your button. For more details and information on adding an action to a button, see "Events" in the "Interactivity" chapter.

> **TIP** *If you wish to test how your button will look and react to your pointer's movement, from the Control menu choose Enable Buttons. You can now use your pointer to test your button's functionality. You can't, however, test most of a button's interactive features; you can only verify its visual response (Up, Down, Over, and Hit states) to pointer movement. After testing your button, turn off the Enable Buttons option to select the button for editing.*

Go To
Play
Stop
Toggle High Quality
Stop All Sounds
Get URL
FS Command
Load/Unload Movie
Tell Target
If Frame is Loaded
On MouseEvent
If
Loop
Call
Set Property
Set Variable
Duplicate/Remove Movie Clip
Drag Movie Clip
Trace
Comment

Figure 7.27
The Add an Action (+) pull-down menu on the Actions tab of the Instance Properties dialog box.

Interactive Symbol Tutorials

 Creating symbols and using instances is a complex and sometimes confusing business. The following interactive tutorial found on the CD-ROM will help you get a better handle on these topics:

Creating Movie Clip. This tutorial walks you through the process of how to create a movie clip and use it multiple time in your project. It will also show you how to assign instance names to each instance of your clip.

The Library

Think how difficult it would be to accomplish anything on your computer if it didn't have a built-in organizational system to help you work with and keep track of your files. Imagine trying to locate a single file among the thousands that reside on your computer's hard drive—you could spend the greater part of a week and still not find what you were looking for. Fortunately, the computer's operating system makes file management fairly painless.

Most operating systems allow you to organize your files in imaginary "folders" that work the same way real folders do. You can open and close them, name and rename them, reorder them, and move them around. In short, you can organize your files in a way that makes sense to *you*. The library in Flash provides a similar benefit.

Flash projects can contain hundreds of items, including symbols, sounds, bitmaps, and video. Keeping track of and working with all of these items would be a daunting task without the library. You work with items in Flash's library in much the same way you do with files on your hard drive.

The Interface

Version 4 of Flash contains a greatly enhanced library that makes finding, organizing, and working with reusable elements in your Flash files easier than ever. To begin our examination of the library, let's take a look at its interface, which can provide all kinds of information about the items in your movie (**Figure 8.1**).

To open the library:

- From the Window menu, choose Library to make the library window appear.

  The library remains open until you close it.

The Library window is made up of the following areas (**Figure 8.1**):

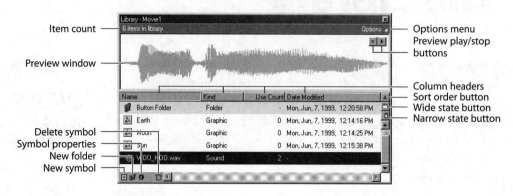

Figure 8.1
The library interface.

Item count. This area shows you the number of items in your library, including individual items and folders.

Options menu. Clicking here opens the Library Options menu, which includes all the commands you need to work with library items. (We discuss these commands later in the chapter.)

Preview window. This window lets you preview the appearance of a particular item and how it plays.

Preview play/stop buttons. Use these to preview any animated items or sounds in your library.

Column headers. These headers describe the content in the information column beneath them, providing the following information:

Name. This is the name of the symbol or of the folder, or it can be the name of the imported file from which the asset was derived (such as in the case of sounds, bitmaps, and QuickTime movies).

Kind. This describes the *kind* of item (graphic, button, movie clip, bitmap, sound, video, or folder).

Use Count. This shows how many instances of a particular item are used in your project.

Date Modified. This indicates the date and time an item was last edited or updated.

TIP *You can adjust the width of any of the headers by placing the pointer between the line that separates them; then, when it turns into a double-sided arrow, click and drag to resize.*

Item list. This hierarchical list includes all of the items in the library.

Sort order. Use this button to sort your items in ascending or descending order.

Wide State button. This button maximizes the library window so that all column headers are visible.

Narrow State button. This button minimizes the library window so that it displays only the most pertinent information. You can use the horizontal scroll bar to scroll through the columns.

New Symbol button. Use this to create a new symbol from the library window. It functions in the same way as the New Symbol command available from the Insert menu on the Flash main menu bar.

New Folder button. Use this to create a new folder in the library directory.

Item Properties button. Use this button to bring up the item's Properties dialog box so that you can adjust the selected item's settings.

Delete button. If you select an item in the library and then press this button, the item will be deleted from your project. But be careful: You cannot undo this action.

Figure 8.2
An item's contextual pop-up menu.

Additional Menus

You'll find a couple of additional menus useful when working with the library:

If you right-click (Windows) or Control-click (Macintosh) an item in the library window, a contextual menu pops up, offering a choice of several tasks that can be performed on that item (**Figure 8.2**).

If you right-click (Windows) or Control-click (Macintosh) the preview window in

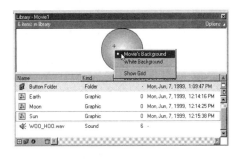

Figure 8.3
The window background contextual pop-up menu.

the library, another contextual menu pops up, allowing you to set how you want the preview window's background to appear (**Figure 8.3**).

Library Items

Put simply, any item that can be used more than once in your Flash movie is placed in the library—a process that's automatic when you're creating symbols inside Flash or importing items such as sounds, bitmaps, and video. Different icons identify the various items (**Figure 8.4**).

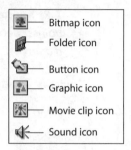

Figure 8.4
Library items and their identifying icons.

Library Management

You can perform all sorts of tasks from within the library window, some of which pertain to the library and others (such as creating new symbols or updating imported files) that are similar to tasks you can perform elsewhere in Flash. Being able to perform them from within the library window is simply a matter of convenience. Let's take a look at some of the library window's functionality.

Creating Items

Items that you can create directly from the library window include new or blank symbols and new folders. Using the library window to create a new symbol produces the same result as selecting New Symbol from the Insert menu on Flash's main menu bar. To add items such as sounds, bitmaps, and video, you must import them using the File Import command.

To create a folder:

1. From the Options menu in the library window select New Folder, or click the New Folder button at the bottom of the library window.

A folder appears on the list of library items.

2. Give the folder a name that will readily identify its contents, such as Navigation Buttons (**Figure 8.5**).

Your new folder is added to the root of the library directory structure, which means it's not inside any other folder.

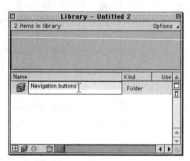

Figure 8.5
Renaming the newly created folder.

To create a new symbol from the library window:

1. From the Options menu in the library window choose New Symbol, or click the New Symbol button at the bottom of the library window.

   The Symbol Properties dialog box appears (**Figure 8.6**).

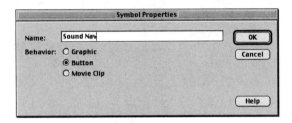

Figure 8.6
Creating a new symbol.

2. Give your new symbol a name, and assign it a behavior.

3. Click OK.

   Your new symbol is automatically added to the library, and you are immediately taken to its timeline and stage so that you can begin adding content. For more information about symbol creation see Chapter 7, "Symbols."

Duplicating symbols

As we mentioned in the chapter on symbols, if you want to create a new symbol that closely resembles an existing one, you can simply duplicate the original, and then edit the duplicate to fit your needs.

To duplicate symbols from the library window:

1. From the list of symbols that appear in the library window, select the one you wish to duplicate.

   The item becomes highlighted.

2. From the Options menu in the library window choose Duplicate to make the Symbol Properties dialog box appear.

3. Name your new symbol, assign a behavior to it, and click OK.

   The new symbol is added to the library. To edit your newly created symbol, see "Working with Library Items" later in this chapter.

Deleting Items

To delete an item from the library:

1. In the library select the item that you wish to delete.

The item—a symbol, sound, bitmap, video, or even a folder—becomes highlighted.

2. From the Options menu on the library window choose Delete, or click the Delete button at the bottom of the library window.

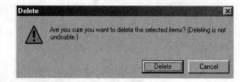

Figure 8.7
The Delete confirmation dialog box.

A Delete confirmation dialog box appears asking if you're sure you want to delete the item (**Figure 8.7**).

3. Click the Delete button.

TIP *You can select multiple items in the library window by Control-clicking (Windows) or Command-clicking (Macintosh) or shift-clicking (both platforms).*

Remember, deleting an item from the library is not undoable, so make sure of your choice before completing the action.

Deleting unused items

If you're like most Flash developers, not all of the symbols you create and the files you import will make it into the final product. However, Flash stores every one of those files and symbols in the library unless you deliberately delete them. Although these unused items will not affect your final exported movie's file size, they will still remain part of your Flash authoring file, making that file unnecessarily large. It's a good idea to do periodic housecleaning to rid the library of all those unused files.

Flash provides a command that allows you to search and select all of the items that aren't actually used in your project. Once you select them, you can delete them simultaneously.

To select and delete unused items:

1. From the Options menu on the library window choose Select Unused Items.

All unused items appear highlighted (**Figure 8.8**).

2. Click the Delete button at the bottom of the library window.

A delete confirmation dialog box appears, asking whether you're sure you want to delete.

3. Click the Delete button.

Renaming Items

Just because an item in the library has a name doesn't mean you can't change it.

To rename an item in the library:

Do one of the following:

- Double-click its name.

- Right-click (Windows) or Control-click (Macintosh), and from the contextual menu that appears, choose Rename.

- Select the item in the library, and then press the Item Properties button at the bottom of the library window.

- From the Options menu on the library window choose Rename.

Working with Symbols in the Library Window

Through the library window, you can quickly see or alter a symbol's properties, change its behavior, and edit its content and timeline. These various tasks perform functions similar to those discussed in the chapter on symbols.

To get a symbol's properties from the library window:

1. In the library window select the symbol.

2. From the Options menu in the library window choose Properties, or click the Properties button at the bottom of the library window.

Figure 8.8
Unused items selected.

To change a symbol's behavior
from the library window:

1. Right-click (Windows) or Control-click (Macintosh) the symbol whose behavior you would like to change.

2. In the contextual menu that appears, choose Behavior and then from the submenu the particular behavior you would like to change this symbol to (**Figure 8.9**).

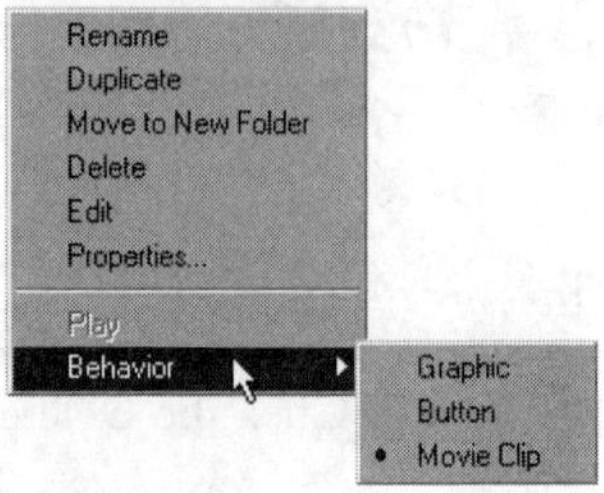

Figure 8.9
Changing the behavior of an item from the library causes any new instances of the symbol to reflect the new behavior.

To enter a symbol's symbol-editing
mode from the library window:

1. In the library window select the symbol; it is highlighted.

2. From the Options menu in the library window choose Edit to open the symbol's stage and timeline for editing, or double-click its icon in the library.

Working with Sounds, Bitmaps, and Videos in the Library Window

Working with sounds, bitmaps, and videos in the library window is only slightly different than working with symbols. You can perform two tasks on these library items: One is to get or change their properties (for example, name and compression settings); the other is to update them to reflect the most current version of the file that was used when they were imported into Flash.

To get or change the properties of a sound,
bitmap, or video from the library window:

1. Select a sound, bitmap, or video item from the library window; it is highlighted.

2. From the Options menu in the library window choose Properties, or click the Properties button at the bottom of the library window.

To update a sound, bitmap, or video file:

1. Select a sound, bitmap, or video item from the library window.

2. From the Options menu on the library window choose Update (**Figure 8.10**) to update the file used in Flash with any changes you made to it externally.

Figure 8.10
Selecting Update from the Options menu will update the selected sound, bitmap, or video file to reflect any changes that have been made to the file outside of Flash.

Viewing and Reorganizing Library Items

The library provides several features that make it easy to find and access the items in your project. Being able to expand or collapse folders, move items from one folder to another, and sort items help you pinpoint a specific library item.

To expand or collapse a folder:

- Double-click the folder's icon to expand or collapse the folder (depending on its current mode).

or

- In the library window select the folder, and from the Options menu choose either Expand Folder or Collapse Folder (depending on its current mode).

To move an item from one folder to another:

1. In the library click the item and begin dragging it.

As you drag the item, the pointer turns into either a circle with a line through it (indicating an area that cannot be dragged to) or as an arrow with a small box in its lower right corner (indicating an acceptable area to drag to) (**Figure 8.11**).

2. Drag the item to the folder you wish to drop it into to, and then release the mouse (**Figure 8.12**).

TIP *You cannot drag and drop items into the same folder where they're currently located; you can, however, drag and drop them into parent or child folders.*

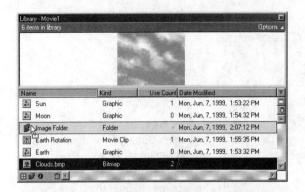

Figure 8.11
Dragging a library item to a folder.

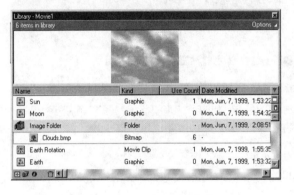

Figure 8.12
The item after being moved to a folder.

To move an item into a new folder:

1. In the library window select an item; it appears highlighted.

2. From the Options menu in the library window choose Move to New Folder.

A dialog box appears, asking you to name your new folder.

3. Give your folder a name, and click OK.

A new folder is created in the library window, and the item you originally selected is automatically placed inside of it.

To sort items in the library:

1. Click a column header to sort the list of library items by that header.

For example, if you click the Name header, library items will be sorted in alphabetical order according to their names.

2. Click the Sort Order button to select whether to sort your items in ascending or descending order.

TIP *Each folder is sorted separately.*

Library Tutorial

 To help you put together all of what you've learned here, we've assembled the following interactive tutorial. They, as well as the resulting source files, are on the accompanying CD-ROM disc:

Working with the Library. This tutorial takes you through a basic tour of the library and shows you how to work with library items in various ways.

Layers

Organization, dimension, and (to a large degree) animation all depend on one of Flash's most basic but powerful features: *layers.* Employed by many graphics programs to improve their ability to handle complex drawings as well as to add depth, layers serve as the ultimate organizational tool in a program such as Flash where objects are placed on top of one another and are animated.

Layers provide numerous benefits. If you never planned to animate more than a single object on the stage, you would have no need for them. However, we know you want to do more than that. You want to see objects go over and under each other so that you get some sense of depth (**Figure 9.1**). Without the dimension and perspective layers provide, you wouldn't be able to achieve that.

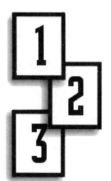

**Figure 9.1
Objects with
layered depth.**

When working with complex scenes and animations, organization is extremely paramount—and layers can help. By placing distinct elements (such as background images or symbols) on individual layers, you make it easy to locate, isolate, and reorder your animation in many ways (**Figure 9.2**). Layers enable you to work on specific areas of your animation without affecting others—and to do so without being distracted by objects on other layers. In this way you avoid accidentally editing or removing an object.

You can use layers for just about everything, including creating symbols, movie clips, and graphics (**Figure 9.3**). However, no matter where you're using them, layers always work the same way.

Figure 9.2
In this image the background image and other elements are placed on individual layers. This makes working with the elements of this scene much easier.

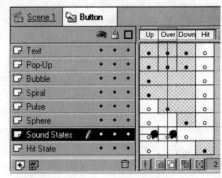

Figure 9.3
Use layers on the main timeline and when creating movie clips, graphic symbols, or even buttons.

Understanding Layers

Layers serve as receptacles for symbols, groups, and other objects. As part of the timeline, layers are placed one on top of another in what is called the "stacking order" (**Figure 9.4**). Objects that reside in the top layer will always appear on the stage above objects contained in the layers below. If the number of layers exceeds the area of the timeline, a scroll bar will appear to the right of the timeline.

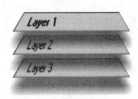

Figure 9.4
Graphic representation of stacking order.

Each layer can contain any number of objects (both stage and overlay level), which have their own *internal* stacking order on that layer (**Figure 9.5**). When you move one layer above or below another layer, its internal stacking order remains intact—but all of those objects appear above or below any objects on layers above or below it, respectively. You can edit objects on multiple layers simultaneously—as long as those objects are not on layers that are locked or hidden. In addition, you can

Figure 9.5
In this illustration both the number 1 and the box are on Layer 1, but the 1 appears above the box.

perform nearly all editing functions (resizing, rotating, erasing, and so on) on objects that exist on multiple layers just as you would edit an object on a single layer. However, you must remember that because the elements are on separate layers, certain events, such as segmenting, cannot occur (for that to take place, the elements must be on the same layer). (For more on segmenting, see that section in Chapter 3, "Drawing.")

With individually animated objects, it's a good idea to place them on separate layers, because sometimes it's a necessity. Flash will not allow you to tween an object unless it's on its own layer. You may, however, have multiple movie clips, graphics, groups, or shapes of any combination on a single layer.

By using layers properly, you can also improve your movie's download time and performance by placing elements that don't change over multiple frames on their own layer, separate from those that do. Take, for example, a scene that includes a plane flying across a background: It's best to place the background on its own layer because it will change little, if at all (**Figure 9.6**). If instead you placed the background and the plane on the same layer, Flash will need to redraw the entire scene (background and plane) on each frame of the timeline. In so doing, performance will degrade unnecessarily since the only thing that's animated—and the only item that needs to be redrawn—is the plane. If you were to place the background on the same layer as the plane, you would need a copy of it on every frame in which the plane's movement changed—dramatically increasing file size. The lesson here? In all cases, big or small, use layers to separate static elements from animated ones.

Figure 9.6
Here, the background is isolated on its own layer so that only the plane is redrawn per each frame of the animation.

In general, creating and using layers is pretty straightforward. However, Flash contains some special layers—guide, motion guide, and mask—that require different techniques for creation and management. We'll deal with those individually later in the chapter.

Creating Layers

When creating a new scene, graphic, movie clip, or button, Flash always creates its timeline with a single layer. Called Layer 1, this layer includes one frame with an empty keyframe (**Figure 9.7**). From this point, you can create a new layer anywhere in the stacking order. And because layer number does not affect file size, you can use as many layers as you need.

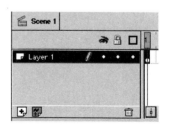

Figure 9.7
Every new scene or symbol begins with a single layer initially named Layer 1.

To create a layer:

1. Click the layer that you want the new layer to go above; it is highlighted.

2. On the Layer control panel, click the Add Layer button (**Figure 9.8**), or right-click (Windows) or Control-click (Macintosh) an existing layer's name bar.

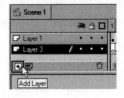

Figure 9.8
The Add
Layer button.

3. From the contextual pop-up menu choose Insert to place a new layer on the timeline.

Whenever you add a new layer to the timeline, Flash automatically adds enough frames to the layer to make it match the longest frame sequence of the timeline (**Figure 9.9**). This means that if Layer 1's longest sequence is 20 frames, Flash will automatically add 20 frames to any new layer created.

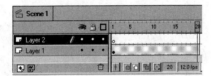

Figure 9.9
When Layer 2 was created, Flash added 20 frames to it to match the same number of frames in Layer 1.

Deleting Layers

You may at times decide you no longer need all of a layer's elements. If this is the case, you can easily delete a layer and all of its associated frames.

To delete a layer:

1. Select the layer you want to delete.

2. From the Layer control panel click the Delete Layer button (**Figure 9.10**), or right-click (Windows) or Control-click (Macintosh) the layer, and from the contextual pop-up menu choose Delete.

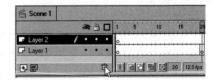

Figure 9.10
The Delete Layer button.

TIP *If you delete the wrong layer, you can always click the Undo button.*

Layer Properties

You can configure layers in a number of ways in one centralized location—the Layer Properties dialog box (**Figure 9.11**). Each layer has a unique set of properties:

Name

Name. Use this text box to assign a name to a layer. (See "Renaming Layers" below.)

Show. Sets whether a layer's contents will be visible on the stage.

Lock. Sets whether the layer's contents can be edited.

Type

Normal. Lets you set the layer type to "normal."

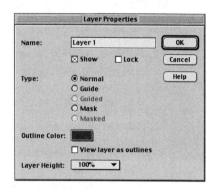

Figure 9.11
The Layer Properties dialog box is where you configure the individual properties of a layer.

Guide. Allows you to set your layer as a motion guide (see "Motion Guide Layers" later in this chapter). This type of layer guides tweened animation on any layers linked to it.

Guided. Sets your layer type as Guided, which means it will be linked to a motion-guide layer. This option is only available to you if the layer whose properties you're adjusting is directly below a motion-guide layer or another linked, guided layer.

Mask. Allows you to set the layer type as a mask (see "Mask Layers" later in this chapter). This type of layer masks objects on any layers linked to it.

Masked. Lets you set the layer type as Masked, which means it's linked to a mask layer. This option is only available to you if the layer whose properties you're adjusting is directly below a mask layer or another linked, masked layer.

Outline Color

Outline Color. Sets the color used for outlining objects on this layer (see "Identifying Objects on Different Layers" in this chapter).

View layer as outlines. Allows you to determine whether the contents of the layer will be visible as outlines.

Layer Height

100%, 200%, 300%. This option allows you to set the height of the layer, which is useful if you're working with waveforms (sounds) in the layer.

To change layer properties:

1. Select the layer whose properties you wish to change.

2. From the Modify menu choose Layer, or right-click (Windows) or Control-click (Macintosh) and from the pop-up menu choose Properties.

The Layer Properties box appears.

3. Make your setting adjustments, and click OK.

The layer reflects your changes.

> **TIP** *The quickest way to access a layer's Property box is to double-click the Layer icon just to the left of the layer's name.*

Renaming Layers

Flash assigns a default name (Layer 1, Layer 2, and so on) to each layer you create. Although you don't need to assign layers different names, layers can lose their organizational benefits if you don't label them according to their associated elements or actions. For example, if you place a background image on a layer, you might want to make it the only element on that layer and name it Background.

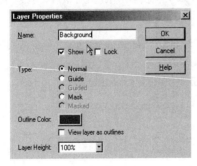

Figure 9.12
Changing the layer's name in the Layer Properties dialog box.

To rename a layer:

1. Right-click (Windows) or Control-click (Macintosh) the layer you would like to rename.

2. From the pop-up menu that appears choose Properties.

3. Type in the name for this layer (**Figure 9.12**), and then click OK.

   The layer name is now displayed.

   TIP *Another, and perhaps quicker, way to complete the same task is to double-click the layer name itself (**Figure 9.13**) and enter a new name.*

Figure 9.13
Changing the layer name by double-clicking it.

Reordering Layers

You can easily change the stacking order of your layers—and by so doing you reorder the objects and animations that reside on those layers.

To reorder a layer:

1. Select the layer you wish to reorder.

   A dark gray line appears along the bottom indicating that layer's position relative to the other layers in the stack (**Figure 9.14**).

2. Drag the layer up or down, and then release the mouse.

   The layer now is in its new position in the stacking order (**Figure 9.15**).

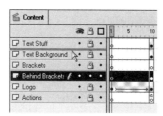

Figure 9.14
Selected layer about to be repositioned.

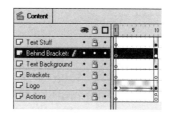

Figure 9.15
Layers after repositioning.

Copying Layers

You may sometimes wish to copy a layer's contents and frame sequences to create a new layer—useful for transferring layers from scene to scene or for transferring layers from one movie to another. You can even simultaneously select all of a scene's layers and paste them elsewhere to duplicate an entire scene. Or you can copy sections of a layer's timeline to create a new layer. Whenever you paste a layer's contents and sequences into the beginning of another layer, that layer automatically takes on the name of the layer from which its contents were derived.

To copy a single layer:

1. If you have not already done so, create an empty layer that can receive the copied layer's contents.

2. On the layer that contains the content you wish to copy, left-click (Windows) or Click (Mac) and drag from Frame 1 through the final frame; then release.

   The contents should appear black to show that they've been selected (**Figure 9.16**).

3. Right-click (Windows) or Control-click (Macintosh) one of the selected frames, and from the Frame pop-up menu choose Copy Frames (**Figure 9.17**).

4. In the empty layer you created earlier, right-click (Windows) or Control-click (Macintosh) Frame 1, and from the Frame pop-up menu choose Paste Frames (**Figure 9.18**).

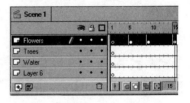

Figure 9.16
The Flowers layer selected for copying.

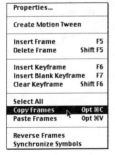

Figure 9.17
Preparing to copy selected frames and keyframes from a layer.

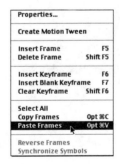

Figure 9.18
Preparing to paste into another layer.

ABI Mouldings

http://www.abimouldings.com

Although a company that specializes in mouldings may seem like an unlikely candidate for having an exemplary Flash site, this one proves that the power of imagination can make the improbable possible. ABI Mouldings' site uses a clean, easily and intuitively navigated site to showcase its products. One particularly interesting feature is that the its well-chosen background music stops the minute you get into any content and picks up again when you return to the main menu. This is a refreshing change from sites that rely on you to search for a mute button on the page. Sound and ambience, like most things in life, are best with moderation.

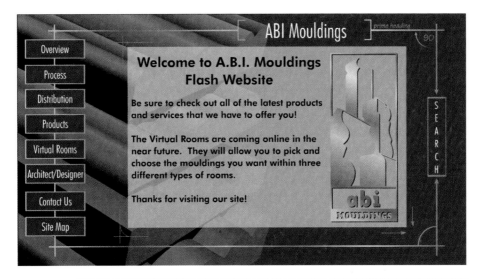

Dirk Rullkoetter

http://www.rullkoetter.de

Dirk shows us that used in moderation, bitmaps can give your Flash project a look and feel that you just can't achieve with vector graphics alone. He employed a creative use for a fly that you have to see to appreciate. The portfolio section of the site uses the Load Movie action to load and display content only as needed, which reduces the site's overall download time.

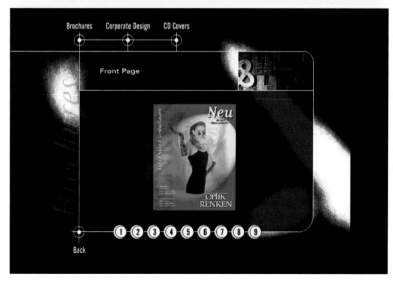

Diverse Web Options

http://www.crazyraven.com/dwo.htm

This site was developed by Crazy Raven Productions and is an example of simple interface design and interactivity. With the target audience being small business, this site displays a technical yet affordable look. The site uses a brief text introduction with an audio track, so the user is ready to enhance his or her own business with a Flashed site. The audio and sound design creates a comfortable atmosphere that keeps the user interested in staying for a while. Taking advantage of the masking and gradient effects in Flash 4, this design demonstrates how you can achieve nice lighting effects and add dimension.

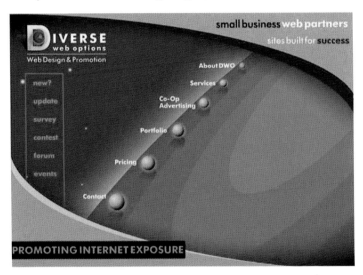

DNA Design

http://www.dnadesign.com

DNA Design uses a mixture of Flash and HTML content to show just how seamless the two can work together. Unless you're paying close attention, you just won't be able to differentiate the two. The DNA site is poetry in motion and doesn't rely on special effects—just a beautiful layout enhanced by Flash's capabilities.

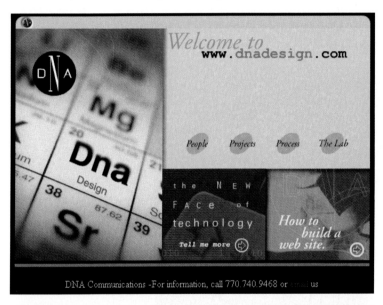

Ego Media

http://www.egomedia.com

Ego Media's site takes an entirely different multimedia approach. Utilizing video footage that has been traced within Flash, the designers make a site and a statement that is original. Unlike most Flash sites that open in a small window, the folks at Ego Media chose to create a site that opens up full screen so that the viewer won't be distracted by the browser's interface.

Eye4u

http://www.eye4u.com

This site is a classic example of precise sound synchronization and navigation construction/reconstruction. One of the most amazing things about this site is that the designers are able to move several large vector images simultaneously, including resizing them, and keep it all perfectly synchronized to the soundtrack, even on a slower machine.

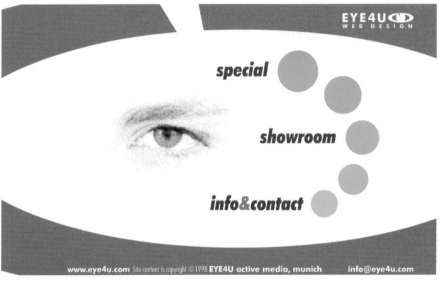

First 9 Months

http://www.pregnancycalendar.com/first9months/

This site doesn't attempt to push the limits of Flash at all. It's purpose is to educate and enter-tain. Watch the various stages of pregnancy from the point of conception all the way to birth. The design and presentation are fascinating. The site utilizes a superb soundtrack and engag-ing text in a well thought out navigation structure. Goes to show that not every Flash site needs to be created with an MTV mentality to be mesmerizing.

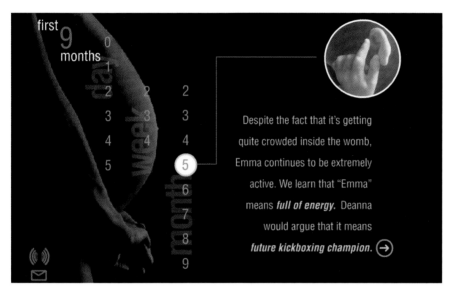

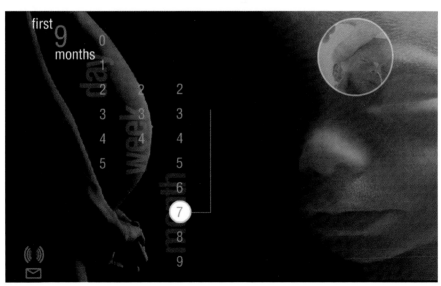

G-Shock

http://www.gshock.com

Blast Radius's G-Shock site demonstrates how to use effective, audience-targeted marketing with clever interface design. The G-Shock site opens with a preloader that will get even those older than the target market excited. It then builds an incredible interface centered on the face of a watch. Beyond great visual design, the watch-like interface—which would typically have limited navigation points—produces intuitive expanding and collapsing subnavigation areas.

Kimble.org

http://www.kimble.org

This site is home base to a well-known former hacker-turned security specialist. It uses sound and animation to present an overall "secret-agent" feel. If you want to see some of the many cool things that you can accomplish simply by using animated buttons, this is the site to visit. The main page is a study in itself of mouseover techniques. Sound is used throughout from mouseovers, to background music, to transitions.

KWHL 106.5

http://www.kwhl.com

This radio site, developed by Crazy Raven Productions, is aimed to take advantage of many of Flash 4's features. Most sections of the site have content that can easily be updated using Flash's new Load Variables action. This gives a tremendous amount of control to the radio station, which wanted to be able to update the site itself. MP3 audio clips are used on the "CD Player" control panel in conjunction with the music reviews section. There is a stunning amount of interactivity to this site. It has to be seen to be appreciated.

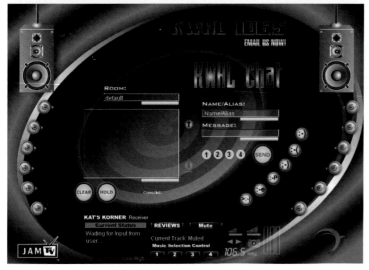

Nashville Predators
NHL Hockey Team
http://design.edge.net/predators

This is an absolutely fun site to visit! As an introduction, it provides an incredible animated sequence that gets you ready for the actual site. This is frame-by-frame animation at its finest. Once you get to the main content of the site, the site continues its theme of building excitement for the team. Navigational elements "slide" into the screen and shake, which gives the viewer a sense of the game. The section of the site with player profiles is pure genius and once again shows what can be accomplished with simple mouseover events.

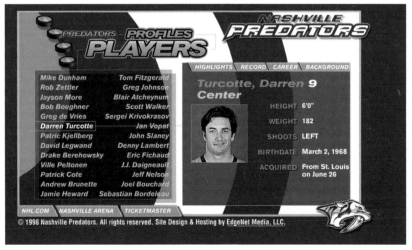

NRG Designs

http://www.nrg.be

NRG Designs is a Flash talent powerhouse. At least three of its sites have received Macromedia's coveted "Shocked Site of the Day," including http://www.kimble.org, which is also highlighted in this color section. NRG's own site has some great examples of Flash interface design coupled with superior sound synchronization. It's uncluttered and simple. Shape tweening is used throughout the site, including a great transition with the company's logo.

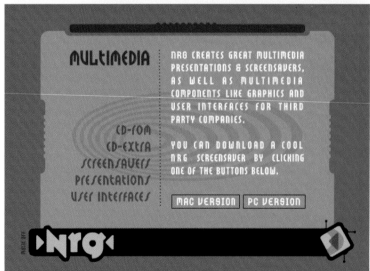

ROSS Video Productions

http://www.rossvp.com

This site was developed by Crazy Raven Productions. It shows how Flash is the only way to go for a fast-paced, in-your-face video production company. From the time the RVP introduction begins, you are being prepared to experience a site—not just view it. Using energetic audio tracks and speeding graphics, this site demonstrates the importance of creating a Web environment for your target audience. Showing the strength of transparency settings and bitmapped graphics in Flash, this design creates a new world for video production companies on the Web.

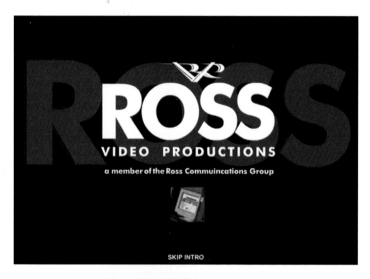

The Media Group

http://themmgroup.com/

The Media Group utilizes a sleek contemporary design that initially gives an overwhelming presence but quickly clears to an incredibly simple navigational system free of clutter. Its use of movement is nothing short of brilliant! This site is an excellent example of how to use text in creative ways.

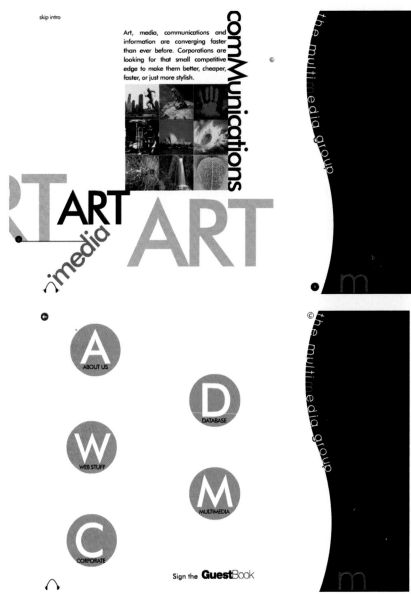

VRLX

http://www.vrlx.net

VRLX provides a mixture of a virtual tour of exotic locations and an immersive online travel magazine. Utilizing multiple technologies, mostly Flash, the site delivers engaging content and sets a mood of class and refinement. Although the actual navigation takes some getting used, to the site launches a help screen that will give you a minitour of how it works as soon as you enter. This is another example of knowing your audience and providing an intriguing experience as well as providing some limited advertising space (also done in Flash) for companies whose products are specific to the target audience.

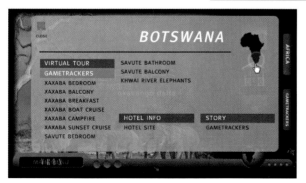

The World is Alive

http://www.crazyraven.com/movie1.htm

The World is Alive is a production by Crazy Raven Productions. It's nearly a 15-minute Flash movie that touts the benefits of getting rid of static content in favor of Flash content. To pull off such a long presentation over the Web, streaming was critical. The movie is carefully put together so that chunks of content are seen for periods of time with little change. This helps facilitate the streaming process. Masks are used for many sequences, including the splash effect prior to the preloader, the focus effect during the rock sequence, and the puzzle piece effect after the rock sequence.

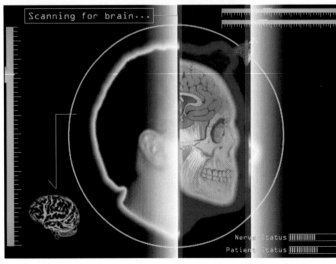

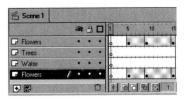

Figure 9.19
Flowers layer copied
to the new layer.

The layer with the pasted contents now has the same name as the layer from which its contents were copied (**Figure 9.19**).

To copy multiple layers:

1. Create one empty layer, which can receive the copied layers' contents.

   Even if you're pasting multiple layers, you only need one empty layer, which takes the top-most position of the layers that you will be pasting in.

2. From the layers whose contents you wish to copy, click and drag from Frame 1 of the top-most layer to the last frame on the bottom-most layer.

   The contents should appear black to show that they have been selected (**Figure 9.20**). You cannot perform this type of edit unless all layers are contiguous.

3. Right-click (Windows) or Control-click (Macintosh) one of the selected frames, and from the Frame pop-up menu choose Copy Frames.

4. In the empty layer you created, right-click (Windows) or Control-click (Macintosh) Frame 1, and then from the Frame pop-up menu choose Paste Frames.

   You now have an exact duplicate of the multiple layers you copied (**Figure 9.21**). Notice that the pasted layers have the same names and relative positions as the layers you copied them from.

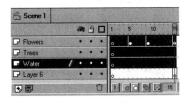

Figure 9.20
The top three layers
are selected.

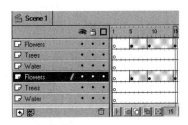

Figure 9.21
A completed copy of
the top three layers.

Identifying Objects on Different Layers

In complex scenes with many layers, keeping track of objects can at times seem like an overwhelming task. Don't despair: Flash has a couple of features that can help speed the process. For one, it allows you to identify an object on a layer by assigning it a colored outline, which appears on that layer's name bar. You can assign a different color to each layer, making it easy to identify objects on individual layers. This way, you can see from the stage which layer an object resides on.

Second, when you select an object on the stage, the name of the layer it resides on will be highlighted in black on the name bar, making it simple to identify a particular layer that may need editing.

To identify objects on layers using colored outlines:

1. Select the layer whose properties you want to change; it is highlighted.

2. From the Modify menu choose Layer, or right-click (Windows) or Control-click (Macintosh) the layer and from the contextual pop-up menu choose Properties.

The Layer Properties box appears.

3. Under the Outline options, select the color you wish to use as the outline color, and check the View layer as outlines option (**Figure 9.22**).

4. Click OK.

The layer now displays its objects as outlines.

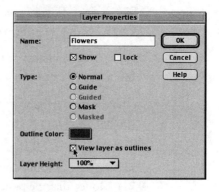

Figure 9.22
The Layer Properties dialog box with View layer as outlines selected.

TIP *You can also accomplish this task by simply clicking the Outline On/Off toggle on the right side of the layer's name bar.*

TIP *When using outline colors to identify objects on a layer, the objects temporarily lose their fill and become outlines. You can still edit them just as you normally would; the only thing that's different is that fills and fill changes will not appear until you turn Outline off.*

TIP *To turn this feature off and return the objects to their normal state, choose Normal Color from the Layer pop-up menu of the layer you wish to return to normal.*

Selecting Everything on a Layer or Multiple Layers

If you need to resize, move, or rotate a complete scene or a number of objects on one or multiple layers, you can select them all in one quick step.

To select every object on all unlocked and visible layers:

1. Move the timeline to the frame with all the objects you wish to select.

2. From the Edit menu choose Select All (**Figure 9.23**).

   This selects all objects on all unlocked and visible layers so that you may edit them simultaneously.

Figure 9.23
Choosing Select All from the Edit menu selects all objects on any unlocked or visible layers.

Layer Modes

Layers have different modes, or *states,* which allow you to work in varying ways. The way in which you edit as well as the stage's appearance while authoring a movie are determined—at least in part—by the layer modes you employ. You can change a layer's layer at any time by clicking the appropriate dot on the layer's name bar. (The exception to this is current layer, which you change by either clicking a layer's name or clicking a stage object that resides on that layer.) Layers have four modes:

Current mode. At any one time, only a single layer can be in current mode. This layer is known as the current layer. Any new object that you draw, paste, or bring onto the stage via the library or by importing is placed on this layer. Whenever you create a new layer, this mode is its initial state. A Pencil icon on the layer's name bar indicates that it is the current layer (**Figure 9.24**).

Figure 9.24
The pencil icon identifies which layer is the current layer.

Figure 9.25
A red X on a layer's name bar indicates that its contents are not visible on the stage.

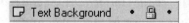

Figure 9.26
A lock on a layer's name bar indicates that its contents are not editable.

Hidden mode. You may occasionally find it useful to hide the contents of a layer or multiple layers when you're trying to focus on a particular part of your scene. A red X on a layer's name bar indicates that it is hidden (**Figure 9.25**).

Locked mode. When a layer is locked, you can see its contents but you can't edit them. You can place your layer in this mode when you feel that its contents are just as you want them and you don't want to edit or delete them accidentally. A lock on the layer's name bar indicates that it is locked (**Figure 9.26**).

Outline mode. If your layer is in this mode, its contents will appear as outlines. A colored outline of a box on the layer's name bar indicates that it is in outline view.

> **TIP** *You can place a layer in multiple modes—for example, making it both locked and hidden.*

Quick Editing with Layers

When working with scenes with numerous layers, you may sometimes wish to view all layers and other times wish to view or edit just one. However, if you're talking about 10, 20, or even 40 layers, you can spend a ridiculous amount of time switching all of these layers' individual modes. That's where "quick edits" come in: You can access these time-saving commands by right-clicking (Windows) or Control-clicking (Macintosh) the layer's name bar and choosing the appropriate command from the contextual menu (**Figure 9.27**).

Figure 9.27
Show All, Lock Others, and Hide Others allow you to quickly make multiple layers visible, hidden, editable, or noneditable.

Show All. Use this command to unlock any previously locked layers in a scene as well as to make visible any previously hidden layers.

Lock Others. Use this command to lock all but the layer whose contextual menu you are using to initiate this command. That layer becomes the current layer (if it wasn't already), and you cannot edit any of the other layers.

Hide Others. Use this to hide all but the layer whose contextual menu you are using to initiate this command. That layer becomes the current layer (if it wasn't already), and you cannot see or edit any of the other layers.

Using Guide Layers

Guide layers can make laying out your Flash movie a breeze: Say you've used Flash (or your favorite graphics program) to create a killer layout—with menu bars and graphics placed just so—that you want to use as the basis for your Flash movie (**Figure 9.28**). If you place your layout on a guide layer in Flash, you can use it as a backdrop for your movie's layout. Although you could accomplish the same thing by placing the graphic on a regular layer as a background, its contents would be included in the exported movie. Guide layers, in contrast, are not exported, which means their contents will not appear in the final product. You can use multiple guide layers in a scene and as many guide layers in your movie as you see fit.

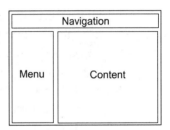

Figure 9.28
Content on a guide layer can be a basic layout you've created and can serve as the basis for how your Flash project will be put together.

To create a guide layer:

1. Once you've created the graphics and placed them on a layer, right-click (Windows) or Control-click (Macintosh) that layer's name bar.

2. From the contexutal menu that appears choose Guide.

   A new icon appears next to the layer's name, indicating that the layer is a guide (**Figure 9.29**). None of this layer's contents will be exported in the final movie.

Figure 9.29
Two intersecting lines on a layer's name bar indicate that it is a guide layer.

Motion Guide Layers

In real life most movement comprises straight and curved motions. Although it's easy to create straight-line movement in Flash, you need to use a motion-guide layer to create curved movements or animations along a path. Say you want to animate a ball symbol so that it appears to be bouncing down a street. First, you would need to place the ball symbol on a regular layer. Then, you would create a path, or line, to simulate the movement you want the ball to follow. Finally, you would associate that path with the ball, so that the ball would follow the line when you animate it. Associating this path or line with the ball is where motion-guide layers come in to play.

Although you place the ball on a regular layer, you must place the path you want the ball to follow on a motion-guide layer (**Figure 9.30**). In fact, the only thing you will ever place on a motion-guide layer is a path. Filled objects have no effect on motion-guide layers, and objects on such layers are invisible in the final product. We'll discuss motion paths—or the paths that are placed on motion-guide layers— in detail in Chapter 10, "Animation." However, you need to know some important things when creating the motion-guide layers where these motion paths will be placed.

A motion-guide layer is always linked or associated with at least one other layer (though it can be linked to as many layers as you want). Linking layers with a motion-guide layer causes any tweened symbols (which you'll learn about in the chapter on animation) on the linked layers to follow the motion path you place on the motion-guide layer. The layer you select when creating a motion-guide layer is the only layer automatically linked

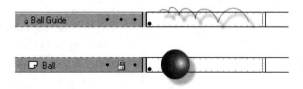

Figure 9.30
You draw a line, or path, on a motion guide layer, which will be followed by any tweened animation on a regular layer that is linked to the motion guide layer.

to it. You can later link as many other normal layers to it as you wish. Any linked layer's name bar will be inset below the motion guide's name bar, thus denoting a hierarchy. A layer that is linked to a motion-guide layer is considered a guided layer.

By default, any new motion-guide layer is placed directly above the layer used to create it. You can reorder a motion-guide layer just as you would a regular layer; however, any layers linked to it will move with it and maintain their relative positions. You may use multiple motion-guide layers in a scene.

To create a motion-guide layer:

1. Click the layer you wish to link to a motion-guide layer; it becomes highlighted.

2. On the Layer control panel click the Add Motion Guide button, or right-click (Windows) or Control-click (Macintosh) the selected layer's name bar, and from the contextual pop-up menu choose Add Motion Guide.

   This creates a motion-guide layer that is above, and linked to, the layer you used to create it. If you now draw a path on the motion-guide layer, tweened symbols on any layers linked to it may follow that path. An icon is placed next to the motion-guide layer's name, indicating its status as a motion guide (**Figure 9.31**).

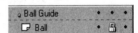

Figure 9.31
An arch with a ball at the end on a layer's name bar identifies the layer as a motion guide.

Although only the current layer is initially linked to the motion guide, you can link as many normal layers to the motion-guide layer as you wish so that all tweened objects on the linked layers share a single path.

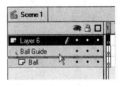

Figure 9.32
Dragging a layer to link it to a motion guide.

To link additional layers to a motion-guide layer:

1. Select the normal layer's name bar to link it to the motion-guide layer.

   A dark-gray line appears along the bottom indicating that layer's position relative to the other layers in the stack (**Figure 9.32**).

2. Drag the layer until the gray line denoting its position appears just below the name bar of the motion-guide layer itself; then release.

   The layer now is linked to the motion guide (**Figure 9.33**).

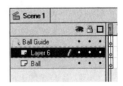

Figure 9.33
Any linked layer's name bar will be inset within the motion guide's name bar, denoting a hierarchy.

To unlink a layer from a motion-guide layer:

1. Select the linked layer's name bar to unlink it from the motion-guide layer.

A dark-gray line appears along the bottom indicating that layer's position relative to the other layers in the stack.

2. Drag the layer until the gray line denoting its position appears either above the name bar of the motion-guide layer itself or below any other normal layer; then release.

The layer now is unlinked from the motion-guide layer.

TIP *Once you've linked several layers to a motion guide, you can reorder them within the linked stack just as you would normal layers.*

TIP *A motion-guide layer can take on any mode that a regular layer can. So, if you wish to hide or lock a guide layer, you may do so—useful if you wish to rid your scene of elements you won't be able to see in the final production anyway.*

Mask Layers

Flash's Mask feature adds a wealth of possibilities to the seemingly endless array of effects you can be achieve with this wonderful animation tool.

Simply put, a mask conceals areas or spaces from view—in much the same way that a wall in your home masks one room from another or that putting your hand in front of your face prevents you from reading this page.

You can also think of a mask as a stencil. When you place a stencil over a surface and spray paint over that stencil, paint is only applied to those areas not covered by the stencil; the rest of the surface is blocked off, or *masked,* from the paint (**Figure 9.34**).

Figure 9.34
A mask works much like a stencil in that it blocks areas from view.

Mask layers work similarly to motion-guide layers in that the content of normal layers linked to a mask layer will only show through areas of the mask layer that have solid objects—for example, a circle, a square, a group, text, or even a symbol. However, a symbol can only contain a single shape or text object. You can animate such objects on the mask layer to create what is essentially a moving mask. You cannot, however, use lines as masks. Normal layers linked to a mask layer actually become masked layers, although they retain all the

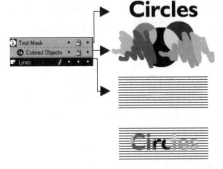

Figure 9.35
Content on layers—even those below the
stack of layers that make up the mask layer
and the ones linked to it—will show through.

capabilities of a normal layer. This means you can use multiple symbols, objects, and text on any linked layers; you can even create an animation on them. Just remember this distinction: A *mask layer* is the layer that includes the actual object used as a mask, and a *masked layer* is the layer affected by the mask. A mask layer can have multiple associated, or *linked,* masked layers.

Mask layers, like motion-guide layers, are initially linked to a single masked layer—the layer that was below the current layer when it was changed to a mask. Also like motion-guide layers, mask layers can have as many linked masked layers as you desire. Only those layers linked to the mask layer will be affected by it. All other layers—even those below the stack of layers that make up of the mask layer and the ones linked to it—will show through (**Figure 9.35**).

To create a mask layer:

1. Right-click (Windows) or Control-click (Macintosh) the name bar of the layer you wish to turn into a mask.

2. From the Layer pop-up menu that appears, choose Mask (**Figure 9.36**).

   An icon appears next to this layer's name and the layer directly below it indicating that they are linked by a mask (**Figure 9.37**). (The upper layer has the mask object; the lower layers include the contents—static or animated—that show through the mask.) By default, these layers are automatically locked.

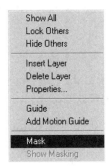

Figure 9.36
Choose Mask from the
Layer pop-up menu.

Figure 9.37
A mask layer and layers
linked to it are identified
by arrow icons.

TIP *You can also convert a normal layer to a mask layer by changing its type through the Layer Properties box, which you access by double-clicking the Normal Layer icon or by choosing Layer from the Modify menu.*

TIP *Remember that the layers linked to the mask layer are the ones whose contents show through the mask itself. By placing a bitmap or animation on one of these layers, you can create many interesting effects.*

TIP *By using multiple masks in a scene, you can create some amazing effects (including kaleidoscope effects). But be careful: Using multiple masks can also be extremely processor intensive.*

Initially, only the layer directly below the mask layer is linked to it. However, you can link as many normal layers to the mask layer as you wish, making them masked layers that share a common mask.

To link additional layers to a mask layer:

1. Select the normal layer's name bar to link it to the mask layer.

   A dark-gray line appears along the bottom indicating that layer's position relative to the other layers in the stack.

2. Drag the layer until the gray line denoting the dragged layer's position appears just below the name bar of the mask layer; then release.

   The layer now is linked to the mask layer.

To unlink a layer from a mask layer:

1. Select the linked layer's name bar you want to unlink from the mask layer.

   A dark gray line appears along the bottom indicating that layer's position relative to the other layers in the stack.

2. Drag the layer until the gray line denoting its position appears either above the name bar of the mask layer or below any other normal layer; then release.

   The layer now is unlinked from the mask layer.

TIP *You can also convert a masked layer to a normal layer (thus unlinking it) by changing the layer type through the Layer Properties box, which you can access by double-clicking the masked layer icon or by choosing Layer from the Modify menu.*

TIP *Once you've linked several layers to a Mask layer, you can be reorder them within the linked stack just as you would normal layers.*

Because both of the layers associated with a mask are locked initially, you must unlock them before you can edit them.

To edit objects on layers associated with a mask:

1. Click the masked layer you wish to edit; it becomes highlighted.

2. Click the lock toggle button on that layer to unlock it.

   You can now edit the layer's contents.

3. When you've completed your edits, right-click (Windows) or Control-click (Macintosh) the layer's name bar, and from the menu that appears choose Show Masking to reestablish the mask effect (**Figure 9.38**) or just lock the layer again.

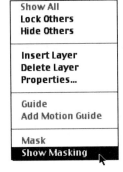

Figure 9.38
After editing a mask layer or a layer linked to it, choosing Show Masking reestablishes the mask effect.

TIP *When editing the contents of any layers affected by the mask, the mask itself may sometimes get in your way. To ease editing on this layer, hide the mask layer using the hidden mode on the layer's name bar. Once you've completed your edits, right-click (Windows) or Control-click (Macintosh) the name bar of one the mask's associated layers, and choose Show Masking from the contextual pop-up menu that appears to reestablish the mask.*

Creative Uses for Masks

You can achieve some of the best effects by using multiple masks, by tweening or animating the object on the mask layer, or by tweening or animating the objects on the linked layers below the mask layer. Here's another thing to keep in mind. The holes that a mask creates are pretty straightforward: You either see the layer beneath the mask, or you don't.

However, you can add some visual finesse to your scene's masks by creating a layer directly *above* the mask and adding a transparent object or gradient (**Figure 9.39**).

Figure 9.39
Use layers above a mask layer to add gradients or other graphical elements to make masked areas visually more interesting.

When animating the object on the mask layer, you can also create a layer *above* the mask layer and put a symbol, group, or other object there to mimic the movement of the object on the mask layer. Here are some additional tricks (you can find examples on the CD-ROM disc):

Magnifying glass and focus effect. With this effect, you provide the sense that the magnifying glass is bringing something into focus, make it larger, or both. By adding animation, you can make it appear that the magnifying glass is moving across the page (**Figure 9.40**).

X-rays. In this interesting effect, a "beam" passes over a normal object to reveal an x-rayed version of it (**Figure 9.41**).

Figure 9.40
Masks allow you to create interesting "magnifying" effects.

Spotlight. You can spot this effect in Flash's own help files. We take it a step further by adding a gradient transparency to make it more lifelike (**Figure 9.42**).

Holes and windows. This effect is best used to create animation or movement inside a window (**Figure 9.43**).

Multiple masks. As you have seen, two normal layers are required to complete the mask effect (creating one mask layer). By placing multiple masks in a scene, you can have one mask effect on top of another mask. This effect is demonstrated in the Holes and Windows sample.

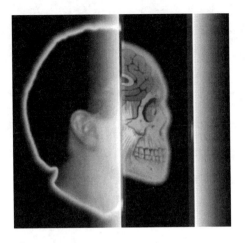

Figure 9.42
Since a mask only allows masked content to be seen or not, we placed a circle with a gradiated transparency above the masked area to give the illusion of diffused lighting.

Figure 9.41
Use masks to make it appear as if you're peering into hidden places.

Layers Tutorials

 Layers, especially mask layers, can be difficult to understand. Therefore, we've put together the following interactive tutorials that you will find on the CD-ROM—along with the source files:

Working with Layers. This tutorial shows you how layers work in general and how to use them effectively in your projects.

X-ray mask. This tutorial shows you how to create an x-ray effect using mask layers.

Figure 9.43
Animating content that is masked creates a sense of depth.

Animation

If all you ever wanted to do was to create Web sites with cool graphics and a few text descriptions, you could easily stick with plain, old HTML. However, although HTML is effective for presenting a message, it does so in a manner that's about as exciting as watching the hair grow on your arms. If you have even an ounce of visual savvy, you'll to want to move beyond HTML and its limitations. Likely, you are interested in Flash because you want to not only bring your message to the world but also *bring it to life*. That, after all, is what animation is all about.

From before the early days of Disney to the current crop of movies with their unbelievable computer-generated graphics, we've long been fascinated by what can be achieved by combining beautiful artwork with movement. Although in life much movement is left to chance, as an animator you determine what happens in a scene and when it happens. Talk about control. You can make birds fly and cartoon characters talk. You can even determine what they say and whether they get their lights punched out for saying it.

All that you've learned about Flash so far means nothing without this chapter's ingredients. This is where the real excitement begins. By animating your message, you make it much more powerful and exciting. And if you do it right, you'll find that you can reach your audience in ways they'll not soon forget. Sound appealing? Read on.

How Animation Works

At one time or another you've probably seen the actual film that makes up a movie. Basically, it looks like a bunch of pictures strung together on what appears to be a strip of plastic. Known as frames, each of these pictures represents a moment in time captured on film. The content of each frame varies ever so slightly from the preceding one, so that when the film is played on a projector, an illusion occurs: Each frame is seen briefly and then replaced so quickly by another that movement appears.

A Flash animation is no different. Just like a motion picture, it comprises individual frames, each slightly different than the preceding one. Special frames known as *keyframes* define where changes in your animation occur—for example, when objects are moved, rotated, resized, added, or removed. Each keyframe can contain any number of symbols or graphics.

When you move the playhead on the timeline or play your movie, the graphic content of each frame is reflected by what can be seen on the stage. When played back at a fast enough speed, the illusion of movement occurs.

Equivalent to the strip of plastic film that makes up a real movie, Flash's timeline includes all of your animation's layers and frames. The timeline can be as long as you wish and play at any speed (frames per second) you wish—within reason (as fast as 120 frames per second). The speed at which any movie, including your Flash movie, plays back is known as frames per second, or fps.

When your Flash movie reaches any keyframe on the timeline, it can perform something regular movies can't: *frame actions*. You set up frame actions to perform such tasks as jumping to other frames and opening URLs in a browser.

Just as in a real movie, the Flash timeline uses scenes to shift from one area of the story to another, allowing you to break your movie's timeline into sections. Needless to say, it's often much easier to manage your movie when sections differ dramatically.

Animation Considerations

When animating in Flash, consider the following:

Not everything moves. When animating an entire scene, be aware of items in the scene that don't move or that move very little. By placing such elements on their own layers of the timeline, you enable your movie to play back faster and you also reduce its file size.

Some things move quicker than others. For example, background elements usually move slower than items in the foreground.

Objects that move or are animated in unique ways should be placed on their own layers. In fact, sometimes Flash requires it.

Animation Methods

Flash actually has two methods of animating: *Frame-by-frame animation,* which gives you greater control over the way graphical content is animated but is more time-consuming, and *tweened animation,* which provides you with less control but is much faster to implement. Let's take a look at both.

Frame-by-frame animation

As the most recognizable and widely used form of animation, the frame-by-frame method is employed for everything from creating animated cartoons to bringing clay figures to life. This type of animation involves taking a snapshot of a frame's content, changing it slightly, taking another snapshot, changing the content again, and so on. When you play these snapshots in quick succession, you see movement and animation. In Flash, this involves moving the timeline to a frame, adjusting the content, moving the timeline to the next frame, adjusting the content, and so on.

With frame-by-frame animation, you edit everything that's visible, giving you control over the way content moves. In addition to being time-consuming, however, this kind of animation can increase your movie's overall file size. So, you should only use it when absolutely necessary—that is, when you need quick movements, such as a mouth moving or hands playing a piano.

We provide a more in-depth discussion of frame-by-frame animation later in this chapter in "Creating Animation."

Tweened animation

Since we use computers to make our jobs easier, there's no reason to manually create an animation that requires smooth transitions in movement, size, rotation, shape, or color when Flash provides a means to do so automatically.

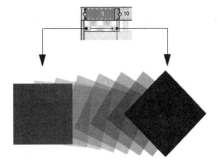

With a tweened animation, you use keyframes to define two points: the graphic's appearance at the beginning of the animation and at the end. You then determine how long it should take (based on frames) for the animation to get from its starting point to its ending. Flash then calculates what the animated graphic should look like in all of the frames in between (hence the name *tweening*) (**Figure 10.1**).

Figure 10.1

In a tweened animation, you define the look of the graphic at the beginning and ending keyframes, and Flash calculates how it should look in the intermediate frames.

As you can see, it's much faster to produce animations using tweening than it is to do so with the frame-by-frame method. What's more, it's much easier to edit tweened animations than it is to edit those created via the frame-by-frame method because there are only two editable frames—the beginning and ending keyframes. Changing either one of these will cause Flash to recalculate the look of all the frames in between. In contrast, you must edit each frame of a frame-by-frame animation.

As you begin to animate, you'll find that tweening works for most animation tasks involving fluid and smooth movements as well as transitions, *or morphing,* of shapes. Frame-by-frame animation works best for delicate, complex, and quick movements. And layers make it possible for you to use both types of animation simultaneously on different graphic elements that appear at the same time in a scene.

Understanding the Timeline

In addition to the stage—where you edit graphic content—the timeline is where the bulk of the animation process takes place. This is where you control your animation's speed, the entry and exit of objects, and the duration (**Figure 10.2**). Most of what you'll learn in this chapter will also apply to animating symbols' timelines (especially graphic and movie-clip symbols).

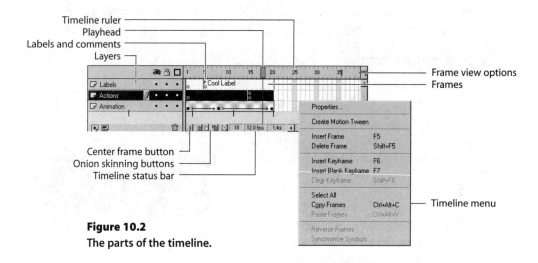

Figure 10.2
The parts of the timeline.

Layers

Although Chapter 9 is dedicated to layers, we think you'll find it helpful to review a couple of points here, especially those that have to do with the relationship between layers, frames, and the stage.

A single frame on the timeline can have multiple layers, the content of which you can view on the stage (**Figure 10.3**). (For more information, see "Putting It All Together" later in this chapter.) This means you can split the various animated elements of each frame's content into individual layers. Just remember that a single frame can comprise hundreds of layers.

You use layers to create complex animations.

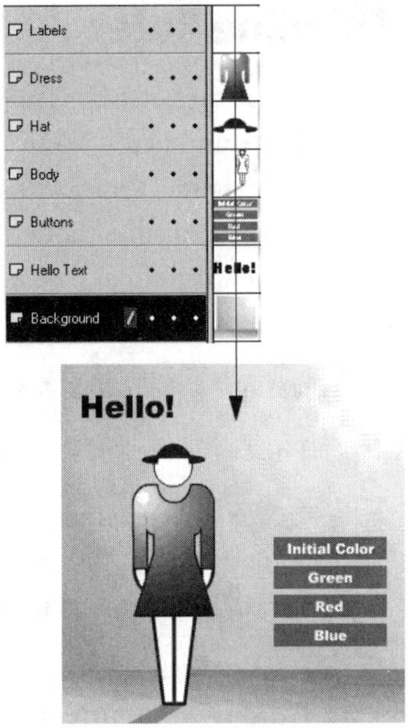

Playhead

The playhead is to the timeline what the Arrow tool is to the stage. It allows you to identify the frame you're editing and to select a frame to work on. You can drag the playhead to *scrub* your movie (that is, to watch it play as you drag back and forth through it). The red vertical line of the playhead stretches across multiple layers to help you identify all of a frame's content.

Figure 10.3
The stage reflects the content of all visible layers.

To move the playhead to a particular frame:

- Click a frame on any available layer, or select a frame on the timeline ruler.

  The playhead jumps to the frame you select.

To scrub the playhead:

- Click and drag the playhead to the left or right.

  As you move the playhead, your movie plays either forward or in reverse, depending on the direction you're dragging.

  TIP *To perform either one of these actions, there must be at least two frames on the timeline. The white and gray rectangular boxes that appear initially on the timeline are not actual frames of your movie. With the exception of the first frame, you must add frames to the timeline. For more on this, see "Inserting Frames" later in this chapter.*

Timeline Ruler

Consisting of two visual parts—frame "ticks" (small vertical lines on the ruler) and frame numbers—the timeline ruler provides an incremented display of frames along the timeline. Only every fifth frame is indicated by a number; the rest are indicated by ticks. Normally, frame numbers are centered between the two ticks that define the frame. Multidigit frame numbers are left aligned to the frame they represent.

Timeline Status Bar

The status area of the timeline provides three pieces of information (**Figure 10.4**):

Current frame. Indicates the frame number whose contents are currently visible on the stage. Also indicates the current position of the playhead.

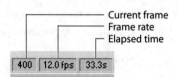

Figure 10.4
The elements of the timeline status bar.

Frame rate. When your movie is not playing, this displays the current frames-per-second setting for your movie. When your movie is playing, this number (which is dynamically updated) reflects the *actual* playback speed. Actual playback speed can differ from the frames-per-second setting you selected in the Movie Properties dialog box—often as the result of processor-intensive animation, which can cause your movie to slow in places.

Elapsed time. Indicates the amount of time (in seconds) between the first frame of your movie and the current frame. The number is dynamically updated as you play your movie in the authoring environment.

Center Frame Button

If you click the Center Frame button, Flash centers the playhead's current frame position on the timeline. So, if you scroll to Frame 900 of a 1000-frame movie while the playhead remains on Frame 200, clicking this button will cause the timeline to quickly scroll back to Frame 200, with the palyhead centered on the timeline (**Figure 10.5**).

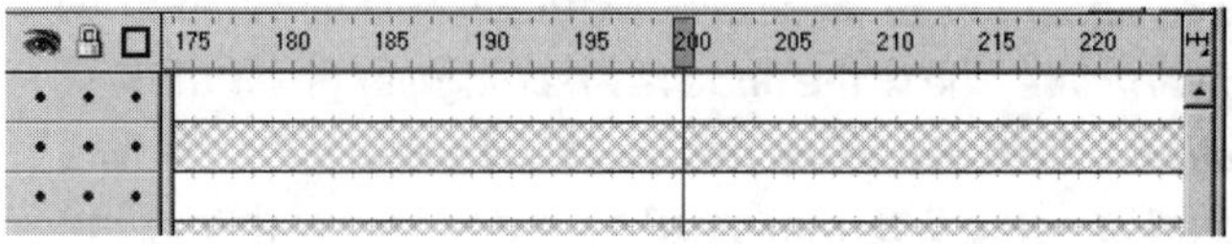

Figure 10.5
The position of the playhead becomes centered on the timeline when you click the Center Frame button.

Frame View Options

The Frame View button allows you to see frames on the timeline in several ways that can help you during different stages of your movie's development. By clicking this button, you are presented with the following options:

Frame Width. Options include Tiny, Small, Normal, Medium, and Large (**Figure 10.6**).

Frame Height. Short is the normal setting.

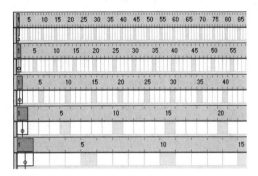

Tinted Frames. By default, sections of frames are tinted different colors to help you distinguish them. You can turn this option on or off (**Figure 10.7**) (see the next section for more details).

Figure 10.6
The effect of the Frame Width setting on the timeline.

Preview. This option causes the graphics of each frame on each layer to be displayed within the boxes on the timeline that represent frames. Flash scales the graphics to fit within the frame boxes (**Figure 10.8**).

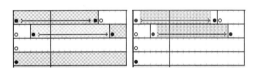

Figure 10.7
With and without tinted frames.

Preview in Context. With one exception, this option is similar to the previous one: The graphics are scaled to show their relative size to the overall movie (**Figure 10.9**).

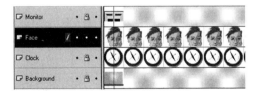

Figure 10.8
The graphics of each frame appear in boxes that represent frames. They are scaled to completely fill the box.

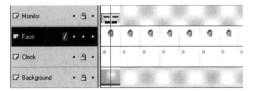

Figure 10.9
The graphics of each frame appear in boxes that represent frames. They are shown in their size relative to the whole movie.

Frames

Dictating each segment of time and movement, frames are at the core of any animation. The number of frames in your movie and the speed at which they're played back determine the movie's overall length.

Frame types

Not all frames are created equal. Different frames types are designed for different animation tasks. Using the timeline's visual features, you should be able to quickly determine a frame's type, which can then help you diagnose problems with your animation.

Empty Frames

Empty frames are not really frames at all but rather rectangular boxes where frames can be placed. Devoid of content, these frames make up the majority of the timeline when you begin your Flash project. Because your movie needs real frames on at least one layer of the timeline to play, it will cease playing once it reaches a point where all layers contain only empty frames (**Figure 10.10**).

Empty frames are indicated by the grid on the timeline (**Figure 10.11**).

Keyframes

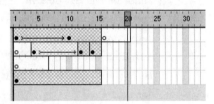

Figure 10.10
This scene will not play past Frame 20 because Frame 21 and beyond (on all layers) contain only empty frames.

Figure 10.11
Empty frames on the timeline.

Keyframes are special frames where you define changes in your animation, including an object's movement and characteristics (for example, size or color), the addition or removal of an object from a scene, and the addition of a frame action. Any time you wish your animation to undergo a visual change or you want an action to occur, you must use a keyframe (for more on this, see "Putting It All Together" later in this chapter).

Obviously, frame-by-frame animations require numerous keyframes since you must edit each frame individually. A tweened animation, on the other hand, requires only two keyframes—one that begins the tween and one that ends the tween. Changes that occur between the beginning and ending keyframes of a tween are calculated by Flash and do not require additional keyframes.

Although most keyframes contain content, they can also be blank—usually the result of removing an object from the animation. Every new project you begin in Flash starts with a blank keyframe on Frame 1 of Layer 1. A regular keyframe is identified by a solid black dot; a blank keyframe is identified by a hollow black dot; and a keyframe with an attached action is identified with a small *a* (**Figure 10.12**).

Regular Frames

Regular frames, also known as static frames, display any content in the last keyframe on the same layer. Confused? Let us explain.

Regular frames must always be preceded by a keyframe on the timeline. The content of this preceding keyframe appears in every regular frame that follows—until another keyframe is encountered.

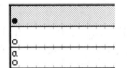

Figure 10.12
A regular keyframe (top), an empty keyframe (middle), and a keyframe with an action attached (bottom).

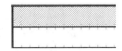

Figure 10.13
Regular frames with content appear gray. Regular frames without content appear white.

A background image that you wish to remain constantly visible in your animation is a perfect example of a place where you might use regular frames. You would place the background on a keyframe at the beginning of the timeline, and then follow it with as many regular frames as you desire—to last the duration of your movie. If, however, you added the background to Frame 1 of your movie but didn't follow it with any regular frames, the background would only be visible in Frame 1. Regular frames that follow filled keyframes (that is, those with content) appear light gray, and regular frames that follow empty keyframes appear white (**Figure 10.13**).

Tweened Frames

To understand how tweened frames work, remember that they don't stand on their own but rather comprise a sequence of frames: at least two keyframes—one that determines a tweened object's appearance at its starting point and one that does so for its ending point—and any number of tweened frames in between. The frames between the two keyframes represent the in-between appearance of that tweened object.

You can perform two types of tweening with Flash: *motion tweening* and *shape tweening*. You use motion tweening to tween the size, position, rotation, and so on of symbols, groups, or text blocks in your animation. You use shape tweening to morph one simple shape into another—for example, smoothly transforming a red circle into a blue square or the letter *T*

Figure 10.14
A shape tween that shows how a circle can morph into a square.

into the letter *I* (**Figure 10.14**). Shape tweening only works with stage-level objects, not symbols or groups. If text is to be used in a shape tween, you must first break it apart.

Simultaneous motion tweening of multiple objects in a scene requires a layer for each tween. Translation? You can't motion tween separate objects on the same layer at the same time. You can, however, tween them simultaneously on different layers.

Motion-tweened frames are identified by at least two keyframes separated by intermediate frames with a black arrow and light-blue background (**Figure 10.15**). Shape-tweened frames are identified by at least two keyframes separated by intermediate frames with a black arrow and light-green background. And a problem tween, such as a missing keyframe, is indicated by a dashed line.

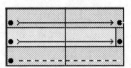

Figure 10.15
A motion tween (top), a shape tween (middle), and a problem tween (bottom).

Labels and Comments

Just as you try to use a name to identify a face in a crowd, a frame label in Flash allows you to quickly identify a keyframe in your movie. This is especially useful when assigning frame or button actions that go to frames within your movie (see Chapter 11, "Interactivity"). Let's look at a scenario where they are invariably valuable, especially in the editing process.

Imagine setting up your movie so that several buttons, when clicked, begin playing your movie at Frame 35. You decide later, however, that you want to shorten the beginning of your movie by five frames. This means the content that once began at Frame 35 will now begin at frame 30; however, the buttons you set up earlier will still go to Frame 35 when clicked—not the result you were looking for. Using a label would alleviate this problem.

Assigning a label to Frame 35, such as "MyLabel," and setting all those button clicks to begin playing your movie from that label would allow you to add and delete frames whenever and wherever you wanted; button clicks would always point to "MyLabel."

Frame comments allow you to write notes, or comments, in frames of your movie, which can then serve as useful reminders of the thought process behind a certain section of the movie's timeline.

Because frame labels are exported with your final movie, they can affect its overall file size. So, you should use short, descriptive labels. Frame comments, in contrast, are not exported and can thus contain as much information as you want.

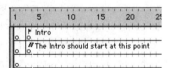

Figure 10.16
A frame label, and a frame comment.

Frame labels are identified by a small red flag followed by the label name (where room on the timeline permits), and frame comments are identified by two green forward slashes followed by the comment text (where room on the timeline permits) (**Figure 10.16**).

To add a label or comment to a keyframe:

1. Click the keyframe once to select it.

2. From the Modify menu choose Frame

The Frame Properties dialog box appears.

3. Click the Label tab to make its options available.

4. Choose a Behavior, and enter the appropriate text in the text box.

5. Click OK.

Depending on the behavior you chose, the keyframe now has a label or comment attached to it.

> **TIP** *If you place your pointer over any frame on the timeline for a moment, a tooltip appears with a description of the frame type. If the pointer is over a frame with a label or comment, the label name or comment text appears.*

Working with frames

Now that you're familiar with the frame types and their functions, it's time to look at the various ways you can work with them on the timeline. Most timeline editing functions are handled via the Timeline menu or Frame Properties dialog box. For more information about using frames, see "Creating and Editing Animations" later in this chapter.

To select an individual frame:

- Click the frame once to select.

When selected, it becomes the current frame, and any commands pertaining to frames will affect it.

To select a range of frames:

- Click the first frame you want to be part of the range and drag to the last frame you want to be included, and then release.

All selected frames appear highlighted (**Figure 10.17**). You can now move, delete, and duplicate them.

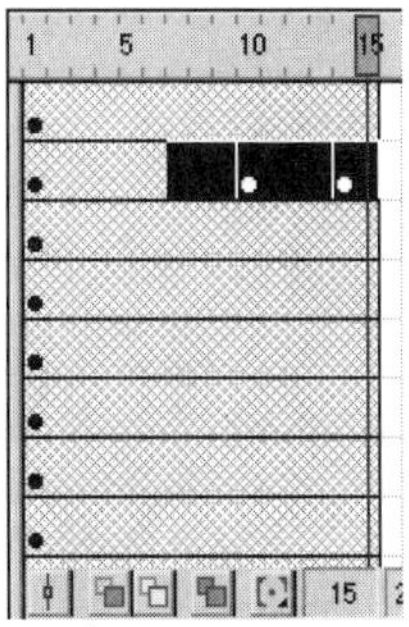

Figure 10.17
A range of selected frames are inverted to show they have been selected.

To add regular frames to the timeline:

1. Select an empty frame on the timeline.

2. Choose Insert > Frame.

Regular frames are added up to the point of the selected empty frame (**Figure 10.18**).

To insert regular frames in the middle of an existing range of frames:

1. Select a single frame or range of frames within the middle of an existing range of frames.

2. Choose Insert > Frames.

The number of frames you selected are inserted onto the timeline (**Figure 10.19**), and the previously selected frames are moved to the right of the newly inserted ones.

To delete frames:

1. Select a single frame or range of frames.

2. Choose Insert > Delete Frame.

To add a keyframe to the timeline:

1. Select an empty or regular frame on the timeline.

2. Choose Insert > Keyframe to add a keyframe.

If the originally selected frame was empty, regular frames are added up to the point of the newly created keyframe. If the originally selected frame was a regular frame, it is simply converted to a keyframe.

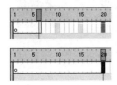

Figure 10.18
When adding frames after selecting an empty frame, regular frames are added up to the point of the selected empty frame.

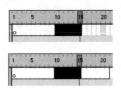

Figure 10.19
The same number of selected frames will be inserted onto the timeline.

To add a range of keyframes to the timeline:

1. Select a range of frames.

2. Choose Insert > Keyframe.

A range of keyframes is added (**Figure 10.20**).

To move or duplicate frames:

1. Select a frame or range of frames.

2. Click and drag the selected frames to a new location on the timeline (**Figure 10.21**).

3. To duplicate the frame or range of frames at a new location, hold down the Control key (Windows) or Command key (Macintosh) while you drag.

To add a frame action:

1. Double-click the keyframe where you would like to add an action.

The Frame Properties dialog box appears.

2. Click the Action tab.

3. Click the Add Action button to add any actions to this frame, and then click OK.

The keyframe now includes a small *a* to indicate an action has been assigned to this frame.

To display the Frame Properties dialog box for a specific frame:

• Double-click a frame on the timeline.

The Frame Properties dialog box appears, allowing you to set labels and comments, add sound to a frame, assign an action to a frame, and adjust tweening parameters.

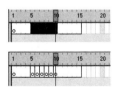

Figure 10.20
When adding keyframes, for every selected frame, a keyframe is inserted.

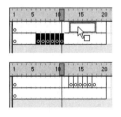

Figure 10.21
Drag selected frames to their new location and release.

Timeline Menu

The context-sensitive Timeline menu provides quick access to a handful of timeline-related commands, including adding and deleting frames, defining frame properties, and creating motion tweens (**Figure 10.22**).

To display the Timeline menu:

- Right-click (Windows) or Control-click (Macintosh) any frame on the timeline to make the Timeline pop-up menu appear.

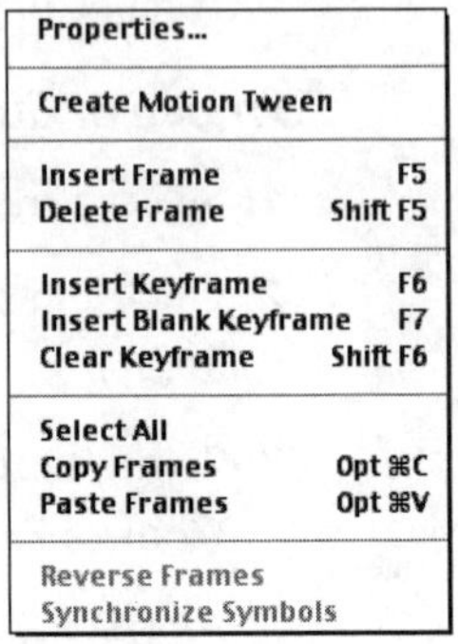

The contextual menu contains the following options:

Properties. Brings up the Frame Properties dialog box, which you can use to add labels and comments, sounds, or actions and to adjust tweening parameters of the frame at the position where the pointer was located when the menu was activated.

Figure 10.22
The Timeline menu.

Create Motion Tween. Uses the current frame's content to automatically create a motion tween. (To do so, it converts any content that is not a graphic symbol into one.)

Insert Frame. Adds a regular frame after the currently selected one. If you select a range of regular frames, the same number of frames will be added to the timeline. If you select an empty frame, regular frames will be added up to the point of the selected empty frame.

Delete Frame. Deletes the currently selected frame. If you select a range of frames, this command deletes all of them.

Insert Keyframe. Inserts a keyframe on the timeline at the point where the pointer was located when you activated the menu. If a regular frame was at this position, the keyframe replaces it; if an empty frame was at this position, a keyframe is inserted and regular frames are added so that there are no empty frames prior to the newly inserted keyframe. A newly inserted keyframe starts out with the same content as the previous keyframe.

Insert Blank Keyframe. Inserts a blank keyframe on the timeline at the position where the pointer was located when the menu was activated. If a regular frame was at this position, the keyframe replaces it; if an empty frame was at this position, a keyframe is inserted and regular frames are added so that there are no empty frames prior to the newly inserted keyframe.

Clear Keyframe. Converts the selected keyframe to a regular frame. If a range of keyframes are selected, this command converts them all.

Select All. Selects all frames on all unlocked and visible layers of the current scene. This is useful for copying and then duplicating entire scenes.

Copy Frames. Copies a frame or range of frames for pasting elsewhere.

Paste Frames. Pastes any frames on the clipboard onto the timeline after the currently selected frame. If the clipboard contains a range of frames across multiple layers, these frames and layers will be pasted onto the timeline in their same relative position.

Reverse Frames. Flips, or reverses, the positions of the currently selected range of frames. The result is reversed playback.

Synchronize Symbols. Synchronizes the starting frame of multiple instances of the same graphic symbol across multiple keyframes on the same layer.

> **TIP** *All of these commands are also available on the Insert and Modify menus on the menu bar. When selected, they affect the currently selected frame or range of frames.*

Onion-Skinning

If you've ever watched a pencil-and-paper animator, you've probably noticed that he or she customarily works with a pencil in one hand and a couple of pages, or eventual frames, of the animation in the other. While drawing on the current frame, the animator will flip among frames that come before and after the current one. This allows the animator to see how the drawing sequence will emulate movement when it is eventually played. Flash provides similar functionality in the form of *onion-skinning,* which allows you to view multiple frames simultaneously and edit them.

To view multiple frames using onion-skinning:

- On the timeline click the Onion Skin button (**Figure 10.23**).

This brings up a set of onion-skinning markers, which appear next to the playhead on the timeline (**Figure 10.24**).

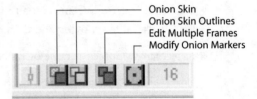

Figure 10.23
The Onion Skin buttons.

The content of all of the frames between these two markers now appear on the stage, some of them before the current frame and some of them after. The current frame is the one over which the playhead is positioned. In this mode, it is the only one whose

Figure 10.24
Onion-skinning markers.

contents are editable. Content on uneditable frames appears dimmed. Dragging the playhead allows you to see onion-skinning on other frames.

TIP *You won't be able to see content on locked or hidden layers when you are using onion-skinning. Thus, locking or hiding layers can help you specify which content is visible and editable when onion-skinning.*

To view onion-skinned frames as outlines:

- Click the Onion Skin Outlines button.

This option works in much the same fashion as the Onion Skin button, with the exception that all content on frames other than the current one appears as outlines. You can assign a different outline color to each layer, which can help you identify which layer's content needs to be edited.

Editing multiple frames

Normally when you are using onion-skinning you can edit only the content of the current frame. By making multiple frames editable while using onion-skinning, you can select, move, rotate, resize, and otherwise alter the content of multiple frames simultaneously.

To make multiple frames editable:

- Click the Edit Multiple Frames button to make the content on all frames between the markers editable.

    Be aware, however, that you can only edit keyframes of tweens in this mode.

Onion-skinning markers

You use the onion-skinning markers to determine the range of frames that are onion-skinned, configuring the markers' positions to suit your needs. Usually, the markers maintain the same position relative to the playhead, although you can also anchor them while the playhead moves. You can adjust onion-skinning markers manually or via the Modify Onion Markers pop-up menu.

To move the onion-skinning markers manually:

- Click a marker handle and drag it to its new position.

    You can't move either marker beyond the playhead.

To modify the onion-skinning markers:

- Click the Modify Onion Markers button.

    This brings up the Modify Onion Markers pop-up menu (**Figure 10.25**), which includes the following options.

Always Show Markers. Normally, onion-skinning markers only appear when onion-skinning is turned on. This option causes them to be displayed whether or not onion-skinning is turned on.

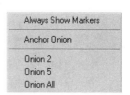

Anchor Onion. Anchors, or locks, the onion-skinning markers in their current position, which means they will remain stationary rather than maintain their relative position to the playhead.

Figure 10.25
The Modify Onion Markers pop-up menu.

Onion 2. Provides a quick method for setting onion-skinning markers two frames before and two frames after the current frame (playhead position).

Onion 5. Lets you quickly set onion-skinning markers five frames before and five frames after the current frame.

Onion All. Onion-skins all of the frames in the current scene. Obviously, this is best used for viewing a limited number of layers; lock or hide certain layers to make them invisible.

Putting It All Together

 Imagine trying to figure out what a 5000-piece puzzle is supposed to look like without any kind of visual reference. Chances are, that puzzle will soon find its way into the nearest fireplace, where you'll happily watch the bugger go up in flames. Like that pesky puzzle, Flash animations comprise many pieces, and you're likely to get confused unless you have some reference for how they are supposed to come together.

To that end, we've constructed a fictional scene to demonstrate most of the items and principles we've discussed as well as to give you a better idea of how to construct your own animation (**Figure 10.26**).

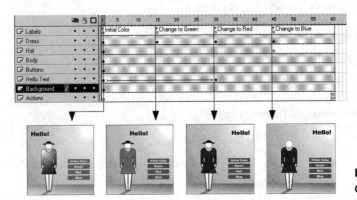

Figure 10.26
Composite animation.

We've included the source files on the CD-ROM disc so that you to follow along.

This scene is made up of eight layers and 60 frames. The four composite pictures represent the way the animation appears on that frame of the timeline. Each layer has a name that corresponds with its content.

The *stacking order* of the layers determines which elements appear above others. For example, the background layer is meant to appear behind everything else, so it is the bottom layer (other than the Action layer, which contains no content).

The Label layer contains four labels, indicated by flags, which highlight portions of the timeline we wished to emphasize. We have assigned Go To actions to the Initial Color, Green, Red, and Blue buttons in the lower right corner of the scene that cause the timeline to jump to the appropriate label when a button is clicked.

Labels can only be assigned to keyframes. Because the labeled keyframes have no graphic content that appears on the stage, they are represented by hollow dots on the timeline. Likewise, the regular frames that follow the keyframes on this layer have no content and thus appear white.

The Dress layer includes four keyframes, each of which represents a place along the timeline where the dress color changes. Because these keyframes contain content that appears on the stage (the dress with different colors), they are represented by solid black dots on the timeline. Likewise, the regular frames that follow these keyframes appear light gray to indicate that their content is the same as that contained in the last keyframe on the layer. Thus, regular Frames 2 to 14 of this layer contain the same content as the keyframe on Frame 1; regular Frames 16 to 29 contain the same content as the keyframe on Frame 15, and so on.

The Hat layer holds the hat graphic. Frame 1 of this layer is where the hat graphic was initially placed. The light-gray regular frames that follow this keyframe indicate that the hat does not change in appearance on the stage until Frame 45, which is a keyframe indicating where the hat graphic is removed from the scene. Since this keyframe, on Frame 45, no longer holds any graphic content, the regular frames that follow it on this layer also have no content, and so appear white.

The Body layer contains the legs, head, and hands of our model, which are initially placed on the keyframe on Frame 1. This keyframe appears as a solid black dot indicating that it contains content. These graphic elements remain static throughout the sequence, hence the lack of keyframes on this layer. The light-gray regular frames on this layer contain the same content as the initial keyframe on Frame 1.

The Buttons layer contains the four buttons that are in the scene, which we initially placed on Frame 1's keyframe and which appears as a solid black dot because it contains content. These graphic elements do not change during the sequence; thus, no additional keyframes are needed on this layer. The light-gray regular frames on this layer contain the same content as the initial keyframe on Frame 1.

The Hello Text layer contains the text *Hello,* which is motion tweened between Frames 1 and 30 to move from the left to the right. On the keyframe on Frame 1, the text is positioned where it should be at the beginning of the tween, and the keyframe on Frame 30 is where the text will be at the end of the tween. Because the text does not move or change from that point forward, no additional keyframes are needed on this layer. The light-gray regular frames that appear after the last keyframe on this layer indicate that the content remains the same from Frame 30 (the position of the last keyframe) to Frame 60.

The Background layer contains our background, which is initially placed on the keyframe on Frame 1. This keyframe appears as a solid black dot indicating that it contains content. These graphic elements remain unchanged throughout the sequence; thus, no keyframes are needed on this layer. The light-gray regular frames on this layer contain the same content as the initial keyframe on Frame 1.

The Action Layer contains two blank keyframes, one at Frame 1 and the other at Frame 60. The keyframe on Frame 1 is there because every layer initially starts with a keyframe that can't be deleted. The keyframe on Frame 60 has a frame action that causes the timeline to go back to the first frame of the animation and begin playing it again. Because the keyframes themselves on the Action layer contain no graphic content, the regular frames that follow them have no content and thus appear white.

Working with Scenes

Scenes provide an easy way to break your movie's timeline into sections of frames. You can also think of scenes as animated "pages," each of which can be different than the previous or following one, though they all belong to the same timeline. A single movie can comprise any number of scenes played in the order you placed them in. And each movie automatically starts with one scene; you manually add (or delete) the rest.

Let's say you have a movie that consists of three scenes: Intro, Body, and Conclusion.

Your movie will first play Intro from beginning to end and then Body and finally the Conclusion, at which point the movie will stop. Keep in mind, however, that you can also easily reorder these scenes to change their flow.

Scenes serve no function other than to help you organize content. A timeline that spans multiple scenes is still considered a singular timeline—important to remember, especially if you're working with and updating variables in a timeline (for more on this, see Chapter 11, "Interactivity"). Scenes are not available for symbols.

Scene Management

Scene management can encompass (among other things) adding and deleting scenes, renaming scenes, and changing the order in which scenes appear in the movie—all of which you can use the Scene inspector to accomplish.

To display the Scene inspector:

- From the Window menu choose Inspectors > Scene.

  The Scene inspector appears (**Figure 10.27**) and lists any scenes in the movie.

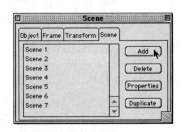

Figure 10.27
The Scene inspector.

To add a scene:

- On the Scene inspector click the Add button.

  or

- From the Insert menu choose Scene.

  Either one of these creates a new scene with the default name Scene appended by a number. The timeline also automatically jumps to frame 1 of your newly created scene.

To delete a scene:

1. On the Scene inspector, select the scene you wish to delete from the scene list.

2. Click the Delete button.

  An alert box asks you to confirm the deletion.

3. Click OK.

  or

1. Go to the scene you wish to delete .

2. From the Insert menu choose Remove Scene.

  An alert box asks you to confirm the deletion.

3. Click OK.

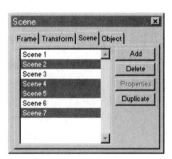

Figure 10.28
Multiple scenes selected
on the Scene inspector.

> **TIP** *Using the Scene inspector, you can delete multiple scenes simultaneously. Simply hold down the Control key (Windows) or the Command key (Macintosh) while selecting multiple scenes from the scene list (**Figure 10.28**). Once all the scenes you wish to delete are selected, click the Delete button.*

To rename a scene:

1. From the scene list in the Scene inspector, select the scene whose name you wish to change.

2. Click the Properties button to bring up the Scene Properties dialog box.

3. Enter a new name for the scene, and click OK.

or

1. From the scene list in the Scene inspector, double-click the scene whose name you wish to change.

   The Scene Properties box appears.

2. Enter a new name for the scene, and click OK.

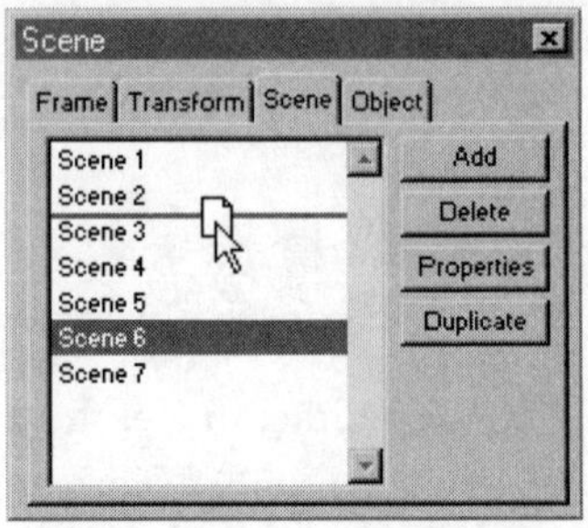

To reorder scenes:

1. From the scene list in the Scene inspector, click and hold the name of the scene you'd like to move.

2. Drag and drop the scene to a new position in the list (**Figure 10.29**).

   The scenes now play sequentially in the order you arranged them in.

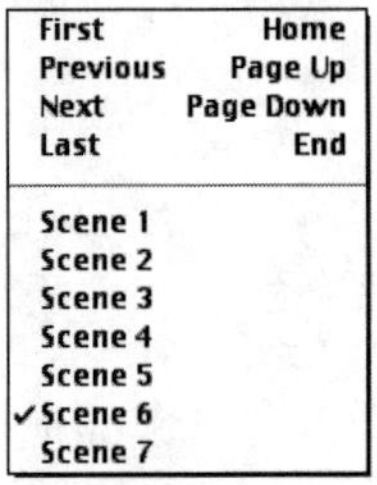

To navigate between scenes:

- From the scene list in the Scene inspector, click the name of the scene you wish to navigate to.

  The timeline automatically jumps to that scene.

  or

- From the View menu choose Go To and then one of the available scenes from the list (**Figure 10.30**).

Figure 10.29
Moving Scene 6 between Scenes 2 and 3.

Figure 10.30
Available scenes are listed on the Go To submenu. The current scene is checked.

Duplicating scenes

Duplicating a scene allows you to make an exact replica of it—including all frames, layers, animations, and sounds—to form a new scene. So, you can use one scene as a starting point for a new one—handy for similar scenes that nonetheless require some editing.

To duplicate a scene:

1. From the scene list in the Scene inspector, click the name of the scene you wish to duplicate.

2. Press the Duplicate button.

   The new scene is given a default name and appears on the scene list.

Creating Animations

At this point you've learned just about all you can about animation without actually beginning the creative process. That's about to change, however. We will now take you through the process of creating three simple types of animations: frame by frame, motion tweened, and shape tweened.

Creating a Frame-by-Frame Animation

Creating frame-by-frame animations usually entails numerous keyframes, each with different content. You can use frame-by-frame animation in conjunction with other forms of animation; you just need to place each type on a separate layer.

To create a simple frame-by-frame animation:

1. Create a new Flash document by choosing File > New.

Your new Flash document initially includes a single layer with one keyframe.

2. Click the Text tool on the Drawing toolbar.

3. From the modifiers that appear, select Times New Roman as the font, 48 as the size, and whatever color you wish.

4. Click the stage to start a text label, and type a capital *H* in the lower left corner of the stage (**Figure 10.31**).

5. Select the next empty frame on the timeline (it appears highlighted), and then choose Insert > Keyframe.

A keyframe is inserted on Frame 2 and contains the same content as Frame 1(our capital *H*).

6. From the Drawing toolbar choose the Arrow tool, and select the text label (if it's not already selected).

7. With the *H* selected, hold down the Shift key and press the up-arrow key three times to move the text object upward.

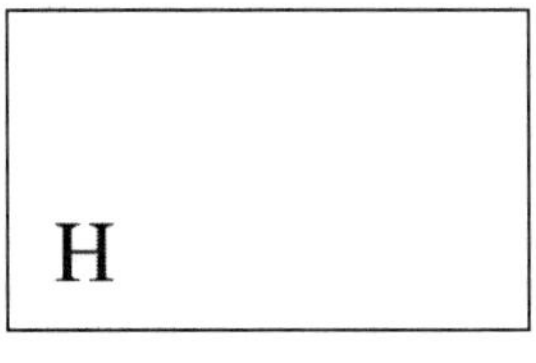

H

Figure 10.31
Place an H in the lower left portion of the stage.

HE

Figure 10.32
Our text object, with an E inserted after the H and moved upwards from its previous position.

8. Select the Text tool again, place its insertion point just after the *H*, and type an *E* (**Figure 10.32**).

9. Repeat Steps 5 through 8 until you have completed the word *HELLO*.

If you move the playhead on the timeline, you can see your animation spring to life.

 Obviously, this is simplified animation. Some frame-by-frame animations consist of many layers with numerous elements requiring movement at each keyframe. The frame-by-frame interactive tutorial on the CD covers this same animation with a few additional techniques.

Creating a Shape-Tweened Animation

Shape tweening, or *morphing*, describes the process of transforming one object into another over a period of time. In Flash, you can morph, or tween, objects' shape, color, transparency, size, and location.

Although Flash will normally attempt to tween two shapes in the most logical manner without any additional input from you, this can sometimes produce undesirable results. When you need control over a shape tween, you can use *shape hints* to select common points on the beginning and ending shapes that correspond to each other in the shape tween.

You cannot shape tween symbols, groups, or bitmaps—only shapes, stage-level objects, and text (and the latter only if you've broken it apart first; see Chapter 3, "Drawing"). Although more than one shape can be tweened on a layer at a time, you'll get better results from using separate layers.

Let's look at how to create a simple animation of a box tweening into the letter *T*. You'll learn how to tween not only shapes but color and location as well. And a little later we show you how to use shape hints to gain more control over the actual tween. An interactive tutorial on the CD demonstrates the way this animation was put together.

To create a shape-tweened animation:

1. Create a new Flash document by choosing File > New.

Your new Flash document initially includes a single layer with one keyframe.

2. On the Drawing toolbar click the Rectangle tool.

3. From the modifiers that appear, select "no outline" and a red fill color.

4. Draw a medium-size square in the middle of the stage.

5. Select the empty frame on Frame 25 of the timeline (it appears highlighted), and then choose Insert > Blank Keyframe.

A blank keyframe is inserted at Frame 25 (**Figure 10.33**).

Figure 10.33
A blank keyframe inserted at Frame 25.

6. With the playhead on Frame 25, select the Text tool on the Drawing toolbar.

7. From the modifiers that appear, select Ariel as the font, enter 150 as the size, and choose any color you wish to use.

8. Click somewhere on the upper right corner of the stage to create a text label, and type a capital *T*.

9. Select the Arrow tool, and the text you just typed is automatically selected.

10. Choose Modify > Break Apart to turn the text into a shape.

11. Double-click the keyframe on Frame 1 to automatically move the playhead back to that frame and open the Frame Properties box for that frame.

12. Click the Tweening tab, and choose Shape from the pop-up menu.

Two additional options appear, Blend Type and Easing (**Figure 10.34**):

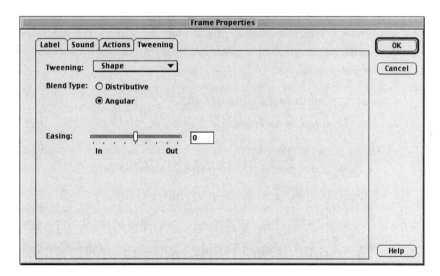

Figure 10.34
The Tweening tab is where you set shape-tween properties.

Blend Type. This lets you set the way the shapes' curves and corners are blended: Distributive is better for blending smooth and curvy shapes; Angular is better for shapes with sharp corners and straight sides.

Easing. Easing is all about acceleration and deceleration. In real life, few objects move at a constant speed. Thus, easing makes a tweened animation move faster or slower at its beginning than it does at its end. Easing In causes the animation to move slower at the beginning of the tween, and Easing Out causes it to move faster at the beginning of the tween. If you place the Easing slider in the middle, motion speed will be constant for the duration of the tween.

13. Set the Blend Type to Angular and leave the Easing slider at its initial setting; then click OK.

The timeline now reflects your shape tween. If you move the playhead back and forth, you can see the tweened animation you just created. Notice that the actual shape is tweened and so are the object's color and position.

> **TIP** *After creating a tweened animation, you can edit the starting or ending keyframe, and Flash will automatically recalculate the tween.*

Shape hints

Although our shape tween work decently, you can achieve greater control over the way your shapes blend by using shape hints.

You can add as many as 26 shape hints—labeled a to z—per tween. Although not absolutely necessary, it's best to position them counterclockwise from the upper left corner of the shapes.

To add shape hints to a shape tween:

1. Place the playhead on Frame 1.

This is where the first keyframe of our tween is located; shape hints must always be added on the first keyframe of a shape tween.

2. Choose Modify > Transform > Add Shape Hint.

This places a shape hint labeled *a* on your initial shape (our red square).

3. Click and drag the shape hint to the side or corner of the shape you wish to use as a reference.

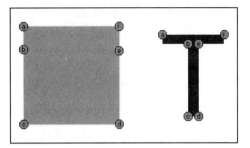

Figure 10.35
Place the shape hint labeled a on the upper left corner of the square.

Figure 10.36
The location of shape hints on the beginning and ending keyframes of the tween.

For our demonstration, move it to the upper left corner of the square (**Figure 10.35**).

4. Place the playhead on Frame 25.

This is where the last keyframe of our tween is located. The shape hint labeled *a* appears on the shape.

5. Click and drag the shape hint to the side or corner of the shape that you wish to correspond with the point you marked on the first shape.

For our demonstration, move it to the upper left corner of the *T*.

You can move the playhead any time you wish to test a shape hint's effect on a tween.

6. Repeat steps 1 through 5 until shape hints appear on the beginning and ending shapes as those shown in **Figure 10.36**.

> **TIP** *Even though it may seem like more work, you should add a shape hint to the beginning shape, set its corresponding point on the end shape, go back to the beginning shape and add another shape hint, set its corresponding point on the end shape, and so on. You'll get unpredictable results if you add several hints to the beginning shape before setting corresponding points on the ending shape.*

> **TIP** *Place your shape hints in a logical order. Illogical placement will produce unpredictable results, defeating their purpose.*

To remove a shape hint:

- Click and drag it off the stage.

  The labels of any other shape hints in use for this tween are updated to reflect the deletion.

To remove all shape hints:

- Place the playhead at the beginning keyframe of a tween, and choose Modify> Transform > Remove All Hints.

  Only the shape hints used for that tween are removed.

To display or hide shape hints:

- Place the playhead at the beginning or ending keyframe of a tween, and choose View > Show Shape Hints.

  This option toggles the visibility of shape hints in a tween.

Creating a Motion-Tweened Animation

Whereas shape tweening allows you to tween simple shapes, motion tweening lets you tween symbols, groups, and text blocks. With the exception of morphing, you can accomplish pretty much the same things with motion tweening as you can with shape tweening. With motion tweening, you can tween size, skew, location, rotation, color, and transparency of symbols and groups—all of which allow you to create many of the great Flash transitions you see on the Web these days. You can also use a motion tween in conjunction with a path (a line of any shape) to create an object that is tweened and follows the direction of the line (see "Motion Tweening Along a Path" for more information).

Let's create a simple animation of a ball whose size, location, rotation, and transparency all change. A bit little later you'll learn how to add a motion path so that the ball can appear to bounce down a street in a nonlinear fashion. The CD includes an interactive tutorial that demonstrates how this animation was put together.

To create a motion-tween animation:

1. Create a new Flash document by choosing File > New.

   Your new Flash document initially includes a single layer with one keyframe.

2. On the Drawing toolbar click the Oval tool.

3. From the modifiers that appear, select "no outline" and a red fill color.

4. Draw a medium-size circle in the lower left corner of the stage.

5. Click the Rectangle tool on the Drawing toolbar.

6. From the modifiers that appear, select "no outline" and a white fill color.

7. Within the red circle you just drew, draw a wide rectangle (**Figure 10.37**).

   This will to help you to later see how rotation works within a motion tween.

Figure 10.37
Draw a wide rectangle within the circle.

8. Select the empty frame on Frame 25 of the timeline, and choose Insert > Frame.

   This inserts 24 regular frames after the keyframe on Frame 1, all of which initially have the same content as the keyframe on Frame 1.

9. Right-click (Windows) or Control-click (Macintosh) the keyframe on Frame 1 to bring up the Timeline pop-up menu.

10. From the contextual menu, choose Create Motion Tween (**Figure 10.38**).

   Because a motion tween only works with symbols, groups, and text blocks, this command automatically converts content of any other type into a symbol and adds it to the library with the name "tween" appended by a number. Since our red ball and white rectangle were simple shapes, Flash converted both to a symbol called "tween 1." The timeline now shows that a motion tween exists, but the dotted line indicates that there's a problem with the tween: The reason for this is that so far, we've only defined the *beginning* of the tween. Let's now define the end of it.

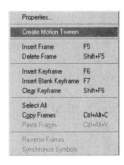

Figure 10.38
Choose Create Motion Tween from the Timeline menu.

11. Move the playhead to Frame 25, which is where we want the tween to end.

12. With the playhead at Frame 25, click the Arrow tool on the Drawing toolbar, and select the red circle on the stage and drag it to the middle right portion of the stage.

   This action automatically adds a keyframe to Frame 25, which completes the motion tween.

13. Move the playhead back and forth to view your animation.

Since we want our animation to spin, shrink, disappear, and speed up as it moves from left to right, we'll take care of the visual edits first (size and transparency), and then edit the movement of the tween (rotation and easing).

To customize a motion tween:

1. Place the playhead at Frame 25.

   Because we want our red ball to be smaller in size and completely transparent at this point in the tween, let's edit it accordingly.

2. On the Drawing toolbar click the Arrow tool, and select the red ball on the stage.

3. Choose Modify > Transform > Scale and Rotate to bring up the Scale and Rotate dialog box.

4. Enter *40* in the Scale box (**Figure 10.39**), and click OK.

   The red ball on Frame 25 reflects that it has been scaled to 40 percent of its original size. We could have entered an amount greater than 100 percent to scale it bigger. If you move the playhead back and forth, you can see the effect of this edit. Let's now make our ball transparent on this keyframe.

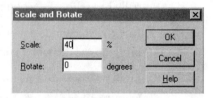

Figure 10.39
Enter 40 as the percentage to scale the red ball.

5. With the Arrow tool still selected, double-click the red ball symbol to bring up the Instance Properties dialog box.

6. Click the Color Effect tab, and choose Alpha from the pop-up menu that appears.

7. Enter *0* in the percentage box, or move the slider all the way to the left.

8. Click OK.

   Even though the ball seems to have disappeared from the stage, it's actually still there—it's just completely transparent. If you move the playhead back and forth, you can see the effect of this edit.

9. To edit how the tween moves double-click the first keyframe on the tween (which in our case is on Frame 1).

   The Frame Properties dialog box appears.

10. Click the Tweening tab to access the tweening properties, and enter the following settings:

Tween scaling: Checked.

Rotate: Clockwise.

Times: 2.

Orient to path direction: Unchecked.

Easing: Move the slider all the way to the left, or enter -100 in the box next to the slider.

Synchronize symbols: Unchecked.

Snap to guide: Checked.

11. Click OK.

Because all of these edits affect the tween's movement, you will only be able to see them when moving the playhead back and forth. Two things to notice about the red ball in the tween: It rotates clockwise twice between the beginning and ending keyframe, and it moves more slowly at the beginning of the tween than it does at its end. This is the result of the Rotation and Easing settings we selected.

Motion-tweening properties

Motion tweens have several adjustable properties, which you can access from the Tweening tab of the Frame Properties dialog box **(Figure 10.40):**

Tweening. Allows you to choose the type of tweening used.

Tween Scaling. If the symbol or group at the beginning and ending keyframes differ in size, checking this option will tween that size difference. Unchecking this option will cause the group or symbol to remain the same size throughout the tween.

Rotate. The options on this pop-up menu let you tween a rotation of the group or symbol between the beginning and ending keyframes:

None. The group or symbol will not rotate.

Automatic. If you rotated the group or symbol in one of the keyframes, this option will tween that rotation in the direction that requires the least amount of motion.

Clockwise/Counterclockwise. These choices rotate the group or symbol clockwise or counterclockwise. The adjacent box indicates the number of full rotations that will be completed over the duration of the tween.

Frame Properties

| Label | Sound | Actions | Tweening |

OK

Cancel

Tweening: Motion ▼

☒ Tween scaling

Rotate: Clockwise ▼ 2 times

☐ Orient to path direction

Easing: ○──────────── -100

In   Out

☒ Synchronize symbols

☒ Snap to guide

Help

Figure 10.40
The Tweening tab, where you can also set motion-tween properties.

Orient to path direction. This is only useful if you are performing a motion tween along a path (see "Motion Tweening Along a Path" later in this section). It allows you to determine whether the base line of a motion-tweened group or symbol remains at the same angle relative to the path throughout the tween (**Figure 10.41**).

Easing. See the "Creating a Shape-Tweened Animation" section above for a explanation of easing.

Synchronize Symbols. See the "Timeline Menu" section above for a explanation of this option.

Snap to Guide. When using a motion guide with a tween, this option causes objects on the keyframes of the tween to snap to the path, or line, on the motion-guide layer (see "Motion Tweening Along a Path" for more information).

Motion Tweening Along a Path

Chances are, you won't want to move every motion-tweened animation in a straight line from Point A to Point B. Not to worry: Flash is able to move a tweened animation along any line you draw or import via motion-guide layers (see Chapter 9, "Layers," for more information). A motion-guide layer simply contains a

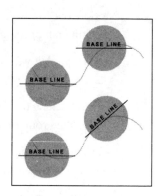

Figure 10.41
The top portion of this graphic illustrates how a tween follows a path with Orient to path direction turned off; the bottom illustrates how it works with it on.

line that's any length, shape, or twist you want. You then link the layer that contains the motion-tweened animation to this layer, and the motion-tweened animation will follow the line you drew.

Using the motion-tweened ball animation we already created, we'll now add a motion path to it to make it appear as if it's bouncing.

To motion tween along a path:

Figure 10.42
The Add Motion Guide button.

1. Select the layer that contains our motion-tweened animation, and click the Add Guide Layer button (**Figure 10.42**).

   This adds a motion-guide layer above the tweened animation layer. A motion-guide layer is always placed above the layer that was the current layer when it was created. The name of the layer with our tweened animation is indented under the name of the motion guide layer above it. This signifies that it is linked to the motion-guide layer. You can link any number of layers to a motion-guide layer.

2. Make the motion-guide layer the current layer (if it isn't already).

3. On the toolbar click the Pencil tool.

   From the Pencil tool modifiers, choose Smooth as the pencil mode, any size and color you wish, and Solid as the line style.

4. Draw a curvy line similar to that shown in **Figure 10.43**.

   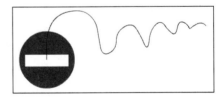

   Figure 10.43
   Draw a curvy line similar to the one shown here. This is the motion path the tween will follow.

   If the Snap to guide option is checked for the tween (which it should be by default), the symbol instances on the beginning and ending keyframes will snap to the closest point along the path.

5. Move the playhead back and forth to see the effect adding a motion guide has had.

To move to the beginning and ending points of a motion tween along a path:

1. Click the Lock control on the motion-guide layer.

   This makes it uneditable.

2. Place the playhead at Frame 1, which contains the beginning keyframe of our tween.

3. Click the Arrow tool on the toolbar, and select the center of the instance of the red ball on the stage and drag it to the end of the path.

It snaps into place as you drag (**Figure 10.44**). You can place the symbol anywhere along the path that you wish—if you drag away from the path, the group or symbol will still snap back onto the path.

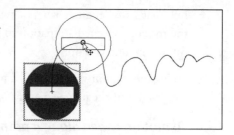

Figure 10.44
The symbol will snap to the path as you drag along it.

4. Move the playhead to the end keyframe of our tween, and perform the same actions as you did in Step 3.

A motion path is never visible when the movie is exported.

To make a motion path invisible:

- To make a motion path invisible within the authoring environment, on the motion-guide layer, click the Eye column.

- Though no longer visible, the linked animations still follow the path.

Using QuickTime Video

At times, nothing can get a point across as effectively as video. Flash's QuickTime capabilities put a whole new dimension of power into your hands: You can mix Flash content with QuickTime video to create interactive videos. And you can control the QuickTime video's timeline with Flash actions to go to specific frames or to play sections, just as you would with regular Flash content. You can even place Flash content, such as buttons and movie clips, on top of a QuickTime video to act as an interface or a way of annotating the QuickTime movie.

Along with the possibilities, however, come some limitations.

QuickTime 4 is the only format that can play back content that combines Flash and QuickTime video: The Flash 4 plug-in does not support this functionality. When creating a Flash project that uses QuickTime video, you must export it to QuickTime format, not Flash, and your audience must have the QuickTime plug-in or player installed on their computers to view it. For more information, see Chapter 13, "Publishing."

The QuickTime 4 plug-in or player only supports Flash 3 functionality at this time; so, Flash 4–specific features will not work when exported to the QuickTime format.

Although visible in the authoring environment, QuickTime video will not appear in your movie when you use the Test Movie feature. To test any Flash project with QuickTime content, you must first export it directly to the QuickTime 4 format.

To import a QuickTime video:

1. From the File menu choose Import.

2. In the Import dialog box, select the video and click Open.

The video is imported into Flash and automatically added to the Library (see Chapter 8, "Library," for more information).

> **TIP** *For organization, it's usually best to place a QuickTime video on its own layer.*

Even though you can import QuickTime video into Flash, you cannot directly edit the video itself; you can only manipulate the movie's timeline. When using button and frame actions to jump to frames in your movie, the QuickTime video frame number corresponds with the Flash frame number. For example, if you place a QuickTime video beginning on Frame 30 of the Flash timeline, Frame 1 of the QuickTime video is referenced as Frame 30 within Flash.

The Flash timeline and the QuickTime timeline are closely linked. The QuickTime timeline will not move unless the Flash timeline also moves. If you import a 50-frame QuickTime video into Flash, you must provide at least 50 frames on the Flash timeline for all the frames of the video to play. If you don't, the video will play to the length of frames provided, and then stop. By using buttons and frame actions, you can jump to various frames of a QuickTime movie much like you can in a regular Flash movie.

Transparent Flash content used on top of a QuickTime video can maintain its transparency at export (**Figure 10.45**).

Because you can see frames of a QuickTime movie within the Flash authoring environment, you can synchronize Flash content and sound with the QuickTime video. Simply scrub the playhead on the Flash timeline to see frames of your QuickTime movie (see "The Playhead" section earlier in this chapter).

Figure 10.45
You can create semitransparent navigational controls for QuickTime movies.

Animation Tutorials

 Animation can be a tricky thing to understand. Therefore, we've put together the following interactive tutorials that you will find on the CD-ROM—along with the source files:

Creating a Frame-by-Frame Animation. This tutorial demonstrates the principles behind frame-by-frame animation.

Creating a Shape-Tweened Animation. Learn how to easily morph one shape into another with this simple tutorial. You'll also see how shape hints are used to help specify how a morphed transition should look.

Creating a Motion-Tweened Animation. We'll create a motion-tweened animation similar to the sample we used in this chapter, and you'll see how size and transparency are tweened. We'll also place this tween along a path to help you better understand the concept of motion guides.

Creating a Preloader. Learn how to create a simple animation that will play while your main movie downloads in the background.

Wave Text. Simulate the cool effect of a wave of text falling into place on the screen.

Interactivity

Humans thrive on interaction. We design our actions to provoke a response. We're more than willing to make utter fools of ourselves just to bring a smile to a baby's face. We love remote controls because we're obsessed with pushing buttons and seeing what happens. But a mute audience, a battery-dead remote control, a frozen computer—these can drive us nuts. If we can't interact with something, we move on to something else. Period.

Which is precisely what you *don't* want the audience of your Flash presentation to do. Sure, you can add sound and animation to capture their attention—we've even taught you how—but if you really want to captivate your viewers, interact with them.

Interactivity is the lifeline between your movie and your audience. You can use it in simple ways to let the viewer control your movie's playback and appearance, or you can employ it in a more advanced fashion to create games, customizable interfaces, forms, and more. However, to do so successfully, we think you should understand a bit of the logic behind advanced interactivity. But don't panic: You don't need to be a computer programmer to add simple interactivity to your presentation; however, a little knowledge can go a long way.

Interactivity in Flash

Three things are needed to make interactivity work in Flash: an *event* that triggers an action, the *action* triggered by the event, and the *target,* or object, that performs the action or is affected by the event.

Not so different than the real world, eh? Think about your alarm clock: When you set it at night, you're programming it to perform an interactive function—the underlying logic of which might look something like this:

Event. The clock reaches the time you set the alarm to go off (which sets the action into motion).

Target. The alarm clock (the object affected by the event).

Action. The alarm sounds (the action performed by the object).

If you can set your alarm, you're on your way to becoming an interactive guru.

To create interactivity with Flash, you use an *ActionScript,* which is simply a set of instructions that defines an event, a target, and an action.

Events

The first thing you need to define to add interactivity to your presentation is the event, which you can trigger in one of in two ways: *deliberately*—meaning something or someone initiates the event by clicking a button, dialing a number, or performing an action—or *based on time*—meaning the event is initiated when a set amount of time has passed. In Flash these are known as mouse/keyboard events (initiated by the user) and frame events (initiated when the timeline reaches a frame during playback).

Mouse events (button actions)

Mouse events occur when your audience interacts with a button instance in your movie. Such events are also known as *button actions* because they are always attached to buttons and they always trigger an action. A user can employ the pointer in any of the following ways to trigger a mouse event (**Figure 11.1**):

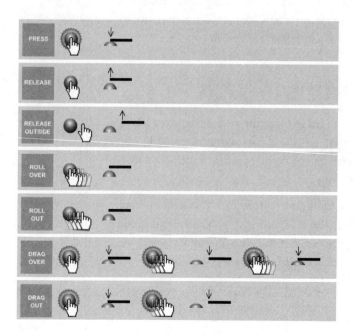

Figure 11.1
The down arrow represents the mouse button being pressed down; the up arrow represents it being released. No arrow represents a mouse event that doesn't require the mouse button to be pressed or released.

Press. Action is triggered when the user moves the pointer over a movie button and presses the mouse button.

Release. Action is triggered when the user moves the pointer over a movie button and clicks and releases the mouse button. (This is the default event for most actions.)

Release Outside. Action is triggered when the user presses a movie button but releases the mouse away from the button.

Roll Over. Action occurs when the user moves the pointer over a movie button.

Roll Out. Action occurs when the user moves the pointer away from a button.

Drag Over. Action occurs when the user places the pointer over a movie button while pressing the mouse button, then drags the pointer away from the movie button (while still pressing the mouse button), and finally moving back over the movie button.

Drag Out. Action occurs when user places the pointer over a movie button, presses the mouse button, and drags away from the movie button (while still pressing mouse button).

Buttons are the only objects in your movie that are affected by these events.

To define a mouse event that triggers an action:

1. Double-click a button instance, or select a button instance and from the Modify menu choose Instance.

The Instance Properties dialog box appears.

2. Click the Action tab.

3. Click the plus sign ("+") to assign an action or actions you want triggered on the mouse event.

4. For our demonstration, choose the Stop action to halt your movie.

The Actions pane shows your completed ActionScript (**Figure 11.2**), which indicates that the action will occur when the button is released. This is the default mouse event Flash assigns to an action when you don't specifical-

Figure 11.2
ActionScript for making a mouse event trigger the movie to stop.

ly choose one. This may not be the mouse event you want to trigger the action, or you may want to use more then one mouse event to trigger it. Let's configure the mouse event more to our liking.

5. In the Actions pane select the On (Release) statement.

It becomes highlighted, and mouse event parameters become available on the right side of the Action dialog box (**Figure 11.3**).

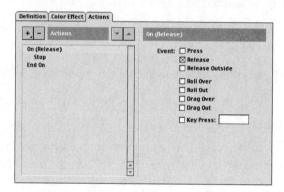

Figure 11.3
Mouse event parameters.

6. Check any mouse events you want to trigger this action.

As you check various events, the On () statement is updated in the Parameter pane.

7. Click OK.

When the movie is played, the action you assigned to this button will be performed when any of the mouse events you checked are triggered.

TIP *Mouse events assigned to one instance of a button have no affect on other instances of the button—even if they're all on the stage at the same time. Each button instance can be assigned different events and actions.*

TIP *You can, if you wish, assign the mouse event before you assign an action to it. Perform Steps 1 and 2 above, but in Step 3 select On MouseEvent to define the mouse event. Then, from the same menu, select an action (Figure 11.4).*

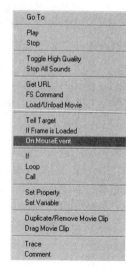

Figure 11.4
Choose the On MouseEvent option first to assign mouse events before setting up an action.

TIP *Many button actions cannot be tested in the authoring environment. To test buttons completely, choose Control > Test Movie.*

Keyboard events

A keyboard event occurs when the user presses a letter, a number, a punctuation mark, a symbol, an arrow, the Backspace, the Insert, the Home, the End, the Page Up, and the Page Down keys. Keyboard events are case sensitive, which means that *A* is not the same as *a*. So, if you assign *A* to trigger an action, *a* will not trigger it.

Keyboard events are attached to button instances. Although you don't need to interact with the button instance, it must be present in a scene for the keyboard event to work (though it doesn't need it to be visible or even present on the stage). It can even reside in the work area of the frame so that it is not visible when the movie is exported (**Figure 11.5**).

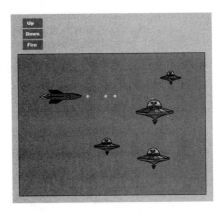

Figure 11.5
Hide buttons that contain keyboard events in areas that will not be seen when the final movie is exported—for example, outside the stage area.

To define a keyboard event that triggers an action:

1. Perform Steps 1 through 5 above (for adding a mouse event).

2. On the Parameter pane of the Action dialog box, check the key-press event.

3. In the small text box next to the key-press option, type the key that will trigger the action (**Figure 11.6**).

4. Click OK.

    When the movie is played, the action you assigned this button instance will be performed when the user presses the key you picked.

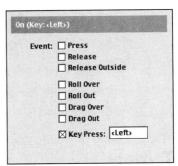

Figure 11.6
Press a key on the keyboard to set the key that triggers an action.

Frame events (frame actions)

Whereas user interaction triggers mouse and keyboard events, the timeline triggers frame events, which are also known as *frame actions* because they are attached to frames and always trigger an action.

Frame events—which are always placed at keyframes—are useful for actions that you want to occur at certain points in time. For example, a Stop action will cause your movie to halt, and a Go To action will cause you movie to jump to another frame or scene on the timeline.

To create a frame event that triggers an action:

1. Double-click the keyframe where you would like the frame event to occur.

The Frame Properties dialog box appears.

2. Click the Action tab.

3. Click the plus sign ("+") to assign an action or actions that you want triggered when the timeline reaches this keyframe.

4. For our demonstration, choose the Stop action, which will cause your movie to stop playing.

The Actions pane displays your completed ActionScript. Notice that even though this is the same action that was assigned to the mouse event we configured earlier, the script is different: It lacks the On (Release) and End On statements, which are only required to define mouse or keyboard events (because both can take so many forms). A frame event can only be triggered one way—by the timeline reaching that frame.

5. Click OK.

When the movie is played, it will perform the action when the timeline reaches this keyframe.

Targets

Now that you know how to use events to trigger an action, you need to learn how to specify which object, or target, will be affected by the event that occurs. Events control three primary targets: the current movie and its timeline, other movies and their timelines (such as movie-clip instances), and external applications (such as a browser). The following sample ActionScripts show how each of these targets can be used to create interactivity. More in-depth explanations follow.

In the following script, a Roll Over (*event*) on a button in the current movie (*target*) causes the movie's timeline to stop playing (*action*).

```
On (Roll Over)
    Stop
End On
```

In the following example, a Roll Over (*event*) on a button in the current movie causes a different movie's timeline—the movie-clip instance MyMovieClip (*target*)—to stop playing (*action*).

```
On (Roll Over)
    Begin Tell Target ("/MyMovieClip")
        Stop
    End Tell Target
End On
```

The following ActionScript opens the user's default browser (*target*)—if it's not already open—and load the specified URL (*action*) when the Roll Over (*event*) is triggered.

```
On (Roll Over)
    Get URL ("http://www.crazyraven.com")
End On
```

> **TIP** *For more information on ActionScripting syntax, see "ActionScripting" later in this chapter.*

Current movie (default target)

The current movie is a *relative* target, which means it contains the button or frame that triggers an action. Thus, if you assign a mouse event to a button, and that event affects the movie or timeline that contains the button, your target is considered the current movie (**Figure 11.7**). If however, you assign a mouse event to a button that affects a movie other than the one that it's a part of, your target becomes a *Tell Target*.

Figure 11.7

When an event, such as a mouse event, causes its own timeline to do something (for example, stop), the target for the event is considered the current movie.

Same principle applies to frame actions. Unless you define a Tell Target as your target, ActionScripts will by default target your current movie for most events. For an example, take a look at the following ActionScript:

```
On (Roll Over)
    Go To and Stop (Scene 5, 20)
End On
```

This ActionScript indicates that a mouse event triggers the action. When the button in your movie is rolled over (*event*), the current movie's timeline (*target*) jumps to Scene 5, Frame 20, and begins playing (*action*) from there.

If you attached the above ActionScript to a button in the main movie—and you didn't use Tell Target to target another movie—the main movie is considered the current movie. If, however, you attached the same Action-Script to a button in a movie-clip symbol—and didn't use Tell Target to target another movie—that movie clip would be the current movie (**Figure 11.8**). Just remember: The current movie—which is where the triggering event originates—is a relative target used in any ActionScript.

Figure 11.8
The context determines the current movie (depending on where an event is triggered).

Other movies (Tell Targets)

A Tell Target is a movie controlled by an event in another movie. Thus, if you assign a mouse event to a movie-clip button so that it affects a different movie clip or time-line than the one that contains the button, your target is considered a Tell Target (**Figure 11.9**). Compare the following ActionScript for controlling a Tell Target with the ActionScript in the previous example used to control the current movie:

```
On (Roll Over)
    Begin Tell Target ("/MyMovieClip")
        Go To Stop (Scene 5, 20)
    End Tell Target
End On
```

This ActionScript indicates that a mouse event triggers the action. When the button in your movie is rolled over (*event*), another movie's timeline (the movie clip called MyMovieClip) (*target*) will jump to Scene 5, Frame 20, and begin playing (*action*) from there.

 If you find the concept of controlling one movie via another confusing, hang in there. We're going to continue to look at these concepts throughout this chapter. For more information, see "Working with Multiple Movies" later in this chapter or review some of the interactive tutorials available on the CD.

Figure 11.9
When an event, such as a mouse event, causes another movie's timeline to react in some way (for example, stop), the target for the event is considered a Tell Target.

> **TIP** *You only use Tell Target to control movie-clip instances or movies that are loaded with the* `Load/Unload Movie` *action within one Flash Player window. You cannot use Tell Target to communicate between two movies placed on an HTML page with separate* `<object>` *or* `<embed>` *tags.*

External (such as a browser or projector)

An *external* target exists outside the realm of your movie. With the Get URL action, for example, you need a Web browser to actually open the specified URL. Three actions can target external sources: Get URL, FS Command, and Load/Unload Movie. All of these actions require the help of an outside application. Targets for these actions can be Web browsers, Flash projectors, Web servers, or other applications (for more information see "Actions," below). The following ActionScript targets a Flash projector window:

```
On (Roll Over)
    FS Command ("fullscreen", "true")
End On
```

This ActionScript indicates that a mouse event triggers the action. When the button in your movie is rolled over (*event*), the projector window becomes full screen. The projector window is considered an application window and thus an external target.

Actions

Actions represent the final pieces of the interactivity puzzle. They allow you to instruct your movies (or external applications) to perform tasks. A single event can trigger multiple actions, which can be performed and executed simultaneously on different targets.

We'll take a brief look at the actions available in Flash and then examine them in depth via some real-world applications. The options in **Table 11.1** can be found by clicking the Add Action button on the Action tab (**Figure 11.10**):

Figure 11.10
Clicking the Add Action button reveals a list of available actions.

Table 11.1
Actions

Action	Description
Go To	Causes a movie to jump to the specified frame or scene on the timeline and stop or begin playing from that point forward.
Play	Causes a movie to begin playing from its current position on the timeline.
Stop	Causes a movie to stop playing.
Toggle High Quality	Turns antialiasing off and on.
Stop All Sounds	Stops all currently playing audio tracks.
Get URL	Opens a browser window with the specified URL loaded, or sends variables to the specified URL.
FS Command	Sends data to the application hosting your Flash movie (such as a browser, projector, Director movie).
Load/Unload Movie	Loads a Flash movie, at the specified URL, within Flash player, or it unloads a previously loaded movie. You can also use it to load variables from a remote file into a movie.
Tell Target	A command that is used as a way of identifying a movie so that you can get it to perform an action.
If Frame Is Loaded	Determines whether a particular frame has been loaded and, if it has, performs an action.

Table 11.1 (continued)

Actions

Action	Description
On Mouse Event	Mouse events are actually triggers rather than actions. For more information, see "Events" earlier in this chapter.
If	Checks to see if a conditional statement is true and, if it is, performs an action.
Loop	Continuously performs an action or set of actions as long as a condition is met. When the condition ceases to be met, the loop stops.
Call	Performs a set of actions attached to a particular frame.
Set Property	Allows you to set various movie properties.
Set Variable	Allows you to create a new variable or update an existing one.
Duplicate/Remove Movie Clip	Allows you to create or remove instances of movie clips dynamically.
Drag Movie Clip	Allows you to make a movie-clip instance draggable in relation to the pointer's movement.
Trace	Displays a custom message when an action is performed. Used primarily to test interactivity. See Chapter 12, "Testing," for more information.
Comment	This option allows you to place comments in your script to help clarify the underlying logic.

Actions in Depth

To take your Flash development to the next level, you're going to need a firmer grasp of the power at your fingertips—and understanding actions in Flash is more than half the battle. Here, we'll show you—in detail—the ways you or your viewer can use actions to control your presentation.

In the following section, we use the terms *expression* and *evaluate* frequently. These require a brief explanation. Most of the actions in Flash have parameters that you must set up for them to function the way you want. For example, the Go To action, which you'll learn about shortly, has a parameter that requires that you identify a frame to go to. This can be a frame number or label. You can enter an exact value such as *25*, or you can set the value of the parameter based on *what value an expression evaluates to*. Do what, you ask? Let's say that in the box that requires you to specify the frame number to go to, instead of simply entering a value of *25*, you enter something like *18 + 7*. *18 + 7* is an *expression* or, in other words, an operation or phrase that *evaluates* to a specific value, in this case 25. Using this expression for the parameter's value would cause the Go To action to go to frame 25 just as if you had directly entered 25. Expressions can take many forms and can evaluate to many types of values, including numbers and text. The purpose of using an expression may not be evident quite yet, but by using them, your movies can take on a life of their own. For more information, see "Using Expressions" later in this chapter.

> **TIP** *You cannot see or test the effect of most actions within the Flash authoring environment. To test interactivity, choose Control > Test Movie from the menu bar.*

> **TIP** *In the following information, timeline, movie, and movie clip are used interchangeably.*

Go To

You use the Go To action to control the position of a movie's timeline, making it jump to a specific frame number, frame label, or scene, where it can stop or play from that point forward (depending on how you set it up).

Parameters

The following parameters are available for this action **(Figure 11.11):**

Scene. Allows you to choose a scene as a starting point for the Go To action. Once you've defined a scene, you can then define a frame number or label within that scene. The scene parameter is not available for symbols. The available options include:

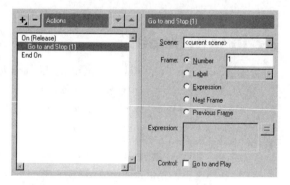

Figure 11.11
Available parameters for the Go To action.

<current scene>. Allows you to choose a frame number or label (see "Frame" below) from the current scene as the point on the timeline to go to.

<next scene>. Causes the action to go to Frame 1 of the next scene. If you select this option, you cannot go to a specific frame number or label in the scene. To do this, you would use Scene_Name.

<previous scene>. Causes the action to go to Frame 1 of the previous scene. If you select this option, you cannot go to a specific frame number or label in the scene. To do this, you would use Scene_Name.

Scene_Name. A listing of scene names appear here; select from the list that appears.

Frame. Based on the scene option you selected, this allows you to choose a specific frame in the scene to go to.

Number. Select a frame number to go to.

Label. Select a frame label in the scene to go to. (The list that appears only offers frame labels available in the current scene.)

Expression. Allows you to dynamically set the destination frame based on what value an expression evaluates to. For more information, see "Using Expressions" later in this chapter.

Next Frame. Causes the timeline to jump to the frame following the one where the action is triggered. This is only available when selecting <current scene> for the scene parameter.

Previous Frame. Causes the timeline to jump to the frame previous to the one where the action was triggered. This option is only available when selecting <current scene> for the scene parameter.

Expression. This text box allows you to type in an expression to dynamically set a frame to go to based on what value the expression evaluates to. Click the equal ("=") button to activate the Expression Editor. For more information, see "Using Expressions" in this chapter.

Control. Once the timeline has jumped to a specific frame, the Control option allows you to specify whether the movie will stop playing at that frame or continue playing from that frame. If you leave this box unchecked, the movie will halt (the default setting).

Sample script

The following script shows a mouse event that causes the current movie to go to Frame 10 of the Intro scene and then begin playing:

```
On (Release)
    Go To and Play (Intro, 10)
End On
```

The following script shows a mouse event in the current movie that causes another movie, a movie clip instance named Brooks, to go to a frame labeled Sleep and then stop:

```
On (Release)
    Begin Tell Target ("Brooks")
        Go To and Stop ("Sleep")
    End Tell Target
End On
```

Real-world use

This is Flash's way of creating hyperlinks within a Flash movie.

Play

The Play action causes a movie to begin playing from its current position. If your movie stops (due to a Stop action or Go To and Stop action), it cannot begin playing again until you use the Play action to start it.

Parameters

Play has no parameters.

Sample script

The following script shows a mouse event that causes the current movie to begin playing from its current position:

```
On (Press)
    Play
End On
```

The following script shows a frame event in the current movie that causes another movie—the movie clip instance named Brooks—to start playing (if it's not already):

```
Begin Tell Target ("/Brooks")
    Play
End Tell Target
```

Real-world use

Use to create start/stop buttons—On (Press) Play, On (Release) Stop.

Stop

The Stop action causes a movie to cease playing. You can use it during any points in the movie that you wish to remain visible for an extended period of time.

Parameters

Stop has no parameters.

Sample script

The following script shows a mouse event that causes the current movie to stop playing:

```
On (Press)
    Stop
End On
```

The following script shows a frame event in the current movie that causes another movie, a movie-clip instance named Brooks, to stop (if it's playing):

```
Begin Tell Target ("/Brooks")
    Stop
End Tell Target
```

Real-world use

Use to create start /stop buttons. Place this action on any keyframes where the movie should be stopped.

Toggle High Quality

The Toggle High Quality action turns antialiasing off and on (**Figure 11.12**), which affects the visual quality and playback speed of your movie. With antialiasing on, visual quality improves but playback slows on older computers. With it off, just the opposite occurs. This action cannot affect a single target. It affects all presently playing movies and movie-clip instances within Flash Player.

Parameters

This action has no parameters. If high quality is already on, setting this action will turn it off, and if it's off, will turn it on.

Sample script

The following script shows a mouse event that causes the high-quality setting of all movies currently playing in Flash Player to be toggled on or off depending on its current setting:

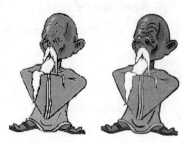

Figure 11.12
Toggling between High Quality in your movie can affect how smooth your graphics appear.

```
On (Release)
    Toggle High Quality
End On
```

Real-world use

To determine view quality, and to turn off antialiasing for intensely animated portions of a movie.

Stop All Sounds

The Stop All Sounds action halts all currently playing audio tracks in all movies and movie-clip instances within Flash Player. This action does not affect the visual aspects of your movie.

Parameters

This action has no parameters.

Sample script

The following script shows a mouse event that stops the audio tracks in all movies and movie clip instances currently playing in Flash Player:

```
On (Release)
    Stop All Sounds
End On
```

Real-world use

To turn off sounds (sound on/off buttons), and to silence a sound track.

Get URL

The Get URL action does one of two things: It either loads a specified URL into a browser window, or it sends variable data to the specified URL. For example, variable data can be sent to a CGI script for processing in the same way an HTML form can. Note that only variables for the *current* movie are sent (see "Working with Multiple Movies" later in this chapter).

Although the Get URL action is mostly for use when placing a Flash movie on a Web page, you can also use it in a Flash projector to automatically open a browser window and display a specified URL.

Parameters

Get URL has the following parameters (**Figure 11.13**):

URL. This is where you define the URL for the Get URL action. It can be a relative path such as mypage.html, or it can be an absolute path such as http://www. mydomain.com/mypage.html.

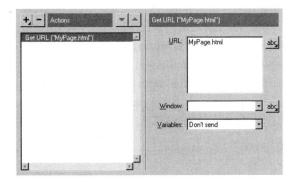

Figure 11.13
Available parameters
for the Get URL action.

If the URL you are "getting" is a CGI script or Cold Fusion template, it could look like http://www.mydomain.com/cgi-bin/myscript.cgi or http://www.mydomain.com/mycftemplate.cfm, respectively.

If your Flash movie is on an HTML page, you can use this area to define a JavaScript function to call—such as javascript:newWindow()—when an event is triggered.

You can dynamically set what URL to get based on what value an expression evaluates to. Click the "abc" button to activate the Expression Editor. For more information, see "Using Expressions" later in this chapter.

Window. Specifies the browser window or HTML frame in which to load and display the specified URL. If you have defined an HTML window or frames with a name and you want the specified URL to load into that window, simply type its name into this box. Otherwise, you can choose among the following options:

self. Loads the specified URL into the window or frame now occupied by the Flash movie.

blank. Opens a new browser window and loads the specified URL into it.

parent. Opens the URL in the parent frame of the current frame.

top. If the Flash movie with the Get URL action is in an HTML frame, this removes the frame set and loads the URL into the browser window.

You can dynamically set the window or frame a URL is loaded into based on what value an expression evaluates to. Click the "abc" button to activate the Expression Editor. For more information, see "Using Expressions" later in this chapter.

Variables. Lets you choose how variables in the current movie are dealt with when using the Get URL action. The following options are available:

Don't send. Doesn't send variables and is best used to simply open a URL.

Send using GET. Sends variables appended to the specified URL. For example, passing two variables, name and age, using the GET method will cause the URL to look like http://www.mydomain.com/mypage.html?name=Derek+Franklin &age=unkown. Thus, if a Flash movie existed on mypage.html, it would be passed the values of name and age and could react to those values in its own way. In other words, you can employ this option to automatically send the values of the variables in a Flash movie on one HTML page to a Flash movie on another HTML page. (This only works well for sending a small number of variables.)

Send using POST. Sends variables separate from the URL, letting you send more variables. On regular HTML pages, this method is most often used to post information collected from a form to a CGI script on the server. In the same way, it can send variable values to a CGI script for processing.

> **TIPS** *When sending variables, only variables from the current movie get sent (not variables from all movies present in the Flash movie window).*

> **TIPS** *For more information about variables, see "ActionScripting" later in this chapter.*

Sample script

The following script shows a mouse event that opens the URL in a new window:

```
On (Release)
    Get URL ("http://www.mydomain.com/mypage.html", window="_blank")
End On
```

The following script shows a mouse event that posts variables to a CGI script on the server.

```
On (Release)
    Get URL ("http://www.mydomain.com/CGI-bin/myscript.cgi", vars=POST)
End On
```

Real-world use

Use on Flash forms and on HTML-driven pages in conjunction with Flash content.

FS Command

FS Command allows your Flash movie to communicate with other programs—say, a Web browser or any program that can host your Flash movie. A host program is simply a program that allows you to embed your Flash movie into it. This command is commonly used to enable a Flash movie to interact with JavaScript on an HTML page.

Without getting too technical, the following shows how to use FS Command to open custom alert boxes:

1. Create a Flash movie with a button that includes a mouse event that triggers an FS Command action.

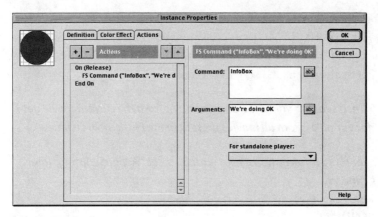

Figure 11.14
The Command and Argument text boxes can contain anything you
wish, depending on what action the FS Command is set to perform.

2. When setting up the FS Command, type *Infobox* in the Command box and
We're Doing OK in the Argument box (**Figure 11.14**).

You make up the command name, which can be anything from *turtle* to
hairspray. It's just a unique identifier.

3. If you wish, you can create a second button with an FS Command action on it
as well. For the second button, simply type *Infobox* in the Command box but
We're not so good in the Argument box. You now have two buttons that use the
same command but different arguments.

When you put your movie on the HTML page, you can also place it on a
JavaScript function that can detect when an FS Command has been activated in
your movie. In our example, we intentionally set up this JavaScript function to
evaluate the FS Command in a way that says, "If the command equals InfoBox,
create an alert box that reads whatever the arguments of the FS Command
were." Thus, depending on which button you click, an alert box opens that
reads either "We're doing OK" or "We're not so good."

Obviously, you can accomplish much more using the FS Command, but it usually
involves a lot more JavaScripting. For most users, Flash's new internal scripting
(ActionScripting) should be more than enough to handle most jobs.

Parameters

This action has the following parameters:

Command. This is a unique name you assign to an FS Command to identify it. It can be anything from *sausage* to *escalator.*

You can dynamically set the command based on what value an expression evaluates to. Click the equal ("=") button to activate the Expression Editor. For more information, see "Using Expressions" in this chapter.

Arguments. If the command requires that any information be passed—for example, to a JavaScript function—you must enter it here. It can take the form of a text string, such as "Hey Bob," or a numeric value, such as 35.

You can dynamically set the arguments to be used based on what value an expression evaluates to. Click the equal ("=") button to activate the Expression Editor. For more information, see "Using Expressions" in this chapter.

For Stand-Alone Player. You can use the following settings to control a Flash projector when distributing your movie as a stand-alone application:

fullscreen. To display a projector so that it can be seen at full screen, choose "true." "False" displays it at the size set in the Movie Properties dialog box.

allowscale. Choose "true" to allow your user to resize the projector window. "False" prevents the window from being resized.

showmenu. Choose "true" to make the projector menu available when the user right-clicks (Windows) or Control-clicks (Macintosh) the projector window. "False" prevents the menu from being displayed.

quit. Quits the projector and closes its window.

exec. Use this command to start an external application from Flash. Enter the directory path to the application in the Argument box.

Sample script

The following script shows a frame event that opens a projector window to full screen:

```
FS Command ("fullscreen", true)
```

Real-world use

To control a projector, and to interact with JavaScript.

Load/Unload Movie

The Load/Unload Movie action allows you to do several things:

Load a new movie into the Flash movie window that will replace an existing movie—which means you can display a new movie without loading a different HTML page.

Load a new movie into the Flash movie window in addition to any existing movies (**Figure 11.15**).

Send the variables of a loaded movie to a CGI script for processing.

Unload a movie that was previously loaded into the movie window using the Load Movie action.

Load a set of variables into a timeline so that it can take any necessary actions as a result of those variables.

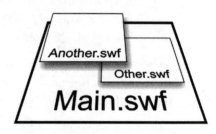

Figure 11.15
Loading movies using the Load Movie action allows you to have multiple .swf files in the Flash Player window at once.

Because the Load/Unload Movie menu item/action is actually a *set* of actions, rather than using sample scripts, we'll show you how to perform each one of the tasks.

Parameters

This action has the following parameters (**Figure 11.16**):

Action. The Load/Unload Movie action/menu item performs three primary actions, which are determined by the following buttons:

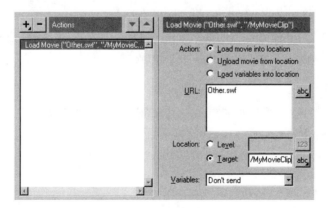

Figure 11.16
Available parameters for the Load/Unload Movie action.

Load movie into location. Loads a new .swf file into the level or target defined. This allows multiple .swf files to be present in the Flash Player window at once. Use this action in conjunction with the GET or POST setting for the Variables parameter to send the variables of the current or targeted timeline to a CGI script specified at the URL parameter.

Unload movie from location. Unloads a movie previously loaded using the Load Movie action.

Load variables into location. Allows you to load a set of variables into a movie from a remote text file that you've created and placed on the server or that have been generated by a CGI script (see "Something Remotely Possible" below). Use this action in conjunction with the GET or POST setting for the Variables parameter to send the variables of the movie specified at the location parameter to a CGI script specified at the URL parameter, which then loads new variable values back into the same movie based on the server's response.

Something Remotely Possible

Loading variables from a remote text file requires that the information in the text file be in a special format so that Flash can read it. This format is known as URLformencoded and can be written manually or outputted by means of a CGI script, Cold Fusion, ASP, or other server scripting languages. Here's an example of how a text file would look:

```
name=John+Doe&age=25&favoritefood=Pizza&married=false
```

Name, age, favorite food, and marital status all represent variable names that should correspond with variable names used in the movie that the text file is being loaded into. Using a plus sign indicates spaces in the variable value. So, John+Doe is actually John Doe when loaded into Flash. Different variables/values are separated by an ampersand. So, this example has four separate variables.

URL. When used with "Load movie into location" this is the directory path to the .swf file to load. It can be a relative path such as mymovie.swf or an absolute path such as http://www.mydomain.com/mymovie.swf. When using this option in conjunction with either the GET or POST settings for the Variables parameter, this parameter specifies the location of the CGI script that the variables of the current or targeted timeline will be sent to for processing. It is grayed out when "Unload movie from location" is selected.

When used with "Load variables into location" this is the directory path to the .txt file to load. It can be a relative path such as myvariables.txt or an absolute path such as http://www.mydomain.com/myvariables.txt. When using the GET or POST settings for the Variables parameter, this parameter specifies the location of the CGI script that the variables of the loaded movie will be sent to.

You can dynamically set the URL to get based on the value an expression evaluates to. Click the "abc" button to activate the Expression Editor.

Location. This parameter defines the level or target that will be affected by the specified action.

Level. Unless loaded into a target (which replaces a movie-clip instance in your current movie with an entire movie [.swf file]), a loaded movie is placed on a level and assigned a level number. Levels can be thought of as layers of separate .swf files stacked on top of each other in the Flash Player window (**Figure 11.17**). The number assigned to a level determines its position relative to all other levels. As the bottom .swf file in the stack, Level 0 usually represents your original movie. Movies can be loaded into levels that already contain another movie. Doing so simply replaces the existing .swf file on that level.

Target. Allows you to load an entire .swf into a space currently occupied by a movie-clip instance. Doing so causes the loaded .swf to inherit all of the movie clip's current properties, including it's name, target path, size, and position (**Figure 11.18**).

You can dynamically set the level or target name in which to load a movie based on the value an expression evaluates to. Click the equal ("=") button to activate the Expression Editor.

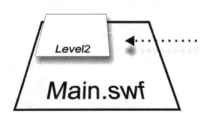

Figure 11.17
Loading a movie into a level places all of its content above any levels below it.

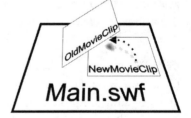

Figure 11.18
Loading a movie into a target allows an .swf file to replace a space originally occupied by a movie-clip instance.

Variables. Lets you choose how variables in a movie are sent to a server. The following options are available:

Don't send. Prevents variables in a movie from being sent if either the Load Movie or Load Variables action is selected.

Send using GET. Sends variables appended to the end of the specified URL. See Get URL for more information.

Send using POST. Sends variables separate from the URL, which means it can transmit a greater number of variables. See Get URL for more information.

To load a new movie into the Flash movie window that replaces an existing movie:

1. Select the "Load movie into location" option.

2. For the URL parameter, enter the directory path to the .swf file you want loaded.

3. For the Location parameter, enter a level number that is currently occupied by another movie, or choose a movie-clip target to replace.

4. In the Variables parameter choose the "Don't send" option.

To load a new movie into the Flash movie window in addition to any existing movies:

1. Select the "Load movie into location" option.

2. For the URL parameter, enter the directory path to the .swf file you want loaded.

3. For the Location parameter, enter a level number that is not occupied by another movie.

When loading movies into levels, the level numbers you choose do not need to be sequential. You can load one movie into Level 6 and then the next one into Level 87.

4. In the Variables parameter choose the "Don't send" option.

To send the variables of a loaded movie to a CGI script for processing:

1. Select the "Load movie into location" option.

2. For the URL parameter, enter the directory path to the CGI script to which you wish to send the variables for processing.

3. For the Location parameter, enter a level number or target path of the movie whose variables you want to send.

4. In the Variables parameter choose the "Send using GET" or "Send using POST" option.

To unload a movie that was previously loaded into the movie window with the Load Movie action:

1. Select the "Unload movie from location" option.

The URL parameter is grayed out.

2. For the Location parameter, enter the level number or target path of the movie you want to unload.

The Variables parameter is grayed out

To load a set of variables into a timeline so that it can take any necessary actions as a result of those variables:

1. Select the "Load variables into location" option.

2. For the URL parameter, enter the directory path to the text file with the variables that will be loaded.

If the text will be generated from a CGI script, enter the path to the script instead.

3. For the Location parameter, enter the level number or target path of the movie whose variables will receive the updated variables.

4. In the Variables parameter, choose "Don't send" if you want variables only to be *retrieved* from the remote file or CGI script.

If you choose the "Send using GET" or "Send using POST" option, current variables for the specified movie will be sent to the server (to a CGI script) and processed. Then, new variables based on the server's response will be loaded back into the specified movie.

Real-world use

Viewing various Flash movies without loading additional HTML pages, and connectivity between Flash and server-based information and processing, which allows for Flash-based forms to be processed or dynamically generated content to easily be displayed within Flash.

Tell Target

The Tell Target command prefaces actions directed toward any timeline other than the current one. You use the Tell Target command—which is always employed in conjunction with an action—to control movies other than the current one, to set or change a variable on another timeline, or to set a property of a specific movie clip instance.

Parameters

This command has only one parameter:

Target. This is where you define the movie that will be targeted for any subsequent actions. A special box appears with a directory of available movie-clip instance targets (**Figure 11.19**). A plus sign ("+") next to a movie clip instance's name indicates that it contains a *child movie clip* which is simply a movie clip instance inside of it (see "Working with Multiple Movies" in this chapter). Click the plus sign to expand the directory. Double-click a target's name if you want it entered as the target.

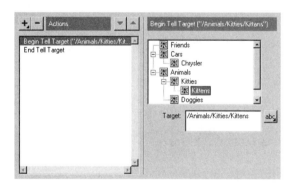

Figure 11.19
A directory of movie-clip instances allows you to easily set a movie clip as your target: Simply double-click a movie clip's name to select it.

TIP *Only child movie-clip instances of the current movie are available in this box. If you wish to target a parent movie clip or another child, you must enter its path. For more information, see "Working with Multiple Movies" later in this chapter.*

You can dynamically choose the target based on the value an expression evaluates to. Click the "abc" button to activate the Expression Editor.

Sample script

The following script shows a mouse event that causes the timeline of a movie-clip instance (MyMovieClip) to jump to the frame label MyFrameLabel and then stop:

```
On (Release)
   Begin Tell Target ("/MyMovieClip")
     Go to and Stop ("MyFrameLabel")
   End Tell Target
End On
```

The following scripts demonstrate the two ways a target can be addressed to perform an action. In the top script the target is defined using the Tell Target command; in the bottom script it's defined via the Set Property command—both scripts perform the same action:

```
On (Release)
   Begin Tell Target ("/MyMovieClip")
     Set Property (" ", X Scale) = "50"
   End Tell Target
End On
```

The second script:

```
On (Release)
   Set Property ("/MyMovieClip", X Scale) = "50"
End On
```

Real-world use

To control one movie from another.

If Frame Is Loaded

If Frame Is Loaded is another command used to preface an action (and it's always used in conjunction with an action). The underlying logic goes something like this: If frame x is loaded, do these actions. If frame x is not loaded, ignore the "If Frame Is Loaded" command. This is known as a conditional statement: The action is only performed if the condition is met.

This command is commonly used to create a loop that constantly checks to see if the back end of a movie has been completely downloaded. This is also known as a *preloader* (see the sample script below).

Parameters

This action has the following parameters (**Figure 11.20**):

Scene. Allows you to choose a scene as a starting point for the If Frame Is Loaded command. Once you've defined a scene, you can define a frame number or label within that scene. The scene parameter is not available for symbols. The available options include the following:

    <current scene>. Allows you to choose a frame number or label from the current scene as the frame to check (see the frame parameter below).

    Scene_Name. Select a name from the list of scene names that appears.

Frame. Based on the scene option you selected, this parameter allows you to determine whether a specific scene has been loaded.

Number. Select a frame number.

Label. Select a frame label in the scene. (The list that appears only offers frame labels available in the current scene.)

Expression. This parameter allows you to type an expression to dynamically set which frame's load status to check based on what value the expression evaluates to. Click the equal ("=") button to activate the Expression Editor. For more information see "Using Expressions" in this chapter.

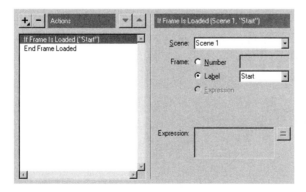

Figure 11.20
Available parameters for the "If Frame is Loaded" action.

Sample script

The following scripts show how a basic preloader is put together. A frame event on Frame 1 of our movie checks whether the frame labeled Start on a scene named MainScene (this is the scene that contains our main animation) has been loaded. If it has, the Go To action is carried out, causing the timeline to start playing your movie from that label forward. If the label has not been loaded, the command is ignored and the timeline continues on to Frame 2 (see below for the script that goes on Frame 2):

```
If Frame Is Loaded (MainScene, "Start")
    Go to and Play (MainScene, "Start")
End Frame Loaded
```

The following script shows a frame event on Frame 2 that simply sends the timeline back to Frame 1 of our movie:

```
Go To and Play (1)
```

This triggers the "If Frame is Loaded" command from the first script. Once again, if the Start frame still hasn't been loaded, the command is ignored, the timeline continues, and the Go To and Play action on Frame 2 is triggered again, which starts the process all over again. This is known as a loop. This loop will continue until the Start label has been loaded, at which point the Go To and Play action on Frame 1 as shown in the first script will be triggered.

> **TIP** *A more dynamic way to create the functionality just described is demonstrated in the sample script for the If command.*

Real-world use

Use to create a preloader or to prevent certain actions from being triggered before the necessary content has been downloaded by the viewer.

On Mouse Event

See "Mouse Events" earlier in this chapter.

If

Use the If command to create a conditional statement: If a condition is met, an action is performed; if the condition is not met, a different action is performed. Take a look at the following conditional statement:

```
If (Outside="rain")
   Go To and Stop ("Bed")
Else
   Go To and Play ("Park")
End If
```

This conditional statement shows that if Outside equals rain, go to bed; however, if Outside equals anything else, go to the park. This may not be the best logic to use. What if it's snowing or there's a tornado? Well, we just need to add a few more conditions. Look at the following example:

```
If (Outside="rain")
   Go To and Stop ("Bed")
Else If (Outside = "sun")
   Go To and Play ("Park")
Else If (Outside = "Snow")
   Go To and Play ("SkiResort")
Else If (Outside = "Tornado")
   Go To and Stop ("Basement")
Else
   Go To and Play ("TV")
   Set Variable: "LifeIsGood" = True
End If
```

This conditional statement, once again, checks the value of Outside; however, it does so with a twist. In our new conditional statement, different actions are possible depending on the condition that's met. This is due to the addition of Else If to our conditional statement. For example, if Outside equals "rain," it's time to go back to bed. If it equals "sun," it's time to go to the park and have fun. If it equals "Snow", it's off to the ski resort. If it equals "Tornado", head for the basement. And if it doesn't equal any of these, go watch TV and update the value of LifeIsGood to true (see "Set Variable" later in this chapter).

Obviously, conditional statements can be much more complex. For more information, see the "ActionScripting" section of this chapter.

Parameters

Various parts of the conditional statement require different parameters.

For the If () part of the statement:

Condition. Enter the condition that you wish to verify. Click the equal ("=") button to activate the Expression Editor. For more information, see "Using Expressions."

Else/Else If. By default, conditional statements do not include Else or Else If clauses. Press the Add Else/Else If clause button to add as many clauses as you wish (**Figure 11.21**).

If you add an Else or Else If clause to your conditional statement, you can click the clause in the Action pane to bring up the following parameters:

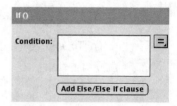

Action. Lets you choose whether an added clause is an Else or Else If clause.

If an Else If clause, the following parameter becomes available.

Condition. Enter the condition that you wish to verify. Click the equal ("=") button to activate the Expression Editor.

Figure 11.21
Press the Add Else/Else If clause button to add additional conditional logic to an If statement.

Sample script

The following script shows a frame event on Frame 2 of a movie that checks to see how many frames have been loaded in your movie and then acts accordingly. The first part of this conditional statement says that if less than 100 frames of your movie have been loaded, go back to Frame 1 and begin playing again. After Frame 1 is played again, Frame 2 is rechecked with this conditional statement. If still less than 100 loaded frames at this point, the timeline goes back to Frame 1 and the process is repeated. Once 100 or more frames have been loaded, the Go To action is triggered instead:

```
If (_framesloaded < 100)
    Go to and Play (1)
Else
    Go to and Play (MainScene, "Start")
End If
```

Real-world use

Adds logic to your Flash movie so that it will perform certain actions if specified conditions are met.

Loop While

You use the Loop While command to perform a series of actions while a condition is true. The logic used in a Loop While statement might look something like this: As long as *x* equals ten, perform these actions repeatedly (loop); however, as soon as *x* no longer equals ten, stop performing those actions and instead perform whatever action follows the Loop While statement. Since the Loop While action continues to perform a set of tasks you set it up to perform while a condition is true, if you don't provide a means for the condition to eventually become false you'll be creating and endless loop, which will keep your movie from functioning properly. See the sample script below for more information. Use the Loop While command for advanced scripting in Flash.

Parameters

Loop While has one parameter:

Condition. Enter the condition that must be true for the loop to continue. Click the equal ("=") button to activate the Expression Editor. For more information, see "Using Expressions."

Sample script

The Loop While action provides for some sophisticated scripting within Flash. The following script shows the concept behind the way it works. The first thing that will happen is a variable named Count is created and given an initial value of 1. Next, you'll see the Loop While statement set up, which basically says that when the count is less than or equal to 10, perform the following actions. Part of the actions that will be performed is the updating of the value of Count by 1 with each iteration of the loop. Thus, after 10 loops Count will equal 11 and the loop will stop.

```
Set Variable: "Count" = 1
Loop While (Count <= 10)
    Actions…
        Set Variable: "Count" = Count + 1
End Loop
```

TIP *The Loop action is not based on time intervals as are other types of loops within Flash: A Loop While action will not loop every second or even every 3 seconds. A Loop While action is usually performed almost instantaneously—regardless of how many times it loops. Use this action primarily to quickly perform repetitive evaluation or creation tasks.*

Real-world use

To dynamically create variables and movie-clip instances, and to check and verify data.

Call

The Call action enables you to create a reusable ActionScript. For example, if each of a set of buttons needs to perform the same set of actions, you could create the action set once and just reference it later (see the sample script below). You simply create a set of actions at a keyframe, which is assigned a frame label so that whenever you need that set of actions to run, you simply "call" that frame label. When a mouse/keyboard event or a frame event triggers a Call action, the timeline doesn't jump to that frame, but the action is executed.

Be aware of several things when using the Call action:

The frame label that is called can exist on any timeline present in Flash Player (see "Working with Multiple Movies" in this chapter).

If a Call action is made to a frame label of a movie not yet loaded, the Call action will be ignored.

If variables from one timeline are to be evaluated by a set of actions on a frame label of another timeline (basically what the Call action does), the variable values must first be passed to that timeline using the Set Variable action. Conversely, if the Call action creates any new values to be used by the timeline that made the call, these values must first be passed back (see the sample script below). For more information, see "Setting and Getting Variable Values for Different Timelines" later in this chapter.

After the set of actions has been executed, any actions following the Call action are resumed.

Parameters

The Call action has a single parameter:

Frame. This is the path and frame label of the frame whose actions you want to use, or call. For more information, see "Identifying Frame Labels" later in this chapter.

You can dynamically choose the frame label to call based on the value an expression evaluates to. Click the "abc" button to activate the Expression Editor. For more information, see "Using Expressions" in this chapter.

Sample script

The following script shows a mouse event that creates a variable named UseInCall with a value of 45. The set of actions at the ActionSet1 keyframe (the Call action) will evaluate this variable's value—and in so doing set the value of a variable named ActSet1Value, which instructs the timeline where to go (**Figure 11.22**).

```
On (Release)
    Set Variable: "UseInCall" = 45
    Call ("ActionSet1")
    Go To and Stop (ActionSet1Value)
End On
```

> **TIP** *Keyframes holding action sets to be used in Calls can be placed anywhere along a timeline—even in a separate scene that the user never views or visits. This is a great way to "store" action sets in one convenient place.*

Real-world use

Use for reusable actions (similar to JavaScript functions).

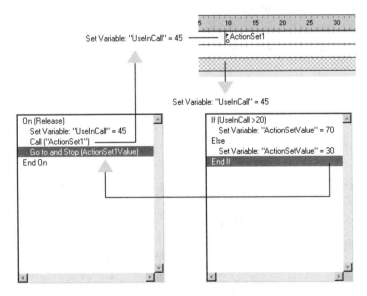

Figure 11.22
A visual representation of the way the Call action works.

Set Property

Using the Set Property action, you can adjust the position, size, rotation, transparency, visibility, and name of any movie in Flash Player while your movie plays.

Parameters

This action has the following parameters (**Figure 11.23**):

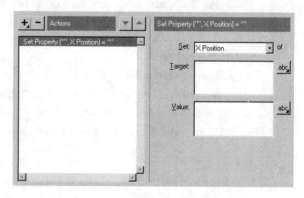

Figure 11.23
Available parameters for the Set Property action.

Set. This list lets you choose which property you wish to adjust. The following properties are available:

X Position. Sets the horizontal position of a movie. The value is based in pixels and is relative to the center point of the movie-clip instance's parent (see "Working with Multiple Movies" in this chapter).

Y Position. Sets the vertical position of a movie. The value is based in pixels and is relative to the center point of the movie-clip instance's parent.

TIP *Normally, x and y positions are relative from the center point of a movie clip instance's parent to the top-left corner of the movie clip instance. Selecting a movie-clip instance and choosing the Use Center Point option on the Object Inspector changes it from the center point of a movie-clip instance's parent to the center point of the movie-clip instance (**Figure 11.24**).*

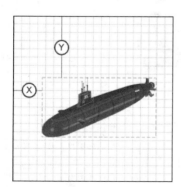

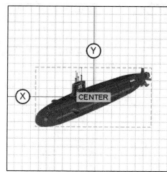

Figure 11.24
Choosing a movie-clip instance and selecting Use Center Point changes the reference point in determining the *x* and *y* positions of movies.

X Scale. Sets the horizontal size of a movie based on a percentage. A value less than 100 reduces the horizontal size; a value greater than 100 increases its size.

Y Scale. Sets the vertical size of a movie based on a percentage. A value less than 100 reduces the vertical size; a value greater than 100 increases its size. (**Figure 11.25**).

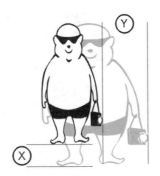

Alpha. Sets the transparency of a movie. A value of 0 makes the movie-clip instance invisible. A value of 100 makes it opaque. Elements in a completely transparent movie remain active, which means you can still interact with them.

Figure 11.25
The X and Y Scale properties let you scale an object's size based on its original size. Values are based on a percentage amount.

Visibility. Sets the visibility of a movie. A value of True, or any nonzero value, makes the movie-clip instance visible; a value of False, or 0, makes it invisible. You cannot interact with elements in an invisible movie.

Rotation. Sets the rotation of a movie-clip instance (in degrees). A negative value rotates the movie clip counterclockwise.

Name. Sets the name of a movie-clip instance, which makes it possible for you to dynamically rename it while your movie is playing. If you change the name of a movie-clip instance, it retains its relative directory path to other movies (see "Working with Multiple Movie" in this chapter).

Three properties affect how all movies play in the Flash movie window. Because they are global properties, you cannot adjust them for individual movies (which is why the Target parameter is grayed out when one of them is selected).

High Quality. Sets the view and playback quality of your movie to one of three values: 0 (low quality), 1 (high quality), or 2 (best quality).

Show Focus Rectangle. Shows a yellow rectangle around buttons in your exported movie as you use the Tab key to navigate them (**Figure 11.26**). A value of True, or any nonzero value, makes the focus rectangle visible, and a value of False, or 0, makes it invisible.

Sound Buffer Time. Sets the amount of streaming sound, in seconds, that should be downloaded before it begins to play.

Target. This is where you define the movie-clip instance whose properties you wish to adjust.

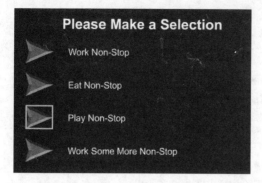

Please Make a Selection

Work Non-Stop

Eat Non-Stop

Play Non-Stop

Work Some More Non-Stop

Figure 11.26
The focus rectangle surrounds
buttons when the Tab key is used
to navigate between them.

You can choose the target based on the value an expression evaluates to. Click the "abc" button to activate the Expression Editor.

Value. This is where you set a value for the selected property.

Sample script

The following script shows a mouse event that sets the transparency of the movie-clip instance named MyMovieClip to 50 percent:

```
On (Release)
    Set Property ("/MyMovieClip", Alpha) = "50"
End On
```

The following script performs the same action differently. A Tell Target command is used to identify the movie-clip instance whose property you wish to change. You do not need to identify the movie-clip instance in the Set Property action.

```
On (Release)
    Begin Tell Target ("/MyMovieClip")
        Set Property (" ", Alpha) = "50"
    End Tell Target
End On
```

Real-world use

For interactive objects and interfaces, and to pan and zoom.

Set Variable

The Set Variable action creates a new variable with the initial value you assign or updates the value of an existing variable. A variable is basically a container that holds a value. Many of us learned this in math class (if we were paying attention). For example, we learned that x=20 or that y=10. This way when we wrote an equation that read x+y=z, we knew that z=30. Bet you didn't realize that those boring classes in high school were prepping you for Flash mastery later in life did you?

In Flash you use variable values to dynamically set various parameter values in other actions—for example which frame numbers to go to, the value of a movie-clip instance property, and even text in a text field (see sample script below).

Parameters

This action has the following parameters:

Variable. The name of the variable you wish to create or update. All variable names must begin with a character; however, the subsequent characters can be letters, digits, or underscores.

You can dynamically choose the variable that you wish to create or update based on the value an expression evaluates to. Click the "abc" button to activate the Expression Editor. For more information, see "Using Expressions" in this chapter.

Value. The value of the variable that you create or update.

You can dynamically set the value of a variable based on the value an expression evaluates to. Click the "abc" button to activate the Expression Editor.

Sample script

The following script shows a mouse event that sets the value of SeeThrough to 45. As soon as you set it, this variable's value is used to set the transparency value of the movie-clip instance MyMovieClip:

```
On (Release)
    Set Variable: "SeeThrough" = "45"
    Set Property ("/MyMovieClip", Alpha) = SeeThrough
End On
```

Real-world use

Use to dynamically generate the text shown in text fields, to dynamically set action parameter values, and to track the number of times an event has been triggered.

Duplicate/Remove Movie Clip

The Duplicate/Remove Movie Clip action dynamically creates or removes movie-clip instances as your movie is playing. When a movie-clip instance is duplicated, the new clip inherits the original's properties but none of its variables (**Figure 11.27**) (see "Working with Multiple Movies" in this chapter). At its creation, a duplicate always begins playing at the first frame, regardless of which frame the original movie clip instance was on when the duplicate action was triggered.

Only movie-clip instances created with the Duplicate action can be removed with this action; movie-clip instances that were originally part of the Flash movie cannot.

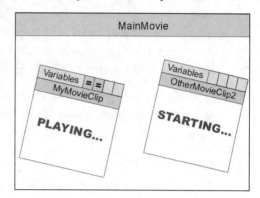

Figure 11.27
A duplicated movie clip inherits all of the original's properties but none of its variables.

Parameters

This action has the following parameters (**Figure 11.28**):

Action. Because you can use this menu choice either to duplicate or remove a movie-clip instance, this parameter lets you choose which action to perform:

Duplicate Movie Clip. Makes a duplicate movie clip instance out of the target defined in the next parameter.

Remove Movie Clip. Removes a previously created duplicate. Because this action deletes a movie clip, the "New name" and "Depth" parameters are grayed out when it is selected.

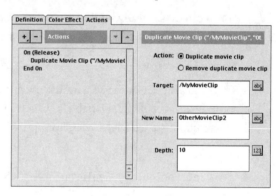

Figure 11.28
Available parameters for the Duplicate/Remove Movie Clip action.

Target. Use this parameter to define the path of the movie-clip instance you wish to duplicate or remove. For more information about paths, see "Working with Multiple Movies" in this chapter.

You can dynamically choose the target based on the value an expression evaluate to. Click the "abc" button to activate the Expression Editor. For more information, see "Using Expressions" in this chapter.

New Name. Lets you set the name of the duplicated movie-clip instance. You only need to enter a name, not a directory path. The duplicated movie clip inherits the same relative path as the original.

You can dynamically name the duplicated movie-clip instance based on the value an expression evaluates to. Click the "abc" button to activate the Expression Editor.

Depth. Depth is a numerical value that represents the stacking depth in which the duplicated movie-clip instance is placed in relation to other duplicated movie-clip instances within the same movie load level. For example, the main movie represents Level 0, or the bottom movie. All other movies appear on top of the main movie. If other movies exist on Levels 1, 2, 3, and so on (see Load/Unload Movie action), a duplicate won't replace a loaded movie on any of these levels even if you duplicate it to depth 1, 2, 3 and so on. A duplicate always appears above the original.

You can choose the depth of the duplicated movie clip instance based on the value an expression evaluates to. Click the "abc" button to activate the Expression Editor.

Sample script

The following script shows a mouse event that causes the movie-clip instance named MyMovieClip to be duplicated. Placed on Level 2, the duplicate is named MyMovieClipClone. When the duplicate is created, its *x* position is changed so that the duplicate doesn't appear directly over the original:

```
On (Release)
   Duplicate Movie Clip ("/MyMovieClip", "MyMovieClipClone", 2)
Set Property ("/MyMovieClipClone",X Position) = 200
End On
```

The following script shows a mouse event on a different button that causes MyMovieClipClone to be removed:

```
On (Release)
   Remove Movie Clip ("/MyMovieClipClone")
End On
```

Real-world use

Use for games or any time you would like movie elements to be dynamically created.

Drag Movie Clip

The Drag Movie Clip action allows users to move a movie-clip instance anywhere in the movie window, which means they can reposition elements of your movie while it's running. The movie-clip instance moves in conjunction with the user's pointer (**Figure 11.29**).

Parameters

This action has the following parameters (**Figure 11.30**):

Figure 11.29
Flash now facilitates drag-and-drop behavior.

Start Drag Operation. Causes the targeted movie clip instance to be dragged (see below). The movie-clip instance will then remain draggable until an event triggers the "Stop drag operation" or another movie clip instance is made draggable. (Only one movie clip instance can be dragged at a time.)

Target. This is where you define which movie-clip instance you wish to be dragged.

You can dynamically choose the target to drag based on the value an expression evaluates to. Click the "abc" button to activate the Expression Editor. For more information, see "Using Expressions" in this chapter.

Constrain to rectangle. By default, the Drag action allows the dragged movie-clip instance to be moved anywhere within the movie window. Using this option, you can restrict its movement to a rectangular area. The left, top, right, and bottom values you enter are based in pixels and relative to the center point of the movie clip's parent (see "Working with Multiple Movies" for more information about parents). When you use this option, you cannot drag the center point of the dragged movie-clip instance beyond this perimeter (**Figure 11.31**).

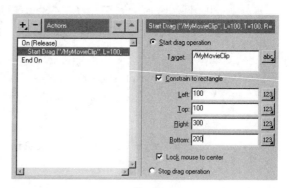

Figure 11.30
Available parameters for the Drag Movie Clip action.

You can dynamically set the coordinates of the constrain rectangle based on the value an expression evaluates to. Click the "123" button to activate the Expression Editor.

Lock Mouse to Center. By default, the movie clip being dragged retains its position relative to the user's pointer when the drag operation began. Selecting this option positions the dragged movie-clip instance directly beneath the center of the pointer while it is moved.

Stop Drag Operation. Halts the drag operation, leaving the movie-clip instance in the position it occupied when the Stop Drag action was triggered.

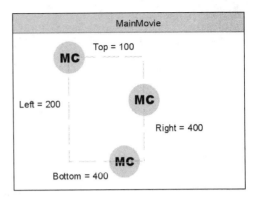

Figure 11.31
Constraining the movement of a movie clip to a rectangle prevents its center from moving beyond the perimeter of the rectangle, based on the dimensions you set.

Sample script

The following script shows a mouse event that causes the movie-clip instance named MyMovieClip to be dragged while being locked in center position with the pointer. As long as this mouse event continues, the movie clip will continue to be dragged. When the second mouse event occurs, the dragging stops.

```
On (Press)
    Start Drag ("/MyMovieClip", lockcenter)
End On
On (Release Outside)
    Stop Drag
End On
```

The following script shows a mouse event that causes MyMovieClip to be dragged within a rectangular area while being locked in center position with the pointer. As long as this mouse event continues, the drag will continue. When the second mouse event occurs, the dragging stops.

```
On (Press)
    Start Drag ("/MyMovieClip", L=250, T=200, R=450, B=400, lockcenter)
End On
On (Release Outside)
    Stop Drag
End On
```

Real-world use

Use for games, drag-and-drop functionality, customizable interfaces, scroll bars, and sliders.

Trace

When an action is performed, this action outputs a custom message—which does not appear in your final movie and has no effect on the rest of the script. This is useful to get a behind-the-scenes look at how your script is functioning—primarily to test interactivity. See Chapter 12, "Testing," for more information.

Parameters

Trace has no parameters other than the message it creates.

You can dynamically create the message based on the value an expression evaluates to. Click the "abc" button to activate the Expression Editor. For more information, see "Using Expressions" in this chapter.

Sample script

The following script shows a mouse event that causes the Count variable to be updated by a value of 1 each time the mouse event occurs and (if testing in Flash's testing environment) the trace message to be output to the Output window:

```
On (Release)
    Set Variable: "Count" = Count+1
    Trace ("The variable is now " & Count)
End On
```

To see a Trace command output to the output window, choose Control > Test Scene or Test Movie. Whenever the event is triggered that your trace is associated with, the Output box in the testing environment will open automatically and display the trace message.

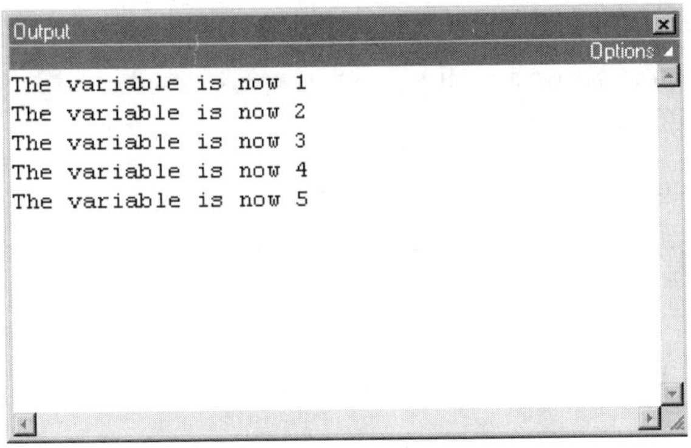

Figure 11.32
The Output box in the Flash testing environment will display any Trace messages you have set up to help test the flow and execution of your ActionScript.

In the testing environment, the trace in the script above will output the set of messages shown in **Figure 11.32**.

Real-world use

To ensure that variables are being updated at the right time and in the correct fashion, and to check the functionality of an ActionScript.

Comment

You can place comments—which are not exported and have no effect on your movie—in your script to help clarify its underlying logic.

Working with Actions

As you've just learned, actions can perform many powerful tasks in your movie. Understanding some of the basic principles of how to work with them can go a long way toward making your own creations more powerful.

Adding actions

Adding an action to an event is a fundamental aspect of making your Flash movie interactive. Although adding actions is usually straightforward, you need to consider a few things when setting them up.

First, Flash can perform multiple actions for any event that may occur. For example, if you want a single mouse event to send the current timeline to Frame 15 while also setting the transparency property of the MyMovieClip movie-clip instance to 50 percent, you would follow the steps outlined below.

To add multiple actions to a single event:

1. Double-click a button to set up a mouse event trigger, or double-click a keyframe to set up a frame event trigger.

For the purpose of our demonstration, select a button.

The Instance Properties dialog box appears.

2. Click the Action tab.

3. Click the plus ("+") button to display the action menu.

4. Since we want a Roll Over mouse event to trigger our action, select the On Mouse Event menu item.

The parameters for this appear on the right side of the Action dialog box.

5. Check the Roll Over checkbox.

Our mouse event is now set. The Action pane displays our mouse event, which appears highlighted.

6. Click the plus ("+") button again, and select the Go To action.

The parameters for this action appear on the right side of the Action dialog box.

7. With the Frame Number radio button selected, enter 15 in the adjacent text box.

8. Click the plus ("+") button to display the list of actions, and select Set Property.

The parameters for this action appear on the right side of the Action dialog box.

9. From the Set list at the top of the Parameters pane, choose Alpha.

10. In the Target box below, enter the target whose property you want to change.

For our demonstration, enter /MyMovieClip, which is our target's name and path (for more information about target names and paths, see "Working with Multiple Timelines" later in this chapter).

11. In the Value box enter the number 50.

12. Click OK.

The button is now configured to perform multiple actions at once.

You could also set it up so that on a single instance of a button, one mouse event did one thing and another did something else The following script borrows from our example; however, instead of using a Roll Over event to trigger both actions, in this script a Roll Over event triggers one action, and a Roll Out event triggers another.

```
On (Roll Over)

   Go To and Stop (15)

End On

On (Roll Out)

   Set Property ("/MyMovieClip", Alpha) = 50

End On
```

A word about nested actions

Nesting is not a difficult concept; however, it is important. By themselves, some Flash actions don't do much. A Tell Target action, for example, allows you to set a target to perform an action; however, a secondary action must tell the target what to do. Using one action within another in this way is known as nesting. Nested actions are indented in the Action pane so that you can identify them as such (**Figure 11.33**).

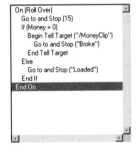

```
On (Roll Over)
   Go to and Stop (15)
   If (Money = 0)
      Begin Tell Target ("/MoneyClip")
         Go to and Stop ("Broke")
      End Tell Target
   Else
      Go to and Stop ("Loaded")
   End If
End On
```

Figure 11.33
Nested actions appear indented in the Action pane so that they are easier to locate.

How you nest actions can affect the way your ActionScript performs. Take a look at the following script:

```
On (Release)

   Tell Target ("/MyMovieClip")

      Go To and Play (20)

   End Tell Target

End On
```

In the preceding script, the Go To action is nested in the Tell Target action, which is nested in the On (Release) mouse event. This script causes MyMovieClip's timeline to go to and play Frame 20 when the On (Release) mouse event occurs. Compare that with the following script:

```
On (Release)

Tell Target ("/MyMovieClip")

End Tell Target

Go To and Play (20)

End On
```

Although this script contains the same ingredients as the previous one, it works differently because the actions are not nested. This script is triggered by a *frame event* (rather than a mouse event), which causes the *current* timeline (not the MyMovieClip timeline), to go to and play Frame 20. The mouse event and Tell Target actions in this script are useless.

The following actions are "nestable," which means they usually require a second nested action to affect the script. Nestable actions always have an accompanying End statement that is automatically inserted into the script, as in the following:

```
Tell Target
    Tell target to do what?
End Tell Target

If Frame is Loaded
    Then do what?
End Frame Loaded

On Mouse Event
    Do What?
End On

If (something is True or False)
    Do What?
End If

Loop While (something is True or False)
    Repeatedly this:
End Loop
```

> **TIP** See "Sequence of Actions" in this section for information about moving actions up or down in the script for nesting purposes.

Deleting actions

If you've found that you've put an action somewhere that it doesn't belong, you can easily remove it from the Action pane.

To delete an action:

Select the action in the Action pane, and click the "-" button at the top of it.

TIP *If you select a command that includes nested actions (such as an On Mouse Event, Tell Target or If statement, all nested actions are removed as well (Figure 11.34).*

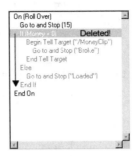

Figure 11.34
Deleting the top-level action in a nest removes all actions nested below it.

Sequence of actions

In Flash—just as in life—actions need to be performed in a specific order for things to take place in a logical and coherent manner. Flash executes actions, from top to bottom, in the order that they appear in the Action pane. If the sequence of actions there isn't quite right, your script may not perform the way you intended.

Take, for example, the following scripts; the first shows the proper order:

```
On (Release)
    Set Variable: "DynamicFrame" = 20
    Go To and Play (DynamicFrame)
End On
```

This script shows a mouse event that creates a variable named DynamicFrame with a value of 20. Once that variable is created, a Go To action is set up to go to a frame number based on the value of DynamicFrame. Because DynamicFrame has been assigned a value of 20, the Go To action will go to Frame 20. This is the proper sequence. In comparison, look at the following script, which switches things around a bit:

```
On (Release)
    Go To and Play (DynamicFrame)
    Set Variable: "DynamicFrame" = 20
End On
```

This script shows a mouse event that triggers a Go To action that is set to go to a frame number based on the value of DynamicFrame. Problem is, according to the sequence of actions, DynamicFrame has not yet been created. In fact, it will not be created until *after* the Go To action; thus, the Go To action does nothing.

The moral here is to be aware of the order in which actions are performed. That order could mean the difference between the success and failure for your script.

To reorder actions:

1. In the Action pane, click once to select the action you want to reorder.

2. Click the up- or down-arrow buttons at the top right of the Action pane to move the action up or down in the overall sequence (**Figure 11.35**).

Cutting, copying, and pasting actions

If you've created the perfect sequence of actions on a keyframe or button and you wish to use it elsewhere, you don't need to redo your efforts. You can simply cut (or copy) and paste.

To cut (or copy) and paste actions:

1. In the Action pane select the actions you wish to cut or copy:

   To select a single action, click it once.

   To select multiple actions, hold down the Control key (Windows) or Command key (Macintosh) while clicking multiple actions.

   To select a range of actions, click the first action in the range, and then hold down the Shift key and click the last action in the range (**Figure 11.36**).

2. Right-click (Windows) or Control-click (Macintosh) a selected action, and from the menu that appears choose Cut or Copy to place the selected action or actions on the system clipboard.

3. Click OK to close the Action dialog box.

Figure 11.35
Press the up- or down-arrow keys above the Action pane to reorder actions.

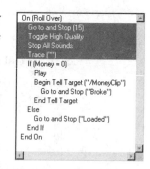

Figure 11.36
You can select a range of actions for cutting, copying, or pasting.

4. Double-click the button or keyframe where you would like to paste these actions.

   Depending on what you double-click, the Instance or Frame dialog box appears.

5. Click the Action tab to make it active.

6. In the Action pane, right-click (Windows) or Control-click (Macintosh), and from the menu that appears choose Paste.

   The cut or copied actions now appear in the current Action pane.

Working with Multiple Movies

It stands to reason that a single Flash movie window, which can contain many movies (the main movie, any movie-clip instances, or any movies loaded into the main movie by means of the Load Movie Action), can include multiple timelines. Each of these movies is a separate entity with its own timeline, variables, and properties. And each is identified in a unique way (**Figure 11.37**).

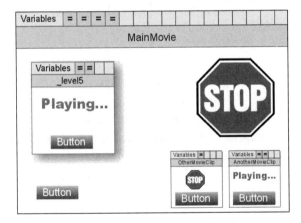

Figure 11.37
The main movie can act independently of any movie clips or levels and vice-versa.

As you've learned, mouse and frame events in one timeline can affect the movement, properties, and variables of any other present timeline. Thus, when you use multiple movie clips simultaneously, you can target multiple timelines to perform an action, providing almost unlimited versatility.

A movie-clip instance can only be targeted while it is present. For example, if a particular movie-clip instance is available in your movie only for 40 frames, it can be considered a target only for those 40 frames.

In addition, you must specifically target a movie if it is to react to events in another movie. Let's look in detail at how to do that.

TIP *Assigning movie-clip instances names so that they can be targeted is discussed in Chapter 7, "Symbols."*

Identifying Targets in ActionScripts

To target a specific timeline, you need to address it. This is accomplished one of four ways: Blank, with a name, with a level number, or with a level and name. This may seem confusing, so let's look at each of these in a little more detail.

Blank

When a target name or level number does not preface an action, the target is understood to be the current movie or timeline. For more information on what is considered to be the current movie, see "Targets" earlier in this chapter.

Targeting the current movie could look like this:

```
On (Release)
    Set Variable: "Derek" = 32
End On
```

Name

You assign names to instances of movie clips to identify them in ActionScripts (see "Defining an Instance" in Chapter 7). By so doing, you make it possible to control them via ActionScripts. An event in the main movie can cause a movie clip to jump to a frame on its timeline, make the movie clip invisible, rotate it, and so on. In contrast, a movie clip that has not been named can play as normal but cannot be targeted. You can give different instances of the same movie clip unique names so that they can be targeted separately (**Figure 11.38**).

And because a movie clip is essentially a Flash movie with its own graphics, buttons, sounds, and timeline, one movie clip can control another via button/keyboard and frame events. A movie clip can even control the main movie.

Figure 11.38
Separate instances of the same movie clip can be targeted differently and act independently of one another if given different names.

When targeting a movie clip in an ActionScript, you must spell its name correctly, but it does not have to be case sensitive (that is, *MyMovieClip* is the same as *mymovieclip.*)

Targeting a movie-clip instance can look like this:

```
On (Press)
    Tell Target ("/MyMovieClip")
        Go To and Stop (20)
    End Tell Target
End On
```

Targeting a movie clip instance inside another movie clip instance would look something like this:

```
On (Press)
    Tell Target ("/MyMovieClip/AnotherMovieClip")
        Go To and Stop (20)
    End Tell Target
End On
```

The "/" before the name of the movie clip denotes the movie clip's directory path. For more information, see "Target Paths" later in this section.

Levels

Whenever you use the Load/Unload Movie action, you are essentially loading another SWF file into an already existing one. This action gives you the option of loading the file onto a specific level such as 1 or 20 or something else. By identifying the level on which you want your move to reside, you make its timeline (and the timelines of any of the movie clips within it) available for targeting. If, for example, you load a movie into Level 5, its content would appear above content in Levels 0 through 4 (0 being the original or main movie).

Targeting a level's main timeline can look like this:

```
On (Release)
    Tell Target ("_level5")
        Go To and Stop (25)
    End Tell Target
End On
```

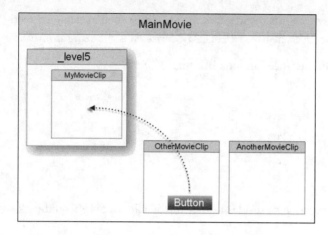

Figure 11.39
Movie clips on any level can be targeted from any other timeline.

Targeting a movie clip instance on another level would look something like this (**Figure 11.39**):

```
On (Release)
  Tell Target ("_level5/MyMovieClip")
    Go To and Stop (25)
  End Tell Target
End On
```

Target paths

In addition to a name, you need an address—or *target path*—to target something in Flash. If you know how to set up hyperlinks on a Web page, you should find learning about target paths a breeze.

In Flash, target paths are based on a hierarchical structure—the same type of structure used to organize the files on your computer or a server.

To help you understand how target paths are derived, let's consider an analogy. You can think of your Flash project in the form of a family structure with your main movie as being the *mother* movie. Now mom has some kids, and she names them Joe, Lucy, and Bob. In Flash, these kids represent movie clip instances inside the main movie and are called *child* movies (see sidebar "Parent-Child Relationships").

Parent-Child Relationships

Just as a real family is built on a hierarchy of parents, children, and even children's children, a Flash movie can contain several movies, any of which can contain several more movies. The relationship between all of these movies is considered a parent-child relationship. A parent is a movie that contains other movies, or children. For example, a parent movie may contain children even though it is a child of another movie itself.

The important thing to realize here is that when you change a parent's properties, its children inherit the same properties. For example, if you make a parent movie transparent, all of its children become transparent. However, the reverse is not true: Changing the properties of a child will not affect its parent.

The following shows how our "family" structure would look within Flash (**Figure 11.40**):

Mother (_level0)

    /Joe

    /Lucy

    /Bob

If you clicked a button in the "Mother" movie to make Lucy invisible, the target path in the script might look like the following:

```
On (Release)
   Tell Target ("/Lucy")
      Set Property ("", Visibility) = 0
   End Tell Target
End On
```

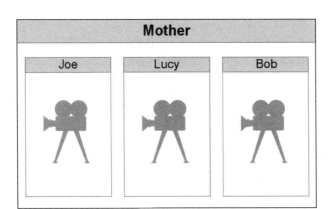

Figure 11.40
The various timelines present within the Flash Player window at any given time can be thought of as a family structure with parent movies containing other movies, or children.

The script below does exactly the same thing but without the Tell Target command. Instead, the target path is actually part of the Set Property statement (both ways work equally well):

```
On (Release)
  Set Property ("/Lucy", Visibility) = 0
End On
```

Now, let's say that Joe has a couple of kids himself. He decides to name them Junior and Youngster. If Joe represents a movie-clip instance, his "kids" represent movie-clip instances within a movie-clip instance.

The overall family structure now looks like this:

Mother (_level0)

    /Joe

        /Junior

        /Youngster

    /Lucy

    /Bob

With this in mind, if you clicked a button in the Mother movie that made Joe's child Junior invisible, the target path in the script would look like the following:

```
On (Release)
  Tell Target ("/Joe/Junior")
    Set Property ("" , Visibility) = 0
  End Tell Target
End On
```

Now let's initiate some power struggles within the family: Mother isn't the only one in control here. Joe can tell Lucy to do something; Bob can tell Junior to do something; and even Youngster can tell Mother (or in his case, grandmother) to do something.

Look at the following illustration and the accompanying sample target paths (**Figure 11.41**):

For a mouse or frame event in Mother to target:

Joe, Lucy, or *Bob.* The target path would be "/Joe" or "/Lucy" or "/Bob".

Junior or *Youngster.* The target path would be "/Joe/Junior" or "/Joe/Youngster".

Figure 11.41
This illustration should help you visualize the hierarchical structure when targeting various movies.

For a mouse or frame event in Bob to target:

Mother. The target would be "../".

Lucy or *Joe.* The target path would be "/Lucy" or "/Joe".

Junior or *Youngster.* The target path would be "/Joe/Junior" or "/Joe/Youngster".

For a mouse or frame event in Lucy to target:

Mother. The target would be "../".

Bob or *Joe.* The target path would be "/Bob" or "/Joe".

Junior or *Youngster.* The target path would be "/Joe/Junior" or "/Joe/Youngster".

For a mouse or frame event in Joe to target:

Mother. The target would be "../".

Lucy or *Bob.* The target path would be "/Lucy" or "/Bob".

Junior or *Youngster.* The target path would be "Junior" or "Youngster".

For a mouse or frame event in Junior to target:

Mother. The target would be "../../".

Lucy or *Bob.* The target path would be "../../Lucy" or "../../Bob".

Joe. The target path would be "../"

Youngster. The target path would be "../Youngster".

For a mouse or frame event in Youngster to target:

Mother. The target would be "../../".

Lucy or *Bob.* The target path would be "../../Lucy" or "../../Bob".

Joe. The target path would be "../"

Junior. The target path would be "../Junior".

The last target paths we're going to look at are those created whenever a new SWF file is loaded into the Flash movie window using the Load/Unload Movie action.

Whenever a new movie (in addition to the main movie already present) is loaded into the Flash movie window, it is given a level number. The original movie is automatically assigned Level 0. Any new movie loaded into a level can be thought of as another parent movie containing child movies.

For our analogy, the structure of a loaded movie placed on level 5 would look like this:

Mother (_level5)

/Kathy

/Ashlie
/Carla

/Jack
/Liz

As you can see, in addition to our original "family" on Level 0, a new family exist on Level 5 (**Figure 11.42**).

To target the main timeline of the movie on Level 5 from any other movies loaded into the Flash Player window, your script might look like this:

```
On (Release)
   Tell Target ("_level5")
      Go To and Stop (10)
   End Tell Target
End On
```

To target the movie clip named Ashlie (which is contained in the movie on Level 5) from any other movie within the Flash Player window, your script might look like this:

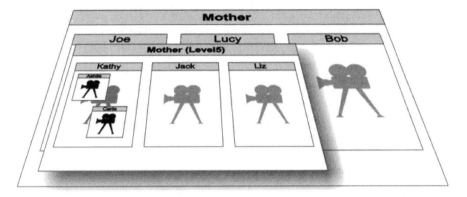

Figure 11.42
Loading another movie into Flash Player introduces a whole new hierarchy.

```
On (Release)
   Tell Target ("_level5/Kathy/Ashlie")
      Go To and Stop ("Bed")
   End Tell Target
End On
```

> **TIP** *Whenever targeting a movie or movie clip on another level, you must always include "_level" and the level number in the target path.*

Target Editor

Flash includes a utility called the Target Editor to help you define target paths. The Target Editor is a visual tool that shows the hierarchy of a movie. You can access it via the following commands and actions: Tell Target, Load/Unload Movie (when loading to a target), Set Property, Duplicate/Remove Movie Clip, and Drag Movie Clip.

To use the Target Editor:

1. Choose the Tell Target command, or select an action where a target must be defined.

2. Click the "abc" button next to the Target parameter box, and then select the Target Editor (**Figure 11.43**).

Figure 11.43
The Target Editor is available anywhere that a target should be defined.

A dialog box appears with a directory of available movie clip targets. If a plus sign ("+") appears next to a movie-clip instance's name, that movie clip has an associated child movie clip. Click the plus sign to expand the directory.

3. Double click a target's name to have it automatically entered as the target.

Only child movie-clip instances of the current movie are available in this box. If you wish to target a parent movie clip or another child, you must enter its path manually.

Setting and getting properties

You perform two essential tasks with a movie's properties: setting them and getting them. To perform either task, you need the movie's name and path.

Setting properties involves changing a movie's property in some way when an event is triggered. The following script shows a frame event in Mother that sets the transparency of the movie clip Junior to 50:

```
Set Property ("/Joe/Junior",Alpha) = 50
```

Or this script:

```
Tell Target ("/Joe/Junior")
    Set Property ("" ,Alpha) = 50
End Tell Target
```

Note that in the above script, the name and path conventions you learned earlier are used in the same way to target a movie so that you can work with its properties.

Getting a movie's properties allows you to evaluate its current state and act accordingly. Continuing with our previous analogy, the following script shows a mouse event in the main movie (Mother) that checks to see if Junior's height is greater than 200. If it is, the width of his parent, Joe, will be set to 20; if not, Joe will be set to 50:

```
On (Roll Over)
    If (GetProperty("/Joe/Junior",_height) > 200)
        Set Property ("/Joe",_width) = 20
    Else
        Set Property ("/Joe",_width) = 50
    End If
End On
```

You don't need to use the Get Property function to obtain the current movie's properties. You only need to use this function when an event in one movie triggers the action to get the properties of another movie. If you wanted to evaluate the state of the current movie (see "Targets" earlier in this chapter), your script might look like this:

```
On (Roll Out)
   If (_alpha > 50)
      Set Property ("", Alpha) = 100
   End If
End On
```

The above script checks the transparency of the current movie, and if it's more then 50 percent transparent, the Set Property action sets that number back to 100 percent. You don't need to identify the current movie in the If statement because the script understands that if a target is not defined, the current movie is the target.

Identifying frame labels

When using the Call action, you need to define the frame label you wish to call. You can call a frame label from any present timeline. To define a frame label, you first need to define the name and path to its timeline, follow it with a colon and then the frame label itself. The following script shows a Call action in the main movie that targets the frame labeled HisRoom in the movie clip Junior (from our previous example):

```
Call ("/Joe/Junior:HisRoom")
```

To target a frame label in the current movie, you only need the frame label:

```
Call ("MyFrame")
```

ActionScripting

Welcome to Flash ActionScripting! You can think of ActionScripting as a basic programming language. With it you program your Flash movies to perform tasks. As with most programming languages, in ActionScripting terms (or words) provide meaning, order lends structure, and punctuation provides context. This may not make sense now, but just hang in there with us, it will become clearer soon.

Variables

Variables make up a basic and important part of just about any programming script. They are, in fact, what facilitates the dynamic software we use today. When creating interactivity with ActionScripting it is no different.

A variable is basically a container that holds a value. Although you may not always be conscious of them, your life is composed of variables. Take, for example, the following:

X = 25

Name = Derek

Age = 29

Income = 500

Best Band = The Beatles

IQ = 47

X, Name, Age, Income, BestBand, and IQ are all variable names, and the information that follows the equal sign is the value of that variable. In ActionScripting the same principles apply. When using the Set Variable action, you might create several variables, as the following script indicates:

```
Set Variable: "Name" = "Derek"
Set Variable: "Age" = 29
Set Variable: "Income" = 500
```

When creating and naming variables in Flash, be aware of the following:

All variable names must begin with a character. The characters that follow can be letters, digits, or underscores. In addition, names are not case-sensitive; so, *MyVariable* is the same as *myvariable.* Names cannot contain spaces. Quotation marks enclose variable names only when you have used the Set Variable action to assign them (Flash inserts them automatically); they do not enclose variables names when used in expressions (see "Using Expressions" later in this chapter).

Each movie or movie clip has a unique set of variables. The variables in a timeline continue to exist, and their values can be set or retrieved, as long as the timeline is present.

An editable text box is assigned a variable name in a different manner than all other variables. Whereas you use the Set Variable action to assign most variable names, text fields are assigned names as one of their properties. The value of a text field (the text it displays) is determined by text the user enters while the movie is playing, or it can be dynamically generated using the Set Variable action. For more information, see "Working with Text Fields" later in this section.

Even though a variable's value may change, its name will always remain the same. For example, at one point in your movie the value of *x* might be 25, and later in your movie it might be 720.

Variable names should make sense. If a variable holds a value for the number of times the user has clicked a mouse button, you could name that variable MouseClicks or something similar.

Values

In Flash, variable values can take the following forms:

Numbers. A number value refers to anything from 0 to 999,999+. An Age variable might have a value of 20, which in ActionScript would look like:

```
Set Variable: "Age" = 20
```

Strings. The term *string* is commonly used in programming languages to denote text values. Typical string values can include anything from "a" to "Hello, what's your name? Does your dog bite, or is it a nice dog?" A string value can contain almost any number of letters (within reason) and can include text, spaces, punctuation, and even numbers. The value "345" can even be thought of as a string value even though it involves numbers. String values that contain numbers are distinguished from actual number values through the use of quotation marks—that is, ActionScripting uses quotation marks to denote strings. Thus, while 1966 is considered a number value, "1966" is considered a string value. Variables that contain string values might look like the following:

```
Set Variable: "PhraseThatPays" = "Flash 4 Rocks!"

Set Variable: "FavoriteWife" = "Kathy"

Set Variable: "FavoriteWifesAge" = "Always 29"
```

Boolean. This type of value refers to whether a condition exists. The two possible Boolean values are True and False. In Flash, False has the numerical equivalent of 0, and True can be any nonzero number. Assigning a Boolean value to a variable in Flash would look something like this:

```
Set Variable: "MacromediaRocks" = True

Set Variable: "MacromediaRocks" = 1
```

Nothing. Though not really a value, this defines the *absence* of a string value. For example, If you can't remember someone's name, your memory as an ActionScript variable might look like this:

```
Set Variable: "Memory" = ""
```

Assigning values

A value is assigned two ways to a variable, either as a "literal" or as an "expression." Take a look at the following *literal* assignments:

```
Set Variable: "Cost" = 25.00
```

Or this one:

```
Set Variable: "Name" = "John Doe"
```

Notice that the values assigned to the variables are not really dynamic. For example, if you wanted to use the value of Cost elsewhere in your ActionScript, it would always have a value of 25.00. Likewise, the value of Name would always be John Doe. Not very exciting. To create more dynamically assigned values, you could use an expression instead. For example:

```
Set Variable: "Product" = 20.00

Set Variable: "Tax" = 5.00

Set Variable: "Cost" = Product + Tax
```

In the preceding script, the value of the Cost variable is Product + Tax—themselves variables. To break Cost into its most basic parts, it could be read "Cost" = 20.00 + 5.00, which would total 25.00. However, if the value of Product changed to 22.00 and the value of Tax became 6.00, the value of Cost would automatically become 28.00 because it's based on the value of Product + Tax. A *literal* is a value explicitly and definitively assigned to a variable, whereas an *expression* is a value based on a phrase that is evaluated (see "Using Expressions" later in this chapter). Here's another example where the value of the variable "Name" is based on an expression:

```
Set Variable: "FirstName" = "John"

Set Variable: "LastName" = "Doe"

Set Variable: "Name" = FirstName & LastName
```

To create a variable and assign it a value:

1. Doulble-click a button instance on the stage or a keyframe on the timeline.

Depending on what you clicked, the Instance or Frame Properties box appears.

2. Click the Action tab.

3. Click the plus ("+") button, and choose Set Variable from the menu that appears.

The Set Variable parameters appears on the right side of the Action dialog box.

4. In the Variable box enter a name to describe the variable.

Do not include quotes; Flash does so automatically.

5. In the Value box, you need to make a choice:

If the value of this variable will be a text string, just enter it (without quotes) into the box. The button to the right of this box shows "abc," which means it treats whatever you enter as a string value (even if you enter something like 465).

If you wish this value to be treated as a number, Boolean value, or even an expression, click the "abc" button, and choose "=" instead (**Figure 11.44**). If you look in the Action pane while you're doing this, you'll see that the quotation marks are removed from the value portion of the assignment (which is necessary when assigning a number, Boolean, or expression as a value).

```
Set Variable: "MyVariable" = "40 +20"
Set Variable: "MyVariable" = 40 + 20
```

Figure 11.44
Removing the quotations from a variable value identifies its value as a number, Boolean, or expression instead of a text string.

6. Click OK.

When the movie is played, this variable is created and becomes part of the current timeline whenever the button is clicked or the frame is reached where you set up the Set Variable action in Step 1.

Setting and getting variable values for different timelines

You can use the Set Variable action to create or update a variable for any movie in the Flash Player window (including movie clips and loaded movies). Just prefix the name of the variable with the path of the timeline when entering the variable's name as described in Step 4 of the previous exercise. For example:

```
/MyMovieClip:MyVariable
```

If you wished to address a variable in a parent movie from one of its "children", it would look more like this:

```
../:MyVariable
```

You apply much the same principle when using variable values from various timelines in expressions. If you wish to create an expression in one timeline using the value of a variable in another, simply use the same syntax found in the previous example. Take a look at the following:

```
If (/MyMovieClip:MyVariable + 50 = 300)
    Go To and Play (20)
End If
```

The passing of variable values between movies (or timelines) is an integral part of using the Call action. At times, this action allows a set of actions on one timeline to evaluate and manipulate variable values from another and then send the manipulated and evaluated variable values back to the originating movie. When using this action, the transfer of variable values between timelines is not automatic; you must send variable data back and forth using the Set Variable action and the proper syntax.

> **TIP** *For more information about creating and using expressions, see "Using Expressions" in this chapter.*

Updating variable values

Once you have created a variable, its value remains available as long as the timeline it's a part of remains present. Think of variables as existing in some invisible place that you'll never see, although they are there whether the timeline is moving or not.

At times, you'll want to update a variable's value—for example, if you want to change its literal value from Joe to Fred, or if you want an expression value updated to track how many times a button had been clicked.

Say an event triggered the creation of the variable described earlier in the exercise for creating a variable. When you created this variable, you named it MyVariable and gave it a value of Hello. If you want to change its value to Goodbye at some point while the movie is playing, you would simply attach another Set Variable action to a mouse or frame event that identifies MyVariable as the variable and Goodbye as the new value it should be updated to. Just remember that when using the Set variable action, Flash checks to see if a variable with the name you assigned already exists. If it doesn't, it creates one; if it does, Flash updates it.

You can update expression-based variable values on a mouse or frame event *without* using another Set Variable action. Take a look at the following script:

```
On (Release)
   Set Variable: "Count" = Count + 1
End On
```

The preceding script updates the value of Count by 1 each time the mouse event occurs. This is because the value of Count is an expression, and the logic behind the expression goes something like this:

When the mouse event occurs, the value of Count equals the current value of Count, plus 1.

To do this, get the current value of count.

The current value is 15 (you can't see this, but take our word for it).

OK, it's 15 so add 1 to it to make it 16.

The next time this mouse event occurs, Flash will check the current value of Count, which is now 16, and then add 1 to it again to make it 17.

The string value of a text field is always displayed in the field, and is updated constantly. Thus, if a text field displays the word *Mushroom,* this is the value of the field; however, if your user types *tomato* into that field, it automatically becomes the new value.

Working with text fields

As you learned in Chapter 4, "Text," text fields are dynamic blocks of text identified by a variable name. You can use this variable name in ActionScripts to evaluate the text your user has typed in a text field. You can also use the variable name to dynamically generate the text that's displayed in the field itself.

For example, imagine a text field on the stage with a variable name of Food. Someone has entered the word *Burger* in it. A button is pushed, and the script below is executed:

```
On (Release)
   If (Food eq "Burger")
      Go To and Play ("Diet")
   Else If (Food eq "Salad")
      Go To and Play ("EatUp")
   End If
End On
```

This script would evaluate that Food equals Burger and cause the timeline to go to the frame labeled Diet.

If you wanted to dynamically generate a message displayed in a text field with a variable name of Message, you could use the following ActionScript (which is triggered by a mouse event). This ActionScript would generate a message based on the text that was entered into a different text field with a variable name of Name. For our demonstration, we enter *Ashlie* in this field:

```
On (Release)
    Set Variable: "Message" = "Hello," & Name & ",
    is your homework finished? "
End On
```

This script would generate the following message in the text field with a variable name of Message when the mouse event occurred:

Hello, Ashlie, is your homework finished?

Using Expressions

Expressions are the heart of any truly dynamic and interactive Flash movie, making each user's experience of your movie unique.

In Flash, an expression is a phrase, or collection of variables, numbers, text, and operators, that evaluates to a value such as a string, number, or Boolean value. Expressions are evaluated to carry out a number of tasks, including setting a variable's value, defining which targets to affect, determining what frame numbers to go to, and dragging. Take a look at the following script, which uses an expression to evaluate which frame number to go to:

```
On (Release)
    Go To and Play (24 + 26)
End On
```

The expression in the preceding script—what 24 + 26 evaluates to—would cause the timeline to jump to Frame 50. Pretty simple, don't you think? You could go even further and create a script that uses an expression to accomplish the same thing in a different way:

```
On (Release)
    Set Variable: "FavoriteNumber" = 24
    Set Variable: "SecondFavNumber" = 26
    Go To and Play (FavoriteNumber + SecondFavNumber)
End On
```

First things first

The first thing you need to determine in writing an expression is what type of value it should return. Should it be a string such as "Hello, there!" or a number such as 560 or a Boolean such as True. The value you select will depend on what you're trying to accomplish.

As you've probably noticed, many action parameters allow you to use expressions when setting their values. If you are going to do this, you need to be aware of the type of value that would normally be used for this parameter so that you can construct your expression accordingly. For example, when using the Get URL action, the URL parameter requires a value such as http://www.mydomain.com/mymovie.swf, which is a string value. If you used an expression to generate the value for this parameter, it would have to evaluate to a string. If, on the other hand, you wanted to set the value for the alpha transparency property of a movie using an expression, it would need to evaluate to a numeric value. Writing an expression that evaluated to *telephone* would not make sense, nor would the alpha setting be set properly.

Numeric Operators

When evaluating numbers (or variables with numeric values), numeric operators do things such as add and subtract. Numeric operators come in two types, arithmetic and comparison. **Table 11.2** provides a list of arithmetic numeric operators and a brief description of their functions.

Table 11.2
Arithmetic Numeric Operators

Operator	Description
+	Adds one numeric value to another numeric value
-	Subtracts one numeric value from another
*	Multiplies one numeric value by another
/	Divides one numeric value by another

Sample script

```
On (Release)
    Set Variable: "Season" = 4
    Set Variable: "Hrs" = 24
    Set Variable: "Mins" = 60
    Set Variable: "MinsASeason" =(365 / Season)*(Hrs * Mins)
End On
```

This script creates four variables and assigns them numeric values. Three of them are assigned literal values, and the forth is based on an expression. Look at this expression using actual values:

$(365 / 4) \star (24 \star 60)$

This breaks down to:

$91.25 \star 1440$

Which further breaks down to:

131400

So, the value of MinsASeason is 131400.

To understand just how dynamic you can get, look at the following script, which accomplishes the same thing as the previous one but uses two variables whose values are based on expressions.

```
On (Release)
    Set Variable: "Season" = 4
    Set Variable: "Hrs" = Season + 20
    Set Variable: "Mins" = 60
    Set Variable: "MinsASeason" =(365 / Season)*(Hrs * Mins)
End On
```

The value of Hrs is based on an expression that evaluates to 24. This value is used in the second expression in the script where the value of Hrs is multiplied by the value of Mins.

Adding and subtracting numeric values is only one way you can manipulate them. Using comparison numeric operators, you can also compare the numeric values of variables—especially when using the If and Loop While commands.

Table 11.3 provides a list of comparison numeric operators and a brief description of their functions.

Table 11.3
Comparison Numeric Operators

Operator	Description
=	Equals
<>	Not Equals
<	Less than
>	Greater than
<=	Less than or equal to
>=	Greater than or equal to

Sample script

```
On (Release)
    Set Variable: "Paycheck" = 200
    Set Variable: "Savings" = 5
    Set Variable: "Bills" = 500
    If (Paycheck + Savings >= Bills)
        Go To and Stop ("Happiness")
    Else
        Go To and Stop ("NotSoHappy")
    End If
End On
```

This script created three variables and assigned them numeric values. The If command checks whether the combined value of Paycheck and Savings is greater than or equal to the value of Bills. If it is, the timeline jumps to a frame labeled Happiness; if not, it jumps to a frame labeled NotSoHappy.

Some things to keep in mind when using numeric operators:

The evaluation of an expression follows what's known as *an order of precedence*. This term refers to the order in which parts of an expression are evaluated. Anything in parenthesis is evaluated first, then anything multiplied or divided, and then anything added or subtracted. Be keenly aware of this rule: The order can affect the end value of an expression.

If you attempt to evaluate a string using numeric operators, Flash will convert the string to a numeric value. The numeric value is based on the number of characters are in the string. For example, 10 + Hello = 15 because the string Hello contains five characters.

> **TIP** *For more on text manipulation, see the Int and Random functions discussed in the "Using Functions" section of this chapter.*

String Operators

When evaluating strings or any variables that hold text values, string operators perform such tasks as concatenation (combining strings) and comparing the values of string values.

Table 11.4 provides a list of string operators and a brief description of their functions.

Table 11.4
String Operators

Operator	Description
""	String
&	Concatenate
eq	Equals
ne	Not equals
lt	Less than
gt	Greater than
le	Less than or equal to
ge	Greater than or equal to

Sample script

Imagine four text fields on the stage with the variable names of First, Last, Age, and Message. Your user typed *John, Doe,* and *30,* respectively, in the first three fields. The user pushes a button, and the following script is executed:

```
On (Release)

    Set Variable: "Message" = "Hello," & First & Last & ".
    You appear to be " & Age & " years old. "

End On
```

When the script is executed, the variable Message displays the following phrase:

"Hello, John Doe. You appear to be 30 years old."

In the expression, the values of the variables First, Last, and Age are concatenated with literal text values surrounded by quotation marks.

Let's look at another script.

Imagine a text field on the stage with a variable name of Password. Someone has entered the text *Boom Bam* into the field. The user pushes a button, and the script below is executed:

```
On (Release)
   If (Password eq "Boom Bam")
      Go To and Stop ("Accepted")
   Else
      Go To and Stop ("AccessDenied")
   End If
End On
```

When this script has executed (based on information entered into the Password text field), the timeline will go to and stop on the frame labeled Accepted.

Note the eq string operator: It—not the equals sign (which is a numeric operator)—evaluates whether a string equals something. If you were to use the equals sign, your script would not evaluate properly.

Comparison operators used for text, such as *lt, gt, le,* and *ge,* are used to determine alphabetical order of words based on their first character. Small characters (*a* to *z*) hold greater value than capital letters (*A* to *Z*). For example, *derek* is greater than *Brooks,* but *Derek* is not.

Some things to keep in mind when using string operators:

Values of strings are case-sensitive: *kathy* does not equal *Kathy.*

Using numeric values in a string expression will cause the numeric value to be automatically converted to a string. For example, the expression "I love to eat " & 10 + 5 & "donuts a day!" results in the string "I love to eat 15 donuts a day!"

> **TIP** *For additional information on text manipulation, see the Substring, Length, Chr, and Ord functions discussed in the "Using Functions" section of this chapter.*

Logical Operators

Logical operators are used in expressions to evaluate whether certain conditions exist. They are used mostly in conjunction with the If and Loop While actions.

Table 11.5 provides a list of logical operators and a brief description of their functions.

Table 11.5
Logical Operators

Operator	Description
and	Logical AND
or	Logical OR
not	Logical NOT

Sample script

```
On (Release)
    Set Variable: "Paycheck" = 1000
    Set Variable: "Decision" = "Buy"
    If (Paycheck >= 1000 and Decision eq "Buy")
        Go To and Stop ("NewComputer")
    Else
        Go To and Stop ("Cry")
    End If
End On
```

The expression in this script checks if the numeric value of Paycheck is equal to or greater than 1000 *and* whether the string value of Decision equals Buy. If they do, go get a new computer; otherwise, cry your brains out! In this script, If evaluates to True, so it's new computer time!

As you'll notice, using a logical operator in the expression allows you to evaluate both numeric and string values and act accordingly.

Using Functions

Available from the Expression Editor, functions are built-in ActionScripting features that create and retrieve dynamic data for use in expressions. We'll look at each function, along with a sample script that uses it functionality.

The scripts that follow in no way exemplify the power available by using these functions or properties. They are simply to help clarify the way they work.

Eval

Syntax: `Eval (VariableName)`

The Eval function is useful to determine the value of a variable that is an expression itself. It allows the name of the variable evaluated to be determined while the movie is playing. This function can be a difficult concept to understand, so take a look at the script below.

```
On (Release)
    If (Eval ("GamePiece" & Number) = 50
    Actions…..
End On
```

This is the same as having an ActionScript that reads:

```
On (Release)
    If (Gamepiece7) = 50
    Actions…..
End On
```

Or an ActionScript that reads:

```
On (Release)
    If (Gamepiece2) = 50
    Actions…..
End On
```

The main difference is that the Gamepiece variable in the first script is dynamic, meaning that the game piece checked is based on the current value of the variable called Number; if that value changes, so does the game piece that is evaluated.

True

Syntax: `True`

This function assigns a Boolean value of True to a variable.

Place the following script on a button to set that it has been clicked:

```
On (Release)
    Set Variable: "Answer1Value" = True
End On
```

On another button you could check this value and take action, depending on whether it's True or False, as the following script demonstrates:

```
On (Release)
    If (Answer1Value)
        Go To and Play ("Correct")
    Else
        Go To and Play ("Wrong")
    End If
End On
```

> **TIP** *The If statement above reads "If (Answer1Value)" rather than "If (Answer1Value = True)"—simply a shorter way of expressing the same thing.*

False

Syntax: `False`

This function assigns a Boolean value of False to a variable. For an example, see the above script for the True function.

Newline

Syntax: `NewLine`

This function begins a new line in an expression.

Imagine a text field on the stage with a variable name of Name, and a user has entered the word *Jim* in the field. The user clicks a button, and the script below is executed:

```
On (Release)
    Set Variable: "Greeting" = "Hello there, "
    Set Variable: "Phrase" = Greeting & Newline & Name & "." & Newline
    & " How are you today? "
End On
```

When this script has executed, based on the information entered into the Name text field, another text field with a variable name of Phrase will display a string that looks like this:

"Hello there,

Jim.

How are you today?"

GetTimer

Syntax: `GetTimer`

The GetTimer function is useful for determining the length of time, in milliseconds, that have elapsed since your movie began playing. This value is based on your computer's system clock and is not affected if your movie's frames-per-second rate slows while playing. Individual movies playing simultaneously in the Flash movie window do not have individual timers; this is a global timer.

Use the GetTimer function to track the amount of time between events in your movie.

The following script creates a double-click behavior for a button:

```
On (Release)
    If (GetTimer - LastClick < 500)
        Go to and Stop (10)
    End If
    Set Variable: "LastClick" = GetTimer
End On
```

Int

Syntax: `Int (number)`

This function extracts the whole number from a numeric value. For example, Int (43.364) becomes 43. If a variable holds a numeric value, you can use the variable name instead of a number literal, such as Int(VariableName).

Use the Int function to eliminate decimal values in your ActionScripts.

In the following script, the expression for Total evaluates to 38:

```
On (Release)
    Set Variable: "FirstNumber" = 19.35
    Set Variable: "SecondNumber" = 2
    Set Variable: "Total" = Int (FirstNumber) * SecondNumber
End On
```

Random

Syntax: `Random (number)`

This function generates a random numeric value within a range you specify. For example, Random (300) will generate a random number between 0 and 299.

Use the Random function to create dynamic, unpredictable behavior. If a variable holds a numeric value, you can use the variable name instead of a number literal, such as Random(VariableName).

In the following script, the movie clip instance named Dice will go to a specific frame between zero and five based on the number that is randomly generated.

```
On (Release)
    Set Variable: "DiceRoll" = Random (6)
    Tell Target ("/Dice")
        Go To and Stop (DiceRoll)
    End Tell Target
End On
```

Substring

Syntax: `Substring (string, index, characters to include)`

This function extracts a portion of a string. The string parameter indicates the string to evaluate, and *index* represents the number of characters from the left of the string to use as a starting point for the extraction. *Characters to include* specifies the number of characters from the index character on.

For example, `Substring ("Macromedia", 4, 4)` evaluates to *rome. Macromedia* is the string; four characters over is *r,* and including four characters from the index equals *rome.* If the third parameter is omitted from the Substring function, all characters after the index are included. Thus, `Substring ("Macromedia", 4)` would evaluate to *romedia.*

If a variable holds a string value, you can use the variable name instead of a string literal, such as `Substring(VariableName, index, characters to include)`.

You would use the Substring function to isolate parts of strings so that they may be evaluated individually from the string itself.

Imagine a text field on the stage with a variable name of Title. A user entered the text *Dr. Frankenstein* in the field and pushes a button, and the script below is executed:

```
On (Release)
    If (Substring(Title, 1, 3) eq "Ms. ")
      Go To and Stop ("DivorceCourt")
    Else If (Substring(Title, 1, 3) eq "Dr. ")
      Go To and Stop ("TheLab")
    Else
      Go To and Stop ("HelloJunior")
End On
```

When this script has executed, based on the information entered into the text field Title, the movie will go to the frame labeled the Lab.

Length

Syntax: `Length (string)`

The Length function creates a numeric value based on the number of characters in a string. The string parameter indicates the string to evaluate. For example, `Length ("Flash")` evaluates to a numeric value of 5 because the word *Flash* is five characters. If a variable holds a string value, you can use the variable name instead of a string literal, such as `Length(VariableName)`.

You can use the Length function to easily check the length of strings—for example, to verify data that must contain a specific number of characters, such as ZIP codes and phone numbers.

Imagine a text field on the stage with a variable name of ZIPCode in which a user has entered the text *46293*. The user pushes a button, and the script below is executed:

```
On (Release)
  If (Length (ZIPCode) = 5
    Set Variable: "Message" = "That is a valid ZIP Code"
  Else
    Set Variable: "Message" = "Please enter a valid ZIP Code. "
  End If
End On
```

When this script has executed, based on the information entered into the ZIPCode text field, another text field with a variable name of Message will display the string "That is a valid ZIP Code."

Chr

Syntax: `Chr (number)`

This function converts a numeric value to its ASCII character equivalent. For example, `Chr (90)` evaluates to Z. If a variable holds a numeric value, you can use the variable name instead of a numeric literal, such as `Chr(VariableName)`.

You can use the Chr function to assign numbers to string values.

Ord

Syntax: `Ord (character)`

This function converts an ASCII character to its numeric equivalent. For example, Ord ("D") evaluates to 68. If a variable holds a string value, you can use the variable name instead of a string literal, such as `Ord(VariableName)`.

You can use the Ord function to assign numeric values to strings.

Properties

Each movie in the Flash Player window has a unique set of properties, which are constantly updated and evaluated so that ActionScripts can make dynamic decisions based on the current value of the movie property.

Properties are available from the Expression Editor.

GetProperty

Syntax: `GetProperty (target, property)`

The GetProperty function provides the current value of a movie's property. Use this function only to retrieve a property value for a movie other than the current one. For example, `GetProperty ("/MyMovieClip", _alpha)` will return a value of 50 if the movie clip named MyMovieClip is 50 percent transparent. If a variable holds a string value. Use the variable name instead of a string literal to set the target or property to evaluate, such as `GetProperty (VariableName, VariableName2)`.

Use the GetProperty function to evaluate a current property of any movie clip, so that your movie can act accordingly.

The following script evaluates the height of MyMovieClip and acts accordingly.

```
On (Release)
  If (GetProperty ("/MyMovieClip", _height)< 300)
    Set Variable: "Message" = "That's a pretty small movie clip"
  Else
    Set Variable: "Message" = "That movie clip is way too big! "
  End If
End On
```

When this script has executed, for our demonstration the height of MyMovieClip is evaluated to be more than 300; thus, a text field with a variable name of Message will display the string "That movie clip is way too big!"

_x

Syntax: _x, or when used with GetProperty, (target, _x)

The x property provides the current horizontal position of a movie clip instance. Based in pixels in the object inspector, the value is stated relative from the top left corner of the movie-clip instance to the top left corner of the movie-clip instance's parent (see the "Parent-Child Relationships" sidebar earlier in this chapter).

Selecting a movie clip and checking Use Center Point on the Object inspector will cause both x and y positions of the movie clip to be a relative amount based on the distance from the center of the movie clip to the center point of its parent (See Set Property action discussed earlier in this chapter).

The following script evaluates the current horizontal position of the current movie and acts accordingly:

```
On (Release)
  If (_x < 200)
    Set Variable: "Message" = "I'm on the left. "
  Else If (_x > 200)
    Set Variable: "Message" = "I'm on the right. "
  Else
    Set Variable: "Message" = "I'm stuck in the middle somewhere. "
  End If
End On
```

When this script has executed, the horizontal position of the current movie is evaluated to be exactly 200; thus, a text field with a variable name of Message will display the string "I'm stuck in the middle somewhere."

_y

Syntax: _y, or when used with GetProperty, (target, _y)

The y property provides the current vertical position of a movie. Based in pixels, the value is relative to the center point of the movie-clip instance's parent (see the "Parent-Child Relationships" sidebar).

Selecting a movie clip and checking Use Center Point on the Object inspector will cause both x and y positions of the movie clip to be a relative amount based on the distance from the center of the movie clip to the center point of its parent. See the script for the x property for an example of how this property works.

_width

Syntax: _width, or when used with GetProperty, (target, _width)

The width property provides the current width of a movie; its value is based in pixels.

The following script evaluates the current width of the current movie and acts accordingly.

```
On (Release)
Set Variable: "NextMeal" = 50
   If (_width + NextMeal >= 400)
     Set Variable: "Message" = "I'm too fat"
   Else If (_width + NextMeal <= 100)
     Set Variable: "Message" = "I'm too skinny. "
   Else
     Set Variable: "Message" = "I'm just right. "
   End If
End On
```

When executed, this script creates a variable named NextMeal and gives it a value of 50. The width of the current movie is determined, and the value of NextMeal is added to it. The combined total is then evaluated to determine whether it's greater than or equal to 400, less than or equal to 100, or somewhere in between. For our demonstration, the width of the movie was determined to be 230, which when combined with 50 equals 280. Thus, a text field with a variable name of Message will display the string "I'm just right."

_height

Syntax: _height, or when used with GetProperty, (target, _height)

The height property provides the current height of a movie; its value is based in pixels.

For an example of this type of script see the sample script for the width property.

_rotation

Syntax: _rotation, or when used with GetProperty, (target, _rotation)

The rotation property provides the rotation of a movie. Based in degrees, the value is relative the movie's parent.

The following script is triggered by the On (Release) mouse event. When triggered, a random numeric value between 0 and 359 is generated for the variable Spin. This value is used to set the rotation for the movie clip named MyMovieClip. In addition, the value of Spin is evaluated: If it is between 0 and 45 degrees, "You spun a 1, you win!" is displayed in a text field with the variable name of Message. Otherwise, "Try Again" is displayed.

```
On (Release)
    Set Variable "Spin" = Random (360)
    Set Property ("/MyMovieClip", Rotation) = Spin
    If ( Spin >= 0 and < 45)
        Set Variable: "Message" = "You spun a 1, you win! "
    Else
        Set Variable: "Message" = "Try again. "
    End If
End On
```

_target

Syntax: _target, or when used with GetProperty, (target, _target)

The target property provides the target name and full path of a movie clip in the form of a string value such as /MainClip/MyMovieClip.

The following script makes the current movie draggable when the On (Press) event occurs and stops it from being dragged when the On (Release) event occurs.

```
On (Press)
    Set Variable: "MovieToDrag" = _target
    Start Drag (MovieToDrag)
End On
On (Release)
    Stop Drag
End On
```

TIP *Place this script on a button that is inside a movie-clip instance to make that movie-clip instance draggable when the button is pressed.*

_name

Syntax: _name, or when used with GetProperty, (target, _name)

The name property provides the name of a movie clip in the form of a string value such as MyMovieClip. This is similar to the target property without the full path being included.

The following script evaluates the name of the current movie clip when the On (Release) mouse event occurs and then outputs it to a text-field variable named MovieName:

```
On (Release)
   Set Variable "MovieName" = _name
End On
```

The result is a text field that displays the movie's name (for example, MyMovieClip).

_url

Syntax: _url, or when used with GetProperty, (target, _url)

This property provides the complete URL for an .swf or any of its child movie clips. You are most likely to use this in conjunction with an .swf that has been loaded into the Flash Player window via the Load/Unload Movie action. For example, if an .swf were loaded into the Flash Player window from the URL http://www.mydomain.com/secondmovie.swf, checking the url property of this movie would return a string value of http://www.mydomain.com/secondmovie.swf.

Using this property ensures that others don't "borrow" your work. You can place a script on Frame 1 of a movie that checks its url property and instructs it to take one action if it was loaded from the "correct" URL and another if it was loaded from the "wrong" URL. In this way you can prevent others from stealing an .swf file from their cache and using it as their own. The following script—which is placed on Frame 1 of your movie—evaluates the url property of the current movie. It will continue to play if the URL is what it should be; if not, however, it will cease playing and jump to (and stop at) the frame labeled Denied:

```
If (Substring (_url, 1, 23) eq "http://www.myserver.com")
   Play
Else
   Go To and Stop ("Denied")
End If
```

In this script, we only need to know whether the first part of the URL, http://www.myserver.com, is what it should be. This is why the Substring function is used. It extracts the first 23 characters returned (the length of the URL you want to check may be different) and sees if they equal what they should. If they do, the movie plays. If not, the user gets sent to a frame that stops the movie from playing and that might have a message such as Access Denied.

_xscale

Syntax: _xscale, or when used with GetProperty, (target, _xscale)

This property provides the percentage a movie or movie clip has been scaled horizontally from its original size as the result of previous Set Property actions where its X Scale property was changed.

When the On (Release) mouse event occurs, the following script evaluates the amount that the movie clip /MyMovieClip has been scaled from its original size. If it is more than 100 percent, it gets reset to 100 percent; otherwise it remains its current size:

```
On (Release)
   If (GetProperty ("/MyMovieClip",_xscale) > 100)
      Set Property ("/MyMovieClip", X Scale) = 100
   End If
End On
```

_yscale

Syntax: _yscale, or when used with GetProperty, (target, _yscale)

The yscale property provides the percentage that a movie or movie clip has been scaled vertically from its original size as the result of previous Set Property actions where its yscale property was changed.

For an example of this type of script, see the xscale script sample above.

_currentframe

Syntax: _currentframe, or when used with GetProperty, (target, _current-frame)

The currentframe property provides the current frame-number position of a timeline for a movie or movie clip.

When the On (Release) mouse event occurs, the following script will send the current movie's timeline forward 20 frames from its current position:

```
On (Release)
   Go To and Stop (_currentframe + 20)
End On
```

_totalframes

Syntax: _totalframes, or when used with GetProperty, (target, _totalframes)

The totalframes property provides the number of frames in a movie or movie clip.

When the On (Release) mouse event occurs, the following script will create the variable TimeToPlay. This variable's value is based on the number of frames in the movie divided by the frame-per-second rate. The Int function is used to remove any decimal places in the calculation. The next variable, Message, is a text field that will display a message based on the value of TimeToPlay:

```
On (Release)
   Set Variable: "TimeToPlay" = Int(_totalframes / 12)
   Set Variable: "Message" = "This movie will take " & TimeToPlay" &
   " seconds to play.
End On
```

If the movie has 240 frames, a text field with a variable name of Message will display the following:

"This movie will take 20 seconds to play."

_framesloaded

Syntax: _framesloaded, or when used with GetProperty, (target, _framesloaded)

The framesloaded property provides the number of frames of a movie that have loaded. This property is similar to the If Frame is Loaded command; however, it allows the number returned to be evaluated in an expression.

This following script is placed on Frame 2 of the timeline. If the number of frames loaded exceeds 200, the timeline will jump to and begin playing Scene 2, Frame 1. Otherwise, the timeline will go to and begin playing from Frame 1 of the current scene. This causes a loop that is not broken until the number of frames loaded exceeds 200.

```
If (_framesloaded > 200)
   Go to and Play (Scene 2, 1)
Else
   Go to and Play (1)
End If
```

_alpha

Syntax: _alpha, or when used with GetProperty, (target, _alpha)

The alpha property provides a movie or movie clip's transparency (expressed as a percent).

The following script evaluates the transparency of the movie clip "dress." If the clip is more than 50 percent transparent, WearSlip? is set to True before going to DanceParty. Otherwise, you go straight to DanceParty.

```
If (GetProperty ("/Dress",_alpha) > 50)
   Set Variable: "/Dress:WearSlip? " = True)
   Go To and Play ("DanceParty")
Else
   Go To and Play ("DanceParty")
End If
```

_visible

Syntax: _visible, or when used with GetProperty, (target, _visible)

The visible property returns a Boolean value of True or False: True if visible, and False if invisible.

Triggered by a frame event, the following script checks the visibility of the movie clip Teacher. If it's not visible, the movie clip Kids is sent to a frame labeled "Recess"; otherwise Kids is sent to "Desk":

```
If (GetProperty ("/Teacher",_visible) = False)
  Tell Target ("/Kids")
    Go To and Play ("Recess")
  End Tell Target
Else
  Tell Target ("/Kids")
    Go To and Stop ("Desk")
  End Tell Target
End If
```

_droptarget

Syntax: _droptarget, or when used with GetProperty, (target, _droptarget)

The droptarget property returns the target path that a dragged movie is currently on top of (**Figure 11.45**), allowing you to emulate drag-and-drop behavior.

Figure 11.45
The droptarget property is the target path of the movie that is currently below a dragged movie. In the case of this illustration, the droptarget for /OldPC is /Trash. This property is constantly updated.

This following script emulates drag-and-drop behavior. When the mouse event On (Press) occurs, the movie clip named MyMovieClip is dragged while being centered to the pointer's position. When the On (Release Outside) mouse event occurs, dragging halts and an expression is used to evaluate the movie clip's position. The movie clip directly beneath the one that is being dragged is always considered the droptarget. In this script, when the drag operation stops, the droptarget is identified. If it equals MyTarget, MyMovieClip becomes invisible; otherwise, nothing happens.

```
On (Press)
   Start Drag ("/MyMovieClip", lockcenter)
End On
   On (Release Outside)
   Stop Drag
      If (GetProperty ("/MyMovieClip", _droptarget) eq "/MyTarget")
      Set Property ("/MyMovieClip", Visibility) = False
   End If
End On
```

_highquality

Syntax: _highquality

The highquality property returns a numeric value of zero, one, or two based on the current playback quality setting. As a global property, it pertains to all movies currently playing in the Flash Player window.

```
If (_highquality = 2)
   Actions…
Else
   Actions…
```

_focusrect

Syntax: `_focusrect`

The focusrect property returns a Boolean value of True or False, depending on whether the focus rectangle property is on or off (see Set Property action earlier in this chapter). As a global property, it pertains to all movies currently playing in the Flash Player window.

```
If (_focusrect = True)
   Actions…
Else
   Actions…
```

_soundbuftime

Syntax: `_soundbuftime`

The soundbuftime property returns a numeric value for the current soundbuffer time setting. The default setting is 5 (for 5 seconds). As a global property, it pertains to all movies currently playing in the Flash Player window.

```
If (_soundbuftime > 15)
   Actions…
Else
   Actions…
```

Special text properties

Because a text field can contain many lines of text, you can use two unique properties for them to, among other things, create scrollbars.

Scroll

Syntax: `VariableName.scroll`

The scroll property is a numeric value that represents the line number of the top-most visible line currently displayed in a text field. So, if the text field has ten lines of text and the user has scrolled to the point where Line 4 is the top-most visible line, the scroll value for this text field would be 4. This value is constantly updated as your movie plays. It can be evaluated in expressions, or you can create buttons that cause the top-most line to jump to wherever you want (see script below).

The following script shows a frame event that uses an expression to evaluate the current Scroll property of the text field with a variable name of MyTextBox. If the value is greater than 3 the movie will stop playing.

```
If (MyTextBox.scroll > 3)
    Stop
End If
```

The following script shows a mouse event that will cause the text field with a variable name of MyTextBox to make Line 6 it's top-most visible line.

```
On (Release)
    Set Variable: "MyTextBox.scroll" = 6
End On
```

maxscroll

Syntax: `VariableName.maxscroll`

The maxscroll property is a numeric value that represents the line number of the top-most scrollable line in a text field. If you have a text field that is high enough only to show two lines of text even though it actually contains five, the maxscroll value is 4. This is because at its highest scroll point, Line 4 is the top-most *visible* line. If a text field contains ten lines of text but can only display four lines at a time, the maxscroll value for this text field would be 7. This is because at its highest scroll point, Line 7 is the top-most *visible* line (**Figure 11.46**).

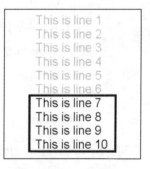

Figure 11.46
Ten lines of text in a text field that can only display four lines at a time would make Line 7 the maxscroll value.

Obviously, the maxscroll value is not a value you set. It's determined by the number of text lines within the text field compared with the number it can display at once. The value can be used in an expression attached to a button instance to create a looping scroll—that is, one in which the text within a text field will scroll when the button is clicked but the scroll starts back at the top automatically when the text reaches its bottom-most point (see the script below).

The following script makes the text field with the variable name MyTextBox go to a line number based on the value of Count, which is updated with each click of the button. Also with each click, the value of Count is compared to the value of

MyTextBox.maxscroll. Once the value of Count equals the value of MyTextBox. maxscroll, the end of the scroll has been reached and Count is reset so that on the next button click the text field will display Line 1 again and start the process all over again:

```
On (Release)
    Set Variable: "Count" = Count +1
    Set Variable: "MyTextBox.scroll" = Count
    If (Count = MyTextBox.maxscroll)
        Set Variable: "Count" = 0
    End If
End On
```

The Expression Editor

The Expression Editor provides a quick way of putting together the expressions that you'll use in your ActionScripts. It gives you access to all of the functions, properties, and operators we discussed earlier. Although you'll find helpful a general knowledge of the way expressions are put together, the Expression Editor will give you guidance along the way.

To use the Expression Editor:

1. Click the parameter field's button, and from the menu that appears choose Expression Editor (**Figure 11.47**).

The Expression Editor appears.

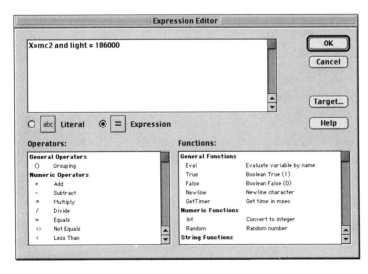

Figure 11.47
The Expression Editor allows you to quickly and easily build expressions.

2. Double-click any individual operator or function names to add them to the expression.

   Double clicking some functions, such as Eval or GetProperty, will place general terms such as target, property, or variable in the expression as a way of indicating where specific information should go.

3. When you wish to set the target of the GetProperty function, select "target," and click the Target button.

4. Select a target from the list by double-clicking its name.

   If the name does not appear on the list, you must enter it.

5. Click OK to close the Target Editor.

6. If you wish to set the property of the GetProperty function, highlight the term *property* and then select the property from the list.

7. Click OK when you are finished using the Expression Editor.

   TIP *Standard editing functions are available in the Expression Editor by right-clicking (Windows) in the expression text area.*

Interactivity Tutorials

To help you put all of these concepts together, we've assembled four interactive tutorials, which you will find on the CD-ROM disc, along with their source files:

Emulating Drag-and-Drop Behavior. This tutorial shows you how to emulate drag-and-drop behavior in your Flash movie.

Creating a Mouse Tracker. This tutorial shows you how to create a movie that contains a mouse tracker, which is simply a simple device that constantly displays the current x and y position of the user's pointer in a couple of text fields.

Whack a Mole. There is no associated video tutorial for this Flash project (.fla). It's included to help you see some of what goes on behind putting together an interactive game in Flash. It uses techniques that you've learned about in this chapter.

Testing

When we were students, this word could make us quake in our tracks or sick to our stomachs—most likely because it was sure to confirm one of three things: that we had goofed off too much, that we weren't quite as perfect as we thought, or (wonder of wonders) that we were *exactly* as perfect as we suspected. Of course, the word we're speaking of is *testing*.

Although it's natural to dread them, tests can actually be good things. Sure, we can "burn the midnight oil," sweat blood studying, or even write the answers on the palms of our hands, but all of these efforts are pointless if we can't make something work in real life. That's where testing can help.

In computer-driven interactive content, mistakes are referred to as *bugs*—and they are often as ugly, annoying, and even devastating as their name implies. Although your project is probably not as complex as a major software product, you'll still more than likely to discover some problems. And unless you want to scare off your audience, you'll need to exterminate the bugs.

One of the keys to becoming a Flash master is understanding the need for testing. It doesn't matter how good you or your project are: If you don't test your work, you're putting your reputation, not to mention your neck, on the line. You should never neglect this vital step in your movie creation, especially considering how easy Flash makes it and how powerful it's testing tools are. Testing is about eliminating mistakes, but it's also about optimizing your movie to make it playback most efficiently.

Getting Ready to Test

Here are some tips to get you started:

Test everything. Never assume something works—even if it seems like a trivial part of your project. All it takes is one mistake to bring your movie to a halt.

Test often. Don't wait until your project is nearing completion—test at every opportunity. It's much easier to isolate problems if you know your movie was working 5 minutes ago. That way, you can pinpoint any glitches to changes you've made within the last few minutes.

Fix bugs in an orderly fashion. Don't attempt to fix a bunch of bugs at once. It's best to fix one or two problems at a time, testing after each. After all, you don't want to create any nasty *new* bugs.

Get a second opinion. Sometimes you're too close to a project to spot obvious problems. One of the best things you can do is have someone else test your project. Because this person won't know what to expect, he or she may stumble upon problems you might have overlooked. Encourage your testers to be brutal and diligent—and don't get upset if they also provide some unsolicited opinions about design and functionality along the way. Swallow your pride and listen: Their opinions may be the opinions of your target audience.

Plan. Don't even approach a project until you've created a basic outline.

Testing Within the Flash Authoring Environment

Although it shouldn't be your first choice for heavy-duty project testing, the Flash authoring environment does accommodate some minor testing. Within the authoring environment you *can* test the following:

Button states. You can test the way buttons look in their up, down, over, and hit states.

Sounds on the main timeline. You can hear sounds placed along the main timeline (including those that are synchronized with on-stage animations) when you play the timeline.

Frame actions along the main timeline. Any Go To, Play, and Stop actions attached to frames or buttons will work on the main timeline (see below for actions that won't).

Animation along the main timeline. Animation along the main timeline (including shape and motion tweens) work. Notice we said *the main timeline;* this does not include animation within movie clips or buttons (see below for more information).

To test a button's visual functionality:

- From the Modify menu choose Enable Buttons.

  With buttons enabled you can place your pointer over them, and they will react visually the way they will in your final movie. Disable this feature to edit instances of buttons.

To test frame actions such as Go To, Stop, and Play:

- From the Modify menu choose Enable Frame Actions.

  With frame actions enabled, Go To, Stop, and Play actions will respond when the timeline is played within the authoring environment (as long as they don't rely on ActionScript expressions or point to URLs).

Within the authoring environment you cannot test the following:

Movie clips. Sounds, animation, and actions that are part of movie clips will not be visible or function. (Only the first frame of a movie clip will appear in the authoring environment.)

Actions. Go To, Play, and Stop are the only actions that work in the authoring environment. This means you can't test interactivity, mouse events, or functionality that rely on any other actions.

Movie speed. Playback within the Flash authoring environment is slower than it will be in your final optimized and exported movie.

Download performance. From within the authoring environment, you can't gauge how well your movie will *stream,* or download, over the Web.

The important thing to remember here is that the above-described limitations are only limitations *within the authoring environment.* Just a couple clicks a way are commands that you can employ to fully test your movie. Let's take a closer look at them.

The Test Movie and Test Scene Commands

Testing *within* the authoring environment is limited. To evaluate movie clips, action scripts, and other important movie elements, you must move outside the authoring environment. This is where the Test Scene and Test Movie commands—both located on the Control menu—can help: They automatically create a working version of the current scene or entire movie and open it in a window where you can test nearly every aspect of it's interactivity, animation, and functionality.

The Test Scene and Test Movie commands generate actual .swf files (just as if you'd exported your authoring file using the Publish feature) and place them in the same directory as the authoring file. If your test file works as it should and you wish to use it as your final file, locate it on your hard drive and upload it to your server.

The export settings with the Test Scene and Test Movie commands are based on the settings on the Flash tab in the Publish Settings dialog box. To change these settings, from the File menu choose Publish Settings and make the necessary adjustments under the Flash tab.

To test the current scene:

- From the Control menu choose Test Scene.

  Flash automatically exports the current scene and opens it in a new window ready for you to test it.

To test the entire movie:

- From the Control menu choose Test Movie.

  Flash automatically exports all of the scenes within the current project and opens the file in a new window ready for you to test it.

The Testing Environment

When using the Test Scene or Test Movie command, you'll notice that although you're still within Flash, the interface has changed. This is because you're now in the testing environment rather than the authoring environment. Although both look similar, they do have differences (**Figure 12.1**):

Tool bars appear but do not function.

The menu bar has changed, as have many of the menu choices (see "Testing Environment Menu Options" later in this chapter).

The Timeline has been replaced with the Bandwidth Profiler, which itself includes a timeline, graph, and other features (see "Understanding the Bandwidth Profiler" later in this chapter.)

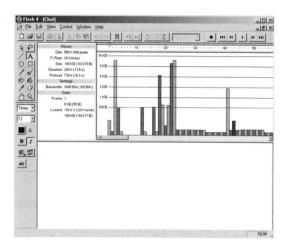

Figure 12.1
The Test Movie environment.

The stage and work area have been replaced with a fully functional copy of the scene or movie you are testing.

> **TIP** *Any time you wish to close this window and return to the Flash authoring environment, from the File menu choose Close.*

Testing Functionality

Testing your movie's functionality can actually be kind of fun since it's fairly easy yet allows you to see how your work is coming together. During this phase of testing, you should view animation for mistakes, press any buttons, and generally give your movie a good run-through. Leave nothing unchecked. And remember: If your movie doesn't work here, it won't work period—the only exceptions are actions that are intended to open URLs or to post variables to a Web server. You need to post your movie to the Web to test these actions.

Besides the hands-on testing you can perform here, the testing environment offers a few additional commands on the menu bar that can assist you in tracking down problems.

List Objects command

The List Objects command provides a complete tally of all objects present in a given frame, including the object type and—if it's a target—its name. This will help you to determine whether all of the objects that should be present are.

To list objects for a particular frame:

1. Move the playhead to a frame.

2. From the Control menu choose List Objects.

The Output window appears with a list of all objects present on the current frame.

List Variables command

The List Variables command provides a complete tally of all variables present—including their value—for a given frame. This will help you to ensure that variables are created and updated properly as the timeline plays.

To list variables for a particular frame:

1. Move the playhead to a frame.

2. From the Control menu choose List Variables.

The Output window appears with a list of all variables present on the current frame, along with their current values.

Output

You use the Output command in conjunction with the Trace action. Every time a Trace action is encountered in your movie, the Output window displays a Trace message. It's easy to use the Trace action to follow the ActionScripting logic within your movie to make sure that it is flowing in the proper manner internally (that is, the intangible or invisible part). For more information, see Chapter 11, "Interactivity."

To display the Output window:

- From the Window menu choose Output to bring up the Output window.

TIP *The Output window will open automatically whenever a Trace action is encountered along the Timeline.*

Testing Download Performance

Testing your movie's functionality is only half the battle. Because the majority of Flash movies are delivered over the Web, you need to plan, design, and create your movie with bandwidth limitations in mind.

To test how well your movie will stream over the Web:

1. With the testing environment open, from the Control menu choose a bandwidth for testing the streaming, or download, performance of your movie (**Figure 12.2**).

2. Make sure you've rewound your movie, and then from the Control menu choose Show Streaming.

   Your movie begins to play as it would over the Web at the connection speed you chose in the previous step.

Although this method can be helpful for locating specific problem areas in the streaming process, sometimes more information can make troubleshooting easier. This is where the Bandwidth Profiler can help.

Figure 12.2
Choosing the bandwidth for testing from the Control menu.

Understanding the Bandwidth Profiler

The Bandwidth Profiler is one of your most important sources of information for testing download performance (**Figure 12.3**). It can provide you with vital statistics that help you pinpoint problem areas in streaming, including information about the size of individual frames in your movie, the amount of time needed from the point where the movie actually starts to stream, and when it has enough information to begin playing.

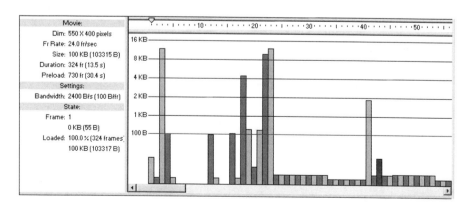

Figure 12.3
The Bandwidth Profiler.

Using the Bandwidth Profiler, you can simulate the actual download experience of someone using a 28.8-Kbps, 33.6-Kbps, or 56-Kbps modem or even a custom setting to simulate the streaming process of an ISDN or LAN connection. By simulating a modem speed, you can detect pauses in streaming caused by content-heavy frames so that you can reedit to get acceptable performance. Perhaps most important, the Profiler saves you the hassle of uploading your movie to the Web and testing it over an actual Web connection.

To display the Bandwidth Profiler:

- From the View menu choose Bandwidth Profiler.

To resize the Bandwidth Profiler:

- Place your pointer over the horizontal bar that separates the Bandwidth Profiler from your movie. When the pointer changes to a double-sided arrow, click and drag to resize.

To help you get the most from the Bandwidth Profiler, let's look at its parts.

The Information Bar section of the Bandwidth Profiler provides all sorts of vital information about the movie or scene you are testing (**Figure 12.4**):

Dim. Your movie's dimension.

Fr Rate. The speed, based on frames per second, at which your movie plays.

Size. The file size of the entire movie (or if testing a scene, its contribution to your movie's overall file size). The number in parentheses represents the exact amount in bytes.

Duration. The number of frames in the movie (or if testing a scene, the number of frames in the scene). The number in parentheses represents the duration of the movie or scene (in seconds as opposed to frames).

Preload. The amount of frames/time (based on the current frames per second) from the point at which the movie begins to download to the time it can begin to play.

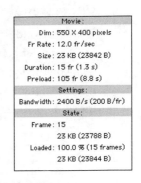

Figure 12.4
The Information Bar section of the Bandwidth Profiler.

Bandwidth. The bandwidth speed being used to simulate an actual download. This figure has no meaning unless it is used in conjunction with the Control > Show Streaming command.

Frame. Displays two numbers: The top one indicates the frame number at which the timeline playhead is currently positioned in the testing environment, and the bottom one indicates the current frame's contribution to your movie's overall file size. The number in parentheses is the exact amount in file size. Move the playhead on the timeline, and the statistics for the individual frames appear here. This information is useful for tracking down particularly large frames.

> **TIP** *You can also navigate to different frames along the timeline simply by clicking the gray bars that represent the frames in the Streaming/Frame by Frame graph area.*

Loaded. The information will only make sense when used in conjunction with the Control > Show Streaming command. This area shows two numbers: The top one indicates the percentage (or number of frames) of the movie that have downloaded, or streamed, in the background at any given point during playback. The bottom number indicates the total amount, in file size, that has been streamed in the background. Watch these figures closely to evaluate your movie's streaming.

Testing Timeline

The testing timeline looks and functions like the one in the authoring environment, with one notable exception—the streaming bar (**Figure 12.5**). When used in conjunction with the Control > Show Streaming command, the streaming bar will reflect the amount (by means of a green bar) of the movie that has downloaded in the background, and the playhead reflects the current playback position. By observing the amount that the streaming bar is ahead of actual playback, you can pinpoint areas or frames that may be causing glitches in streaming. Remember, however, that the testing environment merely *simulates* download and streaming; actual conditions may vary.

Figure 12.5
The testing environment's timeline and streaming bar.

Streaming Graph/Frame by Frame Graph

Depending on the option you choose (View > Streaming Graph or View > Frame by Frame Graph), you are presented with a graphical representation of your movie's frames. The gray blocks represent the frames in your movie; their height represents their size. Areas where no blocks appear indicate frames that do not add anything to your movie's overall file size (empty frames or frames with no movement or interactivity). Each graph has its own advantages:

Frame by Frame graph (**Figure 12.6**). This gives you a graphical representation of the size of individual frames along the timeline.

Streaming graph (**Figure 12.7**). This is good for determining where pauses will occur when the movie is being downloaded over the Web. A block above the red line indicates an area where a pause in the streaming process may occur.

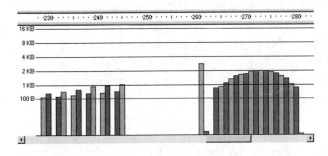

Figure 12.6
The Frame by Frame graph provides a graphical representation of the size of various frames in you movie. Areas where no bars appear represent frames in your movie where nothing changes.

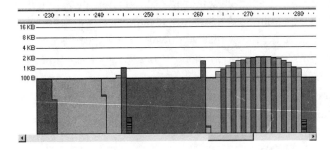

Figure 12.7
The Streaming graph provides a graphical representation of how you movie will stream. In this example, bars above the 100 B line indicate areas in your movie where streaming could possible be interrupted during playback.

Creating Custom Download Speeds

Unfortunately, when talking about the Web, you must always contend with variables when creating content—one of which is bandwidth. When delivering streamed content, bandwidth issues become even more important. Fortunately, Flash allows you to test your movie's Web delivery at different modem speeds (including the most common speeds of 14.4 Kbps, 28.8 Kbps, and 56 Kbps). It also allows you to test at even less common speeds, or speeds you determine, so that you have complete control over the testing process.

To create custom modem speeds to test streaming:

1. From the Control menu choose Customize to bring up the Custom Modem Settings dialog box (**Figure 12.8**).

2. In one of the available Menu text boxes, enter the text you want to appear on the Control menu as a modem speed choice.

3. In the accompanying Bit rate box, enter the bit rate you want this choice to simulate.

4. Click OK.

The custom modem speed you created is now available on the Control menu.

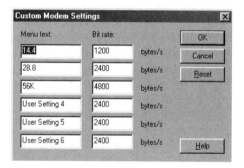

Figure 12.8
The Custom Modem Settings dialog box.

Publishing Your Work

As much as we may deny it, many of us are egomaniacs at heart. When we've worked hard to perfect our Flash movie, few things are as rewarding as having others view and praise it. Whatever the *stated* purpose of our Flash movies, we all share the same goal: to get our movie into the hands of as many people as possible.

Whether you distribute your movie via a Web page or as a stand-alone application, video, or still image, Flash offers ways to automate the process. Let's take a look at the delivery modes and the final production process, so that you can finally begin to experience the joy of a job well done.

Delivery Methods

With Flash's Publish feature, you simply choose the formats in which you want your authoring file delivered, adjust any settings available for that format, click Publish, and—voilà—Flash exports your authoring file to the selected formats and creates the files based on the settings you selected for that format.

Most of what we're going to be talking about next involves the Publish Settings dialog box.

To open the Publish Settings dialog box:

- Choose File > Publish Settings.

Publish Settings

With Flash, you control the way your movie is delivered: You can choose a single method of delivery, such as on an HTML page, or you can choose multiple ways, such as on an HTML page, as a QuickTime movie, and as a Projector. In the last case, the Publish feature creates all of the files simultaneously.

Let's take a look at the options available through the Publish Settings dialog box.

Formats

Choosing the format for movie delivery is the first task in the publishing process. The Formats dialog box (**Figure 13.1**) provides you with several selections:

Type. Checking a format choice (other than Projector) adds a tab to the Publish Settings dialog box. By clicking that tab, you make all of that format's settings available for adjusting.

Filename. You can name any file you create with the Publish feature. If you check "Use default names," the created files will have the same name as the authoring file with the appropriate file extensions. If you leave this unchecked, you can specify file names.

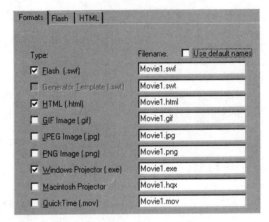

Figure 13.1
The Formats dialog box.

Depending on the template you choose in the HTML dialog box, you may actually need to select more than one format from the Formats dialog box. For example, if you choose an HTML template that detects whether the Flash Player plug-in is installed on the viewer's computer, your Flash movie will be displayed if the plug-in is installed, but a bitmap image (GIF, JPEG, or PNG) will be displayed if the plug-in is not installed. This type of functionality requires an HTML page, a Flash movie file, and an image file. So, in the Formats dialog box, you must select Flash and HTML and GIF, JPEG, or PNG (the choice of image is up to you). This will allow the Publish feature to create all the files (.swf, .html, .gif, .jpeg, or .png) needed for the plug-in detection template to work.

To use any of the Files created by the Publish feature, you must place them in the same directory as your authoring file and upload them to your server. When uploading a set of files that are intended to work together, make sure the files, once uploaded, maintain their relative positions. For example, if your authoring file resides on your hard drive in a folder named Awesome Flash Project, all new files created by the Publish feature will initially reside there as well. When uploading these files, make sure that they all reside in the same folder on your server.

Flash (.swf)

Creating an .swf file is the most common way of delivering a Flash movie. It is also the first step toward getting your movie on the Web (see "HTML" below). When you place your movie on an HTML page in this format, users can view it through a Web browser such as Microsoft's Internet Explorer or Netscape's Navigator or Communicator—as long as the browser has the Flash Player plug-in. You can also use Flash movies in this format with Macromedia Director and Authorware or any program that can host the Flash Player ActiveX control.

When you export your project to a Flash movie, all interactivity and functionality remain intact.

The following settings are available when exporting in this format (**Figure 13.2**):

Load Order. When your movie is being downloaded over the Web, the first frame is visually "constructed" a layer at a time as information arrives in the viewer's browser. This option allows you to set the order in which layers are loaded.

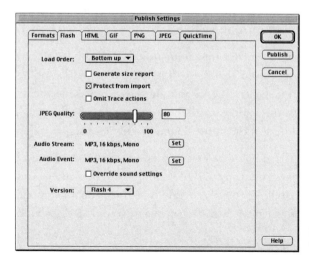

Figure 13.2
The Flash format dialog box.

Bottom Up. Causes the bottom layer to load first, with all subsequent layers following.

Top Down. Causes the top layer first to load first, with all subsequent layers following.

Generate size report. Creates a text file (with a .txt extension in Windows) that contains information about frames sizes in your movie and a list of imported files and fonts. This text file has the same name as the exported movie and resides in the same directory.

Protect from import. Prevents your final exported movie from being reimported into Flash—in other words, it prevents others from claiming your work as their own. This option does not affect the authoring file, just the resulting Flash movie.

Omit trace actions. Removes any Trace actions from the exported Flash movie, preventing others from peering into your code.

JPEG Quality. Allows you to set a default amount of compression that will be applied to all bitmaps in your movie that you have not individually optimized (see Chapter 6, "Bitmaps"). A setting of 0 will export the bitmaps at their lowest quality (which will produce a movie with a smaller file size), whereas a setting of 100 will export them at their highest quality (and consequently produce a movie with a larger file size).

Audio Stream. Lets you set a default amount of compression for all streamed sounds in your movie (that is, those you have not individually optimized; see Chapter 5, "Sound"). The amount shown represents the settings that will be used. To change the settings, click the accompanying Set button. The available settings are the same as those in the Sound Properties dialog box.

Audio Event. Allows you to set a default amount of compression for all event sounds in your movie (that is, those that have not been individually optimized; see "Optimizing Sounds" in Chapter 5). The amount shown represents the settings that will be used. To change the settings, click the accompanying Set button. The available settings are the same as those in the Sound Properties dialog box.

Override sound settings. If you optimized sounds individually in the Sound Properties dialog box, this option overrides any of those settings with the settings you define in the Audio Stream and Audio Event areas of this dialog box. You might want to do this to produce a version of you movie with higher-quality sound for distribution on CD.

Version. Allows you to export your movie so that a previous version of Flash Player can view it. Version-specific features will not work when exporting to an earlier version.

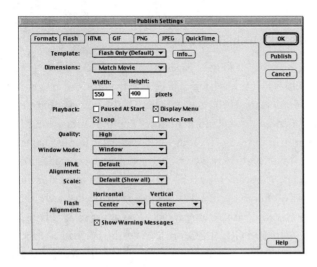

Figure 13.3
The HTML format dialog box.

HTML (.html or .htm)

The HTML format tab (**Figure 13.3**) lets you choose settings that will generate an HTML page containing your Flash movie. You upload the generated HTML page and exported movie file to your server to make it available on the Web.

Publishing to HTML is done in conjunction with publishing your movie to the .swf format (see Flash above) because the exported Flash movie is, at the same time, placed on the generated HTML page.

The HTML code generated by this feature includes the <object> and <embed> tags, which enable your movie to be viewed in Microsoft's Internet Explorer and Netscape's Navigator/Communicator Web browsers, respectively. It also generates the code needed to set your movie's parameters within the HTML page, including alignment, size, and whether it begins to play automatically (for more information see the "Flash and HTML" section later in this chapter).

The following settings are available when exporting in this format:

Template. Flash provides templates used for generating the HTML pages produced from this dialog box. Different templates offer specific functionality. For example, one template simply places your Flash movie on the generated HTML page so that users can only view it through a Web browser if the plug-in is already installed. Another template allows you to do the same thing except that it will first detect whether the plug-in has been installed, and if it hasn't, the template will automatically install it. Other templates include JavaScript for such functions as plug-in detection and cookie creation and detection. For more on templates, see "Understanding Templates" later in this chapter.

Flash Only (Default). Generates an HTML page with your Flash movie embedded in it. This template does not include plug-in detection.

Flash 3 with Image. Creates an HTML page that uses JavaScript to determine whether version 3 of Flash Player has been installed on the user's machine. If it has, your movie will show up on the Web page. If it hasn't, the newest plug-in will be automatically downloaded and installed for Internet Explorer users, and Netscape users will see an image map instead (see "Plug-In Issues" later in this chapter). Any keyframe with buttons that have attached Get URL actions can be used as a basis for the generated image map. To specify which keyframe you wish to use for the image map, label it #Map; if you fail to do this, Flash will automatically create the image map using buttons on the last frame of the movie. You must select Flash 3 as the version number to export to and GIF, JPEG, or PNG on the Format tab for the necessary image map to be generated (see the "Flash Movie" section of this chapter).

Flash 4 with Image. Generates an HTML page that uses JavaScript to detect whether version 4 of the Flash Player has been installed on the user's machine. After that, it performs the same actions as the Flash 3 with Image option does.

Flash with FS Command. Builds an HTML page with your Flash movie embedded in it. It also includes the necessary code for enabling FSCommands to work on the page (see the Actions section in Chapter 11, "Interactivity"). This template does not include plug-in detection.

Image Map. Creates an HTML page with an image map embedded within it. Any keyframe with buttons that have attached Get URL actions can be used as a basis for the generated image map. To specify which keyframe you wish to use for the image map, label it #Map; if you fail to do this, Flash will automatically create the image map using buttons on the last frame of the movie. This option only generates an embedded image map, not an embedded Flash movie. The image generated can be a GIF, JPEG, or PNG, depending on the format you chose on the Format tab of the Publish Settings dialog box.

Java Player. Generates an HTML page that displays a Java-based version of your movie. All of the necessary Java classes are created and should be placed in the same directory as the accompanying HTML page. Flash 2 must be selected as the version to export to (see "Flash Movie" in this section).

QuickTime. Makes an HTML page that displays a QuickTime 4 version of your movie. You must select Flash 3 as the version number to export to on the Flash dialog box, and select QuickTime on the Format tab for the necessary QuickTime movie to be generated.

User Choice. Creates an HTML page with links that let your users decide how they want to see your movie—that is, as a Flash movie or as an image—and then creates a cookie based on that choice. This cookie serves as the basis for how they will view other Flash-enhanced pages they encounter—as movies or images. The Flash movie generated for this option is based on your Flash tab settings (see "Flash Movie" in this section). The image generated can be GIF, JPEG, or PNG, depending on the format you chose on the Format tab of the Publish Settings dialog box.

TIP *Selecting a template and then clicking the Info button opens a small dialog box that displays information about the currently selected template, including name, function, and the formats that you must select and adjust for it to output properly (**Figure 13.4**). To scroll through the dialog box, press the up or down keys on your keyboard.*

Figure 13.4
The Info box provides information about the selected template.

Dimensions. Lets you set the horizontal and vertical dimensions of the movie window in which your movie appears within the HTML page. The movie window is simply the rectangular area in which your movie appears. Since they are basically two different objects (movie and movie window) they can be proportionately different sizes and shapes. Depending on the dimensions you choose with this setting, the movie itself may not always fit exactly edge to edge with the movie window (see "Scale" setting in this section). This setting does not affect the authoring file, just the exported movie as it will appear within the movie window on the HTML page.

Match Movie. Sets the dimensions of your movie window on the generated HTML page to match the dimensions specified in the Movie Properties dialog box.

Pixels. Sets the dimensions of your movie window on the generated HTML page to a specific pixel amount.

Percent. Sets the dimensions of your movie window on the generated HTML page to a percentage amount relative to the browser window through which it is viewed.

TIP *A common practice is to enter percentage values of 100 in each of these boxes so that your Flash movie will appear full-screen in the browser.*

Playback. Provides options that affect what happens at the start, and during playback, of your movie on the HTML page that is generated.

Paused At Start. If you check this, your movie will not begin to play back on the HTML page until the user clicks a button within your movie or selects the Play option from the Flash Player shortcut menu (see "Display Menu" in this section).

Loop. If you check this, your movie will automatically begin to play again when it has played through its last frame.

Display Menu. The Display menu appears in the browser window when your user right-click (Windows) or Control-click (Macintosh) your movie. This menu normally displays options that allow the user to stop, play, and rewind your movie along with a few other settings. If you uncheck this option, you eliminate all of these options and the menu will only display information about Flash Player itself.

Device Font (Windows only). If necessary fonts are not installed on your user's computer, checking this option will substitute antialiased system fonts.

Quality. Because users who view you movie have computers with varying processor speeds, this option lets you determine how processor limitations will affect your movie's playback in terms of speed and visual quality.

Low. This sacrifices visual quality for playback speed. With this, your movie will never be antialiased.

Autolow. With this, antialiasing is turned off initially but turned on to improve visual quality if the user's processor is fast enough to handle it.

Autohigh. With this, antialiasing is turned on initially but turned off to improve playback speed if the frames per second rate drops below the amount set in the Movie Properties dialog box.

High. Maintains even visual quality on computers with slower processors. Antialiasing is always on when this option has been selected. If your movie is animated, bitmaps will not be smoothed; if it is not animated, they will be.

Best. Bitmaps are always smoothed, and antialiasing is always on.

Window Mode (Windows only). Allows you to take advantage of capabilities only available in a Windows version of Internet Explorer with Flash Player ActiveX control installed.

Window. Providing the best playback performance, this option plays your movie within its own rectangular area on the HTML page. For more information on this and the next two options, see "Flash and HTML" later in this chapter.

Opaque. Allows you to move elements on the HTML page behind the rectangular area of the movie without having them show through. Use this option in conjunction with dynamic HTML layers.

Transparent Windowless. Causes the background color of your Flash movie (as set in the Movie Properties dialog box) to become transparent so that the background of the HTML page on which your movie is embedded will show through. This setting, though interesting, provides the slowest playback performance—use it sparingly.

HTML Alignment. Determines the alignment of your movie in relation to other elements on the page. It will not have any visible effect unless you reedit the generated HTML page and place other elements, such as text or graphics, alongside your movie. The available options are Default, Left, Right, Top, and Bottom.

Scale. If you've selected width and height settings for the actual movie window (in the Dimensions setting) that differ from those in the Movie Properties dialog box, your movie elements (which were designed for a specific size) may not fit perfectly within the new dimensions of your movie window. This determines how the movie will look within the boundaries of the movie window you have specified.

Default (Show All). Makes your movie visible within the movie window. All elements are scaled proportionately to fill the movie window. Borders or elements on the work area may appear between movie elements and the movie window if the window's proportions differ from the movie's original size.

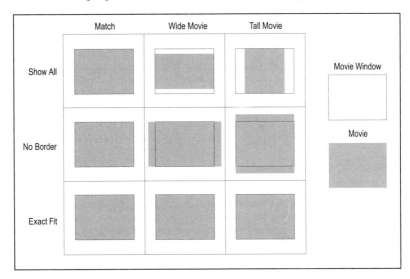

Figure 13.5
The effects of different scale settings.

No Border. Scales your movie proportionately so that it fills the movie window and no borders appear. As a result, elements of your movie may be cropped and not visible within the movie window.

Exact Fit. Disproportionately scales your movie to fit the dimensions of the movie window. Thus, your movie may appear squashed or bloated, depending on how the movie window's proportions differ from the movie itself (**Figure 13.5**).

Flash Alignment. These options determine your movie's alignment within the movie window and are used in conjunction with the Show All and No Border settings. Borders may appear between the movie and the movie window when you employ the Show All setting; this option affects which borders appear. For example, if you use vertical/horizontal alignment settings of center/center, the movie will be placed in the center of the movie window, and borders will appear on all four sides of the movie window. If, however, you use vertical/horizontal alignment settings of top/left, the movie will be placed in the top left portion of the movie window, and borders will only exist on the bottom right sides of the movie window. Remember, these borders only exist if the movie window differs from those of the actual movie.

When using the No Border setting, your movie is scaled proportionately to fill the movie window, becoming larger than the movie window and possibly forcing parts of your movie to be hidden. The Flash alignment settings let you determine which

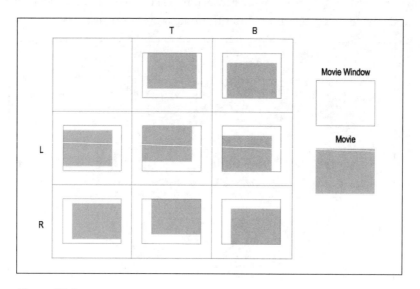

Figure 13.6
The effect that different alignment settings will have on you movie if it doesn't fill the movie window completely.

areas are visible. For example, if you use vertical/horizontal alignment settings of bottom/right, the movie will be placed in the bottom right corner of the movie window, and sections of the top left portion of the movie will not be visible. If, however, you choose vertical/horizontal alignment settings of top/center, the movie will be placed in the top center portion of the movie window, and sections of the bottom, left, and right portions of the movie will not be visible (**Figure 13.6**).

Show Warning Messages. When using templates, this will display a warning message indicating that the template being used requires that you select additional publish formats or adjust publish settings.

GIF (.gif)

GIFs are the most popular form of graphics used on the Web. This is because they are compressed and—unlike other Web graphic formats such as JPEGs and PNGs—can be animated. You would create a GIF from the Flash authoring file in two scenarios: If you wanted to use Flash as a GIF creation tool for HTML pages, or if you wanted to use a GIF file as a replacement for a Flash movie on a Web page because the user didn't have the plug-in. Either way, Flash makes it simple. The following options are available when creating GIFs (**Figure 13.7**).

Dimensions. Lets you set the vertical and horizontal dimensions (in pixels) of the GIF that is created. "Match movie" creates a GIF that has the same dimensions as those set for the movie in the Movie Properties box. If you check this option, the Width and Height boxes will have no effect and will be grayed out. If you leave this option unchecked, you can enter a new size for the exported GIF. You only need to enter either the width or the height because Flash will always export an image that maintains the aspect ratio of the original.

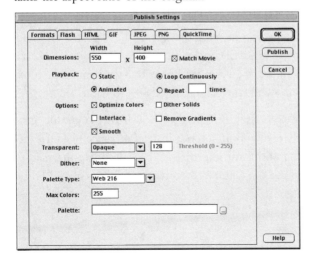

Figure 13.7
The GIF format dialog box.

Playback. Lets you choose whether the exported GIF will be static or animated and, if animated, how it will play.

Static. To create a nonanimated GIF based on a single keyframe in your movie, choose this. Label a keyframe #Static to make it the one that is exported. (If you don't do this, Flash will use the first frame of the movie.)

Animated. To create an animated GIF based on your movie or a section of it, choose this option. You can specify the range of frames exported by giving the first and last keyframe of the range the labels #First and #Last, respectively. If you do not do this, the entire movie will be exported, which could result in a huge file. Interactivity and sound are lost when exporting to GIF.

Loop Continuously. By checking this, your animated GIF will automatically, and continuously, replay when it has reached its last frame during playback.

Repeat Times. If you check this, your animated GIF will automatically begin to play again—as many times as you specify—when it has reached the last frame during playback.

The following options determine the visual appearance of your GIF:

Optimize Colors. Choosing this can reduce the file size of the resulting GIF by removing any unused colors from its color table. When using an Adaptive palette, this has no effect.

Dither Solids. Dithers solid colors, gradients, and images. For more information, see "Dither," below.

Interlace. Causes the GIF to be displayed in stages—as if it's coming into focus—when it is downloaded over a slow connection.

Remove Gradients. Gradients can increase the size of the exported GIF and are usually poor quality. Selecting this will convert all gradients to solid colors based on the first color of the gradient. So, if an area is filled with a gradient going from white to blue, selecting this option will convert that filled area to white only.

Smooth. Antialiases the exported GIF. This creates a slightly larger file, but elements of the image, especially text, appear smooth instead of jaggy. If your exported GIF has a transparent background, turning this off can eliminate the halo effect that sometimes appears around the edges of the image when it is placed on a multicolored background.

Transparent. A transparent GIF is an image that is partially transparent, so when it is placed on a Web page, that page's background can be seen through any area of the GIF that is transparent. The following transparency settings determine which parts of the exported GIF are transparent.

Opaque. Makes the entire rectangular area of the image opaque. The exported image will appear on the HTML page the way it does in Flash.

Transparent. Makes the background of the exported GIF transparent. This means that any portion of the movie's background that can be seen in Flash will now become transparent.

Alpha. This handles colors in your movie that have an alpha amount applied to them (these are semitransparent colors used in your movie). Enter a number between 0 and 255 (which corresponds to the 0 to 100% alpha slider in the Color window; so, a value of 128 for this setting is equal to 50 percent in the color window) in the threshold box. Any colors with alpha values above the amount you enter will be exported as opaque; any colors with alpha settings below the amount will be exported as transparent.

Dither. A GIF file, by nature, has a limited color palette (256 colors max). If the GIF you are exporting uses colors not available on the current palette, dithering can help approximate those colors by mixing available colors. This process tricks the eye into believing that more colors are shown than actually are. Before you use dithering, though, be aware of two things: It can increase the file size of your exported image and, in some cases, can look bad on low-resolution monitors.

If you do not use dithering, any colors that are not available on the current palette will be replaced with the closest available color. If you go with this option, be sure to check the exported file because you sometimes get unexpected results.

None. Exports your image without using dithering.

Ordered. Dithers the exported image at a reasonable quality with a minimal change in file size.

Diffused. Creates the highest-quality dithering and also the biggest increase in file size.

Palette Type. Because GIF files have a limited palette of colors, you must choose the right one so that your exported file's color is as accurate as possible. The following options provide a great deal of control in palette selection.

Web 216. If you've used mostly Web-safe colors in your project, this will provide the best results. It produces a GIF file based on the 216-color palette used by Microsoft and Netscape browsers.

Adaptive. Creates a custom palette based on the colors in the image—the result is more accurate colors than those produced by the Web 216 palette. The downside is that the resulting image file is also larger. By decreasing the number of maximum colors available (see the Max Colors option below), you can minimize file size.

Web Snap Adaptive. Uses the best parts from the two previous palette options. It creates a custom palette based on colors in the image; however, Web-safe colors are substituted for custom colors whenever possible.

Custom. If you created a custom palette (with an .act file extension) in another application (such as Macromedia's Fireworks), you can use this palette when exporting your image to GIF. Press the button with the ellipse (...) to locate the palette you wish to use.

Max Colors. When using either an Adaptive or Web Snap Adaptive palette option where a custom palette is created when the image is exported, this allows you to set the maximum number of colors that will be created. Fewer colors result in a smaller image file but less color accuracy. More colors result in a larger file size but better color accuracy.

JPEG (.jpeg or .jpg)

GIFs are great for creating simple, small images with few colors. However, if you want to export an image that renders gradients well and is not hindered by a limited color palette, JPEGs are the way to go. The JPEG format dialog box (**Figure 13.8**) gives you the ability to export photographic-quality images that are compressed to maintain a relatively small file size. The main difference between JPEGs and GIFs is that JPEGs can't be exported as animated graphics. In addition, they don't export images with few colors well.

JPEG images can only be exported as static, or nonanimated, images. Label a keyframe #Static to make it the keyframe that is exported. Otherwise, Flash will use the first frame of the movie.

Dimensions. Lets you set the vertical and horizontal dimensions, in pixels, of the JPEG that is created. "Match movie" will create a JPEG with the

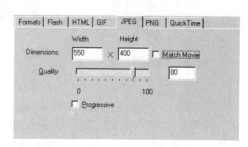

Figure 13.8
The JPEG format dialog box.

same dimensions as those set for the movie in the Movie Properties box. If you check this option, the Width and Height boxes will have no effect and will be grayed out. If you leave this option unchecked, you can enter a new size for the exported JPEG.

Quality. Allows you to set the amount of compression that will be applied to the exported JPEG. A setting of 0 will export the JPEG at its lowest visual quality, which will produce an image with the smallest file size; a setting of 100 will export the JPEG at its highest visual quality, which will result in an image with the largest file size.

Progressive. Similar to the Interlace option for GIFs, this will cause the JPEG to be displayed in stages—as if it's coming into focus—when it is downloaded over a slow connection.

PNG (.png)

The PNG format dialog box (**Figure 13.9**) allows you to export an image to a relatively new standard in graphics that offers numerous advantages over GIFs, especially when it comes to compression, color capabilities, and transparency. (For more information, see the "Using PNGs" section of the Chapter 6, "Bitmaps.") Keep in mind, however, that PNGs are not yet widely used or supported, so use discretion when exporting to this format.

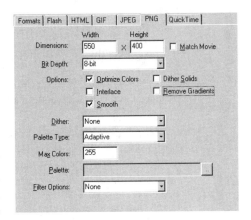

Figure 13.9
The PNG format dialog box.

Like JPEGs, PNG images can only be exported as static, or nonanimated, images. Label the keyframe that you wish to import as #Static so that Flash will use it rather than the first frame of the movie.

Dimensions. Lets you set the vertical and horizontal dimensions, in pixels, of the PNG that is created. "Match movie" will create a PNG with the same dimensions as those set for your movie in the Movie Properties box. If you check this option, the Width and Height boxes will grayed out. If you leave it unchecked, you can enter a new size for the exported PNG.

Bit Depth. Bit depth determines the number of colors that will be used in the exported image. The lower the bit depth, the smaller the resulting file size.

8-bit. Produces an image file with a maximum palette of 256 colors. Dithering options are only available when this setting is selected (otherwise, they are grayed out).

24-bit. Produces an image file with a maximum palette of more than 65,000 colors. Highly accurate color is achieved with this setting, though at a cost of an increased image file size.

24-bit with Alpha. Produces an image file with a palette of millions of colors as well as 256 values of transparency. Highly accurate color and transparency effects are achieved with this setting, once again, at a cost of an increased file size.

You can use the following options to adjust your PNG's appearance.

Optimize. This option can reduce the file size of the resulting PNG by removing any unused colors from the PNG's color table. When using an Adaptive palette, this option has no effect.

Dithers. Dithers solid colors, gradients, and images.

Interlace. Lets the PNG display in stages when it is downloaded over a slow connection.

Remove Gradients. Gradients can increase the size of the exported PNG and are usually poor quality. Selecting this option will convert all gradients to solid colors based on the first color of the gradient.

Smooth. Antialiases the exported PNG. This creates a slightly larger file, but elements of the image appear smooth rather than jaggy.

Dither. If you choose a bit depth of 8 bits (see "Bit Depth" in this section), the available color palette can contain a maximum of 256 colors. If the PNG you are exporting uses colors not available on the current palette, dithering can help approximate these colors by mixing available colors. The following options are available for dithering:

None. Exports your image without using dithering.

Ordered. Causes the exported image to be dithered at a reasonable quality but with little impact on its file size.

Diffused. Produces the highest-quality dithering but also has a greater impact on file size than the Ordered option.

Palette Type. When exporting your image using a bit depth of 8 bits, only a limited palette of colors is available; thus, it's important that you choose the right palette so that the colors in your exported file are as accurate as possible. The following options provide a great deal of control in color palette selection.

Web 216. If you've used mostly Web-safe colors in your project, this option will provide the best results. It produces a PNG file based on the 216-color palette used by Internet Explorer and Netscape browsers.

Adaptive. Creates a custom palette based on the colors in the image—the result is more accurate colors than those produced by the Web 216 palette. The downside is that the resulting image file is also larger. By decreasing the number of maximum colors available (see the Max Colors option below), you can minimize file size.

Web Snap Adaptive. Uses the best parts from the two previous palette options. It creates a custom palette based on colors in the image; however, Web safe colors are substituted for custom colors whenever possible.

Custom. If you created a custom palette (with an .act file extension) in another application, you can use this palette when exporting your image to PNG. Press the button with the ellipse (…) to locate the palette you wish to use.

Max Colors. When using either an Adaptive or Web Snap Adaptive palette option where a custom palette is created when the image is exported, this option allows you to set the maximum number of colors that will be created. Fewer colors result in a smaller image file but less color accuracy. More colors result in a larger file size but better color accuracy.

Filter Options. During compression, a PNG image goes through a "filtering" process that enables it to be compressed in the most efficient manner. Choose a filter that gives you the best results in both image quality and file size—a process that may require some experimentation. The available options include None, Sub, Up, Average, and Paeth.

QuickTime (.mov)

Thanks to cooperation between Apple and its QuickTime software and Macromedia and its Flash, you can now combine the interactive features of Flash with the multimedia and video features of QuickTime to produce a single QuickTime 4 movie that anyone with the QuickTime 4 plug-in can view.

> **TIP** *You can only combine Flash and QuickTime content when exporting to the QuickTime 4 format but not when creating a Flash movie. The Flash 4 plug-in cannot read or play back QuickTime movies or content. Also, be aware that only Flash 3–specific functionality is available when using Flash in a QuickTime movie. When exporting to QuickTime, make sure you have selected Version 3 from the Version pop-up menu on the Flash tab of the Publish Settings dialog box. For more information see Using QuickTime Video in Chapter 10, "Animation."*

Any Flash content you export to a QuickTime video is known as the Flash track. No matter how many layers are in your actual Flash project, they are all considered part of a single Flash track.

The following options are available in the QuickTime format dialog box (**Figure 13.10**):

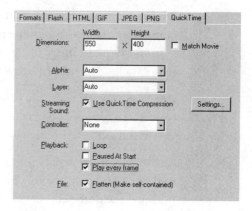

Figure 13.10
The QuickTime format dialog box.

Dimensions. Lets you set the vertical and horizontal dimensions, in pixels, of the file that is created. "Match movie" will create a QuickTime movie with the same dimensions as those set for your movie in the Movie Properties box. If you check, the Width and Height boxes will be grayed out. If you leave unchecked, you can enter a size for the QuickTime movie.

Alpha. Determines the transparency mode of the Flash track in the QuickTime movie. Alpha settings used within the Flash movie are not affected by this setting.

Auto. With this option, if the Flash track appears over other tracks, it becomes transparent; if it's the bottom or only track in the movie, it becomes opaque.

Alpha Transparent. Makes the Flash track transparent, so that you can see any content below it.

Copy. Makes the Flash track opaque, obscuring any content beneath it.

Layer. Lets you set where the Flash track will appear in relation to other tracks in the QuickTime movie.

Top. Places the Flash track above any other tracks in the QuickTime movie.

Bottom. Places the Flash track below any other tracks in the QuickTime movie.

Auto. Detects whether Flash content has been placed in front of imported QuickTime content, and if so, places the Flash track on top. (If not, the Flash track is placed on bottom.)

Streaming Sound. Converts streaming audio in the Flash move to a QuickTime sound track using the settings available through the Settings button. (Since these are Quick-Time settings, you must refer to the QuickTime documentation for more information.)

Controller. Allows you to select which QuickTime controller will be used to play back the exported QuickTime movie; your choices are None, Standard, or QuickTime VR.

Loop. Allows you to specify whether the exported QuickTime movie will play from beginning to end and then start over. Deselecting this option will cause the exported QuickTime movie to play once and stop.

Pause At Start. If you check this option, your QuickTime will not begin to play until the viewer presses a button within your movie or the Play button on the QuickTime control panel.

Play every frame. Slower machines sometimes skip frames of your movie to maintain the timeline's flow. By selecting this option, you cause every frame to be seen, regardless of the effects on playback. This option also disables any sound in the exported QuickTime movie.

Flatten (Make self-contained). If you select this option, the Flash content and imported video content will be combined in a self-contained QuickTime 4 movie. Otherwise, the QuickTime movie will reference any imported video files externally.

Projectors (.exe or .hqx)

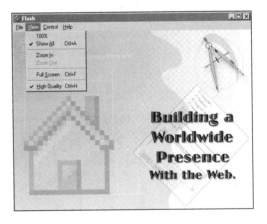

Projectors are stand-alone files (and applications in and of themselves) that can play on just about any computer, regardless of whether the Flash plug-in is installed. The projector file contains your Flash movie and everything needed to play it. This means you can you can create a Flash movie, turn it into a projector, and then distribute it widely. To view the movie, all users need to do is start it (like any other application), and the projector will open in its own application window and begin to play (**Figure 13.11**).

Figure 13.11

A Projector is a stand-alone application with its own menu bar—in other words, a self-contained version of your movie.

A projector can open URLs, load and unload movies, update variables, and more. You don't need much marketing savvy to understand the potential they provide—multimedia business presentations, Web sites on-a-disk, "Flashmercials." The list goes on and on.

No settings are available when creating projectors using the Publish Settings dialog box; however, this doesn't mean you can't configure projectors. Using button and frame actions such as Toggle High Quality and, especially, FS Commands, you can tailor your projector to your needs. For more information, see "FS Commands" in Chapter 11, "Interactivity."

New to Flash 4 is the ability to create both Windows and Macintosh projectors from either operating system. However, be aware that when creating a Macintosh projector from a Windows machine, you will need to convert the Mac projector file you create from its initial exported form to an application file that a Macintosh can read. This is easy to do on a Macintosh using a file-encoding program (Macromedia recommends BinHex). Once converted, your projector/movie is ready for distribution.

Previewing Your Settings

If you want to create the best Flash presentation possible, testing is a necessary evil. Thank goodness, then, for the Publish Preview command, which allows you to preview what you have exported, or created, based on the settings you selected in the Publish Settings dialog box.

The Publish Preview command creates and places temporary preview files into the same directory as your Flash authoring file. However, it does not automatically delete them when you've finished previewing; they remain on your drive until you remove them.

To preview you settings using Publish Preview:

1. From the Publish Settings dialog box, select the formats and adjust the settings according to your needs.

2. Click OK.

3. From the File menu choose Publish Preview to open a submenu with the following options (**Figure 13.12**):

Default. This varies depending on the settings you select in the Publish Settings dialog box.

Flash. Opens your movie in Flash's own testing environment (see Chapter 12, "Testing.")

HTML. Opens your default browser with a preview of the Web page that will be created when you publish your project. It contains all of the HTML required to make the movie look and work as it should, based on the settings and template you chose.

GIF. Opens your default browser with a preview of the GIF image that will be generated based on the settings you selected in the Publish Settings dialog box.

JPEG. Opens your default browser with a preview of the JPEG image that will be generated based on the settings you made in the Publish Settings dialog box.

PNG. Opens your default browser with a preview of the PNG image that will be generated based on the settings you made in the Publish Settings dialog box.

Projector. Opens your Flash movie in its own Projector window.

QuickTime. Opens a QuickTime version of your movie inside QuickTime Player.

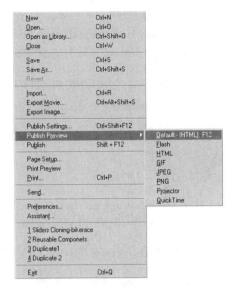

Figure 13.12
The Publish Preview submenu provides options for previewing the settings you selected in the Publish Settings dialog box.

TIP *For a QuickTime preview to work, you must have QuickTime 4 installed on your machine. For more information, visit Apple's Web site at http://www.apple.com/quicktime/.*

Exporting

Using the Publish feature is not the only way to create images or movies from your authoring file. Exporting allows you to accomplish almost the same thing, though it's geared for using Flash-created content in other applications such as a photo-editing or vector-drawing program.

Exporting as a movie

Exporting your authoring file to a movie allows you to do one of two things: You can convert your animation to an animation file format such as Flash, QuickTime, Windows AVI, or an animated GIF (yes, this is pretty much exactly what can be done with the Publish feature, just so you're not confused). Or you can export each frame of your animation as a separate static image file. When exporting in this manner, each file you create is given a name you assign appended by a number indicating its position in the sequence. So, if you provide a file name such as "myimage" for a JPEG sequence and your movie consists of ten frames, the resulting files would be named myimage1.jpg through myimage10.jpg.

To export your animation as a movie or sequence:

1. From the File menu choose Export Movie to bring up the Export Movie dialog box.

2. Name the exported movie, and choose a file type.

3. Click OK.

   Depending on the file type you selected, an additional Export dialog box may appear. For information on these setting see "Export Settings" in this section.

4. Adjust any of the settings in this dialog box, and click OK.

Exporting as an image

Exporting as an image allows you to create a single image file based on the currently displayed frame. If exported in a vector format, you can open this image in a drawing program such as Macromedia FreeHand, Adobe Illustrator, or CorelDraw for further editing. If exported as a bitmap, you can open the image in a photo-editing program such as Adobe Photoshop or Corel Photo-Paint for further editing.

To export a single frame as an image:

1. From the File menu choose Export Movie to bring up the Export Image dialog box.

2. Name the exported image, and choose a file type.

3. Click OK.

   Depending on the file type you selected, an additional Export dialog box may appear. For information on these setting see "Export Settings" in this section.

4. Adjust any of the settings in this dialog box, and click OK.

Export Settings

As you've probably figured out by now, when exporting to most file types, you have several configuration options. The file types discussed here are those found in the Save as type pop-up menu on the Export Movie/Export Image dialog boxes (**Figure 13.13**).

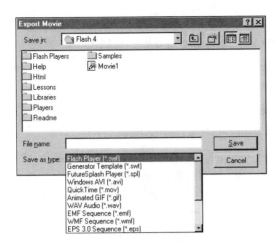

Figure 13.13
The Export Movie dialog box with a list of supported export file types.

Flash Player (*.swf). The settings here are the same as those available from the Flash tab on the Publish Settings dialog box.

Generator Template (*.swt). With one exception, the settings here are the same as those available from the Flash tab on the Publish Settings dialog box:

Create External Font Files. Because a Generator template is dynamic (that is, it can be changed on the fly), creating external font files allows sets of fonts to be created externally from the Generator template and then loaded as needed. This helps reduce the overall size of the template file.

FutureSplash Player (*.spl). This is the file format used by Flash prior to Macromedia's acquisition. The settings here are the same as those available from the Flash tab on the Publish Settings dialog box.

Windows AVI (*.avi) (Windows only). This format will export your movie as a Windows video; however, all interactivity will be lost, and the Mac OS does not support this format. The following options are available (**Figure 13.14**):

Dimensions. Lets you set the vertical and horizontal dimensions, in pixels, of the AVI. If the Maintain Aspect Ratio option is checked, you must enter the width or the height dimension, and Flash will export the AVI so that it maintains the aspect ratio of the original movie. If you leave the option unchecked, you can enter values that change the proportions of the exported AVI.

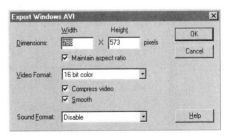

Figure 13.14
The Export Windows AVI dialog box.

Video Format. Lets you set the color depth of the exported movie. A lower color depth results in a smaller exported file, though at cost in image quality.

Compress Video. If you select this, you can set additional compression options for the exported file.

Smooth. Antialiases the exported AVI, creating a slightly larger file but one in which image elements—especially text—will appear smooth rather than jaggy.

Sound Format. Lets you set the sample rate and size of the sound track as well as whether it will be exported in mono or stereo (see "Understanding Sound" in Chapter 5, "Sound"). The smaller the sample rate and size, the smaller the exported file—though sound quality will be sacrificed.

QuickTime (*.mov). The settings here are the same as those available from the Flash tab on the Publish Settings dialog box.

QuickTime video (*mov) (Macintosh Only). Allows you to export your movie in the older QuickTime 3 format. Be aware, however, that exporting to this format is not the same as exporting to QuickTime 4: All Flash interactivity will be lost, and Flash elements will be converted from vector graphics to bitmaps. The following options are available (**Figure 13.15**).

Size. Lets you set the vertical and horizontal dimensions, in pixels, of the QuickTime movie that is created. If you check the Maintain Aspect Ratio option, you need only enter the width or height dimension, and Flash will export the QuickTime movie so that it retains the aspect ratio of the original movie. If you leave this option unchecked, you can enter values that will change the proportions of the exported QuickTime movie.

Format. Lets you set the color depth of the exported movie.

Smooth. Selecting this option antialiases the exported QuickTime movie.

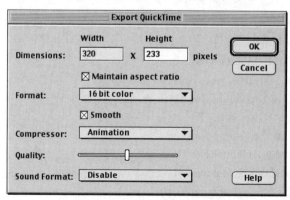

Figure 13.15
The Export QuickTime video dialog box.

Compressor. Allows you to select the standard QuickTime compressor.

Quality. Allows you to set the amount of compression that will be applied to your movie when it is exported to the QuickTime format.

Sound Format. Lets you set the sample rate and size of the sound track as well as whether it is exported in mono or stereo (see "Understanding Sound" in Chapter 5, "Sound"). The smaller the sample rate and size, the smaller the exported file—though sound quality will be sacrificed.

Animated GIF (*.gif). With two exceptions, the settings here are the same as those available from the GIF tab on the Publish Settings dialog box:

Resolution. Resolution is the size of the image based on its width in pixels (dots per inch, or dpi). Obviously, changing the resolution affects the pixel size of your movie, so if you adjust one setting, the other will reflect the change. Click the Match Screen button to make the exported images match the size of the movie as it appears on your screen. A resolution of 72 dpi is usually sufficient for most graphics you can view on your computer.

Colors. Allows you to set the number of colors that will be used to create the exported image. Although fewer colors create a smaller file, image quality suffers. The Standard Colors option uses the Web-safe 216-color palette and usually gives the best results.

WAV Audio (*.wav)(Windows only). If you export your movie in this format, only the sound file will be exported. There are two definable options:

Sound Format. Lets you set the sample rate and size of the soundtrack and whether it's exported in mono or stereo.

Ignore Sound Events. Checking this will exclude Event sounds from the exported sound file.

EMF Sequence/Enhanced Metafile (*.emf) (Windows only). This format allows you to export both vector and bitmap information in a single file, so that it can be imported into other applications.

WMF Sequence/Windows Metafile (*.wmf) (Windows Only). This Windows format for importing and exporting graphics among applications does not include any adjustable settings.

EPS 3.0 Sequence/EPS 3.0 (*.eps). EPS is a popular format for placing image files within page-layout programs. The current frame is exported when using this option.

Adobe Illustrator Sequence/Adobe Illustrator (*.ai). This vector format allows you to export vector elements of your movie so that they can be brought into a vector-drawing program to be edited further. When exporting using this format, you are prompted for which version of Illustrator you would like to export to.

DXF Sequence/DXF (*.dxf). This 3D format lets you export elements of your movie so that they can be brought into a DXF-compatible program for further editing.

PICT sequence/PICT (*.pict) (Macintosh Only). This format allows you to export vector or bitmap information in a file so that it can be imported into other applications. The following options are available (**Figure 13.16**):

Dimensions. Lets you set the dimensions, in pixels, of the PICT. Enter only the width or the height, and Flash will retain the aspect ratio of the original image in the exported image.

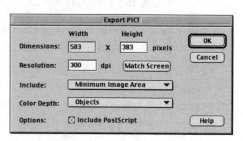

Figure 13.16
The Export PICT dialog box.

Resolution. Click the Match Screen button to make the exported images match the size of the movie as it appears on your screen.

Include. Allows you to choose which elements of your movie will be included in the exported PICT file. If you choose Minimum Image Area, the exported PICT file will be just big enough to include the graphic elements in the current frame. If you choose Full Document Size the entire movie will be exported so that the PICT file dimensions match those found in the Movie Properties dialog box. You can use this setting as an alternative to the Dimensions setting.

Color Depth. This pop-up box serves two purposes: It allows you to determine whether the PICT graphic will be object-based (a vector) or bitmap-based. And if it is bitmap-based, it allows you to set color depth.

Include PostScript. If you choose to export a PICT file as object-based, including PostScript information will optimize the graphic for PostScript printing.

Bitmap Sequence/Bitmap (*.bmp). This format allows you to create bitmapped images for use in other programs. The following options are available:

Dimension. Lets you set the vertical and horizontal dimensions, in pixels, of the bitmap that is created. You can enter either the width or the height because Flash will retain the aspect ratio of the original image in the exported image.

Resolution. Click the Match Screen button to make the exported images match the movie as it appears on your screen.

Include. Pick which elements of your movie will be included in the exported bitmap. Note that the Minimum Image Area option has no effect when exporting as a bitmap sequence.

Color Depth. Lets you set the color depth of the exported bitmap. A lower color depth results in a smaller exported file but at a cost in image quality.

Smooth. Antialiases the exported bitmap, creating a slightly larger file but one in which image elements—especially text—will appear smooth rather than jaggy.

JPEG Sequence/JPEG (*.jpeg). With one exception, this option includes the same settings as those found on the JPEG tab in the Publish Settings dialog box:

Resolution. Click the Match Screen button to make the exported images match the size of the movie as it appears on your screen.

GIF Sequence/GIF (*.gif). With two exceptions, the settings here are the same as those available on the GIF tab in the Publish Settings dialog box:

Resolution. If you click the Match Screen button, the exported images matches the size of the movie as it appears on your screen.

Colors. Allows you to set the number of colors that can be used to create the exported image.

PNG Sequence/PNG (*.png). With two exceptions, the setting here are the same as those available on PNG tab in the Publish Settings dialog box:

Resolution. Click the Match Screen button to make the exported images match the movie as it appears on your monitor.

Include. Pick which elements of your movie will be included in the exported bitmap.

Flash and HTML

You can normally place a Flash movie on an HTML page automatically by using the Publish feature. However, if you wish to build your pages or are interested in creating custom templates, you should know how Flash integrates with HTML.

HTML Tags

As with most things browser related, Microsoft's Internet Explorer and Netscape's Communicator/Navigator each has its own tag requirements that you must follow to display your movie properly on an HTML page. To place a movie on a page so that Internet Explorer can interpret it correctly, use the <OBJECT> tag; for Communicator, use the <EMBED> tag. You can use these tags separately or together on the same page, and you can also use them in conjunction with other HTML content. Each of these tags has additional attributes, or parameters, that affect the look and playback of your movie. The following describes how to place your movie on an HTML page using each tag on separate pages first and then both tags on the same page.

<OBJECT> tag

If you were to place your movie on an HTML page using the <OBJECT> tag, it would look similar to this:

```
<HTML>
<HEAD>
<TITLE>Using the Object Tag</TITLE>
</HEAD>
<BODY>


<OBJECT CLASSID="clsid:D27CDB6E-AE6D-11cf-96B8-44553540000"
WIDTH="400" HEIGHT="400" CODEBASE="http://active.macromedia.com/
flash4/cabs/swflash.cab#version=4,0,0,0">
<PARAM NAME="MOVIE" VALUE="coolflashmovie.swf">
<PARAM NAME="PLAY" VALUE="true">
<PARAM NAME="QUALITY" VALUE="best">
<PARAM NAME="LOOP" VALUE="false">
</OBJECT>


</BODY>
</HTML>
```

Now, let's take a closer look. Within the opening <OBJECT> tag, we find four attributes in the form of ATTRIBUTE="value." These include the CLASSID, WIDTH, HEIGHT, and CODEBASE attributes. Once again, these attributes are contained within the opening <OBJECT> tag and are all required for your movie to appear on the page. After the opening <OBJECT> tag, we find a set of <PARAM> tags. Although the <OBJECT> tag actually places your movie on the page, the <PARAM> tags affect the way it looks and plays. For more information about all of these attributes as well as the <PARAM> tags, see "HTML Tag Reference" later in this chapter.

<EMBED> tag

If you were to place your movie on an HTML page using the <EMBED> tag, it would look similar to this:

```
<HTML>

<HEAD>

<TITLE>Using the Embed Tag</TITLE>

</HEAD>

<BODY>


<EMBED SRC="coolflashmovie.swf" WIDTH="400" HEIGHT="400" PLAY="true"
QUALITY="best" LOOP="false" PLUGINSPAGE="http://www.macromedia.com/
shockwave/download/index.cgi?P1_Prod_Version=ShockwaveFlash">

</EMBED>

</BODY>

</HTML>
```

You will notice two differences in the way the <OBJECT> and <EMBED> tags are used:

The <EMBED> tag consists of only ATTRIBUTE="value" settings, which are within the opening <EMBED> tag. These are equivalent to the <OBJECT> tag's <PARAM> settings.

There are no CLASSID or CODEBASE attributes because these are unique to the <OBJECT> tag. Instead, the <EMBED> tag includes a PLUGINSPAGE attribute, which is unique to it. For more information about all these attributes as well as <PARAM> tags, see "HTML Tag Reference" later in this chapter.

<OBJECT> and <EMBED> tags together

Chances are you'll want both Microsoft and Netscape browser users to be able to view your movie from the same page. You can facilitate this by using the <OBJECT> and <EMBED> tags in tandem. The following example illustrates how to do so:

```
<HTML>

<HEAD>

<TITLE>Using the Object and Embed Tags Together</TITLE>
```

```
</HEAD>

<BODY>


<OBJECT CLASSID="clsid:D27CDB6E-AE6D-11cf-96B8-44553540000" WIDTH=
"400" HEIGHT="400" CODEBASE="http://active.macromedia.com/flash4/cabs/
swflash.cab#version=4,0,0,0">

<PARAM NAME="MOVIE" VALUE="coolflashmovie.swf">

<PARAM NAME="PLAY" VALUE="true">

<PARAM NAME="QUALITY" VALUE="best">

<PARAM NAME="LOOP" VALUE="false">

<EMBED SRC="coolflashmovie.swf" WIDTH="400" HEIGHT="400" PLAY="true"
QUALITY="best" LOOP="false" PLUGINSPAGE="http://www.macromedia.com/
shockwave/download/index.cgi?P1_Prod_Version=ShockwaveFlash">

</EMBED>

</OBJECT>

</BODY>

</HTML>
```

When using the <OBJECT> and <EMBED> tags together on the same page, it's a good idea to enter the same values for both. This will ensure that you movie looks and plays the same in most major browsers.

HTML Tag Reference

The following key will help you to understand the various tags and parameter settings that can affect the way your movie looks and acts on an HTML page.

MOVIE

Required.

The directory path to the Flash movie to be loaded; it can be either a relative or an absolute path. An <OBJECT>-only attribute.

Possible values: YourMoviesName.swf or http://www.yourdomain.com/
                 YourMoviesName.swf

Sample: <PARAM NAME="MOVIE" VALUE="coolflashmovie.swf"> or
                 <PARAM NAME="MOVIE" VALUE="http://www.crazyraven.com/
                 coolflashmovie.swf">

Template variable: $MO

SRC

Required.

The directory path to the Flash movie to be loaded; it can be either a relative or an absolute path. An <EMBED>-only attribute.

Possible values: YourMoviesName.swf or `http://www.yourdomain.com/YourMoviesName.swf`

Sample: `SRC="coolflashmovie.swf"` or `SRC="http://www.crazyraven.com/coolflashmovie.swf">`

Template variable: `$MO`

WIDTH

Required.

This value indicates the width of your movie window within the browser. You may enter a specific pixel amount or a percentage of the browser window.

Possible values: 18–2880 pixels or 0%–100%

Sample: `WIDTH="400"` or `WIDTH="75%"`

Template variable: `$WI`

HEIGHT

Required.

This value indicates the height of your movie window within the browser. You may enter a specific pixel amount or a percentage of the browser window.

Possible values: 18–2880 pixels or 0%–100%

Sample: `HEIGHT="400"` or `HEIGHT="75%"`

Template variable: `$HE`

CLASSID

Required.

The Flash Player ActiveX control identification number, which tells Internet Explorer which ActiveX control to initiate. An `<OBJECT>`-only attribute.

Possible values: `D27CDB6E-AE6D-11cf-96B8-44553540000` (must be entered exactly as shown)

Sample: `CLASSID="D27CDB6E-AE6D-11cf-96B8-44553540000"` (must be entered exactly as shown)

Template variable: not applicable.

CODEBASE

Required.

The URL where the Flash Player ActiveX control can be downloaded if it is not already installed on your users Internet Explorer browser. An `<OBJECT>`- only attribute.

Possible values: `http://"download.macromedia.com/pub/shockwave/cabs/flash/ swfflash.cab#version=4,0,13,0"` (must be entered exactly as shown)

Sample: `CODEBASE=http://"download.macromedia.com/pub/shockwave /cabs/flash/swfflash.cab#version=4,0,13,0"` (must be entered exactly as shown)

Template variable: not applicable (value is not configurable).

PLUGINSPAGE

Required.

The URL where the Netscape plug-in can be downloaded if it is not already installed on your user's Netscape browser. An `<EMBED>`-only attribute.

Possible values: `http://www.macromedia.com/shockwave/download/index.cgi? P1_Prod_Version=ShockwaveFlash` (must be entered exactly as shown)

Sample: `PLUGINSPAGE="http://www.macromedia.com/shockwave/ download/index.cgi?P1_Prod_Version=ShockwaveFlash"` (must be entered exactly as shown)

Template variable: not applicable (value is not configurable).

ID

Optional.

A name that identifies your movie on the page for use in scripting (not to be confused with ActionScript). If no scripting is used in conjunction with Flash, you don't need to fill in this attribute. An <OBJECT>-only attribute.

Possible values: Any name. May not include spaces. When using a template variable, this value is derived from the name of the authoring file.

Sample: ID="MyMovie"

Template variable: $TI

NAME

Optional.

A name that identifies your movie on the page for use in scripting. If no scripting is used in conjunction with Flash, you don't need to fill in this attribute. An <EMBED>-only attribute.

Possible values: Any name. May not include spaces. When using a template variable, this value is derived from the name of the authoring file.

Sample: NAME="MyMovie"

Template variable: $TI

SWLIVECONNECT

Optional.

When using FS Commands in conjunction with JavaScripting within a Netscape browser, Java must be turned on for these FS Commands to work. This attribute either enables (true) or disables (false) Java. Java does not need to be enabled for normal JavaScripting purposes on pages that do not pertain to FS Commands. Enabling it otherwise can slow down the time it takes for your movie to begin playing. The default setting is false. An <EMBED>-only attribute.

Possible values: TRUE. This enables Java.
                   FALSE. This disables Java.

Default setting: FALSE

Sample: SWLIVECONNECT="false"

Template variable: not applicable (must be set in the template code).

PLAY

Optional.

Controls whether your movie begins playback immediately upon being loaded or waits for user interaction.

Possible Values: TRUE. Your movie will begin playing as soon as the first frame has loaded completely.

FALSE. Your movie will wait for user interaction to begin playing.

Default setting: TRUE

Sample for <OBJECT> tag: `<PARAM NAME="PLAY" VALUE="true">`

Sample for <EMBED> tag: `PLAY="true"`

Template variable: `$PL`

LOOP

Optional.

Controls your movie's behavior once it reaches the last frame during playback.

Possible values: TRUE. Your movie will return to the first frame and begin playing again.

FALSE. Your movie will play once and then stop at the last frame.

Default setting: TRUE

Sample for <OBJECT> tag: `<PARAM NAME="LOOP" VALUE="true">`

Sample for <EMBED> tag: `LOOP="true"`

Template variable: `$LO`

QUALITY

Optional.

Lets you determine how certain processor limitations will affect your movie's playback in terms of speed and visual quality.

Possible values:	LOW. Sacrifices the visual quality of your movie to maintain playback speed. With this option, your movie will never be antialiased.
	AUTOLOW. Antialiasing is initially turned off but will be turned on to improve visual quality if the user's processor is fast enough to handle it.
	AUTOHIGH. Antialiasing is initially turned on but will be turned off to improve playback speed if the frames per second rate drops below the amount set in the Movie Properties dialog box.
	HIGH. Maintains even visual quality on computers with slower processors. Antialiasing is always on when this option has been selected. If your movie is animated, bitmaps will not be smoothed; if it is not, they will be.
	BEST. Bitmaps are always smoothed, antialiasing is always on, and frames are never skipped due to processor limitations.
Default setting:	HIGH
Sample for `<OBJECT>` *tag:*	`<PARAM NAME="QUALITY" VALUE="best">`
Sample for `<EMBED>` *tag:*	`QUALITY="best"`
Template Variable:	`$QU`

BGCOLOR

Optional.

Sets the background color of the movie window, overriding the color assigned to your movie in the Movie Properties dialog box.

Possible values: Any hexadecimal color value.

Default setting: The color of the movie background as assigned in the Movie Properties dialog box.

Sample for `<OBJECT>` *tag:*   `<PARAM NAME="BGCOLOR" VALUE="#0099ff">`

Sample for `<EMBED>` *tag:*   `BGCOLOR="#0099ff"`

Template variable: `$BG`

SCALE

Optional.

If the width and height settings you selected for the actual movie window differ from those set for the movie in the Movie Properties dialog box, movie elements (which were designed for a specific size) may not fit perfectly within the new dimensions you set for the movie window. This option determines how the movie will look within the boundaries of the movie window as you specified.

Possible values: SHOWALL. This makes your movie completely visible within the area you defined for the movie window. All elements are scaled to fit within the movie window. Borders may appear between movie elements and the movie window if the movie window's dimensions differ from the movie's original size.

                                     NOBORDER. This scales your movie proportionately so that it fills the entire area of the movie window—no borders appear. As a result, movie elements may be cropped and not visible from within the movie window.

                                     EXACTFIT. This disproportionately scales your movie to fit exactly the dimensions of the movie window. Your movie may appear squashed or bloated depending on how much the movie window's dimensions differ from the actual movie.

Default setting:	SHOWALL
Sample for <OBJECT> tag:	`<PARAM NAME="SCALE" VALUE="showall">`
Sample for <EMBED> tag:	`SCALE="showall"`
Template variable:	`$SC`

SALIGN

Optional.

This attribute allows you to set the alignment of your movie within the movie window if their dimensions differ.

Possible values:	T. Aligns your movie vertically to the top edge of the movie window and center it horizontally.
	B. Aligns your movie vertically to the bottom edge of the movie window and center it horizontally.
	L. Aligns your movie horizontally to the left edge of the movie window and center it vertically.
	R. Aligns your movie horizontally to the right edge of the movie window and center it vertically.
	TL. Aligns your movie to the top left corner of the movie window.
	TR. Aligns your movie to the top right corner of the movie window.
	BL. Aligns your movie to the bottom left corner of the movie window.
	BR. Aligns your movie to the bottom right corner of the movie window.
Default setting:	If this attribute is not specified, your movie will be placed in the center of the movie window.
Sample for <OBJECT> tag:	`<PARAM NAME="SALIGN" VALUE="tl">`
Sample for <EMBED> tag:	`SALIGN="tl"`
Template Variable:	`$SA`

BASE

Optional.

Allows you to set the URL used as a basis for relative links within your movie. Thus, if you movie resides in a directory such as http://www.yourdomain.com/flash/ and you want all relative links in the movie to be referenced from http://www.adifferentdomain.com/, you would enter the latter domain as the BASE attribute's value.

Possible value:s	Any URL.
Default setting:	Same directory as the movie.
Sample for <OBJECT> tag:	`<PARAM NAME="BASE" VALUE=" http://www.adifferentdomain.com/">`
Sample for <EMBED> tag:	`BASE=" http://www.adifferentdomain.com/"`
Template Variable:	`$SA`

MENU

Optional.

Allows you to determine which options are available on the Flash Player pop-up menu that appears when your user right-clicks (Windows) or Control-clicks (Macintosh) the movie in the browser window.

Possible values:	TRUE. Displays all the available menu items.
	FALSE. Displays only the About Flash menu item.
Default setting:	TRUE
Sample for <OBJECT> tag:	`<PARAM NAME="MENU" VALUE="true">`
Sample for <EMBED> tag:	`MENU="true"`
Template Variable:	`$ME`

WMODE

Optional.

Allows you to take advantage of capabilities available only on a Windows version of Internet Explorer that has the Flash Player ActiveX control installed. This attribute is not available for the `<EMBED>` tag.

Possible values: WINDOW. Plays your movie within its own rectangular area on the HTML page, providing the best playback performance.

OPAQUE. Allows you to move elements on the HTML page behind the rectangular area of the movie without having them show through. Use this option in conjunction with dynamic HTML layers.

TRANSPARENT. Causes the background color of your Flash movie (as set in the Movie Properties dialog box) to become transparent so that the background of the HTML page on which your movie is embedded will show through. This setting, though cool, provides the slowest playback performance. Use it sparingly.

Default setting: WINDOW

Sample for `<OBJECT>` *tag:* `<PARAM NAME="WMODE" VALUE="opaque">`

Template Variable: `$WM`

Setting Up the Server

When your movie is downloaded over the Web, two things are sent over the connection that enable viewers to see your movie: The first, and most obvious, is the movie file itself. The second is the movie's MIME (which rhymes with dime) type, which a Netscape browser needs to determine which plug-in to use to play your movie. Without this MIME type, your movie may not be displayed properly—or at all—in a Netscape browser (this is not an issue with Internet Explorer). It may even cause the browser—and your computer—to crash, so be sure to take the proper steps to avoid this.

Setting of the MIME type is done on the server which delivers your movie. Thus, unless you're the administrator of your own server, you'll probably never need to do this yourself. You will, however, need to call your ISP or talk to the server administrator so that they can set the MIME type for your site.

When setting up the MIME type for Flash content, you need to know the MIME type itself (application/x-shockwave-flash) and the Flash file extension (.swf).

You only need to set MIME types once, and they should cover all Flash content within your site. With these two necessary ingredients, your movie delivery is complete.

Plug-In Issues

It used to be that a plug-in was simply the thing at the end of the lamp cord that allowed it to access the power in the outlet. Then science advanced, and *plug-in* took on an additional meaning—that of an air freshener which used 120 volts of electricity to heat up a hardened chunk of perfume to make a room smell "fresh." Thank god for modern science. Today *plug-in* has yet another meaning, which is the one we're interested in: When Netscape introduced version 2 of its browser, it added the ability to *plug in* new features to increase functionality.

All browsers have built-in capabilities that enable users to read text, view pictures, hear sounds, and more. Early on, however, browser developers realized that they could make their products more useful by allowing other developers to add functionality—a concept already employed by such programs as Macromedia Director and FreeHand and Adobe Photoshop.

But how, you ask, does the plug-in get integrated with the browser? Several come pre-installed, but if you view a page that requires a plug-in that your browser does not have, it will either ask you if you want to download it or it will download it automatically. Once the plug-in has been downloaded and installed, you can see the page as it was meant to be viewed.

To see Flash content, you need the Flash plug-in. And with each new version of Flash, comes a new version of the plug-in. This is necessary, for example, because a Flash 3 plug-in will not be able to understand any of Flash 4's new scripting capabilities. Now, this is not to say that you can't view a Flash 4 presentation using the Flash 3 plug-in. It just means that if you want to use all of the groovy new features of Flash 4, you will need to have the Flash 4 plug-in installed.

Currently, more than 100 million users—or 75 percent of those online—have the Flash plug-in installed. However, because it's so new, relatively few people have the latest version (Flash 4) installed. Your hurdle is convincing users that it's worth their time to download and install it.

The Front-Door Approach

Figure 13.17
The Get Flash button.

One of the best things you can do is to tackle the problem at your site's front door—that is, its home page. It's effective to indicate somewhere that your site uses Flash 4 to create an exciting experience. To enjoy it users need to have the Flash 4 plug-in or they need to get it. Place the Get Flash button somewhere on that page and link it to Macromedia's download site at http://www.macromedia.com/shockwave/download/index.cgi?P1_Prod_Version=ShockwaveFlash (**Figure 13.17**). Clicking the button will take users to a well-executed page that explains the plug-in's benefits and its download procedure. It will also include a link so that the user can download the plug-in. Once a user has downloaded and installed the plug-in, he or she can return to your site and view it in all its glory.

Go with What Works

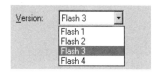

Figure 13.18
You can select a version number for export from the Flash format tab in the Publish Settings dialog box.

If you want to have an interesting Flash-driven site yet keep plug-in download to a minimum, the solution is simple: Design for Flash 3—at least until the majority of users have Flash 4. This, of course, means avoiding the features that are unique to Flash 4.

Keep in mind, however, that you can export Flash 4–created content using the Flash 3 format (**Figure 13.18**). Even though the Flash 4–specific features won't work in Flash 3, everything else—including Mouse Events, Tell Targets, and more—will.

Provide an Alternative

Maybe you only want to provide Flash content for those who have the plug-in installed, though you don't want to require it for Web users to visit your site. If that's the case, provide an alternative: You can create a Flash-driven version of your site *and* an HTML version (**Figure 13.19**). This way, if the plug-in is not installed on your user's computer, he or she can still visit the HTML version without a hitch.

Figure 13.19
Some sites let viewers choose whether they want to view an HTML or Flash version of the site.

However, we don't really recommend this approach because maintaining two sites can be a headache. If you think you're up to it, though, don't let us stop you.

Bold and Beautiful

If you truly don't care about potentially annoying your users, go ahead and set up your Flash 4 site so that it automatically installs the latest version of the plug-in—it also puts your site way ahead of those who are just too chicken try this method. Besides, they'll thank you for it in the end. A Flash 4 site can be one of the coolest and most advanced sites out there, but only if you're not afraid to use it and force it on your viewers. If you offer a way out, some people will take it.

Understanding Templates

Once you begin using Flash to create numerous movies to go on Web pages, you'll really appreciate the addition of templates to Flash 4.

You need to set numerous HTML settings and parameters if you want your movie to look and function properly. There are width and height settings, playback options, and even JavaScript in some cases. Some of us use custom HTML pages (with custom JavaScript perhaps) to place our Flash content. With the exception of a few changing attributes, these custom HTML pages could be used for many Flash movies. After all, writing plug-in detection scripts and filling in parameters every time you want to place a Flash movie on a Web page—especially if you only want to change a few things— quickly becomes tedious. However, by using templates in conjunction with the Publish feature, you can easily fill in attributes that affect not only what movie goes on the page but also how your movie will look and play back in the Web browser. You can even eliminate the need to edit an HTML page with a Flash movie. This is because the template is created once with variables placed in specific places within the template. Using the Publish feature, you then fill in specific information (`<OBJECT>` and `<EMBED>` attributes) concerning the way you want this movie to appear and play back in the browser window. When you publish to HTML, the variables, in the template you select, are replaced with the information you entered. The resulting document is an HTML page with your movie embedded. You could easily use the same template, enter different settings in the HTML tab of the Publish settings dialog box, and output a new HTML page.

The Process

You go through three stages when creating and using templates:

Creating the template.

Selecting a template and filling in the settings on the HTML tab of the Publish Settings dialog box.

Publishing from Flash, which generates an HTML page that is a product of the template you chose and the settings you adjusted.

Creating a template

A Flash template is simply a text file that contains both HTML code (which never changes) and template code, or variables (which are not the same as the variables used in ActionScripts). Flash includes prebuilt templates, which are sufficient for most users' needs; however, you can create as many templates as you want.

Creating a template is really no different than creating a standard HTML page. The only difference is that you replace specific values pertaining to a Flash movie with variables that begin with a dollar sign. If you need to use the dollar sign for some other purpose other than as a template variable, prefix it with a back slash (\$). For a complete list of template variables, see **Table 13.1** at the end of this section.

In the meantime, take a look at the following sample template code:

```
$TTCool Template
$DS
This Cool Template
is to help you understand
how to use variables.
$DF
<HTML>
<HEAD>
<TITLE>$TI</TITLE>
</HEAD>
<BODY bgcolor=$BG>
```

```
$MU

$MT

<OBJECT CLASSID="clsid:D27CDB6E-AE6D-11cf-96B8-44553540000" WIDTH=
"$WI" HEIGHT="$HE"CODEBASE="http://active.macromedia.com/flash4/cabs/
swflash.cab#version=4,0,0,0">

<PARAM NAME="MOVIE" VALUE="$MO">

<PARAM NAME="PLAY" VALUE="$PL">

<PARAM NAME="QUALITY" VALUE="$QU">

<PARAM NAME="LOOP" VALUE="$LO">


<EMBED SRC"$MO" WIDTH="$WI" HEIGHT="$HE" PLAY="$PL" QUALITY="$QU"
LOOP="$LO" PLUGINSPAGE="http://www.macromedia.com/shockwave/download/
index.cgi?P1_Prod_Version=ShockwaveFlash">

<NOEMBED><IMG SRC=$IS WIDTH=$IW HEIGHT=$IH usemap=$IU BORDER=0>
</NOEMBED>

</EMBED>

</OBJECT>

</BODY>

</HTML>
```

Now let's take a closer look at each section of this template.

```
$TTCool Template
```

The name Cool Template will be what appears in the template pop-up menu on the HTML tab of the Publish Settings dialog box.

```
$DS

This Cool Template

is to help you understand

how to use variables.

$DF
```

Anything between $DS and $DF is what appears in the Info box that you access by clicking the Info button on the HTML tab of the Publish Settings Dialog box.

```
<HTML>

<HEAD>
```

```
<TITLE>$TI</TITLE>

</HEAD>
```

This is the standard way of beginning an HTML document. The $TI variable between the <TITLE> tags represents the page title as it will appear on the Web browser. This is derived from the file name of the movie placed on the page. Thus, if your movie is named CoolFlashMovie.swf, your page will be entitled CoolFlashMovie.

```
<BODY bgcolor=$BG>
```

This will cause the HTML page that is generated to have the same background color as your movie.

```
$MU
```

This template variable will place a list of the URLs used in your movie on the generated HTML page.

```
$MT
```

This template variable will place a list of text used in your movie on the generated HTML page so that search engines can index your movie's content. This is output between HTML comment tags.

```
<OBJECT CLASSID="clsid:D27CDB6E-AE6D-11cf-96B8-44553540000" WIDTH=
"$WI" HEIGHT="$HE" CODEBASE=http://"download.macromedia.com/pub/
shockwave/cabs/flash/swfflash.cab#version=4,0,13,0"
```

You will notice the WIDTH and HEIGHT parameters of the <OBJECT> tag have been replaced with template variables.

```
<PARAM NAME="MOVIE" VALUE="$MO">

<PARAM NAME="PLAY" VALUE="$PL">

<PARAM NAME="QUALITY" VALUE="$QU">

<PARAM NAME="LOOP" VALUE="$LO">
```

Different attributes, or parameters, of the <OBJECT> tag have been substituted with template variables.

```
<EMBED SRC="$MO" WIDTH="$WI" HEIGHT="$HE" PLAY="$PL" QUALITY="$QU"
LOOP="$LO" PLUGINSPAGE="http://www.macromedia.com/shockwave/download/
index.cgi?P1_Prod_Version=ShockwaveFlash">
```

The different attributes of the <EMBED> tag have been replaced with template variables.

```
<NOEMBED><IMG SRC=$IS WIDTH=$IW HEIGHT=$IH usemap=$IU
BORDER=0></NOEMBED>
```

For browsers that don't support the plug-in, the `<NOEMBED>` tag provides an alternative image that Flash automatically generates when you publish. You'll notice the template variables that are used.

```
</EMBED>
</OBJECT>
</BODY>
</HTML>
```

These are the tags you need to finish creating your template. Although this template does not use every possible template variable, it should still give you a pretty good idea of how template variables are used in conjunction with HTML.

Template variables can be used in conjunction with other HTML content, including JavaScript, Cold Fusion, Active Server Pages, and more. Any template variables used within any syntax of these programming languages will be replaced with actual movie and image values when you publish your movie, based on the values you've entered on the HTML tab of the Publish Settings dialog box.

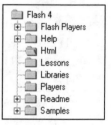

Figure 13.20
Place all custom templates in the HTML folder of the Flash 4 directory.

Save your template (as an HTML document if you wish; see "The Published HTML Page" later in this section for information about file extensions) and place it in the HTML folder of the Flash 4 program directory (**Figure 13.20**). Once you have created a template and placed it in this folder, it becomes available from the template pop-up menu on the HTML tab of the Publish Settings dialog box.

Entering Publish settings

Now that you've created a template, you can use it for any movie in conjunction with the Publish feature.

Using an example authoring file (MapUSA.fla) that we wish to publish to HTML, we'll adjust the settings for our demonstration (**Figure 13.21**). All of these settings relate to a template variable that, when published, will be replaced with the values you set. Once you have entered all of the necessary values, click the Publish button to complete the process.

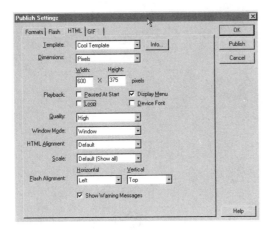

Figure 13.21
The values entered on the HTML format tab of the Publish Settings dialog box are the values that will replace corresponding template variables when you publish.

The published HTML page

When publishing your movie, you need to be aware of two things: the name of the published HTML that is created and its location.

The name of the published HTML page will be a combination of your movie's file name and the file extension you gave the template. For example, if your movie's file name is MapUSA.swf and the file name of your template is cooltemplate.html, the resulting file name of the published HTML page will be MapUSA.html. If the template's file extension were .cfm (Cold Fusion), the resulting file name of the published HTML page would be MapUSA.cfm.

The published HTML page and all of its associated files can be found in the same directory as the authoring file that was used at the time of publishing.

The HTML of the published HTML page will appear similar to the following example. Compare it with the HTML of the original template to help understand how the template itself and the settings adjusted in the Publish Settings dialog box merge to become the final HTML document:

```
<HTML>

<HEAD>

<TITLE>MapUSA</TITLE>

</HEAD>

<BODY bgcolor=#FFFFFF>


<A HREF="http://www.usa.com"></A>

<A HREF="http://www.america.com"></A>

<!-This is a map of the USA ->

<OBJECT CLASSID="clsid:D27CDB6E-AE6D-11cf-96B8-44553540000" WIDTH=
"600" HEIGHT="375" CODEBASE="http://active.macromedia.com/flash4/cabs/
swflash.cab#version=4,0,0,0">

<PARAM NAME="MOVIE" VALUE="MapUSA.swf">

<PARAM NAME="PLAY" VALUE="true">

<PARAM NAME="QUALITY" VALUE="high">

<PARAM NAME="LOOP" VALUE="false">

<EMBED SRC="MapUSA.swf" WIDTH="600" HEIGHT="375" PLAY="true" QUALI-
TY="high" LOOP="false" PLUGINSPAGE="http://www.macromedia.com/
shockwave/download/index.cgi?P1_Prod_Version=ShockwaveFlash">

<NOEMBED><IMG SRC="MapUSA.gif" WIDTH=600 HEIGHT=375 usemap="#MapUSA"
BORDER=0></NOEMBED>

</EMBED>

</OBJECT>

</BODY>

</HTML>
```

Template Variables

Table 13.1 is a complete list of the variables you can use in creating your own templates. Keep in mind that template variables are case sensitive, so $tt will not work, but $TT will.

Table 13.1
Template Variables

Parameter	Variable	Parameter	Variable
Template title	$TT	Image height (unspecified image type)	$IH
Template description start	$DS	Image file name (unspecified image type)	$IS
Template description finish	$DF		
Width	$WI	Image map name	$IU
Height	$HI	Image map tag location	$IM
Movie	$MO	QuickTime width	$QW
Name, ID, or Title	$TI	QuickTime height	$QH
HTML Alignment	$HA	QuickTime file name	$QN
Looping	$LO	GIF width	$GW
Play	$PL	GIF height	$GH
Quality	$QU	GIF file name	$GS
Scale	$SC	JPEG width	$JW
Salign	$SA	JPEG height	$JH
Wmode	$WM	JPEG file name	$JN
Devicefont	$DE	PNG width	$PW
Bgcolor	$BG	PNG height	$PH
Movie Text	$MT	PNG file name	$PN
Movie URLs	$MU	Generator variables <OBJECT> tag	$GV
Parameters for <OBJECT>	$PO	Generator variables <EMBED> tag	$GE
Parameters for <EMBED>	$PE		
Image width (unspecified image type)	$IW		

Publishing Tutorial

 To help you put all of this information together—and we know there's a lot—we've created the following interactive tutorial, which you will find on the CD-ROM disc, along with the resulting source file:

Publishing Your Movie. This tutorial guides you through the steps of publishing your movie, including setting values in the Publish Settings dialog box, previewing the settings, and doing a final publish.

Planning Your Project

You've always dreamed of building your own house. It will be right on the beach so that you can listen to the sounds of the ocean as the sun sets each night. Just out the back door will be your favorite surf break. And you and your friends will hang out by the barbecue drinking Margaritas. Life will be good.

Since you've already got the place designed in your head, you don't waste any time getting to the local hardware store to pick up some lumber, tools, a couple of commodes (the house will have two full baths, after all), and some appliances. But wait: You realize you can't tackle this project alone—you begin to ask for assistance. By the end of the day, you've rounded up a slew of helpers. Work starts in the morning.

However, when morning rolls around, you realize that you forgot to find out if any of your helpers are actually qualified. No matter: The important thing is to finish your house by the end of the day, so that the Margarita fest can begin at sundown. Everyone arrives as promised, and you give them their instructions: "I want a two-story, four-bedroom, two-bath house … Now get to work!"

It's a beautiful day, the temperature is perfect, and coolers of Gatorade ring the property. Your house is coming together nicely, and all is going swimmingly. By the afternoon, you discover you're ahead of schedule! Finally the last nail has been hammered, the final shingle put in place. It's time to celebrate.

> Then you hear a crash. You get outside just in time to watch your dream home collapse like a house of cards.
>
> The problem? You forgot the foundation.
>
> Devastated, you realize that poor planning has robbed you of everything: time, money, dignity.
>
> Don't let this happen to you.

In Flash, you'll soon realize, planning is no less important than it is in building a house. When creating a Flash presentation, you must keep in mind several factors that can affect the final product. To get a firm grasp of the issues, we suggest you turn to one of the best tools we know of—questions. Ask lots of them and really listen to the answers. Start with the sidebar "Basic Planning Questions."

Basic Planning Questions

- Will the movie be streamed from the Internet or as a stand-alone player?

- If stand-alone, will it be distributed on disk or CD?

- Will the movie be a presentation, an interactive information tool, or a combination of both?

- What, if any, is the extent of the interactivity?

- Other than vector art, what types of media are required (bitmaps, music, sounds, movies)?

- What is the target market?

- What is the production's budget?

Another important consideration in planning a Flash project—perhaps *the* most important consideration—is *message*: what it is you're trying to convey and how best to get that idea across. Although creativity is important, you'll need to back up your brilliant ideas with thought and research. Remember: Your job as a Flash developer is to create a presentation that will sway the viewer. Often bells and whistles aren't enough; sometimes they're too much—you'll need to figure out how to channel your energies in the most efficient and effective manner. In this chapter you'll learn about some of the things to consider before you even open Flash as well as how to squeeze every bit of potential from your work: Let's begin.

Processor Considerations

Hollywood has a way of distorting reality. Just as tons of teenage girls drool at the thought of being trapped on a sinking *Titanic* with Leonardo DiCaprio, anyone who regularly uses a computer must salivate over the speed at which computers run in the movies. In Hollywood's vision of the world, every home computer is connected to the Net, you never have to boot your machine, and that desktop box contains enough power to coordinate a shuttle mission, find a cure for cancer, and crunch out the graphics for *Jurassic Park*—all at the same time!

Well, here's the cruel reality: Processor speed—which today can range from 66 MHz to faster than 500 MHz—is a major determinant of computer power. And this means that what takes 1 second to show up on the 500-MHz machine could take 10 seconds or longer on a slower machine (**Figure 14.1**). As you can imagine, this is a major factor in animation. On slow computers, your animated movie will probably end up looking choppy. And you can forget about those cool motion effects. All is not lost, however: Even though you can't anticipate every possibility in creating your movie, you can take some steps to minimize the effect slower machines will have on your movie's playback. For starters:

Avoid animating too many things at once. By *too many,* we mean mainly large objects that require a lot of screen space to move. Although it's tempting to animate everything at once, all you need to do is play your movie on a slow computer to realize that a little self-control is in order—that is, if you can stay awake long enough to watch your movie to play.

Animate in the smallest area possible. Not surprisingly, it takes less processing power to animate something small than it does to animate something large. You can usually animate several small things simultaneously without too much trouble. So, instead of making that monster object rotate, make it smaller and do something else creative with it. And if you do decide to animate a large object, avoid animating anything else on the screen at the same time. This way, you free up resources to handle the large object.

Avoid tweening too many objects at once. Although tweening can be a real time-saver in developing your Flash project, it eats up a lot of resources. Use tweening all you can; just be sure not to use it all at once.

By following these guidelines, you can avoid overstressing a slow processor.

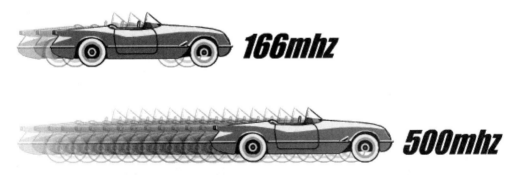

Figure 14.1
The speed at which your presentation will play varies
depending on the processor speed of a particular machine.

Movie Size Considerations

You can balance your craving for super-dazzling presentations with processor limitations by making your movie smaller: All you need to do is change its dimensions. A full-screen movie will play much slower than one half that size (that is, if it contains animation).

Once again, this isn't to say you can't create full-screen presentations. Sometimes it's more important to use all that screen space than it is to have many things moving across the screen.

If, for example, you're trying to showcase the beauty and craftsmanship of a product, you may well want to adopt the full-screen approach and cut back on the animation. However, if instead you want to evoke a sense of excitement through movement, you should probably employ smaller dimensions for your movie so that you can use animation without overburdening your viewers' processors.

Yet another approach makes it possible for you to get the best of both worlds: That is, you can create a full-screen presentation with colorful, imaginative, and effective *static* (or nonmoving) content, and just animate a portion of the screen at a time. If you want to display a big picture of your products that changed occasionally, you could simply animate some content next to each product picture, providing a workable compromise.

Choosing a Movie Speed

On one of the old *I Love Lucy* shows, Lucy and Ethel get jobs packing chocolates into boxes as they come off an assembly line. In this classic TV moment the humor stems from a malfunctioning conveyor belt that begins spitting out chocolates faster then Lucy and Ethel can process them—in the end, the two resort to stuffing candies in their mouths to keep pace. A huge mess—and much hilarity—ensue.

The lesson here is that faster is not always better. While it would be nice to think that by upping your movie's frame rate, you could create videolike transitions that never skipped, jumped, or appeared choppy, Flash's reliance on processor speed means this is not always possible. In fact, a higher frame rate can sometimes even harm your presentation.

No matter what frame rate you choose, each processor can handle information only so quickly—and because so many factors are involved, you can't possibly know just how fast that is. If a particular computer can render your movie at a maximum rate of 20 fps, setting Flash's fps setting to 100 won't improve matters. That computer will *still* show your movie at 20 fps—max. Now, a faster computer may be able to play the same movie at 100 fps, but few of us own the supermachines capable of this.

So upping a movie's speed doesn't help; in fact, it could even slow things down. Here's how: Let's say your presentation is 10 seconds long. At 12 fps, 120 frames (10 seconds x 12 frames per second) need to be played through from beginning to end. If you increase your fps rate to 20, you will have 200 frames from start to finish—or an additional 80 frames to draw over the course of your presentation. While slower computers can handle 120 frames over 10 seconds fairly easily, those additional 80 frames could slow your movie to a crawl because they make more than 50 percent more work for the computer to accomplish in the same 10 seconds (or over the course of your presentation). *Now* can you see how you could end up with precisely the opposite effect you were trying to achieve?

So, what's a reasonable frame rate? The default setting of 12 is usually a good rate to try, with 20 fps at the high end and 24 fps the absolute maximum you should consider. (Of course, this is just our humble opinion.) The only exception to this rule would be if you were to export your Flash presentation as a video file such as QuickTime or Windows AVI. Because these formats are not as processor intensive, you can pump up the frame rate without too many problems.

We don't want you to think you can't produce impressive results within these parameters. Quite the opposite is true: Many examples of beautiful and exciting Flash content have been created using these guidelines. All it takes is some planning.

Defining Your Audience

When it comes to putting together effective presentations, one of the best things—if not *the* best thing—you can do is to watch television commercials! Try to figure out how and why they are doing certain things, and one of the first things you'll notice is that certain types of commercials play only at specific times. Watch a male-oriented program (say a football game), and you'll notice that most of the adds involve trucks, scantily clad women, and beer—sometimes all three. Watch a program with a predominantly female audience (say the Miss America pageant), and you'll see that most of the commercials deal in some fashion with flowers, families, and love. And watch the Cartoon Network (our favorite) and you'll see commercials touting highly sweetened corn meal, high-octane sodas, and the latest in action figures. Chances are you won't see a commercial about investing on the Cartoon Network. And what good would it do to show a body lotion commercial between timeouts in a basketball game. Few guys care about smooth skin; thus, advertising dollars would be wasted.

Another thing to notice about commercials is their use of imagery. You won't find an older gentleman in a three-piece suit promoting the benefits of marshmallow-laced cereal; though you're more than likely to come across a cartoon character doing the same. And when it comes to selling trucks, a mud-soaked pickup making its way across the Grand Canyon conveys just the sort of rugged durability potential buyers are likely to seek. On the other hand, a scene of a vehicle barreling down the highway at a breakneck speed is probably a more appropriate approach for selling a sports car.

To get the most out of your project, do what TV advertisers do: *Define your audience.* Figure out who makes up the target audience you're trying to reach, and then define your message. Use adjectives to describe your audience, and then ask questions to determine the best approach.

Do you want to promote, entertain, inform, or convince? Or are you striving for a combination of all four?

What do you want your audience to think after viewing your presentation?

Is it more important to give a visual presentation or a textual one?

Do you want to build a new image or reuse an existing one?

Do you have overwhelming facts to back up your message?

You could ask many other questions, depending on how you want the viewer to react to your movie and what it is you're trying to promote. Once you've gathered this information, you should write a statement that describes your goal in one sentence. Something like, "We want to get kids addicted to our sugar-coated product based on the fact that it's the 'in' thing to do."

And one more thing: *Use humor whenever, wherever appropriate.*

Once you've defined your audience and refined your message, you need to establish some project guidelines. Say you've been commissioned to create a Flash-based Web site for a company that wants to promote the benefits of its new vitamin, Perfectium2000. After discussing the project with the folks at the company, you've determined that your audience consists of men and women, ages 20 to 50, who are healthy but concerned about maintaining optimal health. The company wants to get out the message that by taking Perfectium2000 and eating well, folks can maintain the high energy levels required for an active lifestyle; it also wants to show that this is easy to do. Your client already has a large base of faithful users, but it wants to attract new customers.

If you're using such adjectives as *healthy, active, athletic,* and *informed* to describe your audience, what kind of imagery comes to mind? Sports, healthy-looking people, an organized home life, smiles, bright colors, facts and figures, the great outdoors, successful people? Any of these images are appropriate for your site because they are all things your target audience will relate to. And use movement wherever possible.

Your client also wants new customers to realize that its vitamin regimen is an easy program to start and maintain. Thus, you could contrast a busy lifestyle with a vitamin regimen that takes only minutes a day. Put a small timer on the page with a quickly rotating second hand. To show that the product is safe, present some data along with your images of happy people. To show that it's effective, provide testimonials or show before-and-after pictures. Use morphing to turn fat letters (which may be part of a headline) into skinny ones, thereby planting the subliminal message that big turns to small with the help of this product.

The important thing is to understand your audience and your message. Then, you can let your imagination run wild.

Storyboarding

Nearly everyone has seen or created a storyboard—it's just the terminology that's specific to moviemaking. If, for example, you've created a budget, you've created a storyboard. Likewise, if you've seen architectural blueprints, you've seen storyboards. A storyboard simply provides an easy means to lay out ideas and content—to determine what works best and to pinpoint potential problems.

For multimedia, a storyboard represents the entire project, denoting general layout, navigation, movement, images used, interactive elements (and their uses), sequence duration, sound and audio placement and synchronization, and link and button functions. Although this may sound like an overwhelming amount of things to consider, all are issues that will arise at some point in the development process. If you storyboard a project, at least you'll see them coming. Need more to convince you? Consider these benefits:

They're easy to create—you can even use pencil and paper.

They require few resources and materials.

Anyone can create one, even nondesigners.

They allow you to anticipate—and prevent—problems.

They enable you to explore numerous design options.

They serve as a common point of reference for design teams and clients, spurring input and discussion.

Figure 14.2 shows a sample of the storyboard discussed in the following paragraphs. (A blank copy is also included on the CD as storyboard2.ai, in Adobe Illustrator format).

Because Flash allows you to create your content in scenes, we strongly recommend that you think of your content in that way, not only in Flash but also in the storyboarding process—it's an excellent way to break up content. The first step in the storyboarding process is to give your scene a name, such as Home/Opening (or for a non-Web presentation, simply Opening).

Next, define your scene's duration (in seconds), and then write down whatever fps setting you choose. If you plan to create a scene with interactivity but no animation, put *0* here. Once you've chosen the duration and fps, you can determine the number of frames the scene will contain. Write this number in the Total FPS section. You may sometimes run into time constraints here—for example, having to keep a scene under 30 seconds because it's an introduction to a Web page. If you know of such constraints, you'll be better able to plan the scene's progression.

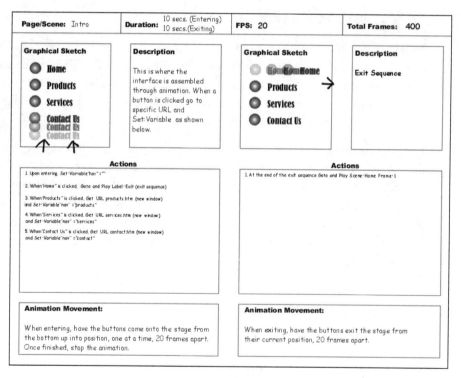

Figure 14.2
Using a storyboard helps you to visualize the look and flow of your presentation prior to devoting too much actual production time to it. This provides a means to work out details and helps you to avoid costly mistakes.

In the next step you get to doodle a bit, drawing a rough idea of what should occur at the beginning of the scene. Here, draw as many of the scene's objects (buttons, pictures, and such) as you can. You may even wish to add color and textures, though these aren't required. This is after all supposed to be a time-saving tool.

Next, provide a description of how it all works, in the section labeled Description. Describe how objects interact with each other, how their movements are animated, how they exit the scene, and the feeling you're trying to convey.

As you can see, this is a simple process—and one where you easily can catch mistakes and make revisions. Of course, scenes can get more complex, so you can use as many worksheets per scene as necessary. Just remember: Try to show concepts rather than details—those can be added when you actually start creating in Flash.

Metaphors

Have you ever thought about the way you work with your computer? After you've worked with one long enough, you tend to do things automatically without actually thinking about *how* you're doing them. But, for a moment, let's ponder the subject anyway. Consider a typical graphics program, such as Macromedia Fireworks and Adobe Photoshop. If you look at its interface, you'll see that it's made up of a bunch of buttons, tabs, palettes, and brushes as well as a clean, white canvas—all of which are really just bits of computer information presented to look like traditional artist tools. And all of which would disappear in an instant if the power went out—though they'd just as certainly reappear once power returned.

Even though the interface is made up of intangible objects, we're thankful for the way it helps us get things done. Imagine having to create an image by entering the appropriate computer code. Using an interface that simulates real-world tools makes it easier for us to understand how to create beautiful *digital* images that can be every bit as spectacular as one we can actually put our hands on.

We use such metaphors all the time when working with computers, putting tasks into contexts that make them understandable and thus easy to carry out. Interface designers know how important metaphors are—to make things easy and to make them *obvious*. Which should be your goal in creating Flash content.

Need some help thinking of metaphors for your own designs? Be aware of a couple of things: One, metaphors are not always necessary or even appropriate. Even

Photoshop or Fireworks requires that you sometimes enter information via your keyboard. (Sometimes it's best to make user interaction as straightforward as possible.) And when using metaphors, it's best to simulate things that move or change—that is, that can be clicked, moved, picked up, selected, felt, and heard. You can use buttons and levers (that make clicking sounds when pressed), flashing lights, gauges, doors, animals, staplers, speakers, knobs, and all kinds of other stuff. Try to make the viewer forget that he or she is actually staring at a computer monitor.

For example, let's say you're creating the interface for a building supply Web site. To build a page, on clicking a navigation button, you could initially show a blueprint of what the page should look like and then go around the page with a hammer (of course, a Flash-based hammer) "nailing" it together. Your navigation buttons could consist of power switches that turn off the lights in one room and turn them on in another. Let your imagination run wild so that you can capture the attention of your audience and make your presentation enjoyable.

Transitions

Generally, people don't do well with instantaneous or immediate change—we usually like to ease our way into situations. For most of us, even getting out of bed is a major transition that requires time and determination to pull off—and still we sometimes fail. The point is, we use transitions constantly to deal with change. Your Flash project should be no different.

Using transitions to transform objects, or even whole scenes, in your movie creates a smooth-flowing presentation. While you may sometimes want to create a shock effect or give the feeling of "popping" into the scene, you don't want your presentation to turn into a simple slideshow—especially when you can do so much more.

Using the many tools and techniques we've discussed thus far, you can create any of these as transitions in Flash: fade in, fade out, size bigger, size smaller, slide in, slide out, rotate/spin, flip, skew, blink, bounce, morph, pulse, wave, color change, add, subtract, blind, scramble, residual, and focus.

You can combine two or three of these transitions for even greater effect.

Streaming

Despite the benefits of streaming, many Flash developers fail to make use of it. You've probably encountered the infamous "Now Loading…" sequence that sometimes plays when a page with Flash content begins to load into your browser. Affectionately referred to as "preloaders," these sequences are actually animations displayed before your main movie has loaded. In other words, the animation is *preloaded*. (An interactive tutorial explaining how to create a preloader is included on the CD-ROM disc.) Such preloaders are not bad in and of themselves. However, there is a problem if you have to wait 5 to 10 minutes for the main content to begin, as you watch one of these sequences, only to realize that once the main part of the movie does begin to play the download is actually complete. Where, in all this, was streaming utilized? You might as well put a 1-MB video file on the page, and have your visitors download that.

To reap the benefits of streaming, you need to consider a few things in the planning process.

> **TIP** *Before going over the following information, you may want to review the "How Streaming Works" section in Chapter 12, "Testing Your Movie."*

Imagine the parking nightmare that would occur at the Indianapolis 500 if the parking lot gates didn't open until all 250,000 spectator cars were lined up and waiting. This means that at even 249,999 cars the lots would still be closed until the last car showed up and then, and only then, would everyone start parking. Not a very smart use of resources. Talk about road rage! Fortunately, the gate opens early, so some cars are being parked as others are filing in. This continues at an even pace so that when the last car shows up, the previous 249,999 cars are already parked.

In much the same way, streaming delivers part of your movie over the Web while the rest continues to download in the background. If you plan it just right, you can usually have your preload sequence play for just a short time before the main section of your movie begins.

The difference between the car analogy and streaming your movie is that cars are generally all about the same size while the frame sizes in your movie can vary wildly: Although some may have 20 KB of content, others may have none; so it takes some frames longer to download then others. For your movie to stream as seamlessly as possible, you need to apply a few basic buffering techniques when planning your presentation's flow.

If you have downloaded all of your movie's 80 frames in the background but have only actually viewed the first 50, 30 frames are *buffered,* or already downloaded but waiting to be played. The trick to maintaining a smooth streaming presentation is to keep this buffer amount as high as possible. In our example, the buffer amount is 30 frames. Although this may seem like a lot, if your movie is playing at 15 frames per second, that buffer amount will be eliminated in just 2 seconds. If zero frames are buffered, your presentation will come to a screeching halt at that point—and stay that way until the streaming process builds the buffer back up.

Things that can quickly eat away at your buffer include sections of your movie that contain bitmaps, sounds, fonts, or a section of frames (in a row) with a lot of content that changes or moves within a short period of time.

To maintain a reasonable buffer:

Use offsetting. Include reasonably long stretches where your animation changes very little. Make creative use of vector graphics or text as well as previously used symbols over a long stretch of frames as a prelude to a section that introduces a lot of new content.

Use bitmaps and sounds sparingly, and use symbols generously. Symbols, symbols, symbols: Use them whenever you can.

Use a preloader. This is the most common way to maintain a decent buffer. Preloaders usually contain little content and are often simple. This means that a good deal of your movie can download in the background while the preloader keeps your audience occupied. The buffer amount will usually increase substantially during this process. Remember: You don't need to buffer, or download, the whole movie before it plays. Use a preloader simply to get the streaming process going and working smoothly.

First impressions are important, and on the Web one of the things people hate most is waiting. If it takes too long for action to occur on a Flash-enhanced page, viewers may well get frustrated and go elsewhere—never to return. However, any type of Web content takes time to download and display. With Flash, you can make this process a lot less tedious by making it seem like part of the show.

You should never create preloaders that display the Now Loading message for more than 5 percent to 10 percent of the duration of the entire movie. But pay attention: Your preloader can actually stretch as long as necessary to create a decent sized buffer—you simply need to make it look like an interesting part of the overall presentation.

You accomplish this by starting simple: Use creatively animated vector graphics rather than bitmaps. If you must use bitmaps, make sure they're small and use them sparingly. Text, on the other hand, you can use generously, inserting quotes or short bits of information that the viewer can read while the movie downloads in the background. But remember that each new font you use can add a lot to the download, so use them sparingly as well. And finally, use short sounds, if any at all.

For more on how to create a preloader, see Chapter 11, "Interactivity," and go through the "Creating a Preloader" tutorial on the CD-ROM.

Hopefully, you now see the importance of good planning before actually even starting Flash. Sure, you can create Flash content without taking into consideration any of the things we've discussed, and you may well be able to pull off a mediocre success, but you should always remember that without a good foundation, nothing will stand for very long. Build your projects on a good foundation. It may take some adjustments on your part, especially if you're the type that likes to jump right in, but in the long run you'll save time and a whole lot of frustration.

Keyboard Shortcuts

FILE MENU

Command	Windows	Macintosh
New	Control-N	Command-N
Open	Control-O	Command-O
Open as Library	Control-Shift-O	Command-Shift-O
Close	Control-W	Command-W
Save	Control-S	Command-S
Save As	Control-Shift-S	Command-Shift-S
Import	Control-R	Command-R
Export Movie	Control-Alt-Shift-S	Command-Shift-Option-S
Print	Control-P	Command-P
Quit	Control-Q	Command-Q

EDIT MENU

Command	Windows	Macintosh
Undo	Control-Z	Command-Z
Redo	Control-Y	Command-Y
Cut	Control-X	Command-X
Copy	Control-C	Command-C
Paste	Control-P	Command-P
Paste In Place	Control-Shift-V	Command-Shift-V
Clear	Delete	Delete
Duplicate	Control-D	Command-D
Select All	Control-A	Command-A
Deselect All	Control-Shift-A	Command-Shift-A
Copy Frames	Control-Alt-C	Command-Option-C
Paste Frames	Control- Alt-V	Command-Option-V
Edit Symbols	Control-E	Command-E

VIEW MENU

Command	Windows	Macintosh
100%	Control-1	Command-1
Show Frame	Control-2	Command-2
Show All	Control-3	Command-3
Outlines	Control-Alt-Shift-O	Shift-Option-Command-O
Fast	Control-Alt-Shift-F	Shift-Option-Command-F
Antialias	Control-Alt-Shift-A	Shift-Option-Command-A
Antialias Text	Control-Alt-Shift-T	Shift-Option-Command-T
Timeline	Control-Alt-T	Command-Option-T
Work Area	Control-Shift-W	Command-Shift-W
Rulers	Control-Alt-Shift-R	Shift-Option-Command-R
Grid	Control-Alt-Shift-G	Shift-Option-Command-G
Snap	Control-Alt-G	Command-Option-G
Show Shape Hints	Control-Alt-H	Command-Option-H

GO TO SUBMENU

Command	Windows	Macintosh
First	Home	Home
Previous	Page Up	Page Up
Next	Page Down	Page Down
Last	End	End

INSERT MENU

Command	Windows	Macintosh
Create Symbol	F8	F8
Frame	F5	F5
Delete Frame	Shift-F5	Shift-F5
Key Frame	F6	F6
Blank Key Frame	F7	F7
Clear Key Frame	Shift-F6	Shift-F6

MODIFY MENU

Command	Windows	Macintosh
Instance	Control-I	Command-I
Frame	Control-F	Command-F
Movie	Control-M	Command-M
Font	Control-T	Command-T
Paragraph	Control-Shift-T	Command- Shift-T
Align	Control-K	Command-K
Group	Control-G	Command-G
Ungroup	Control-Shift-G	Command- Shift-G
Break Apart	Control-B	Command-B

STYLE SUBMENU

Command	Windows	Macintosh
Plain	Control-Shift-P	Command-Shift-P
Bold	Control-Shift-B	Command-Shift-B
Italic	Control-Shift-I	Command-Shift-I
Align Left	Control-Shift-L	Command-Shift-L
Align Center	Control-Shift-C	Command-Shift-C
Align Right	Control-Shift-R	Command-Shift-R
Justify	Control-Shift-J	Command-Shift-J

KERNING SUBMENU

Command	Windows	Macintosh
Narrower	Control-Alt-Left	Command-Option-Left
Wider	Control-Alt-Right	Command-Option-Right
Reset	Control-Alt-Up	Command-Option-Up

TRANSFORM SUBMENU

Command	Windows	Macintosh
Scale and Rotate	Control-Alt-S	Command-Option-S
Remove Transform	Control-Shift-Z	Command-Shift-Z
Add Shape Hint	Control-H	Command-H

ARRANGE SUBMENU

Command	Windows	Macintosh
Bring To Front	Control-Shift-Up-Arrow	Command-Shift-Up-Arrow
Move Ahead	Control-Up-Arrow	Command-Up-Arrow
Move Behind	Control-Down-Arrow	Command-Down-Arrow
Send To Back	Control-Shift-Down-Arrow	Command-Shift-Down-Arrow
Lock	Control-Alt-L	Command-Option-L
Unlock All	Control-Alt-Shift-L	Command-Option-Shift-L

CURVES SUBMENU

Command	Windows	Macintosh
Optimize	Control-Alt-Shift-C	Command-Option-Shift-C

CONTROL MENU

Command	Windows	Macintosh
Play	Enter	Enter
Rewind	Control-Alt-R	Command-Option-R
Step Forward	>	>
Step Backward	<	<
Test Movie	Control-Enter	Command-Enter
Test Scene	Control-Alt-Enter	Command-Option-Enter
Enable Frame Actions	Control-Alt-A	Command-Option-A
Enable Buttons	Control-Alt-B	Command-Option-B
Mute Sounds	Control-Alt-M	Command-Option-M

WINDOW MENU

Command	Windows	Macintosh
New Window	Control-Alt-N	Command-Option-N
Inspector	Control-Alt-I	Command-Option-I
Library	Control-L	Command-L

CONTROLLING LAYERS AND KEYFRAMES

To	Windows	Macintosh
Move a keyframe	Control-drag	Control-drag
Link or unlink a layer to a mask or motion guide layer	Alt-click a layer icon	Option-click a layer icon

DRAWING SHORTCUTS

To	Windows	Macintosh
Set fill and line attributes for all tools with the dropper tool	Shift-click with the dropper tool	Shift-click with the dropper tool
Create a new corner handle	Control-drag a line	Option-drag a line
Move a selected element by 1 pixel	Arrow keys	Arrow keys
Move a selected element by 8 pixels	Shift-Arrow keys	Shift-Arrow keys
Toggle between zoom in and zoom out while the magnifier tool is selected	Alt	Option
Drag a copy of the selected element	Control-drag	Option-drag
Drag the stage with the hand tool	Press Spacebar and drag	Press Spacebar and drag

Spring-Loaded Tools

Hold down the keys below to temporarily activate certain tools. When the key is released, the previous tool is reactivated.

To temporarily activate this tool	Windows	Macintosh
Arrow	Control	Control
Lasso	Tab	Tab
Hand	Spacebar	Spacebar
Magnifier zoom-in	Control-Spacebar	Command-Spacebar
Magnifier zoom-out	Control-Shift-Spacebar	Command-Shift-Spacebar

SWITCHING TOOLS

To switch to this tool	Press	To switch to this tool	Press
Arrow	A	Brush	B
Text	T	Paint Bucket	U
Rectangle	R	Eraser	E
Oval	O	Dropper	D
Pencil	P	Magnifier	M
Ink Bottle	I	Lasso	L

Flash Resources

Flash Tutorials, How To Sites, and Source Files

Macromedia
http://www.macromedia.com/support/flash/

Crazy Raven Productions, tutorials
http://www.crazyraven.com/Tutorials/flash.htm

Raven University, coming soon!
http://www.ravenuniversity.com/

FlashLite
http://www.flashlite.net

BertoFlash
http://www.bertoflash.nu

FlashMaster
http://www.flashmaster.nu/

FlashZone
http://www.flashzone.com

Macromania
http://www.users.bigpond.com/xtian/welcomenew.html

Moock WebDesign Flash
http://colinmoock.iceinc.com/webdesign/flash/index.html

Pixelate Performance Site Design and Service
http://www.pixelate.bc.ca/flash/

Asmussen Interactive, the Flash Guide
http://www.lunarmedia.com/asmussen/tutorials/index.html

Canfield Studios, Flash 3 samples
http://www.canfieldstudios.com/Flash3/index.html

Designs by Mark, Flash 3 tutorials
http://designsbymark.com/flashtut.htm

Ens, tutorials and demos
http://www.enetserve.com/tutorials/

Webmonkey, multimedia collection
http://www.hotwired.com/webmonkey/multimedia/?tw=frontdoor

Web Review, A Quick-Start Guide to Flash 3
http://www.webreview.com/wr/pub/98/07/31/index.html

FlashPlanet
http://www.flashplanet.com

ShockFusion
http://www.shockfusion.com

Discussion Groups

Forums
macromedia.com

Flash Pad
http://www.flasher.net/flashpad.html

Flash discussion
http://www.devdesign.com/flash/

Flash Site Submissions

Quintus, Flash Index
http://qfi.ucc.nl/

The Flash Challenge
http://165.90.193.31/

Index

getting properties for, 298-299
loading/unloading, 260-264
parent-child relationships in,
    292-297
planning, 395-407
QuickTime videos combined with,
    236-238
scaling the movie window, 353-354
scrubbing, 207
setting properties for, 33, 298
size considerations for, 398-399
testing, 336
using symbols from, 156
working with multiple, 289-299
identifying targets in ActionScripts,
    290-299
See also Flash movies
moving
frames, 215
library items into folders, 177-178
objects, 70-71
the timeline, 26
MP3 audio compression, 130-131
MPEG compression, 130-131
multimedia
evolution of, 1-2
streaming content and, 4
vector graphics and, 2-4

N

NAME attribute, 377
name property, 323
naming
layers, 185
movie-clip instances, 290-291
variables, 300-301
See also renaming
navigating between scenes, 224
nesting
actions, 285-286
groups, 69
Newline function, 314-315
<NOEMBED> tag, 390
Normal mode (Eraser tool), 47
normal selecting, 56
number values, 301
numeric operators, 307-310
arithmetic, 307
comparison, 309
sample scripts, 308, 309

O

<OBJECT> tag, 372-373
using with <EMBED> tag,
    373-374
Object Inspector, 27
placing objects using, 70-71
scaling or resizing objects using, 72

objects
aligning, 75-77
creating, 51-55
cutting and copying, 85
deleting, 85
deselecting, 59
duplicating, 83
editing, 70-86
erasing, 83-84
flipping, 80
identifying on layers, 190
listing, 338
locking/unlocking, 85-86
moving, 70-71
overlay-level, 36, 49, 50-51
pasting, 84-85
removing transformations from,
    80-81
reshaping, 81-82
resizing, 71-72
rotating, 77-79
scaling, 72
selecting, 55-59
skewing, 77-79
snapping applied to, 82-83
stage-level, 36, 49, 50, 51-55
text, 106-107
types of, 49-51
offsetting, 406
On MouseEvent action, 242
nesting, 286
onion-skinning feature, 217-219
editing multiple frames, 218-219
markers for, 219
viewing frames, 218
operators
logical, 312
numeric, 307-310
string, 310-311
Optimize Curves dialog box, 89
optimizing
colors, 356, 360
graphics
    bitmap, 135-139
    vector, 89-90
sounds, 127-131
Ord function, 319
order of precedence, 309
Orient to path direction option, 234
outline-mode layer, 192
outlines
colors for, 185
font, 113-114
identifying objects on layers with,
    190
lines compared to, 61
turning into fillable shapes, 68

viewing layers as, 185, 192
viewing onion-skinned frames as,
    218
Output window, 338
Oval tool, 40
Fill Color modifier, 40, 64
ovals, creating, 53
overlay-level objects, 36, 49, 50-51
changing the stacking order of, 51
converting to stage-level objects, 50
cutting and copying, 85
deleting, 85
duplicating, 83
flipping, 80
locking, 85-86
moving the center point of, 77
pasting, 84-85
removing transformations from,
    80-81
rotating and skewing, 77-79
snapping applied to, 82-83
symbol instances as, 163
See also stage-level objects

P

Paint Behind mode (Brush tool), 43
Paint Bucket tool, 45
adding fills with, 65
editing fills with, 65-66
Fill Color modifier, 45, 64
Gap Size modifier, 45, 64
Lock Fill modifier, 45, 64
Transform Fill modifier, 45, 64
Paint Fills mode (Brush tool), 43
Paint Inside mode (Brush tool), 43
Paint Normal mode (Brush tool), 43
Paint Selection mode (Brush tool), 43
palettes
changing background colors with,
    26
custom, 358, 361
for GIF files, 357-358
importing and exporting, 98-99
for PNG images, 360-361
Web-safe, 93-94
paragraph formatting, 108
Paragraph modifier (Text tool), 103
Paragraph Properties dialog box, 108
parameters
for HTML tags, 374-383
for template variables, 393
parent-child relationships, 292-297
password fields, 111
Paste in Place command, 85
pasting
actions, 288-289
frames, 217
objects, 84-85